Moving Beyond Prejudice Reduction

Moving Beyond Prejudice Reduction

Pathways to Positive Intergroup Relations

Edited by
Linda R. Tropp
and Robyn K. Mallett

American Psychological Association • Washington, DC

Published by
American Psychological Association
750 First Street, NE
Washington, DC 20002
www.apa.org

To order
APA Order Department
P.O. Box 92984
Washington, DC 20090-2984
Tel: (800) 374-2721; Direct: (202) 336-5510
Fax: (202) 336-5502; TDD/TTY: (202) 336-6123
Online: www.apa.org/books/
E-mail: order@apa.org

In the U.K., Europe, Africa, and the Middle East, copies may be ordered from
American Psychological Association
3 Henrietta Street
Covent Garden, London
WC2E 8LU England

Typeset in Goudy by Circle Graphics, Inc., Columbia, MD

Printer: Edwards Brothers, Inc., Ann Arbor, MI
Cover Designer: Mercury Publishing Services, Rockville, MD

The opinions and statements published are the responsibility of the authors, and such opinions and statements do not necessarily represent the policies of the American Psychological Association.

Library of Congress Cataloging-in-Publication Data

Moving beyond prejudice reduction : pathways to positive intergroup relations / edited by Linda R. Tropp and Robyn K. Mallett. — 1st ed.
    p. cm.
 Includes bibliographical references and index.
 ISBN-13: 978-1-4338-0928-6
 ISBN-10: 1-4338-0928-1
 1. Prejudices. 2. Discrimination. 3. Intergroup relations. I. Tropp, Linda R. II. Mallett, Robyn K.

 BF575.P9M68 2011
 305—dc22

                 2010030130

British Library Cataloguing-in-Publication Data

A CIP record is available from the British Library.

Printed in the United States of America
First Edition

doi: 10.1037/12319-000

CONTENTS

Contributors .... *ix*

Introduction: Charting New Pathways to Positive
Intergroup Relations 3
Linda R. Tropp and Robyn K. Mallett

I. Reconceptualizing Intergroup Attitudes 19

Chapter 1.   What Can Tolerance Teach Us About Prejudice?
               Profiles of the Nonprejudiced 21
               Robert W. Livingston

Chapter 2.   Measuring Positive Attitudes Toward Outgroups:
               Development and Validation of
               the Allophilia Scale 41
               Todd L. Pittinsky, Seth A. Rosenthal,
               and R. Matthew Montoya

v

II. Motivations and Expectations Across Group Boundaries.............. 61

Chapter 3. Understanding the Intergroup Forecasting Error........... 63
            Robyn K. Mallett, Dana E. Wagner,
            and Patrick R. Harrison

Chapter 4. Approaching Versus Avoiding Intergroup Contact:
            The Role of Expectancies and Motivation 81
            David A. Butz and E. Ashby Plant

Chapter 5. Focusing Beyond the Self: Goal Orientations
            in Intergroup Relations 99
            Katya Migacheva, Linda R. Tropp,
            and Jennifer Crocker

III. Closeness and Inclusion in Cross-Group Relationships............. 117

Chapter 6. Cross-Group Friendships: How Interpersonal
            Connections Encourage Positive
            Intergroup Attitudes....................................... 119
            Kristin Davies, Stephen C. Wright,
            and Arthur Aron

Chapter 7. Friendship and Social Interaction
            With Outgroup Members............................. 139
            Elizabeth Page-Gould
            and Rodolfo Mendoza-Denton

Chapter 8. Is Multiculturalism Bad for African Americans?
            Redefining Inclusion Through the Lens
            of Identity Safety... 159
            Valerie Purdie-Vaughns and Gregory M. Walton

IV. Applications to Postconflict Reconciliation 179

Chapter 9. Achieving Forgiveness and Trust
            in Postconflict Societies: The Importance
            of Self-Disclosure and Empathy 181
            Hermann Swart, Rhiannon Turner,
            Miles Hewstone, and Alberto Voci

Chapter 10.   Promoting Intergroup Reconciliation
               in Conflicts Involving Direct or Structural
               Violence: Implications of
               the Needs-Based Model................................ 201
               Arie Nadler and Nurit Shnabel

Chapter 11.   Intergroup Forgiveness and Reparation in Chile:
               The Role of Identity and Intergroup Emotions............ 221
               Roberto González, Jorge Manzi, and Masi Noor

Conclusion: Positive Thoughts About Positive Approaches
to Intergroup Relations.. 241
Samuel L. Gaertner and John F. Dovidio

Index 261

About the Editors... 271

CONTRIBUTORS

Arthur Aron, PhD, Department of Psychology, Stony Brook University, Stony Brook, NY

David A. Butz, PhD, Department of Psychology, Morehead State University, Morehead, KY

Jennifer Crocker, PhD, Department of Psychology, The Ohio State University, Columbus

Kristin Davies, PhD, Department of Behavioral Sciences, York College, City University of New York, Jamaica

John F. Dovidio, PhD, Department of Psychology, Yale University, New Haven, CT

Samuel L. Gaertner, PhD, Department of Psychology, University of Delaware, Newark

Roberto González, PhD, School of Psychology, Pontificia Universidad de Chile, Santiago

Patrick R. Harrison, MA, Department of Psychology, Loyola University Chicago, Chicago, IL

Miles Hewstone, PhD, Department of Experimental Psychology, University of Oxford, Oxford, England

Robert W. Livingston, PhD, Kellogg School of Management, Northwestern University, Evanston, IL

Robyn K. Mallett, PhD, Department of Psychology, Loyola University Chicago, Chicago, IL

Jorge Manzi, PhD, School of Psychology, Pontificia Universidad de Chile, Santiago

Rodolfo Mendoza-Denton, PhD, Department of Psychology, University of California, Berkeley

Katya Migacheva, MSc, Department of Psychology, University of Massachusetts Amherst

R. Matthew Montoya, PhD, Center for Public Leadership, Kennedy School of Government, Harvard University, Cambridge, MA

Arie Nadler, PhD, Department of Psychology, Tel Aviv University, Tel Aviv, Israel

Masi Noor, PhD, Department of Applied Social Sciences/Psychology, Canterbury Christ Church University, Canterbury, England

Elizabeth Page-Gould, PhD, Department of Psychology, University of Toronto Scarborough, Toronto, Ontario, Canada

Todd L. Pittinsky, PhD, Center for Public Leadership, Kennedy School of Government, Harvard University, Cambridge, MA

E. Ashby Plant, PhD, Department of Psychology, Florida State University, Tallahassee

Valerie Purdie-Vaughns, PhD, Psychology Department, Columbia University, New York, NY

Seth A. Rosenthal, PhD, Center for Public Leadership, Kennedy School of Government, Harvard University, Cambridge, MA

Nurit Shnabel, PhD, Department of Psychology, Tel Aviv University, Tel Aviv, Israel

Hermann Swart, PhD, Department of Psychology, University of Stellenbosch, Stellenbosch, South Africa

Linda R. Tropp, PhD, Department of Psychology, University of Massachusetts Amherst

Rhiannon Turner, PhD, Institute of Psychological Sciences, University of Leeds, Leeds, England

Alberto Voci, PhD, Dipartimento di Psicologia Applicata, Universita degli Studi di Padova, Padova, Italy

Dana E. Wagner, MA, Department of Psychology, Loyola University Chicago, Chicago, IL

Gregory M. Walton, PhD, Department of Psychology, Stanford University, Stanford, CA

Stephen C. Wright, PhD, Psychology Department, Simon Fraser University, Burnaby, British Columbia, Canada

Moving Beyond Prejudice Reduction

INTRODUCTION: CHARTING NEW PATHWAYS TO POSITIVE INTERGROUP RELATIONS

LINDA R. TROPP AND ROBYN K. MALLETT

In 1963, Martin Luther King Jr. stood before an enthusiastic crowd of civil rights supporters and described an ideal state of intergroup relations: that one day "little black boys and black girls will be able to join hands with little white boys and white girls as sisters and brothers" (Washington, 1992, p. 105). His dream was characterized not only by the absence of intergroup strife but also by the presence of connection and friendship across group boundaries. Since his famous speech, the United States has made some progress toward that dream. Generally, intergroup violence is less common, and the call for peaceful relations between groups has grown. Indeed, even following 3 days of riots in 1992 that started after three White Los Angeles police officers were acquitted of beating an African American motorist, Rodney King, he himself pleaded for a halt to the violence:

> Can we get along? Can we stop making it, making it horrible for the older people and the kids? . . . It's just not right. . . . It's not going to change anything. We'll, we'll get our justice. . . . Please, we can get along here. We all can get along. I mean, we're all stuck here for a while. Let's try to work it out. (Mydans, 1993)

Still, we can question whether progress has stalled. Though violence between groups has decreased, friendship and integration between groups has not necessarily increased. Beverly Tatum's (1997) book *Why Are All the Black Kids Sitting Together in the Cafeteria?* notes that, to some extent, King's dream has become a reality—elementary school children frequently interact across racial lines. Yet by the time they reach high school, students' educational and social experiences are often largely segregated (Frankenberg & Orfield, 2007). For example, an analysis of interviews of 59,000 high school students found that of the nearly one million friendship pairs in the sample, only a few hundred were interracial (Hallinan & Williams, 1989). Children and adolescents are still more likely to choose same-race friends than cross-race friends (DuBois & Hirsch, 1990; Hallinan & Teixeira, 1987), and cross-race friendships can be harder to sustain over time (Aboud, Mendelson, & Purdy, 2003). Tatum suggests such segregation occurs because students have become increasingly aware of race and are unsure of how to address the issue with their peers. Uncertainty about how to negotiate interactions with people from different social groups can grow with them into adulthood and pose a formidable barrier to future positive contact.

However, looking back at the history of research on intergroup relations, one might initially think that prejudice is the sole problem. If we could just reduce prejudice, the work suggests, then we should be able to improve intergroup relations. To be sure, the existence and persistence of prejudice are highly problematic. We must continue to build on decades of past research to further our understanding of its genesis and the consequences that prejudice can have for everyday life experiences and outcomes (Ashburn-Nardo, Monteith, Arthur, & Bain, 2007; Dovidio, Glick, & Rudman, 2005; Swim, Hyers, Cohen, Fitzgerald, & Bylsma, 2003).

But the problem of achieving positive intergroup relations is more complex than simply reducing prejudice. Recent studies reveal the multifaceted nature of intergroup relations, such as the benefits of positive attitudes toward other groups, the importance of recognizing differing views of intergroup relationships, the anxieties we may have about cross-group interactions, the discrepancies between our interest in contact and our willingness to reach out across group boundaries, not knowing how others might respond, or whether we would feel that we belong. Indeed, emerging programs of research have begun to converge in identifying the many ways in which our construals, motivations, expectations, and emotional responses impact our intergroup experiences and relationships, far beyond the effects of prejudiced attitudes (e.g., Devine, Evett, & Vasquez-Suson, 1996; Frey & Tropp, 2006; Mendoza-Denton, Downey, Purdie, Davis, & Pietrzak, 2002; Plant & Devine, 2003; Shelton, Richeson, & Vorauer, 2006; Stephan & Stephan, 1985; Vorauer, 2006).

In the present volume, we therefore focus beyond the goal of reducing prejudice to explore what other factors might be necessary to improve relations between groups. This book brings together original contributions from leading scholars in social psychology who have begun to examine the motivations and processes that underlie people's ability to develop positive and meaningful relationships across group boundaries. As one of the earliest researchers to assess intergroup attitudes, Emory Bogardus (1928), stated that

> public attention is usually given to racial prejudice rather than to its counterpart, racial good will. But the more spectacular and melodramatic phenomena do not deserve to receive all the attention; the origins and development of racial friendliness also merit consideration. (p. 77)

In line with this view, the present volume compels us to move beyond our field's traditional focus on prejudice reduction, to consider novel approaches to studying intergroup attitudes and strategies that we can use to improve relations between groups.

EARLY APPROACHES TO STUDYING INTERGROUP RELATIONS

Early theorists such as Gordon Allport (1945, 1954) and Muzafer Sherif (Sherif & Sherif, 1953; Sherif, Harvey, White, Hood, & Sherif, 1954/1961) encouraged psychologists to investigate strategies that could effectively reduce intergroup prejudice. In his landmark book *The Nature of Prejudice*, Allport (1954) wrote what has become the most influential statement of intergroup contact theory, noting that intergroup contact holds the potential either to exacerbate or reduce prejudice. His early research revealed numerous factors, such as unpleasant childhood experiences and social influences, that could heighten intergroup prejudice (Allport & Kramer, 1946). Hence, he emphasized conditions that could be established in the contact situation (e.g., equal status between groups, support of institutional authorities) to effectively reduce intergroup prejudice.

Sherif also recognized the potential for contact between groups to increase or decrease prejudice, and he and his colleagues demonstrated both tendencies in their classic Robbers Cave field study (see Sherif et al., 1954/1961). Situations structured to produce competition between the groups led to intergroup prejudice and hostility and spurred further intergroup competition. By contrast, situations that provided opportunities for the groups to work together cooperatively toward common goals were effective in reversing these tendencies and even in encouraging friendly relations to develop across group boundaries.

Such approaches to understanding the origins of prejudice and the potential for prejudice reduction are well established and well documented in the research literature (see Pettigrew & Tropp, 2005; Stephan & Stephan, 2001). But as we reflect on such strategies and their supportive evidence, we might begin to question whether prejudice reduction has always been the singular goal. Indeed, close inspection of early work on prejudice reveals many examples in which researchers employed a wide range of indicators to assess the nature and tone of intergroup relationships. For example, LaPiere (1934) did not simply ask hotel and restaurant owners to report whether they held prejudiced attitudes toward Chinese people; he also tested whether Chinese clientele would be welcome at their establishments. Though often construed as a measure of "prejudice," Bogardus's (1928) well-known scale actually assesses people's willingness to accept members of other ethnic, religious, and national groups into their neighborhoods, homes, and close friendship circles. Additionally, Deutsch and Collins (1951) examined not only the degree to which White housewives held prejudices against Blacks but also how they felt about living in an integrated housing community. And beyond asking White police officers to report attitudes toward their Black peers, Kephart (1957) examined how these officers would feel about taking orders from Black officers and having Black officers join their formerly all-White police districts.

These early examples demonstrate great variability in how researchers sought to understand multiple dimensions of intergroup relationships, reaching far beyond the goal of prejudice reduction. Yet, somehow, we have perpetually constrained the framing of this work to retain a focus on prejudice and prejudice reduction as the guiding force for our field (for a related discussion, see Devine et al., 1996).

CONTEMPORARY APPROACHES TO PREJUDICE AND INTERGROUP RELATIONS

Indeed, most of our research from the past several decades has focused on negative processes and obstacles in intergroup relations (see Fiske, 1998; Shelton et al., 2006; Sidanius & Pratto, 1999). For example, extensive social psychological research shows that our tendencies to categorize people on the basis of race, gender, and age are natural and inevitable consequences of social perception (see Macrae & Bodenhausen, 2000). Once categorization occurs, stereotypic beliefs and prejudicial attitudes associated with social categories readily come to mind and subsequently shape our judgments of and behaviors toward others (e.g., Bargh, 1999; Devine, 1989; Dovidio & Gaertner, 2004; Stephan & Stephan, 2000). Research has also revealed a range of motivational factors that perpetuate people's tendency to harbor biases against other groups, including the need to confirm one's self-worth or the value of one's group (e.g., Fein & Spencer, 1997; Tajfel & Turner, 1986) and the need to reduce uncertainty about who we are and where we stand in the world (e.g., Hogg, 2007). Moreover, other perspectives explore the resilient nature of prejudice, by highlighting how the mere presence of other groups can provoke intergroup biases (e.g., Turner et al., 1987) and the persistence of dominance and hierarchical relations between groups (e.g., Sidanius & Pratto, 1999).

Yet other work from recent decades has identified the many ways in which intergroup prejudice has evolved into less conspicuous forms. As overt forms of prejudice become increasingly difficult to detect, researchers have set out to create new measures to assess more covert, subtle forms of prejudice (e.g., Henry & Sears, 2002; McConahay, Hardee, & Batts, 1981; Pettigrew & Meertens, 1995). Rather than simply possessing uniformly negative attitudes toward Blacks, many White Americans who believe they are nonprejudiced egalitarians may hold conflicting positive and negative attitudes of which they may be unaware (Gaertner & Dovidio, 1986; Glick & Fiske, 1996). New procedures have also been developed and studied extensively to identify hidden dimensions of intergroup prejudice and bias, including tests of association and activation of group-based stimuli (e.g., Dovidio, Kawakami, Johnson, Johnson, & Howard, 1997; Fazio, Jackson, Dunton, & Williams, 1995; Greenwald, Poehlman, Uhlmann, & Banaji, 2009).

These bodies of research have greatly enhanced our understanding of prejudice and how the seemingly natural processes that induce prejudice can pose formidable barriers between groups. Further research along these lines has therefore sought to identify strategies that can effectively combat and diminish prejudice, such as by making people aware of their biases (Czopp, Monteith, & Mark, 2006), training people to reduce biased responding (e.g., Kawakami, Dovidio, Moll, Hermsen, & Russin, 2000; Kawakami, Dovidio, & Van Kamp, 2007), and enhancing their cross-group experiences (e.g., Brown & Hewstone, 2005; Gaertner & Dovidio, 2000; Pettigrew & Tropp, 2006).

EMERGING APPROACHES TO PREJUDICE AND INTERGROUP RELATIONS

Nonetheless, it appears that relatively little work has moved beyond the central goal of reducing prejudice, to consider different ways in which we can conceptualize intergroup attitudes and explore strategies that enhance feelings of acceptance and inclusion across group boundaries (see Stephan & Stephan, 2001). We believe it is now time to expand our efforts and take a more positive approach to improving intergroup relations.

Emerging research has begun to shift away from the common focus on prejudice reduction to consider novel approaches to understanding and promoting positive intergroup relations, both in contexts of diverse yet largely segregated societies (see Nagda, Tropp, & Paluck, 2006) and in contexts where groups have long been in conflict (see Nadler, Malloy, & Fisher, 2008). For example, some of this work highlights new ways of conceptualizing intergroup attitudes and the ways in which we resist bias and develop positive feelings toward other groups (Devine, Plant, Amodio, Harmon-Jones, & Vance, 2002; Livingston & Drwecki, 2007; Pittinsky, Montoya, Tropp, & Chen, 2007). Other new work explores the motivations that underlie our interest in relations with other groups (Butz & Plant, 2006; Mallett, Wilson, & Gilbert, 2008), and how forging relationships across group boundaries can facilitate feelings of inclusion and acceptance (Mendoza-Denton & Page-Gould, 2008; Purdie-Vaughns, Steele, Davies, Ditlmann, & Crosby, 2008; Walton & Cohen, 2007; Wright, Aron, McLaughlin-Volpe, & Ropp, 1997). New perspectives have also begun to explore processes by which we can begin to achieve reconciliation between conflicting groups, such as by promoting forgiveness and mutual understanding (e.g., Čehajić, Brown, & Castano, 2008; Hewstone, Cairns, Voci, Hamberger, & Niens, 2006; Manzi & González, 2007; Shnabel & Nadler, 2008).

Integrating the best of these emerging perspectives, this book guides psychologists' thinking about how we can extend our work beyond prejudice reduction to enhance our potential for achieving positive intergroup relations. Contributors to this edited volume explore these issues through four primary themes.

RECONCEPTUALIZING INTERGROUP ATTITUDES

Part I of this volume concerns *reconceptualizations in how we think about and study intergroup attitudes*. Rather than focusing on what makes people biased, Robert W. Livingston (Chapter 1) explores factors that lead people to become nonbiased in evaluations of other groups. He reviews theory and provides empirical evidence to suggest ways in which people vary in their susceptibility to forming negative associations with groups, in relation to individual differences, psychological motivations, and practice in making other kinds of associations. He concludes that, for many people, racial prejudice is not the result of devaluing or disliking people from a different social group. Rather, some individuals are simply more susceptible to negative conditioning. With practice and the proper motivation, people may be able to break those associations and form more positive racial attitudes.

Todd L. Pittinsky, Seth A. Rosenthal, and R. Matthew Montoya (Chapter 2) then move beyond typical distinctions in assessment of negative attitudes to examine varying dimensions of positive attitudes toward outgroups, which they refer to as *allophilia*. They present evidence showing that positive and negative intergroup attitudes are not direct opposites and that allophilia comprises five dimensions: Affection, Comfort, Kinship, Engagement, and Enthusiasm. They conclude that to understand the range of benefits that result from holding positive attitudes toward outgroups, psychologists must become more precise in our predictions and measurement. Doing so reveals that positive attitudes are stronger predictors of support for charities and assistance programs that help disadvantaged groups than are negative attitudes.

MOTIVATIONS AND EXPECTATIONS
IN CROSS-GROUP RELATIONS

Part II's theme shifts us from our tendency to focus on avoiding other groups to examine the *motivations and expectations that underlie positive relations with members of other groups*. Robyn K. Mallett, Dana E. Wagner, and Patrick R. Harrison (Chapter 3) consider how, although we often expect the worst, our experiences of intergroup contact tend to be more positive than we initially imagine. Building from social psychological research on affective forecasting, these authors show how influential expectations can be in cross-group relations, and they identify strategies for improving people's expectations to promote more successful and enjoyable cross-group interactions. They suggest targeting three factors that contribute to overly negative expectations: reliance on stereotypes, individual differences in sensitivity to group membership, and appreciation of how the situation constrains one's experience. Their research shows that simply considering overly negative expectations smoothed upcoming instances of interracial contact and increased the formation of interracial friendships.

Relatedly, David A. Butz and E. Ashby Plant (Chapter 4) examine why people often attempt to avoid intergroup contact and what predicts their motivations to approach interactions with members of other groups. In so doing, they demonstrate how negative emotional responses, such as anger, hostility, anxiety, and self-efficacy concerns, can curb our motivation for intergroup contact and how, by alleviating such negative responses, we can encourage more positive, approach-oriented intergroup behavior. Differences in internal or external motivations to control prejudice can also affect whether a person frames an interaction with a member of another group as a threat to be avoided or a challenge to be approached. Framing such interactions as a challenge increases the likelihood of actively working through and eventually overcoming even negative expectations.

Katya Migacheva, Linda R. Tropp, and Jennifer Crocker (Chapter 5) then discuss how the motivations and goals one adopts can either enhance or diminish the potential for achieving positive cross-group relations. Using the distinction between egosystem and ecosystem motivations as a guiding framework, they emphasize how focusing on oneself can foster anxieties about intergroup contact, whereas focusing on learning from others and attending to their needs can facilitate more positive contact experiences. The authors consider the extent to which these goals are held independently in everyday contexts and how we can promote goals focused on compassion and learning, even under conditions of conflict.

FORGING CROSS-GROUP RELATIONSHIPS

Part III explores how *forging relationships across group boundaries* can foster feelings of inclusion and acceptance. Kristin Davies, Stephen C. Wright, and Arthur Aron (Chapter 6) summarize a decade of research on the many benefits of cross-group friendships for creating positive shifts in intergroup attitudes. Describing results from cross-sectional, meta-analytic, and experimental studies of cross-group friendships, they reveal how close cross-group relationships increase the extent to which we include people from different social groups, and therefore the other social group, as part of our self-concept. They examine how self-expansion occurs in certain types of intergroup contact and how it produces positive effects, such as enhancing intergroup liking and empathy and encouraging greater support for disadvantaged groups.

Taking this theme further, Elizabeth Page-Gould and Rodolfo Mendoza-Denton (Chapter 7) discuss processes by which cross-group friendships benefit both majority and minority group members. Cross-group friendships can foster not only interest in intergroup contact but also feelings of institutional acceptance. Feeling that one belongs at an institution is especially critical for members of historically devalued groups because a feeling of belonging can enhance rates of retention and graduation. With longitudinal data and experimental studies, these authors show that cross-group friendships can reduce anxiety about future cross-group interactions and foster a sense of belonging among traditionally devalued groups, along with demonstrating empirically the processes that underlie such positive outcomes of cross-group friendships.

Concluding this section, Valerie Purdie-Vaughns and Gregory M. Walton (Chapter 8) describe how a focus on inclusiveness can promote feelings of trust within diverse institutions, which can have important implications for both academic and intergroup outcomes among historically devalued groups. These authors propose that we should view diversity through the lens of *identity safety*, such that different groups should have the potential to experience institutional contexts in similar ways, while at the same time acknowledging the varied perspectives and experiences that different groups bring to each context. Thus, provocatively suggesting that not all forms of multicultural-ism are equally beneficial, they address common limitations of multicultural ideologies and discuss how the concept of identity safety may usefully be applied in diverse organizations.

APPLICATIONS TO POSTCONFLICT RECONCILIATION

Part IV of this volume explores how these themes may be *applied to post-conflict reconciliation* concerns to promote forgiveness and understanding between groups. Hermann Swart, Rhiannon Turner, Miles Hewstone, and Alberto Voci (Chapter 9) consider several psychological processes that serve as cornerstones for both intergroup relations and reconciliation in postcon-flict societies. In particular, these authors contend that past conflict can per-petuate intergroup hostilities unless the groups involved can learn to forgive each other and foster trusting relationships. Presenting findings from studies in South Africa, Northern Ireland, and the United Kingdom, they show how high-quality contact experiences that include opportunities for reciprocal self-disclosure and empathic responding can facilitate the development of inter-group forgiveness and trust.

Arie Nadler and Nurit Shnabel (Chapter 10) further explore these issues by attending to the psychological needs of each group in the postcon-flict relationship. They present a needs-based model of reconciliation and results from several studies to demonstrate the importance of addressing the distinct needs for empowerment among victims and acceptance among per-petrators. Because members of disadvantaged and advantaged groups approach reconciliation with different goals, even positive messages of acceptance or empowerment may backfire if they do not address the group's primary need. Properly tailored communication between groups with histories of conflict goes beyond merely reducing conflict to actually increase willingness to coop-erate and work against discrimination.

Roberto González, Jorge Manzi, and Masi Noor (Chapter 11) add to this section by discussing how identities and intergroup emotions contribute to processes of forgiveness and reconciliation. Exploring the context of political violence in Chile, these authors describe how, when groups in conflict focus only on their own group identities, conflict is likely to persist and the poten-tial for forgiveness is diminished. But framing group identities at the inclu-sive, superordinate level (i.e., Chileans) will lead to emotional responses of empathy and trust that support forgiveness and willingness to repair relations.

It is our hope that by bringing these perspectives together in one vol-ume, the field of psychology can begin to chart new directions for research that emphasize positive pathways to improved intergroup relations. To this end, we have invited two prominent intergroup scholars, Samuel L. Gaertner and John F. Dovidio, to synthesize and comment on the work presented across the four sections of this book. In doing so, they highlight points of connection across the chapters and suggest avenues for future research. They also conclude their chapter with suggestions for how some of the research described in the volume may be used to inform social policy that seeks to build positive relations and more inclusive societies.

Looking back over the progress that we have made toward Martin Luther King Jr.'s dream in the past 40 years, we still have a way to go. As King said, "we must make the pledge that we shall always march ahead. We cannot turn back" (Washington, 1992, p. 103). On this journey, psychological research has primarily taken the well-traveled pathway to prejudice reduction. This road has allowed us to discover important insights about the roots and nature of prejudice and conflict. Yet it has also bypassed potentially important pathways that could take us beyond prejudice reduction to intergroup trust and acceptance. The purpose of this volume is to highlight the bridges and side roads created by recent research that chart new pathways for investigation. Reconceptualizing how we study intergroup attitudes, motivating interest in relations between groups, forging cross-group relations that can encourage feelings of inclusion and acceptance, and promoting intergroup forgiveness and understanding have the potential to change the landscape of intergroup relations. These new pathways can be used to explore intergroup relations that are characterized by subtle disruptions in interpersonal contexts or by the more systemic barriers that pervade our social institutions.

The editors' hope is that staking out these new pathways will allow us to go beyond mere prejudice reduction and take steps forward to realize Martin Luther King Jr.'s dream. That is, rather than simply reducing prejudice and conflict, we may enhance mutual liking, trust, and friendship between groups.

REFERENCES

Aboud, F. E., Mendelson, M., J., & Purdy, K. T. (2003). Cross-race peer relations and friendship quality. *International Journal of Behavioral Development, 27*, 165–173. doi:10.1080/01650250244000164

Allport, G. W. (1945). Human nature and the peace. *Psychological Bulletin, 42*, 376–378. doi:10.1037/h0054600

Allport, G. W. (1954). *The nature of prejudice*. Cambridge, MA: Perseus Books.

Allport, G. W., & Kramer, B. M. (1946). Some roots of prejudice. *Journal of Psychology, 22*, 9–39.

Ashburn-Nardo, L., Monteith, M. J., Arthur, S. A., & Bain, A. (2007). Race and the psychological health of African Americans. *Group Processes & Intergroup Relations, 10,* 471–491. doi:10.1177/1368430207081536

Bargh, J. A. (1999). The cognitive monster: The case against the controllability of automatic stereotype effects. In S. Chaiken & Y. Trope (Eds.), *Dual-process theories in social psychology* (pp. 361–382), New York, NY: Guilford.

Bogardus, E. S. (1928). *Immigration and race attitudes.* Boston, MA: Heath.

Brown, R., & Hewstone, M. (2005). An integrative theory of intergroup contact. In M. P. Zanna (Ed.), *Advances in Experimental Social Psychology* (pp. 255–343). San Diego, CA: Academic Press.

Butz, D. A., & Plant, E. A. (2006). Perceiving outgroup members as unresponsive: Implications for approach-related emotions, intentions, and behavior. *Journal of Personality and Social Psychology, 91,* 1066–1079. doi:10.1037/0022-3514.91.6.1066

Čehajić, S., Brown, R., & Castano, E. (2008). Forgive and forget? Antecedents and consequences of intergroup forgiveness in Bosnia and Herzegovina. *Political Psychology, 29,* 351–367. doi:10.1111/j.1467-9221.2008.00634.x

Czopp, A. M., Monteith, M. J., & Mark, A. Y. (2006). Standing up for a change: Reducing bias through interpersonal confrontation. *Journal of Personality and Social Psychology, 90,* 784–803. doi:10.1037/0022-3514.90.5.784

Deutsch, M., & Collins, M. (1951). *Interracial housing: A psychological evaluation of a social experiment.* Minneapolis: University of Minnesota Press.

Devine, P. G. (1989). Stereotypes and prejudice: Their automatic and controlled components. *Journal of Personality and Social Psychology, 56,* 5–18. doi:10.1037/0022-3514.56.1.5

Devine, P. G., Evett, S. R., & Vasquez-Suson, K. A. (1996). Exploring the interpersonal dynamics of intergroup contact. In R. M. Sorrentino & E. T. Higgins (Eds.), *Handbook of motivation and cognition* (Vol. 3, pp. 423–464). New York, NY: Guilford.

Devine, P. G., Plant, E. A., Amodio, D. M., Harmon-Jones, E., & Vance, S. L. (2002). The regulation of explicit and implicit race bias: The role of motivations to respond without prejudice. *Journal of Personality and Social Psychology, 82,* 835–848. doi:10.1037/0022-3514.82.5.835

Dovidio, J. F., & Gaertner, S. L. (2004). Aversive racism. In M. P. Zanna (Ed.), *Advances in experimental social psychology* (Vol. 36, pp. 1–52). San Diego, CA: Academic Press.

Dovidio, J. F., Glick, P. S., & Rudman, L. A. (Eds.). (2005). *On the nature of prejudice: Fifty years after Allport.* Malden, MA: Blackwell.

Dovidio, J. F., Kawakami, K., Johnson, C., Johnson, B., & Howard, A. (1997). On the nature of prejudice: Automatic and controlled processes. *Journal of Experimental Social Psychology, 33,* 510–540.

DuBois, D. L., & Hirsch, B. J. (1990). School and neighborhood friendship patterns of Blacks and Whites in early adolescence. *Child Development, 61*, 524–536. doi:10.2307/1131112

Fazio, R. H., Jackson, J. R., Dunton, B. C., & Williams, C. J. (1995). Variability in automatic activation as an unobtrusive measure of racial attitudes: A bona fide pipeline? *Journal of Personality and Social Psychology, 69*, 1013–1027.

Fein, S., & Spencer, S. J. (1997). Prejudice as self-image maintenance. Affirming the self through derogating others. *Journal of Personality and Social Psychology, 73*, 31–44.

Fiske, S. T. (1998). Stereotyping, prejudice, and discrimination. In D. T. Gilbert, S. T. Fiske, & G. Lindzey (Eds.), *Handbook of social psychology* (4th ed., Vol. 2, pp. 357–411). New York, NY: McGraw-Hill.

Frankenberg, E., & Orfield, G. (Eds.). *Lessons in integration: Realizing the promise of racial diversity in American schools.* Charlottesville: University of Virginia Press.

Frey, F. E., & Tropp, L. R. (2006). Being seen as individuals versus as group members: Extending research on metaperception to intergroup contexts. *Personality and Social Psychology Review, 10*, 265–280. doi:10.1207/s15327957pspr1003_5

Gaertner, S. L., & Dovidio, J. F. (1986). The aversive form of racism. In J. F. Dovidio & S. L. Gaertner (Eds.), *Prejudice, Discrimination, and Racism* (pp. 61–89). Orlando, FL: Academic Press.

Gaertner, S. L., & Dovidio, J. F. (2000). *Reducing intergroup bias: The common ingroup identity model.* Philadelphia, PA: Psychology Press.

Glick, P., & Fiske, S. T. (1996). The ambivalent sexism inventory: Differentiating hostile and benevolent sexism. *Journal of Personality and Social Psychology, 70*, 491–512.

Greenwald, A. G., Poehlman, T., Uhlmann, E. L., & Banaji, M. R. (2009). Understanding and using the Implicit Association Test: III. Meta-analysis of predictive validity. *Journal of Personality and Social Psychology, 97*, 17–41.

Hallinan, M. T., & Teixeira, R. A. (1987). Opportunities and constraints: Black-White differences in the formation of interracial friendships. *Child Development, 58*, 1358–1371. doi:10.2307/1130627

Hallinan, M. T., & Williams, R. A. (1989). Interracial friendship choices in secondary schools. *American Sociological Review, 54*, 67–78. doi:10.2307/2095662

Henry, P. J., & Sears, D. O. (2002). The symbolic racism 2000 scale. *Political Psychology, 23*, 253–283.

Hewstone, M., Cairns, E., Voci, A., Hamberger, J., & Niens, U. (2006). Intergroup contact, forgiveness, and experience of "The Troubles" in Northern Ireland. *Journal of Social Issues, 62*, 99–120. doi:10.1111/j.1540-4560.2006.00441.x

Hogg, M. A., (2007). Uncertainty-identity theory. In M. P. Zanna (Ed.), *Advances in experimental social psychology* (pp. 69–126). San Diego, CA: Elsevier.

Kawakami, K., Dovidio, J. F., Moll, J., Hermsen, S., & Russin, A. (2000). Just say no (to stereotyping): Effects of training in the negation of stereotypic associations on stereotype activation. *Journal of Personality and Social Psychology, 78,* 871–888. doi:10.1037/0022-3514.78.5.871

Kawakami, K., Dovidio, J. F., & van Kamp, S. (2005). Kicking the habit: Effects of nonstereotypic association training and correction processes on hiring decisions. *Journal of Experimental Social Psychology, 41,* 68–75.

Kawakami, K., Dovidio, J. F., & Van Kamp, S. (2007). The impact of counter-stereotypic training and related correction processes on the application of stereotypes. *Group Processes & Intergroup Relations, 10,* 139–156. doi:10.1177/1368430207074725

Kephart, W. M. (1957). *Racial factors and urban law enforcement.* Philadelphia: University of Pennsylvania Press.

LaPiere, R. T. (1934). Attitudes vs. actions. *Social Forces, 13,* 230–237.

Livingston, R. W., & Drwecki, B. B. (2007). Why are some individuals not racially biased? Susceptibility to affective conditioning predicts nonprejudice toward Blacks. *Psychological Science, 18,* 816–823. doi:10.1111/j.1467-9280.2007.01985.x

Macrae, C. N., & Bodenhausen, G. V. (2000). Social cognition: Thinking categorically about others. *Annual Review of Psychology, 51,* 93–120. doi:10.1146/annurev.psych.51.1.93

Mallett, R. K., Wilson, T. D., & Gilbert, D. (2008). Expect the unexpected: Failure to anticipate similarities leads to an intergroup forecasting error. *Journal of Personality and Social Psychology, 94,* 265–277. doi:10.1037/0022-3514.94.2.94.2.265

Manzi, J., & González, R. (2007). Forgiveness and reparation in Chile: The role of cognitive and emotional intergroup antecedents. *Peace and Conflict, 13,* 71–91.

McConahay, J. B., Hardee, B. B., & Batts, V. (1981). Has racism declined in America? It depends on who is asking and what is asked. *Journal of Conflict Resolution, 25,* 563–579.

Mendoza-Denton, R., Downey, G., Purdie, V. J., Davis, A., & Pietrzak, J. (2002). Sensitivity to status–based rejection: Implications for African American students' college experience. *Journal of Personality and Social Psychology, 83,* 896–918. doi:10.1037/0022-3514.83.4.896

Mendoza-Denton, R., & Page-Gould, E. (2008). Can cross-group friendships influence minority students' well being at historically White universities? *Psychological Science, 19,* 933–939.

Mydans, S. (1993, March 9). Jury could hear Rodney King today. *The New York Times,* p. 12.

Nadler, A., Malloy, T., & Fisher, J. D. (2008). Intergroup reconciliation: Dimensions and themes. In A. Nadler, T. Malloy, & J. D. Fisher (Eds.), *Social psychology of intergroup reconciliation* (pp. 3–13). New York, NY: Oxford University Press. doi:10.1093/acprof:oso/9780195300314.003.0001

Pettigrew, T. F., & Meertens, R. W. (1995). Subtle and blatant prejudice in Western Europe. *European Journal of Social Psychology, 57,* 57–75.

Pettigrew, T. F., & Tropp, L. R. (2005). Allport's intergroup contact hypothesis: Its history and influence. In J. F. Dovidio, P. Glick, & L. Rudman (Eds.), *On the nature of prejudice: Fifty years after Allport* (pp. 262–277). Malden, MA: Blackwell.

Plant, E. A., & Devine, P. G. (2003). The antecedents and implications of interracial anxiety. *Personality and Social Psychology Bulletin, 29,* 790–801. doi:10.1177/0146167203029006011

Nagda, B., Tropp, L. R., & Paluck, E. (Eds.). (2006). Reducing prejudice and promoting social inclusion: Integrating research, theory, and practice on intergroup relations. *Journal of Social Issues, 62,* 439–451. doi:10.1111/j.1540-4560.2006.00467.x

Pettigrew, T. F., & Meertens, R. W. (1995). Subtle and blatant prejudice in Western Europe. *European Journal of Social Psychology, 57,* 57–75.

Pettigrew, T. F., & Tropp, L. R. (2005). A meta-analytic test of intergroup contact theory. *Journal of Personality and Social Psychology, 90,* 751–783. doi:10.1037/0022-3514.90.5.751

Pittinsky, T. L., Montoya, R. M., Tropp, L. R., & Chen, A. (2007). How and when leader behavior affects intergroup liking: Affect, approval, and allophilia. In C. Anderson, B. Mannix, & M. Neale (Eds.), *Affect and groups: Research on managing groups and teams* (Vol. 10, pp. 125–144). San Diego, CA: Elsevier.

Plant, E. A., & Devine, P. G. (2003). The antecedents and implications of interracial anxiety. *Personality and Social Psychology Bulletin, 29,* 790–801. doi:10.1177/0146167203029006011

Purdie-Vaughns, V., Steele, C. M., Davies, P. G., Ditlmann, R., & Crosby, J. R. (2008). Social identity contingencies: How diversity cues signal threat or safety for African Americans in mainstream institutions. *Journal of Personality and Social Psychology, 94,* 615–630.

Shelton, J. N., Richeson, J. A., & Vorauer, J. D. (2006). Threatened identities and interethnic interactions. *European Review of Social Psychology, 17,* 321–358. doi:10.1080/10463280601095240

Sherif, M., Harvey, O. J., White, J. B., Hood, W. R., & Sherif, C. W. (1961). *Intergroup conflict and cooperation: The Robbers Cave experiment.* Norman: University of Oklahoma Book Exchange. (Original work published 1954)

Sherif, M., & Sherif, C. W. (1953). *Groups in harmony and tension.* New York, NY: Harper & Row.

Shnabel, N., & Nadler, A. (2008). A needs-based model of reconciliation: Satisfying the different emotional needs of victim and perpetrator as a key to promoting reconciliation. *Journal of Personality and Social Psychology, 94,* 116–132. doi:10.1037/0022-3514.94.1.116

Sidanius, J., & Pratto, F. (1999). *Social dominance: An intergroup theory of social hierarchy and oppression.* New York, NY: Cambridge University Press.

Stephan, W. G., & Stephan, C. W. (1985). Intergroup anxiety. *Journal of Social Issues, 41,* 157–175. doi:10.1111/j.1540-4560.1985.tb01134.x

Stephan, W. G., & Stephan, C. W. (2000). An integrated threat theory of prejudice. In S. Oskamp (Ed.), *Reducing prejudice and discrimination* (pp. 23–46). Hillsdale, NJ: Erlbaum.

Stephan, W. G., & Stephan, C. W. (2001). *Improving intergroup relations*. Thousand Oaks, CA: Sage.

Swim, J. K., Hyers, L. L., Cohen, L. L., Fitzgerald, D. C., & Bylsma, W. H. (2003). African American college students' experiences with everyday racism: Characteristics of and responses to these incidents. *Journal of Black Psychology, 29*, 38–67. doi:10.1177/0095798402239228

Tajfel, H., & Turner, J. C. (1986). The social identity theory of intergroup behavior. In S. Worchel & W. G. Austin (Eds.), *Psychology of intergroup relations* (pp. 7–4). Chicago, IL: Nelson-Hall.

Tatum, B. (1997). *Why are all the Black kids sitting together in the cafeteria?* New York, NY: Basic Books.

Turner, J. C., Hogg, M. A., Oakes, P. J., Reicher, S. D., & Wetherell, M. S. (1987). *Rediscovering the social group: A self-categorization theory*. Oxford, England: Basil Blackwell.

Vorauer, J. D. (2006). An information search model of evaluative concerns in intergroup interaction. *Psychological Review, 113*, 862–886. doi:10.1037/0033-295X.113.4.862

Walton, G. M., & Cohen, G. L. (2007). A question of belonging: Race, social fit, and achievement. *Journal of Personality and Social Psychology, 92*, 82–96. doi:10.1037/0022-3514.92.1.82

Washington, J. M. (Ed.). (1992). *I have a dream: Writings and speeches that changed the world: Martin Luther King, Jr.* New York, NY: HarperCollins.

Wright, S. C., Aron, A., McLaughlin-Volpe, T., & Ropp, S. A. (1997). The extended contact effect: Knowledge of cross-group friendships and prejudice. *Journal of Personality and Social Psychology, 73*, 73–90. doi:10.1037/0022-3514.73.1.73

I

RECONCEPTUALIZING INTERGROUP ATTITUDES

1

WHAT CAN TOLERANCE TEACH US ABOUT PREJUDICE? PROFILES OF THE NONPREJUDICED

ROBERT W. LIVINGSTON

It is the pathology of bigotry and not the wholesome state of tolerance that, as a rule, interests social scientists. It is not surprising, therefore, that we know less about tolerance than about prejudice.
—Gordon Allport, *The Nature of Prejudice* (1954)

As Allport observed, social scientific research has focused nearly all of its attention on understanding prejudice, partly because of the recognition that prejudice is problematic, perhaps even "pathological." Although prejudice is widely considered to be morally reprehensible by contemporary Western standards, it is far from abnormal in a statistical sense. On the contrary, copious research suggests that intergroup bias is the rule rather than the exception. Discriminatory bias is universally present across history, region, and culture (e.g., Sidanius & Pratto, 1999), is observable across most individuals (e.g., Nosek, Banaji, & Greenwald, 2002), and is "logical" and functional insofar as it serves to enhance the power and privilege of the dominant group (Sidanius & Pratto, 1999). In short, prejudice is both common and "rational" in many respects. Indeed, a more provocative question concerns the plausibility of *nonprejudice* and its underlying mechanisms.

In the present chapter, I discuss evolutionary and psychological factors that contribute to the ubiquity of prejudice. Although there are various forms of prejudice, this chapter focuses primarily on the unique and complex nature of racial bias in the 21st century. I then turn the question to whether there exist individuals who do not hold racial biases, in any form, and if so, which psychological traits and mechanisms might explain the absence of bias. I conclude the chapter with a discussion of the implications this research has for prejudice reduction.

ORIGINS OF INTERGROUP BIAS

In the present section, I briefly discuss a number of psychological (i.e., evolutionary/cognitive) and social (i.e., sociopolitical/structural) theories of intergroup prejudice and discrimination. Rather than providing a comprehensive overview of the origins of prejudice, this section highlights some theoretical explanations for the ubiquity of bias.

From an evolutionary standpoint, it is clear that humans evolved to live and function within the context of social groups (e.g., Caporael & Brewer, 1991). It is equally clear there is a distinction between "insiders" who belong to the group (i.e., *ingroup* members) and "outsiders" who do not belong (i.e., *outgroup* members). The tendency to categorize individuals into ingroups and outgroups and to favor members of the ingroup is well documented (for a review, see Brewer & Brown, 1998). As postulated by social identity theory (Tajfel, Billig, Bundy, & Flament, 1971; Tajfel & Turner, 1986), the tendency to join social groups and to favor the ingroup over outgroups is a fundamental human tendency. Indeed, ingroup bias can be obtained even for *minimal groups,* or meaningless categories that are artificially created and randomly assigned (Tajfel & Turner, 1986). These findings suggest that the condition of simply being in a group is sufficient to evoke differential feelings between the ingroup and an outgroup, regardless of any conflict over resources or history of intergroup strife. In short, being "different" from others is enough to produce bias.

But what if everyone could be a member of the same group? Would prejudice then disappear? Indeed, there is certainly evidence that categorization into overarching, "superordinate" groups (e.g., "humankind") can effectively reduce intergroup prejudice (Gaertner & Dovidio, 2009; Gaertner, Mann, Murrell, & Dovidio, 1989). The problem, however, is that superordinate categorizations are not likely to spontaneously occur or endure because they do not satisfy humans' basic desire to identify with more "exclusive" groups. According to optimal distinctiveness theory, people prefer "medium-sized" groups that satisfy both the need for assimilation and the need for differentiation (see Brewer, 1991). The *need for assimilation* refers to people's need, as social animals, to be affiliated with others and to feel that they are part of a group. On the other hand, the *need for distinctiveness* reveals people's desire for recognition of their uniqueness and individuality. Because uniqueness can exist only in contrast with something (or someone) else, the need for differentiation requires a focus on salient differences between the ingroup and outgroup, even when the similarities are much more numerous (e.g., Irish Catholics vs. Irish Protestants, or Castilian Spaniards vs. Basque Spaniards). Although ingroup boundaries are flexible (e.g., both of the aforementioned groups could simply identify as Irish or Spanish, respectively), homogeneity may lead to subgroup differentiation in order to satisfy a need for differentiation. The implication is that a highly inclusive self-categorization (e.g., "humankind") would be most likely to occur and endure in the event of an alien invasion. Until then, the need for differentiation ensures that there will always exist people who are *perceived* as being "different" (even if they are not truly different in the grander scheme).

Once in place, categories can lead to *accentuation*, or the exaggeration of differences between categories or groups (Campbell, 1967; Tajfel & Wilkes, 1963). Thus, people will tend to see distinct social groups as being more different than they really are, by virtue of categorization per se. Another social cost of perceiving individuals as representing categories is the activation of stereotypes and prejudice, particularly at the nonconscious or automatic level (Devine, 1989). Researchers have also found that categorization can lead to stereotyping, which is a functional device for simplifying an exceedingly complex world (Allport, 1954; Macrae, Milne, & Bodenhausen, 1994). The disadvantage is that the mere categorization of people automatically activates stereotypes, leading to oversimplified perceptions of outgroup members (Macrae et al., 1994) and subsequent negative evaluation and prejudice (Devine, 1989).

In addition to microlevel psychological factors, there are macrolevel social and structural factors that contribute to prejudice. Some theories, such as realistic group conflict (Bobo, 1988; LeVine & Campbell, 1972), argue that the mere presence of discrete groups increases the likelihood of prejudice and discrimination because of competition over scarce resources. Evidence for realistic group conflict was obtained in the classic Robbers Cave Experiment, in which two groups of boys at a summer camp began to develop strong antipathies toward each other when scarcities stimulated competition (Sherif et al., 1954/1961). Discriminatory bias can also emerge when resources are plentiful, given the desire for relative status and power and the opportunity to dominate the outgroup. According to social dominance theory (Sidanius & Pratto, 1999), every human society has been organized by group-based social hierarchies based on (a) age, (b) gender, or (c) arbitrary sets (e.g., ethnicity, clan, caste, and social class). Although specific organizational structures vary by history, region, and culture, two characteristics that all large-scale societies share is that (a) some groups are more privileged than others, and (b) the privilege is based on socially constructed *legitimizing myths* rather than actual merit. As the term suggests, legitimizing myths are untrue beliefs that people accept as mechanisms to explain why one group is more privileged than another (e.g., meritocracy, divine right of kings, caste or karma, genetic inferiority). These beliefs also rationalize the exploitation and denigration of lower status groups.

There are many other theories and variables that explicate the origins of prejudice, such as the condition of human mortality/fear of death (Greenberg, Solomon, & Pyszczynski, 1997), the need for self-esteem (Fein & Spencer, 1997; Wills, 1981), anger, frustration, and/or scapegoating (DeSteno, Dasgupta, Bartlett, & Cajdric, 2004; Hovland & Sears, 1940), the formation of illusory correlations (Hamilton & Gifford, 1976), and lack of exposure to or contact with outgroups (Zajonc, 1968; Pettigrew & Tropp, 2006). Indeed, there are so many explanations for prejudice that one begins to wonder whether there are any individuals who are able to avoid the potent concoction of evolutionary, psychological, motivational, and structural elements that predispose us to disfavor those who are different.

Nature of Modern Prejudice

Although there is strong evidence that humans are "wired" for prejudice, there is perhaps equally strong evidence that people value justice, fairness, and cooperation (e.g., Lind & Tyler, 1988). The question is whether these values can override prejudiced "default" responses. Research on the active self-regulation of prejudice is mixed, with work showing both success and failure at regulating prejudice responses (e.g., Monteith & Walters, 1998; Richeson & Trawalter, 2005; von Hippel, Silver, & Lynch, 2000). What is important, however, is that the desire to regulate prejudice (independent of success) has created new forms of racial prejudice, loosely referred to as *modern prejudice*. Unlike old-fashioned forms of prejudice that were common in the pre–Civil Rights era, more modern forms of prejudice, often referred to as *symbolic racism* (Sears, 1988), *subtle racism* (Pettigrew & Meertens, 1995), or *aversive racism* (Dovidio & Gaertner, 2004; Gaertner & Dovidio, 1986), do not involve overt manifestations of prejudice. For this reason, Blacks may experience uncertainty or ambiguity as to whether they have been a victim of prejudice in any given situation (Crocker & Major, 1989). The subtle nature of modern prejudice also makes it difficult to gauge the magnitude of racial progress (for a discussion, see Eibach & Ehrlinger, 2006). Has prejudice disappeared, or has it simply assumed a more subtle, insidious form?

Many of the aforementioned theories assume that the latter is true. Although these various theories have meaningful differences, they all share the notion that modern prejudice is some combination of well-intentioned ideological values or acknowledged nonprejudiced norms (i.e., the desire to not appear prejudiced), mixed with anti-Black affect. For example, according to aversive racism theory (Gaertner & Dovidio, 1986), White prejudice toward Blacks is the combination of egalitarian values and anti-Black affect. Because most Whites are truly egalitarian (i.e., they believe that everyone should be treated equally), holding anti-Black affect is "aversive" to them. To avoid threats to the self-concept, Whites push their anti-Black affect into the subconscious and show discriminatory bias only when behaviors can be rationalized on some basis other than race.

In one study by Gaertner and Dovidio (1986), half of the White participants were put in a situation in which they could offer help to a Black man and half were assigned to a condition in which they could offer help to a White man. The experiment also manipulated whether participants had an excuse for not helping (e.g., in a hurry, other bystanders nearby). Results demonstrated no difference in the helping of a Black vs. White man when participants had no excuse for not offering help, but White participants offered assistance to the White man significantly more often than to the Black man when they could explain their behavior by some external factor other than race (e.g., "I was in a hurry"). Their interpretation of these results was that participants discriminated only when they could rationalize their behavior, thereby preserving their egalitarian self-image. However, the important conclusion of the study is that White participants *did* discriminate on the basis of race, even if they were unaware of their racial discrimination (see Gaertner and Dovidio's concluding chapter in this volume for a new look at this classic research).

Aversive racism theory, combined with groundbreaking research by Devine (1989) demonstrating a dissociation between conscious and automatic prejudice, set the stage for decades of research on implicit prejudice (for a review, see Fazio & Olson, 2003). The hallmark of implicit prejudice is that it is not measured by self-reports. Rather than asking participants to respond to a series of scales or ratings that indicate how prejudiced they might be (e.g., "I would not mind if my roommate were African American"), implicit prejudice is assessed by tasks, such as asking participants to press computer keys in response to words, faces, or names. For example, the Implicit Association Test (IAT; Greenwald, McGhee, & Schwartz, 1998) measures prejudice by having participants classify Black and White names or faces and pleasant or unpleasant words using one of two keys. The assumption is that participants will be faster to complete the task when "Black" is paired with "unpleasant" and "White" is paired with "pleasant," compared with when "Black" and "pleasant" and "White" and "unpleasant" are paired, because Black is cognitively associated with negativity. While very few Whites show evidence of anti-Black bias when attitudes are measured explicitly via self-report (Fazio, Jackson, Dunton, & Williams, 1995), the inverse is true when attitudes are measured implicitly (Devine, 1989; Fazio et al., 1995), with over 80% of Whites showing significant evidence of anti-Black bias on the IAT (Nosek et al., 2002).

Not surprisingly, there has been considerable disagreement surrounding the validity of implicit (as well as explicit) measures of racial attitudes (see

Blanton et al., 2009; Greenwald et al., 2009, for discussions). Likewise, there is disagreement over which measure represents the "true" indicator of racial bias. Devine (1989) argued that individuals who consciously disavow prejudice can be nonprejudiced even if their nonconscious or automatic responses to Blacks are negatively biased. On the other hand, Fazio and colleagues (1995) defined "truly" nonprejudiced individuals as those who do not show automatically activated negative associations to African Americans, and they suggested that self-report measures provide a distorted or inaccurate estimate of racial bias. Dovidio, Kawakami, Johnson, Johnson, and Howard (1997) argued that both types of measures can be valid but may tap qualitatively distinct attitudes and predict different discriminatory outcomes. Although a detailed discussion of the differences between implicit and explicit prejudice is beyond the scope of this chapter, I believe that both types of measures tap valid, but qualitatively distinct, forms of prejudice. Therefore, I operationalized nonprejudice in terms of low or null bias on both implicit and explicit measures.

EXISTENCE OF NONPREJUDICE

The aforementioned propensities, incentives, and conditions for racial bias raise the question of whether it is possible to *not* be biased. The answer depends on a number of factors, such as whether it is theoretically possible to be psychologically devoid of an attitude or emotion, and if so, whether the nonratio scales used in psychology can measure its absence. It also depends on the temporal stability of prejudice—that is, do people always experience the same levels of prejudice, or can it vary? Finally, is nonprejudice an all-or-nothing construct, or do prejudice and nonprejudice vary along some continuum? Detailed answers to these provocative questions would require separate chapters to address adequately. Briefly stated, I believe that it is possible to be functionally nonprejudiced even if one cannot be nonprejudiced in an absolute (zero) sense. Prejudice is also malleable. As discussed in many of the chapters in the volume, much work has already shown that racial attitudes, even implicit biases, can be influenced by a number of intrapersonal and situational factors (see also Dasgupta & Greenwald, 2001; Lowery, Hardin, & Sinclair, 2001). Finally, nonprejudice represents a unique range within a distribution. In other words, although prejudice is a continuum, I believe that there is something qualitatively distinct about people who have the functional equivalent of no prejudice, compared with individuals who range from significantly above zero to extremely high levels of prejudice. To use a different metaphor, veritable piano virtuosos possess a uniqueness—perhaps on a neural level—that distinguishes them from all others who play the piano, regardless of whether these others play quite well, somewhat well, or not well at all. However, these are ultimately empirical questions that will, one hopes, be addressed in future research endeavors.

To date, only two studies have directly investigated nonprejudice—both using individual difference approaches. Phillips and Ziller (1997) examined the construct of universal orientation as an antecedent of nonprejudice. Livingston and Drwecki (2007) explored individual differences in affective learning style as one mechanism underlying nonprejudice.

Universal Orientation: Cognitive Attention Toward Similarity

The first empirical study of nonprejudice, conducted by Phillips and Ziller (1997), challenged the "inevitability of prejudice" assumption by building on the theoretical claims of Allport (1954) that a *tolerant personality* was characterized by the lack of quick or persistent categorization of people into discrete categories. Phillips and Ziller (1997) conceptualized nonprejudice as the tendency to attend to and accentuate similarity rather than difference between the self and others. Their research led to the development of the concept of *universal orientation*, which assumes that the key to nonprejudiced thought is the integration, rather than differentiation, of the self and others (see also Purdie-Vaughns & Walton and González, Manzi, & Noor, this volume). Specifically, the authors defined universal orientation as "a theory of self in which there is selective attention to self-other similarities, accompanied by accentuation of these similarities and resulting in an integration of self and others" (Phillips & Ziller, 1997, p. 422). Phillips and Ziller (1997) created the Universal Orientation Scale to tap the tendency to focus on similarity rather than difference. Research statements included: "The similarities between males and females are greater than the differences," "I tend to value similarities over differences when I meet someone," "I have difficulty relating to persons who are much younger than I (reverse-scored)," and "Everyone in the world is very much alike because in the end we all die." The authors found that universal orientation was negatively correlated with several self-report measures of prejudice, while being positively correlated with measures of empathy, perspective-taking, and humanitarianism. Universal orientation also predicted accentuation in judgments of similarity between the self and diverse others.

Consistent with the universal orientation findings, Livingston and Drwecki (2007) found that nonprejudiced individuals (operationalized as low or null bias on both implicit and explicit measures of prejudice [roughly 7% of the population of White college students in the United States]) have a lower propensity for categorization compared with ordinary individuals. We gave participants a version of the "who-said-what" paradigm (Taylor, Fiske, Etcoff, & Ruderman, 1978) in which they viewed mundane statements made by three

White males and three Black males and were later asked to match the comment to the individual who made it. Three response outcomes are possible: (a) accuracy—participants accurately identify the individual who made the statement, (b) within-category error—participants misattribute a statement made by one individual to another individual of the same race, and (c) between-category error—participants misattribute a statement made by one individual to another individual of a different race. By comparing the frequency of within-category versus between-category errors, one can ascertain the extent to which individuals utilize race as a basis for encoding the information that is presented. Results demonstrated that nonprejudiced individuals were much less likely than ordinary individuals to commit within-category errors.

On the surface, these results seem to contradict the "colorblindness" literature, which has found that individuals who do not "see" race tend to be *more* prejudiced than those who subscribe to *multiculturalism*, the notion that race should be both acknowledged and celebrated. For example, Richeson and Nussbaum (2004) found that participants exposed to messages advocating a multicultural approach to reducing racial conflict showed lower levels of implicit and explicit bias relative to participants exposed to more colorblind approaches. Similarly, Apfelbaum, Sommers, and Norton (2008) found that avoidance of the topic of race during an interracial interaction positively predicted racial bias (i.e., negative nonverbal behavior). However, it is possible that there is a qualitative difference between so-called colorblindness, on the one hand, and categorization propensity, on the other. What Apfelbaum et al. (2008) referred to as *strategic colorblindness* involves "avoidance of talking about race—or even acknowledging racial difference in an effort to avoid the appearance of bias" (p. 918). However, what is measured in the who-said-what paradigm is the tendency to perceive the race of another person. Put simply, one form of colorblindness is political and the other is cognitive. It is possible that "colorblind" people actually encode race but do not want to acknowledge its presence. On the other hand, nonprejudiced individuals may not encode race spontaneously but will acknowledge it in relevant situations. Future research will further disentangle the subtle distinctions between these two processes. In the meantime, what can be argued is that seeing race is not necessarily bad, nor will it inevitably lead to bias. Consequently, Livingston and Drwecki (2007) explored the possibility that what distinguishes nonprejudiced from ordinary individuals is not just attention to difference but, rather, the tendency to attach negativity to difference.

Affective Orientation: Susceptibility to Affective Conditioning

Because one source of attitude formation is associative learning (Zanna, Kiesler, & Pilkonis, 1970), it is plausible that mechanisms underlying the formation of general affective associations might also govern the formation of racial biases. A long history of attitude research has implicated classical conditioning as a mechanism by which attitudes can be acquired and maintained (Cacioppo, Marshall-Goodell, Tassinary, & Petty, 1992; Staats & Staats, 1958; Zanna et al., 1970), and more recent research has shown that conditioning processes are closely tied to the genesis of racial attitudes (Olson & Fazio, 2001, 2006; Olsson, Ebert, Banaji, & Phelps, 2005). Livingston and Drwecki (2007) explored how individual differences in affective learning style correlate with individual differences in the acquisition of negative attitudes toward Blacks, given the widespread societal negativity of Blacks (Ruscher, 2001).

To assess individual differences in susceptibility to affective conditioning (SAFCON), Livingston and Drwecki (2007) designed a paradigm that tapped variability in the propensity to acquire both positive ($SAFCON_{pos}$) and negative ($SAFCON_{neg}$) affective information. In the task, evaluatively neutral stimuli (i.e., Chinese ideographs) are paired with objectively positive, negative, or neutral pictures in a random and balanced fashion. The question of interest is the extent to which participants develop positive or negative attitudes toward each individual ideograph as a function of the affective valence of the picture with which it was paired. For instance, if participants especially disliked ideographs that were paired with negative photos, then they are said to be high in susceptibility to negative conditioning or $SAFCON_{neg}$. Conversely, if the especially liked ideographs that were paired with positive photos, then they were classified as being high in susceptibility to positive conditioning, or $SAFCON_{pos}$ (for a detailed description, see Livingston & Drwecki, 2007).

Livingston and Drwecki (2007) found that nonprejudiced individuals possess an affective learning style that is distinct from that of the rest of the population. Specifically, nonprejudiced individuals were more likely than ordinary individuals to form positive associations with neutral stimuli in a classical conditioning paradigm, but they were less likely to form negative associations with neutral stimuli. This effect held true even when controlling for the categorization effect discussed in the previous section. A follow-up study demonstrated that individual differences in affective orientation did not predict nonprejudice toward all outgroups; instead, affective orientation uniquely predicted attitudes toward Blacks. In this study, participants were given measures of implicit and explicit prejudice toward Blacks, Whites, and Latinos, in addition to the SAFCON measure and other personality and individual difference measures. Results indicated that individuals who were nonbiased toward Blacks also tended to be nonbiased toward Latinos ($r = .58$) and Asians ($r = .56$). However, the predictors of racial nonbias were different for the three groups. Whereas SAFCON was related to nonbias toward Blacks, such that individuals with lower susceptibility to negative conditioning tended to be more nonbiased toward African Americans ($r = .22$, $p = .055$), this relationship was not significant for either Latinos ($r = .15$) or Asians ($r = .03$).

These results have interesting implications for the ongoing debate regarding prejudice as a single, general attitude or as a qualitatively distinct attitude that is a function of the target group. Our findings offer support for both the prejudice-as-a-general-attitude model (Allport, 1954; Crandall, Eshleman, & O'Brien, 2002) and content-specific models of prejudice (Alexander, Brewer, & Livingston, 2004; Cottrell & Neuberg, 2005; Fiske, Cuddy, Glick, & Xu, 2002). Individuals who were nonprejudiced toward one group tended to be nonprejudiced toward other groups, consistent with the prejudice-as-general-attitude model. However, the specific mechanisms underlying of the general positive evaluations varied across groups, and that finding supports the notion of more textured and nuanced differences in the quality of racial attitudes.

Other Factors Predicting Nonprejudice

Livingston and Drwecki (2007) also tested the possibility that nonbiased individuals actually hold the same biases as ordinary individuals but are better self-regulators. Previous work has shown that greater inhibitory ability is related to less bias against African Americans, whether inhibition is measured via performance on cognitively demanding tasks (Richeson & Trawalter, 2005), age-related inhibitory differences (von Hippel, Silver, & Lynch, 2000), or manipulated via alcohol (Bartholow, Dickter, & Sestir, 2006). This relationship has been found to exist on both implicit (Bartholow et al., 2006; Richeson & Trawalter, 2005) and explicit (von Hippel et al., 2000) measures of racial bias. Furthermore, it has been shown that internal and external motivations to regulate prejudice can reduce implicit and explicit bias (Devine, Plant, Amodio, Harmon-Jones, & Vance, 2002; Plant & Devine, 1998). Thus, greater inhibitory ability among nonbiased individuals may be evidence that these individuals are simply more able to regulate their racial biases. Livingston and Drwecki (2007) measured self-regulation by assessing inhibitory ability on the Stroop task. This task measures the amount of time it takes for participants to read a color word (e.g., GREEN) as a function of whether the word is written in a consistent or inconsistent hue (e.g., green or red, respectively). Poor inhibitory ability is evidenced by the tendency to read the word much more slowly when it is written in an inconsistent versus consistent hue. In this study, the authors obtained no difference between ordinary and nonbiased participants' inhibitory ability. However, a significant correlation between explicit prejudice and inhibitory ability ($r = -.22$, $p < .02$) was obtained, indicating that individuals who scored higher on a measure of explicit prejudice tended to have lower inhibitory ability.

We have also examined relationships between nonbias and political conservatism. Although the nature of political conservatism is a matter of great political, social, and philosophical debate, there exists consensus regarding the fundamental components of conservatism. Core conservative ideology involves (a) the tendency to resist change and to preserve the status quo and (b) a relatively high tolerance for inequality (Jost, Glaser, Kruglanski, & Sulloway, 2003). Prior research has established both conceptual and empirical links between conservatism and racial bias; indeed, several lines of research have obtained correlations between conservatism and prejudice (Jost et al., 2003; Sears & Henry, 2003; Son Hing et al., 2008). It is clear that we also obtained a link between conservatism and nonprejudice. Whereas ordinary participants tended to be either liberal or conservative, nonprejudiced participants were almost exclusively liberal.

In summary, the data surrounding the nature of nonprejudice yield a complicated but interesting story. Being truly nonprejudiced seems to involve at least two basic psychological processes: (a) lower attention to racial differences and (b) lower propensity to form negative associations. The data indicate that these are independent processes. Nonprejudice also involves other factors such as political conservatism and inhibitory ability. However, these tended to correlate most strongly with explicit components of racial bias compared with implicit components. Building on the current focus on affective orientation, I next explore possible implications for prejudice reduction employing this route.

IMPLICATIONS FOR PREJUDICE REDUCTION: ORIGINS AND MALLEABILITY OF AFFECTIVE ORIENTATION

One question that emerges from the aforementioned research concerns the origins of SAFCON. How do individuals develop an affective learning style that emphasizes positive over negative information? One possibility we are exploring is that positive affective orientation is the result of early childhood socialization. The assumption is that individuals raised in caring, nurturing environments will develop affective orientations that are more positive than individuals raised in hostile, unsafe, or abusive environments. There is much research linking the impact of social experience to cognitive and neural development. For example, the work of Seth Pollak and colleagues has shown that abused children are more adept than nonabused children at detecting anger in visually ambiguous faces (Pollak & Sinha, 2002). Similarly, these researchers have found that early childhood experience affects attentional and hormonal processes that influence social behavior (Pollak, Vardi, Bechner, & Curtin, 2005).

There is also experimental evidence supporting the notion that how one is treated can affect one's affective orientation. Research by Smith et al. (2006)

has shown that context can moderate *negativity bias*—the robust tendency of humans to allocate greater perceptual attention to negative stimuli compared with positive stimuli. They provided experimental evidence showing that participants who were treated kindly showed a positivity bias compared with participants who were treated unkindly. These results suggest that individuals adapt their affective and perceptual orientations to suit the demands of the environment in which they are located. When there is the possibility and likelihood of threat, attention to negativity is adaptive. However, when there is only reward, focusing attention on negativity may cause one to forgo valuable opportunities. Thus, the preponderance of threat/reward in the environment should orient people toward negative or positive information (Smith et al., 2006).

We have also obtained evidence that SAFCON is malleable. A recent study by Hunsinger and Livingston (2010) tested whether susceptibility to affective conditioning could be modified by meditation. Participants were randomly assigned to a meditation condition or a control/nonmeditation condition. Participants assigned to the meditation condition were provided with detailed instructions about engaging in a particular kind of meditation called *Metta* or loving-kindness meditation. This form of Buddhist meditation involves repeating to oneself a series of phrases that are first directed toward the self, then to familiar others, and finally to all humans. When the phrases were first directed toward the self, the meditator repeated the following series of phrases:

> *May I may be safe from danger.*
>
> *May I be happy and peaceful.*
>
> *May I be healthy.*
>
> *May I be free from suffering.*

This series of phrases was repeated for several minutes. Then, the first-person pronoun was interchanged with words or pronouns referring to others in subsequent iterations. While repeating the phrases, the meditator aimed to form a genuine desire for these things to happen as well as a positive affective response to the self. Participants were instructed to do their best to focus on the phrases for 20 min. When other thoughts arose, participants were instructed to acknowledge the presence of those thoughts and reorient their attention back to the phrases.

Results from Hunsinger and Livingston (2010) show that short-term loving-kindness meditation practice significantly affected the degree to which participants were prone to positive affective conditioning. Those in the meditation condition showed higher SAFCON$_{pos}$ scores at the end of the meditation trials, compared with individuals in the control condition. Moreover, the effect of meditation on increasing positive affective learning style was particularly effective for chronically angry individuals (see DeSteno et al., 2004). Specifically, our data revealed that trait anger moderated the relationship between meditation group and positive affective conditioning. For those in the control condition, higher chronic anger predicted lower susceptibility to positive affective conditioning; in contrast, in the meditation condition, positive affective orientation did not differ as a function of chronic anger (Hunsinger & Livingston, 2010). In sum, meditation created a buffer for the deleterious effects of chronic anger on positive affective conditioning.

DISADVANTAGES OF POSITIVE AFFECTIVE ORIENTATION: VICTIMIZATION AND VULNERABILITY?

A second issue worth considering concerns the potential disadvantages of positive affective orientation. Are individuals who are less susceptible to negative conditioning more susceptible to danger because of their relative insensitivity to negative cues in the environment? Does positive affective orientation produce Pollyannas whose rose-colored glasses render them blind and susceptible to real-world hazards? I investigated this issue in a recent study in which individuals were asked to report the frequency with which they experienced a number of mishaps, such as being taken advantage of, being fired from a job, running out of gas while driving, being mugged, making a late payment on a credit card, being bitten by a dog, getting bad grades, and so on. What the data show is that individuals with a positive affective orientation were no more likely than other individuals to experience negative outcomes, and in many cases were less likely to experience negative outcomes.

A colleague who is a well-known cognitive psychologist recounted to me a personal anecdote that seemed to elucidate one process by which Pollyannas are able to avoid negative outcomes—namely, a cycle of kindness. This individual (who I suspect is high in both positive affective orientation and nonprejudice) was picnicking in New York's Central Park with his wife and granddaughter when a strange man approached them. They smiled and warmly greeted the stranger, who subsequently began to interact amicably with their granddaughter. After several minutes of otherwise benign interaction, the stranger unsheathed a large knife. He calmly explained to the family that his original intention had been to rob them at knifepoint. However, in light of all of the kindness and respect that they had shown him, he had had a change of heart and decided against the idea. He nonchalantly walked away, leaving the family stunned and shaken. Aside from being a disturbing account of the dangers that lurk in Central Park, the moral of the story is that so-called Pollyannas can sometimes *cause* a reduction in the level of threat in their environments.

CONCLUSION

What, then, can the nature of nonprejudice teach us about prejudice? For starters, the results suggest that there are different forms of nonprejudice, each with its unique set of antecedents. What allows an individual to be nonprejudiced toward African Americans may be distinct from the source of nonprejudice toward Asian Americans. Conversely, the causes of prejudice toward these groups may differ as well. Given the goal of the present volume, the first step to charting pathways toward improved intergroup relations may be to recognize that prejudice is not a monolithic phenomenon. The nature of sexist attitudes toward women is quite distinct from the nature of racist attitudes toward Blacks (see Fiske, Cuddy, Glick, & Xu, 2002). Thus, the existence of a simple solution is unlikely.

Second, the extant results suggest that prejudice may be more visceral than rational. If racial bias is the product of lower level affective processes, then the extent to which it can be regulated successfully by values or motives alone is not clear. The inability to regulate lower level affect via higher order reasoning can be found in many mundane scenarios. Imagine, for instance, that someone with a strong aversion to lima beans learns that three servings of lima beans per day will greatly reduce the risk of certain cancers and heart disease. While motivated individuals could alter their behavior to increase dietary intake of lima beans to three daily servings, it is unlikely that the same motivation would alter visceral reactions to the flavor of lima beans. Although it is possible for individuals to acquire tastes that were once aversive, they almost always achieve that through a process of repetitive exposure and reconditioning rather than sheer force of will. Similarly, researchers have found that (implicit) racial biases are not readily attenuated by egalitarian values or motives (Gaertner & Dovidio, 1986). However, these attitudes might be altered via experience-based reconditioning achieved through positive contact (Pettigrew & Tropp, 2006) or interracial dating (Olsson et al., 2005), for example. On the other hand, the reduction of sexism toward women might require a completely different intervention, given that sexism does not involve negative affect toward women so much as internalized prescriptions of power and gender roles (see Glick & Fiske, 1996).

In conclusion, it is unlikely that individuals hold racial biases out of malice or failure to recognize the virtues of intergroup tolerance. Rather, prejudice may be the consequence of lower level affective processes that are not readily modifiable by higher order reasoning. If one source of prejudice toward Blacks is negative images in the culture, then those with an "immunity" to the formation of negative associations are most likely to be nonprejudiced toward Blacks. One widely cited assumption in the prejudice literature is that everyone is exposed to and aware of cultural negativity toward Blacks (Devine, 1989).

However, it is possible that nonbiased individuals are able to avoid internalizing known negative associations with Blacks as a result of their resistance to the acquisition of negative affective associations in general. Nevertheless, it is possible that individuals without chronically low susceptibility to negative conditioning could achieve nonprejudice through (chronic) practice, meditation, selective attention, or interpersonal experiences that gradually recondition attitudes. Indeed, Dasgupta and Greenwald (2001) demonstrated that even implicit attitudes could be improved by exposing participants to positive, rather than negative, Black exemplars. Similarly, Olson and Fazio (2006) reduced implicit bias towards African Americans by pairing Black faces with positive stimuli. All in all, a number of studies have indicated that affective, environmental, educational, and interpersonal contexts that orient individuals toward positive achievements or experiences involving African Americans can decrease racial bias (Dasgupta & Greenwald, 2001; Ito, Chiao, Devine, Lorig, & Cacioppo, 2006; Olsson et al., 2005, Olson & Fazio, 2006; Rudman, Ashmore, & Gary, 2001). The take-home point is that, although a small minority of individuals are "naturals" when it comes to being nonprejudiced, it is quite possible for anyone to improve his or her racial attitudes. However, like most acquired skills (e.g., piano playing), prejudice reduction requires practice and the right context, in addition to motivation and desire, to be successful.

REFERENCES

Allport, G. W. (1954). *The nature of prejudice*. New York, NY: Addison Wesley.

Apfelbaum, E. P., Sommers, S. R., & Norton, M. I. (2008). Seeing race and seeming racist? Evaluating strategic colorblindness in social interaction. *Journal of Personality and Social Psychology, 95*, 918–932. doi:10.1037/a0011990

Alexander, M. G., Brewer, M. B., & Livingston, R. W. (2005). Putting stereotype content in context: Image theory and interethnic stereotypes. *Personality and Social Psychology Bulletin, 31*, 781–794. doi:10.1177/0146167204271550

Bartholow, B. D., Dickter, C. L., & Sestir, M. A. (2006). Stereotype activation and control of race bias: Cognitive control of inhibition and its impairment by alcohol. *Journal of Personality and Social Psychology Bulletin, 90*, 272–287. doi:10.1037/0022-3514.90.2.272

Blanton, H., Klick, J., Mitchell, G., Jaccard, J., Mellers, B., & Tetlock, P. E. (2009). Strong claims and weak evidence: Reassessing the predictive validity of the IAT. *Journal of Applied Psychology, 94*, 567–582. doi:10.1037/a0014665

Bobo, L. (1988). Group conflict, prejudice, and the paradox of contemporary racial attitudes. In P. A. Katz and D. Taylor (Eds.), *Eliminating racism: Profiles in controversy* (pp. 85–114). New York, NY: Plenum Press.

Brewer, M. B. (1991). The social self: On being the same and different at the same time. *Personality and Social Psychology Bulletin, 17,* 475–482. doi:10.1177/0146167291 175001

Brewer, M. B., & Brown, R. J. (1998). Intergroup relations. In D. T. Gilbert, S. T. Fiske, & G. Lindzey (Eds.), *The handbook of social psychology* (4th ed., Vol. 2, pp. 554–594). New York, NY: McGraw-Hill.

Cacioppo, J. T., Marshall-Goodell, B. S., Tassinary, L. G., & Petty, R. E. (1992). Rudimentary determinants of attitudes: Classical conditioning is more effective when prior knowledge about the attitude stimulus is low than high. *Journal of Experimental Social Psychology, 28,* 207–233. doi:10.1016/0022-1031(92)90053-M

Campbell, D.T. (1967). Stereotypes and perception of group differences. *American Psychologist, 22,* 817–829.

Caporael, L., & Brewer, M. B. (1991). The quest for human nature: Social and scientific issues in evolutionary psychology. *Journal of Social Issues, 47,* 1–9.

Cottrell, C. A., & Neuberg, S. L. (2005). Different emotional reactions to different groups: A sociofunctional threat-based approach to "prejudice". *Journal of Personality and Social Psychology, 88,* 770–789. doi:10.1037/0022-3514.88.5.770

Crandall, C. S., Eshleman, A., & O'Brien, L. (2002). Social norms and the expression and suppression of prejudice: The struggle for internalization. *Journal of Personality and Social Psychology, 82,* 359–378. doi:10.1037/0022-3514.82.3.359

Crocker, J., & Major, B. (1989). Social stigma and self-esteem: The self-protective properties of stigma. *Psychological Review, 96,* 608–630.

Dasgupta, N., & Greenwald, A. G. (2001). On the malleability of automatic attitudes: Combating automatic prejudice with images of admired and disliked individuals. *Journal of Personality and Social Psychology, 81,* 800–814. doi:10.1037/0022-3514.81.5.800

DeSteno, D., Dasgupta, N., Bartlett, M. Y., & Cajdric, A. (2004). Prejudice from thin air: The effect of emotion on automatic intergroup attitudes. *Psychological Science, 15,* 319–324. doi:10.1111/j.0956-7976.2004.00676.x

Devine, P. G. (1989). Stereotypes and prejudice: their automatic and controlled components. *Journal of Personality and Social Psychology, 56,* 5–18. doi:10.1037/0022-3514.56.1.5

Devine, P. G., Plant, E. A., Amodio, D. M., Harmon-Jones, E., & Vance, S. L. (2002). The regulation of explicit and implicit race bias: The role of motivations to respond without prejudice. *Journal of Personality and Social Psychology, 82,* 835–848. doi:10.1037/0022-3514.82.5.835

Dovidio, J. F., Kawakami, K., Johnson, C., Johnson, B., & Howard, A. (1997). On the nature of prejudice: Automatic and controlled processes. *Journal of Experimental Social Psychology, 33,* 510–540. doi:10.1006/jesp.1997.1331

Dovidio, J. F., & Gaertner, S. L. (2004). Aversive racism. In M. P. Zanna (Ed.), *Advances in experimental social psychology* (Vol. 36, pp. 1–52). San Diego, CA: Academic Press.

Eibach, R. P., & Ehrlinger, J. (2006). Keep your eyes on the prize: Reference points and racial differences in assessing progress toward equality. *Personality and Social Psychology Bulletin, 32,* 66–77.

Fazio, R. H., Jackson, J. R., Dunton, B. C., & Williams, C. J. (1995). Variability in automatic activation as an unobstrusive measure of racial attitudes: A bona fide pipeline? *Journal of Personality and Social Psychology, 69,* 1013–1027. doi:10.1037/0022-3514.69.6.1013

Fazio, R. H., & Olson, M. A. (2003). Implicit measures in social cognition research: Their meaning and use. *Annual Review of Psychology, 54,* 297–327.

Fein, S., & Spencer, S. J. (1997). Prejudice as self-image maintenance: Affirming the self through derogating others. *Journal of Personality and Social Psychology, 73,* 31–44. doi:10.1037/0022-3514.73.1.31

Fiske, S. T., Cuddy, A. J. C., Glick, P., & Xu, J. (2002). A model of (often mixed) stereotype content: Competence and warm respectively follow from perceived status and competition. *Journal of Personality and Social Psychology, 82,* 878–902. doi:10.1037/0022-3514.82.6.878

Gaertner, S. L., & Dovidio, J. F. (1986). The aversive form of racism. In J. F Dovidio & S. L. Gaertner, *Prejudice, discrimination, and racism* (pp. 61–89). San Diego, CA: Academic Press.

Gaertner, S. L., & Dovidio, J. F. (2009). A Common Ingroup Identity: A categorization-based approach for reducing intergroup bias. In T. Nelson (Ed.), *Handbook of prejudice* (pp. 489–505). Philadelphia, PA: Taylor & Francis.

Gaertner, S. L., Mann, J. A., Murrell, A. J., & Dovidio, J. F. (1989). Reduction of intergroup bias: The benefits of recategorization. *Journal of Personality and Social Psychology, 57,* 239–249. doi:10.1037/0022-3514.57.2.239

Glick, P., & Fiske, S. T. (1996). The ambivalent sexism inventory: Differentiating hostile and benevolent sexism. *Journal of Personality and Social Psychology, 70,* 491–512. doi:10.1037/0022-3514.70.3.491

Greenberg, J., Solomon, S., & Pyszczynski, T. (1997). Terror management theory of self-esteem and cultural worldviews: Empirical assessments and conceptual refinements. *Advances in Experimental Social Psychology, 29,* 61–139. doi:10.1016/S0065-2601(08)60016-7

Greenwald, A. G., McGhee, D. E., & Schwartz, J. L. K. (1998). Measuring individual differences in implicit cognitions: The Implicit Association Test. *Journal of Personality and Social Psychology, 74,* 1464–1480. doi:10.1037/0022-3514.74.6.1464

Greenwald, A. G., Poehlman, T. A., Uhlmann, E. L., & Banaji, M. R. (2009). Understanding and using the Implicit Association Test: III. Meta-Analysis of predictive validity. *Journal of Personality and Social Psychology, 97,* 17–41. doi:10.1037/a0015575

Hamilton, D. L., & Gifford, R. K. (1976). Illusory correlation in interpersonal perception: A cognitive basis of stereotypic judgments. *Journal of Experimental Social Psychology, 12,* 392–407. doi:10.1016/S0022-1031(76)80006-6

Hovland, C. I., & Sears, R. R. (1940). Minor studies in aggression: VI. Correlation of lynchings with economic indices. *Journal of Psychology, 9,* 301–310.

Hunsinger, M., & Livingston, R. W. (2010). Unpublished data. University of Massachusetts Amherst.

Ito, T. A., Chiao, K. W., Devine, P. G., Lorig, T. S., & Cacioppo, J. T. (2006). The influence of facial feedback on race bias. *Psychological Science, 17,* 256–261. doi:10.1111/j.1467-9280.2006.01694.x

Jost, J. T., Glaser, J., Kruglanski, A. W., & Sulloway, F. J. (2003). Political conservatism as motivated social cognition. *Psychological Bulletin, 129,* 339–375. doi:10.1037/0033-2909.129.3.339

LeVine, R. A., & Campbell, D. T. (1972). *Ethnocentrism: Theories of conflict, ethnic attitudes, and group behavior.* New York, NY: Wiley.

Lind, E. A., & Tyler, T. R. (1988). *The social psychology of procedural justice.* New York, NY: Plenum.

Livingston, R. W., & Drwecki, B. B. (2007). Why are some individuals not racially biased? Susceptibility to affective conditioning predicts nonprejudice toward Blacks. *Psychological Science, 18,* 816–823. doi:10.1111/j.1467-9280.2007.01985.x

Lowery, B. S., Hardin, C. D., & Sinclair, S. (2001). Social influence effects on automatic racial prejudice. *Journal of Personality and Social Psychology, 81,* 842–855.

Macrae, C. N., Milne, A. B., & Bodenhausen, G. V. (1994). Stereotypes as energy-saving devices: A peek inside the cognitive toolbox. *Journal of Personality and Social Psychology, 66,* 37–47. doi:10.1037/0022-3514.66.1.37

Monteith, M. J., & Walters, G. L. (1998). Egalitarianism, moral obligation, and prejudice-related personal standards. *Personality and Social Psychology Bulletin, 24,* 186–199. doi:10.1177/0146167298242007

Nosek, B. A., Banaji, M. R., & Greenwald, A. G. (2002). Harvesting implicit group attitudes and beliefs from a demonstration Web site. *Group Dynamics, 6,* 101–115. doi:10.1037/1089-2699.6.1.101

Olson, M. A., & Fazio, R. H. (2001). Implicit attitude formation through classical conditioning. *Psychological Science, 12,* 413–417. doi:10.1111/1467-9280.00376

Olson, M. A., & Fazio, R. H. (2006). Reducing automatically activated racial prejudice through implicit evaluative conditioning. *Personality and Social Psychology Bulletin, 32,* 421–433. doi:10.1177/0146167205284004

Olsson, A., Ebert, J. P., Banaji, M. R., & Phelps, L. (2005, July 29). The role of social groups in the persistence of learned fear. *Science, 309,* 785–787. doi:10.1126/science.1113551

Pettigrew, T. F., & Meertens, R. W. (1995). Subtle and blatant prejudice in Western Europe. *European Journal of Social Psychology, 25,* 57–75. doi:10.1002/ejsp.2420 250106

Pettigrew, T. F., & Tropp, L. R. (2006). A meta-analytic test of intergroup contact theory. *Journal of Personality and Social Psychology, 90,* 751–783. doi:10.1037/0022-3514.90.5.751

Phillips, S. T., & Ziller, R. C. (1997). Toward a theory and measure of the nature of nonprejudice. *Journal of Personality and Social Psychology, 72,* 420–434. doi:10. 1037/0022-3514.72.2.420

Plant, E. A., & Devine, P. G. (1998). Internal and external motivation to respond without prejudice. *Journal of Personality and Social Psychology, 75,* 811–832. doi:10. 1037/0022-3514.75.3.811

Pollak, S. D., & Sinha, P. (2002). Effects of early experience on children's recognition of facial displays of emotion. *Developmental Psychology, 38,* 784–791. doi:10.1037/ 0012-1649.38.5.784

Pollak, S. D., Vardi, S., Bechner, A. M. P., & Curtin, J. J. (2005). Physically abused children's regulation of attention in response to hostility. *Child Development, 76,* 968–977. doi:10.1111/j.1467-8624.2005.00890.x

Richeson, J. A., & Nussbaum, R. J. (2004). The impact of multiculturalism versus color-blindness on racial bias. *Journal of Experimental Social Psychology, 40,* 417–423. doi:10.1016/j.jesp.2003.09.002

Richeson, J. A., & Trawalter, S. (2005). Why do interracial interactions impair executive function? A resource depletion account. *Journal of Personality and Social Psychology, 88,* 934–947. doi:10.1037/0022-3514.88.6.934

Rudman, L. A., Ashmore, R. D., & Gary, M. L. (2001). "Unlearning" automatic biases: The malleability of implicit prejudice and stereotypes. *Journal of Personality and Social Psychology, 81,* 856–868. doi:10.1037/0022-3514.81.5.856

Ruscher, J. B. (2001). *Prejudiced communication: A social psychological perspective.* New York, NY: Guilford Press.

Sears, D. O. (1988). Symbolic racism. In P. Katz & D. Taylor (Eds.), *Eliminating racism: Profiles in controversy* (pp. 53–84). New York, NY: Plenum.

Sears, D. O., & Henry, P. J. (2003). The origins of symbolic racism. *Journal of Personality and Social Psychology, 85,* 259–275. doi:10.1037/0022-3514.85.2.259

Sherif, M., Harvey, O. J., White, J. B., Hood, W. R., & Sherif, C. W. (1961). *Intergroup conflict and cooperation: The Robbers Cave experiment.* Norman: University of Oklahoma Book Exchange. (Originally published 1954.)

Sidanius, J., & Pratto, F. (1999). *Social dominance: An intergroup theory of social hierarchy and oppression.* Cambridge, England: Cambridge University Press.

Smith, N. K., Larsen, J. T., Chartrand, T. L., Cacioppo, J. T., Katafiasz, H. A., & Moran, K. E. (2006). Being bad isn't always good: Affective context moderates the attention bias toward negative information. *Journal of Personality and Social Psychology, 90,* 210–220. doi:10.1037/0022-3514.90.2.210

Son Hing, L. S., Chung-Yan, G. A., Hamilton, L. K., & Zanna, M. P. (2008). A two-dimensional model that employs explicit and implicit attitudes to characterize prejudice. *Journal of Personality and Social Psychology, 94,* 971–987. doi:10.1037/ 0022-3514.94.6.971

Staats, A. W., & Staats, C. (1958). Attitudes established by classical conditioning. *Journal of Abnormal and Social Psychology, 57,* 37–40. doi:10.1037/h0042782

Tajfel, H., Billig, M. G., Bundy, R. P., & Flament, C. (1971). Social categorization and intergroup behaviour. *European Journal of Social Psychology, 1*, 149–178.

Tajfel, H., & Turner, J. C. (1986). The social identity theory of intergroup behaviour. In S. Worchel & W. G. Austin (Eds.), *Psychology of intergroup relations* (pp. 7–24). Chicago, IL: Nelson-Hall.

Tajfel, H., & Wilkes, A. L. (1963). Classification and quantitative judgment. *British Journal of Psychology, 54*, 101–114.

Taylor, S. E., Fiske, S. T., Etcoff, N. L., & Ruderman, A. J. (1978). Categorical and contextual bases of person memory and stereotyping. *Journal of Personality and Social Psychology, 36*, 778–793. doi:10.1037/0022-3514.36.7.778

von Hippel, W., Silver, L., & Lynch, M. (2000). Stereotyping against your will: The role of inhibitory ability in stereotyping and prejudice among the elderly. *Personality and Social Psychology Bulletin, 26*, 523–532. doi:10.1177/0146167200267001

Wills, T. A. (1981). Downward comparison principles in social psychology. *Psychological Bulletin, 90*, 245–271. doi:10.1037/0033-2909.90.2.245

Zajonc, R. B. (1968). Attitudinal effects of mere exposure [Supplement]. *Journal of Personality and Social Psychology Monograph, 9*, 1–27. doi:10.1037/h0025848

Zanna, M. P., Kiesler, C. A., & Pilkonis, P. A. (1970). Positive and negative attitudinal affect established by classical conditioning. *Journal of Personality and Social Psychology, 14*, 321–328. doi:10.1037/h0028991

2

MEASURING POSITIVE ATTITUDES TOWARD OUTGROUPS: DEVELOPMENT AND VALIDATION OF THE ALLOPHILIA SCALE

TODD L. PITTINSKY, SETH A. ROSENTHAL, AND R. MATTHEW MONTOYA

What does it mean to *like* members of racial, ethnic, religious, or other groups to which you do not belong? The terms typically used to describe feelings toward outgroups—*racism, sexism, homophobia,* and so on—reflect the pervasively negative perspective from which research on attitudes toward outgroups is typically conducted and the singularly negative vocabulary with which these attitudes are discussed (see Pittinsky, 2009a, 2009b, 2010; Pittinsky & Maruskin, 2008). Describing the positive counterparts to negative feelings toward outgroups can be difficult; even naming them is a challenge. Terms such as *tolerance, acceptance,* and *respect* are offered as the best conceptual opposites of intergroup hate and prejudice and, consequently, as the desired goals of efforts to improve intergroup relations (see Bennett, 2001).

But are tolerance, acceptance, and respect really the opposites of scourges such as racism and sexism? The bias in psychology for the study of negative attitudes toward outgroups and the relative dearth of work on positive attitudes make this an unexpectedly difficult question to answer (Dienstbier, 1970; Phillips & Ziller, 1997; Wright & Taylor, 2003). However, some theory and research suggest that there are positive attitudes that go beyond these states; one can have truly positive attitudes toward members of an outgroup. Unfortunately, in research and in practice, we tend to focus

41

more on understanding and reducing negative attitudes—or on achieving states of tolerance, acceptance and respect—than on understanding and promoting positive attitudes. Although it is critical to understand and reduce negative attitudes, because they are particularly likely to spark hateful acts across racial, ethnic, national, religious, and other forms of difference, it is also critical to understand and promote positive attitudes. This is because positive attitudes are particularly likely to spark proactive and prosocial behaviors (see Pittinsky, 2009b). Is it enough to reduce tension and hatred between groups through our understanding of negative intergroup attitudes? Or should we aim for a loftier goal—truly bringing diverse groups together by understanding and promoting positive intergroup attitudes?

We term such positive attitudes toward members of an outgroup *allophilia*, derived from the Greek for "like or love for the other." Theory suggests that, unlike negative attitudes toward outgroups, which may have evolved to alert humans to respond to negative stimuli with safety-related social behaviors (e.g., fight, flight, or freeze responses), positive outgroup attitudes may have evolved to help humans build social resources by developing bonds and alliances through approach-related social behaviors (see Cacioppo & Berntson, 1994; Fredrickson, 1998, 2001). Research needs to account for allophilia in order to understand the full range of attitudes—and their associated behaviors—that individuals may exhibit toward outgroup members (Pittinsky, 2009a, 2009b, 2010; Pittinsky & Simon, 2007).

A crucial first step toward integrating positive attitudes into research on attitudes toward outgroups is to determine the best way to measure those positive attitudes. There are many scales to choose from if one wishes to measure negative attitudes. They range in scope from the "old-fashioned" view that an outgroup is inherently inferior, to the more "modern" view that an outgroup is being undeservedly coddled by society (McConahay, 1986). But can we simply reverse-score one of these negative attitude scales to measure a positive attitude? Does an individual's low score on a measure of negative attitudes toward an outgroup imply a high score on a measure of positive attitudes toward that group?

There is a strong reason to answer "no." The theory of functional separability (e.g., Cacioppo & Berntson, 1994) provides evidence that, for two reasons, positive and negative attitudes are generally not simply reversible, and thus are not interchangeable (Cacioppo & Berntson, 1994; Cacioppo, Gardner, & Berntson, 1997; Green & Goldfried, 1965; Jordan, 1965; Osgood, Suci, & Tannenbaum, 1957; see also Pittinsky, Rosenthal, & Montoya, 2010, for a summary of supporting research).

First, positive and negative attitudes are nonbipolar; that is, appearances (and often their very names) aside, positive and negative attitudes do not necessarily lie at opposite ends of a unidimensional spectrum. For instance, ratings of "good" and "happy" are more strongly correlated with each other ($r = .55$)

than with their supposed opposites (good–bad, $r = -.30$; happy–sad, $r = -.18$; Green & Goldfried, 1965). If the good–bad and happy–sad relationships were the polar opposites they are often assumed to be, their correlations would be much stronger, approaching -1.00. But because their correlations are in fact so weak, judgments of goodness cannot be determined simply by reverse scoring judgments of badness, nor can one's level of happiness be said to be the opposite of one's level of sadness.

Second, positive and negative attitudes are nonreciprocally activated; that is, a change in a negative attitude does not necessarily coincide with an equivalently countervailing change in the corresponding positive attitude. We can see this in ordinary circumstances; one can, over time, develop a negative attitude about a friend while still feeling the same positive attitudes toward him or her (Rodin, 1978). Another reason is that positive attitudes are accessed more spontaneously than are negative attitudes (Herr & Page, 2004). And because positive attitudes may change at different times and rates than negative attitudes, the current level of a positive attitude cannot be inferred from the reverse of a score on a measure of a current negative attitude.

More important than these technical and measurement-oriented issues is the finding that positive and negative attitudes differ in their ability to predict positive and negative behaviors (see Pittinsky et al., 2010). Specifically, positive attitudes appear to act as predispositions to approach responses, whereas negative attitudes act as predispositions to avoidance and withdrawal responses; thus the attitude–behavior links are *valence congruent* (Cacioppo & Berntson, 1994; Cacioppo et al., 1997; Cacioppo, Gardner, & Berntson, 1999). Positive attitudes are more likely to predict positive behaviors, whereas negative attitudes are more likely to predict negative behaviors. These functionally separate positive and negative attitude–behavior links can occur automatically (Chen & Bargh, 1999) and are evident in the different neurological systems involved in the assessment of a stimulus as friendly or hostile (LeDoux, 1995).

In the specific case of attitudes toward outgroups, research indicates that positive and negative attitudes are indeed nonbipolar (Patchen, Hofmann, & Davidson, 1976; Triandis, 1964; Woodmansee & Cook, 1967) and have valence-congruent relationships to behavior (Pittinsky et al., 2010). It is clear, then, that positive and negative attitudes toward outgroups must be measured separately. Yet there has been no programmatic study of the forms and behavioral effects of positive attitudes toward outgroups.[1]

---

[1]Katz and Hass (1988) identified and measured what they termed *pro-Black* attitudes. However, the pro-Black attitudes they investigated were not direct positive attitudes, but rather were mediated by feelings of sympathy and helpfulness toward African Americans based on recognition of the widespread prejudice against them. Although sympathetic attitudes about a group are certainly not negative attitudes (Schuman & Harding, 1963; Woodmansee & Cook, 1967), neither are they direct positive attitudes (Czopp & Monteith, 2006). This may be why, for instance, higher scores on the Pro-Black Scale are not necessarily linked to increased support for pro-Black policies such as raising the number of college scholarships for African Americans (Eisenstadt, Leippe, Stambush, Rauch, & Rivers, 2005).

Pittinsky et al. (2010) began to fill this gap in the literature by exploring the differential influences on behavior of positive and negative attitudes toward outgroups. They found that positive attitudes were more effective than negative attitudes in predicting positive behaviors (e.g., allocating charity donations to the group, intervening in socially risky ways on behalf of members of the group). Conversely, negative attitudes, measured using traditional prejudice and racism scales, were more effective than positive attitudes in predicting negative behaviors (e.g., support for ending antidiscrimination policies). In other words, the psychological theory of valence congruence was supported; positive behaviors were predicted better by how much individuals liked members of another group than by how little they disliked members of that group. In contrast (and as is more widely known), negative behaviors were predicted better by how much individuals disliked members of another group than by how little they liked members of that group.

If research is to account for positive as well as negative attitudes toward outgroups, it cannot rely solely on standard measures that capture only the presence or absence of negative attitudes, such as xenophobia, prejudice, and racism. Yet social psychology has generally "seemed uninterested" in measuring and understanding positive attitudes and their effects (Wright & Taylor, 2003, p. 433). In our research, we developed a scale to account for such positive attitudes: the Allophilia Scale. The purpose of this chapter is to introduce and further develop that scale.

We also explore the factor structure of positive attitudes toward outgroups as a step toward understanding how different facets of positive attitudes are related to different positive behaviors. Applied to intergroup relations, the tripartite model of attitudes (D. Katz & Stotland, 1959; Rosenberg, Hovland, McGuire, Abelson, & Brehm, 1960) postulates that one's evaluation of a particular social group includes three components: affective (one's emotional response toward the group), behavioral (one's tendency to act in particular ways toward members of the group), and cognitive (one's thoughts and beliefs about the group). Past research indicates the importance of a multi-faceted assessment of an individual's attitudes, which suggested to us that the Allophilia Scale should contain items that assess the affective, behavioral, and cognitive components of an individual's evaluations of an outgroup. However, the cognitive component of attitudes toward outgroup members often consists of stereotypes (e.g., Devine, 2001). Although stereotypes can appear to be positive, the research literature casts some doubt on whether they truly reflect positive attitudes. For instance, research has shown that complimentary stereotypes of African Americans (e.g., that they are musical and athletic) can be positively related to negative prejudices toward them (Czopp & Monteith, 2006). Similarly, benevolent sexism (e.g., the belief that women are more innocent and better than men) can be positively related to more familiar hostile types of sexism (Glick & Fiske, 1996; Glick et al., 2000). We therefore focused on affective and behavioral, but not cognitive, assessments of positive attitudes toward outgroup members as we developed the Allophilia Scale.

DEVELOPMENT OF THE ALLOPHILIA SCALE

Scale Development and Factor Structure

By developing the Allophilia Scale, we have striven to foster research on positive attitudes toward outgroups by offering researchers a common construct and a tool for operationalizing that construct. To ensure that the scale reflects the many facets of the experience of allophilia, we used an exploratory and qualitative bottom-up approach, rather than a theory-driven top-down approach, to generate the scale's items. We surveyed 195 participants, who were diverse in terms of sex, race, age, education, citizenship, and experience with members of various outgroups. They were asked to write down at least three open-ended positive feelings one might have about members of an outgroup or behaviors one might exhibit toward members of an outgroup. After removing similar, repetitious, and unusable responses from an initial pool of more than 500, we retained 34 responses for further study as potential scale items.

We needed to shorten this list even further to achieve a parsimonious measure of positive attitudes toward outgroup members. We therefore recruited a sample of 200 U.S. citizens through an online survey-sampling service. There were 109 women and 91 men; ages ranged from an 18- to 20-year age group to a 61- to 65-year age group ($Mdn = 36$–40 years). Participants responded to the 34 potential scale items (presented in random order) as they pertained to attitudes toward African Americans as an outgroup on a 1 (*strongly disagree*) to 6 (*strongly agree*) scale. Because the study concerned attitudes toward African Americans as an outgroup, African American and other Black participants were not included in the sample.

We performed a principal-components analysis on the resulting data and, by examining the scree plot, determined that there may be as many as five meaningful subtypes of positive attitudes toward outgroups. The data were then reanalyzed, using maximum likelihood extraction with direct oblimin rotations. The results suggested that a five-factor solution, which accounted for approximately 71% of the variance, yielded the most interpretable factor structure. The final five-factor scale consisted of 17 items and accounted for approximately 75% of the scale's variance. The subscales all exhibited good internal consistency; alpha coefficients ranged from .88 to

.92. The final version of the Allophilia Scale is reported and described in Table 2.1.[2]

We confirmed the factor structure of the Allophilia Scale using a second sample of 379 U.S. citizens recruited through an online survey-sampling service. There were 176 women, 183 men, and 20 of unidentified gender; ages ranged from an 18- to 20-year age group to a 66-and-over age group (Mdn = 36–40 years). Again, because the study concerned attitudes toward African Americans as an outgroup, African American and other Black participants were excluded from the sample.

We conducted a confirmatory factor analysis to test the factor structure. We tested a single-factor model (allophilia as a unidimensional construct; Model 1), a benchmark five-factor model (a first-order model in which all factors are allowed to correlate with one another; Model 2), and the model that theoretically represents the structure of the Allophilia Scale (a second-order model in which the five factors are indicative of a higher order general allophilia factor; Model 3).

Levels of fit were assessed by the root mean square error of approximation (RMSEA) and the comparative fit index (CFI). As predicted, the unidimensional model (Model 1) provided a poor fit for the Allophilia Scale items; RMSEA = .15, CFI = .83. In contrast, the two models representing five-factor solutions for the scale (Models 2 and 3) provided acceptably good fit; RMSEA = .06 and .08, respectively; CFI = .97 and .95, respectively (see Browne & Cudeck, 1993; Hu & Bentler, 1999).[3] The good fit of the five-factor confirmatory factor analysis helps verify the exploratory factor analysis results, indicating that a five-factor interpretation of allophilia is robust and replicable.

The subscales derived from the five factors were named for the themes of their content: Affection (positive affective evaluations of outgroup members), Comfort (a feeling of ease with outgroup members), Kinship (a feeling of closeness with outgroup members), Engagement (a tendency to seek to affiliate and interact with outgroup members), and Enthusiasm (having emotionally heightened positive attitudes about outgroup members).

---

[2]The Allophilia Scale appears to have the same five-factor structure when applied to other outgroups as well. For instance, in research using the scale to measure positive attitudes toward Latinos, an unpublished principal components analysis of the responses of 275 non-Latinos yielded the same five factors (see Pittinsky et al., 2010).

[3]To examine the relative fit of the different models, we compared differences in chi-square fit indices, using the corresponding differences in degrees of freedom. Both five-factor models (Models 2 and 3) provided a significantly better fit that did the single-factor model (Model 1); $\chi^2_{diff}(10) = 772.27, p < .001$ and $\chi^2_{diff}(5) = 654.52, p < .001$, respectively. Model 2 also provided a better fit than did Model 3; $\chi^2_{diff}(5) = 117.75, p < .001$. This was not particularly surprising or noteworthy, however, for two reasons. First, no model with the same five factors as the benchmark model (Model 2) but with different relationships between those factors can provide a better fit than the benchmark model (Fletcher, Simpson, & Thomas, 2000; Marsh & Hocevar, 1985). Further, when chi-square statistics are used to compare models with each other, they are influenced by sample size and can therefore be overly liberal in indicating significant differences in fit between models (Marsh & Hau, 1996).

TABLE 2.1

Allophilia Items, Factor Loadings, Subscale Intercorrelations and Reliabilities, Means, and Standard Deviations

Item no.	Item	Factor loadings					M	SD
		Factor 1	Factor 2	Factor 3	Factor 4	Factor 5		
1.	In general, I have positive attitudes about [members of outgroup].	**.88**	.03	.07	-.10	.03	4.39	1.31
2.	I respect [members of outgroup].	**.79**	.04	-.03	.06	.03	4.52	1.18
3.	I like [members of outgroup].	**.64**	.15	-.08	.14	.08	4.54	1.18
4.	I feel positively toward [members of outgroup].	**.57**	.19	.02	.14	.05	4.19	1.32
5.	I am at ease around [members of outgroup].	.01	**.81**	.09	.00	.06	4.05	1.33
6.	I am comfortable when I hang out with [members of outgroup].	.13	**.77**	.17	.02	-.11	4.00	1.41
7.	I feel like I can be myself around [members of outgroup].	.15	**.69**	-.06	.08	.05	4.06	1.40
8.	I feel a sense of belonging with [members of outgroup].	-.09	.20	**.75**	.00	.18	2.98	1.32
9.	I feel a kinship with [members of outgroup].	.08	.08	**.72**	.10	-.05	3.21	1.36
10.	I would like to be more like [members of outgroup].	.07	.02	**.62**	.13	.09	2.88	1.33
11.	I am truly interested in understanding the points of view of [members of outgroup].	-.09	.20	-.10	**.81**	.13	4.00	1.37
12.	I am motivated to get to know [members of outgroup] better.	.14	-.04	.26	**.71**	-.11	3.57	1.31
13.	To enrich my life, I would try and make more friends who are [members of outgroup].	.11	-.09	.15	**.68**	.04	3.59	1.32
14.	I am interested in hearing about the experiences of [members of outgroup].	.13	.15	.05	**.52**	.20	3.85	1.39
15.	I am impressed by [members of outgroup].	.19	.08	.07	.14	**.58**	3.65	1.26
16.	I feel inspired by [members of outgroup].	.21	-.05	.29	.07	**.52**	3.52	1.35
17.	I am enthusiastic about [members of outgroup].	.20	.01	.28	.13	**.33**	3.47	1.26

Subscale correlations and reliabilities

Affection	.92				
Comfort	.73	.91			
Kinship	.64	.72	.89		
Engagement	.78	.67	.62	.92	
Enthusiasm	.76	.76	.75	.63	.88

Note. Item loadings for "home" factors are in bold. Factor 1 = Affection, Factor 2 = Comfort, Factor 3 = Kinship, Factor 4 = Engagement, Factor 5 = Enthusiasm. Alpha coefficients reported on the diagonal. All correlations significant at $p < .001$. Items are rated on a 6-point scale: 1 = *strongly disagree*, 2 = *disagree*, 3 = *slightly disagree*, 4 = *slightly agree*, 5 = *agree*, 6 = *strongly agree*. $N = 200$.

Together, these five factors begin to answer this chapter's opening question: What is it like to experience allophilia for the members of another group? They are compatible with the tripartite model of attitudes (e.g., D. Katz & Stotland, 1959; Rosenberg et al., 1960); Affection, Comfort, Kinship, and Enthusiasm consist of affective evaluations, whereas Engagement consists of behavioral evaluations. As noted earlier, cognitive evaluations were excluded from the scale early in the process.

It also may be instructive to approach the Comfort and Enthusiasm subscales from other theoretical perspectives. For instance, the Comfort subscale may be understood as indicative of low negative affective arousal (e.g., Watson & Tellegen, 1985), and the Enthusiasm subscale may be viewed as a group-level example of idealizing infatuation (i.e., intense positive emotions directed toward a dissimilar other; e.g., McClanahan, Gold, Lenney, Ryckman, & Kulberg, 1990).

The Allophilia Scale's Relationship to Other Measures

To understand how the Allophilia Scale compares with other constructs related to attitudes toward outgroup members, it is instructive to know how it relates statistically to those constructs. We expected allophilia to be positively related to two constructs that focus on inclusiveness and similarity between groups: *recategorization* (redefining outgroup members as members of an inclusive, superordinate group; Gaertner et al., 1999; Gaertner, Mann, Murrell, & Dovidio, 1989; see also Purdie-Vaughns & Walton; González, Manzi, & Noor; and Gaertner & Dovidio in this volume) and *universal orientation*, which Phillips and Ziller (1997) described as an "orientation in interpersonal relations whereby perceivers selectively attend to, accentuate, and interpret similarities rather than differences between the self and others" (p. 420) and which they referred to as a precursor to what they termed *nonprejudice* (see also Livingston, this volume, for a detailed discussion of nonprejudice). Both constructs differ theoretically from allophilia, which stresses positive feelings that emerge *despite* the existence of separate group identities, in that positive feelings are believed to flow instead from feelings of inclusiveness or similarity between individuals or groups. In contrast, although positive and negative attitudes toward outgroups are not empirical opposites, as we made clear earlier, we did expect the Allophilia Scale to correlate negatively with prejudice and racism measures to some degree.

Finally, we expected allophilia to have little or no relationship with *decategorization*, the tendency to view people as individuals rather than as group members (Gaertner et al., 1999, 1989). Although decategorization is believed to be a path to positive attitudes, it plays down the very group identities on which allophilia (as well as prejudice and racism) is founded.

The same participants who completed the Allophilia Scale for the confirmatory factor analysis also completed the following three measures of orientation to groups and differences and four measures of racism or prejudice.

Measures of Orientation to Groups and Differences

The item "To what extent do you feel like members of your ethnic group and African Americans are members of one group?" measured recategorization, and the item "To what extent do you feel like members of your ethnic group and African Americans are separate individuals?" measured decategorization, both on a 1 (*not at all*) to 7 (*very much*) scale (see Gaertner et al., 1999, 1989). The Universal Orientation Scale (Phillips & Ziller, 1997) includes 20 items, such as "I tend to value similarities over differences when I meet someone," rated on a 1 (*does not describe my opinion very well*) to 5 (*describes my opinion very well*) scale.

Measures of Racism or Prejudice

The Old-Fashioned Racism Scale (McConahay, 1986) measured explicit prejudices based on "traditional" racist values of group inferiority, and the Modern Racism Scale (McConahay, 1986) measured beliefs that African Americans are not the victims of discrimination, are overly demanding, and receive undeserved special treatment, both with seven items rated on a scale of 1 (*strongly disagree*) to 7 (*strongly agree*). The Symbolic Racism Scale (Henry & Sears, 2002) measured the interaction of affective components of modern types of racism (e.g., feelings of discomfort, uneasiness, and disgust) with beliefs that African Americans violate important traditional norms by failing to be self-sufficient, with eight items rated on a 1- to-4 scale with varied anchors linked to the content of each item. The Color-Blind Racism Scale (Neville, Lilly, Duran, Lee, & Browne, 2000) measured the extent to which individuals believe that race is not, and should not be, consequential, with 20 items rated on a scale of 1 (*strongly disagree*) to 7 (*strongly agree*).

Correlations between the Allophilia Scale and related scales are reported in Table 2.2. They indicate that as allophilia increased, participants had a more universal orientation and endorsed stronger recategorization of outgroup members into the ingroup. Conversely, increased allophilia was related to lower scores on each of the prejudice and racism measures. Allophilia also exhibited a small but significant negative relationship to decategorization (viewing people as individuals rather than as members of groups). In all but one case, the Allophilia Scale correlated with the validity scale in the predicted direction (allophilia was predicted to be unrelated

TABLE 2.2
Correlations Between Allophilia and Related Constructs

Variable		Factors							M	SD
	1	2	3	4	5	6	7	8		
Allophilia Scale	.96								3.80	1.01
Universal Orientation	.40	.71							3.41	0.42
Recategorization	.42	.26	—						3.94	1.76
Decategorization	−.16	−.08	−.30	—					5.04	1.76
Old-Fashioned Racism	−.57	−.35	−.27	.05	.79				2.44	1.09
Modern Racism	−.53	−.22	−.14	.08	.66	.85			3.21	1.20
Symbolic Racism	−.50	−.17	−.08	.05	.41	.73	.86		2.52	0.57
Color-Blind Racial Attitudes	−.41	−.13	−.02	−.01	.32	.67	.80	.87	3.63	0.75

Note. All correlations $r ≥ ±.10$, $p < .05$. Alpha coefficients are reported on the diagonal. Dashes indicate single-item measures with no alpha reliability coefficient to report. $N = 379$.

to decategorization, but the two measures proved to have a small negative correlation). In no case was the Allophilia Scale redundant with another scale (i.e., it was not within the 95% confidence interval of a ± 1.00 correlation with any scale, even when correlations were adjusted to account for attenuation due to low reliability), indicating that the Allophilia Scale measures a unique construct. This is supported by the findings of Pittinsky et al. (2010) that the Allophilia Scale, when tested simultaneously with various racism and prejudice measures, independently predicted positive behaviors toward African Americans. Overall, the Allophilia Scale converged appropriately with measures of negative attitudes toward outgroups and with measures of attitudes toward groups and humankind in general that are theoretically linked to positive attitudes toward outgroups.

The ability to apply the Allophilia Scale and, by extension, the construct of allophilia, to groups other than African Americans is supported by previous research, which indicates that positive attitudes toward numerous other outgroups are important for generating positive behaviors toward those outgroups. In this research, the Allophilia Scale has predicted positive behaviors toward diverse outgroups, including Latinos, multiracial individuals, the French, and both Jewish and Arab Israeli citizens. Specifically, Pittinsky et al. (2010) found that allophilia toward Latinos predicted the act of allocating larger donations to a Latino charity better than did anti-Latino feelings and attitudes and better than stereotyped pro-Latino beliefs. Pittinsky and Montoya (2009) found that allophilia toward people with one White and one Black parent predicted support for them to have access to the types of social assistance programs that are available to Black Americans. Support for these policies, as well as for official recognition of "multiracial" as a unique racial category, was strongest among people who combined high allophilia toward multiracials with strong beliefs in equality. The Allophilia Scale was also used to identify reciprocal positive attitudes in a real-world applied setting. It identified positive attitudes of Jewish Israeli citizens toward Arab Israeli citizens and vice versa and indicated that these attitudes were crucial antecedents of procoexistence beliefs on both sides (Pittinsky, Ratcliff, & Maruskin, 2008).

Finally, Pittinsky, Montoya, Tropp, and Chen (2007) indicated that allophilia is not necessarily a static attitude; it can be influenced by circumstances. The researchers found that allophilia toward the French people was influenced by whether a French leader was perceived to have acted in a positive or negative way to a devastating earthquake in southern Asia *and* by whether the French people were perceived as approving or disapproving of their leader's actions. Allophilia toward the French was highest among those who perceived the French people as approving of positive actions by their leader.

Allophilia Subscales' Unique Relationships With Positive Outcomes

The subscales of the Allophilia Scale clearly represent statistically robust subtypes of positive attitudes toward outgroups. But to be meaningful subtypes, they each must have unique relationships with different theoretically relevant outcomes as well.

We expected the Affection subscale (generalized positive feelings toward the outgroup) to be uniquely related to *Reciprocal Affection*—the hope that one's positive affective assessment of an outgroup is both shared by those close to one and reciprocated by members of the outgroup (see Swart, Turner, Hewstone, & Voci, this volume, for a discussion of the importance of cross-group, reciprocal feelings and behaviors). We expected the generalized feelings of Comfort with outgroup members to be uniquely related to *Social Ease*—reports that social experiences with outgroup members are emotionally positive and low in negative arousal. The generalized feelings of Kinship with outgroup members were predicted to have a unique relationship to specific feelings of *Social Closeness* that one might feel when one is with members of the outgroup. Engagement, the general inclination to affiliate behaviorally with outgroup members, was expected to have a unique relationship with the desire to facilitate *Learning* more about outgroup members. Finally, the Enthusiasm subscale was expected to have a unique relationship with intense feelings of *Inspiration* that one might experience in an emotionally heightened, infatuated state.

To test these predictions, 222 students from three large public universities in the upper Midwest were recruited through an online survey-sampling service. There were 125 women and 97 men; ages ranged from 18 to 26 years ($M =$ 20.2 years, $SD = 1.71$). Because the study concerned attitudes toward African Americans as an outgroup, African American and other Black participants were not included in the sample. Participants first completed the Allophilia Scale and then the items that constituted the outcome scales, which were presented in random order. All items were rated on a 1 (*strongly disagree*) to 6 (*strongly agree*) scale. (See Exhibit 2.1 for the complete list of outcome items.)

Correlations between the composite Allophilia Scale and subscales and the outcome scales are presented in Table 2.3. The composite Allophilia Scale and each of its subscales were significantly correlated with each of the outcome scales. This indicates that each outcome scale was related to generalized positive feelings toward the outgroup. More germane to the validity of the subscales is the fact that, in all but one case, each outcome scale had a significantly stronger relationship (i.e., a stronger correlation, $p < .05$) with the Allophilia subscale with which it was theoretically linked than with any other subscale. Specifically, Reciprocal Affection was more strongly related to the Affection subscale ($r = .68$) than to any other subscale (except for Enthusiasm, with which the difference in the strength of relationship reached

EXHIBIT 2.1
Items in Outcome Scales

Outcome scale	Items
Reciprocal Affection	1. I hope that my family and friends have positive feelings about African Americans. 2. African Americans would accept me for who I am. 3. I feel accepted by African Americans.
Social Ease	1. I find it easy to talk to African Americans. 2. There is no awkwardness for me when I'm around African Americans. 3. I am not at all self-conscious when I am around African Americans.
Social Closeness	1. I feel like I'm "at home" when I'm with African Americans. 2. I feel like I fit in when I spend a lot of time with African Americans. 3. I feel a real connection with African Americans.
Learning	1. I really want to expand my knowledge of African Americans' perspectives. 2. It would be enjoyable to learn more about African Americans. 3. I would like to learn about African American history.
Inspiration	1. I am awed by African Americans. 2. I idealize African Americans. 3. I idolize African Americans.

the $p = .06$ level); Social Ease was more strongly related to the Comfort subscale ($r = .70$) than to any other subscale; Social Closeness was more strongly related to the Kinship subscale ($r = .72$) than to any other subscale; Learning was more strongly related to the Engagement subscale ($r = .76$) than to any other subscale; and Inspiration was more strongly related to the Enthusiasm subscale ($r = .57$) than to any other subscale.

These results indicate not only that a composite Allophilia Scale score provides a valid measure of positive attitudes toward outgroups but also that the Allophilia subscales provide semi-independent measures of the factors that constitute allophilia. Assessing these factors using the allophilia subscales is especially valuable because it can help researchers study the consequences of specific positive attitudes and make precise predictions about the particular behaviors that such specific attitudes will generate.

CONCLUSION

We developed the Allophilia Scale as a means of moving beyond research on prejudice reduction by promoting programmatic research on positive attitudes toward outgroups. Such research is critical because theory (e.g.,

TABLE 2.3
Correlations Between Allophilia Subscales and Outcome Variables

		Allophilia subscales							
Variable	Allophilia	Affection	Comfort	Kinship	Engagement	Enthusiasm	M	SD	α
Reciprocal Affection	.72	.68[a]	.56	.58	.55	.61[a]	4.29	0.85	.69
Social Ease	.60	.52	**.70**	.48	.40	.42	3.77	1.08	.84
Social Closeness	.72	.55	.61	**.72**	.52	.58	3.29	1.07	.84
Learning	.63	.49	.25	.43	**.76**	.58	3.99	1.10	.88
Inspiration	.52	.37	.24	.48	.47	**.57**	2.92	1.00	.84

Note. All correlations $r \geq \pm.14$, $p < .05$. Correlations presented in bold are of significantly greater magnitude ($p < .05$) than correlations with all other Allophilia subscales in that row except for cells marked with [a], for which the significance level of the difference between correlation magnitudes is $p = .06$. $N = 222$.

Cacioppo & Berntson, 1994) and research (e.g., Pittinsky et al., 2010) suggest that the circumscribed study of negative attitudes toward outgroups is not sufficient to understand the effects of positive attitudes toward outgroups; positive and negative attitudes must be conceptualized and measured independently. It is becoming increasingly clear that the key to promoting positive intergroup relations is to shift the focus away from whether members of one group *dislike* members of another group and, instead, to place the focus squarely on how much the members of one group *like* the members of another group. We believe that the Allophilia Scale is an important tool that can serve as a backbone to this paradigm shift.

The study of positive attitudes toward outgroups may even have some methodological benefits compared with the study of negative attitudes. In general, positive states may be expressed more spontaneously than negative states (Herr & Page, 2004) and by a wider range of individuals (Gross, John, & Richards, 2000). In addition, research participants are more willing to express positive outgroup attitudes than negative ones (Fiske, Xu, Cuddy, & Glick, 1999). Positive outgroup attitudes are also less inhibited by conscious processing than are negative outgroup attitudes; thus, they are more likely to be "expressed and experienced in [their] 'raw' form" (Crandall & Eshleman, 2003, pp. 414–415).

Measuring positive and negative attitudes separately also increases precision, allowing researchers to differentiate ambivalent (i.e., strong but conflicted) from indifferent (i.e., weak) attitudes. These different attitude states would both appear near the midpoint of a single, negative (or positive) attitude scale, making them indistinguishable (Green & Goldfried, 1965; Kaplan, 1972). For the small "cost" of including both positive and negative attitude measures in research on attitudes toward outgroups, researchers can develop more accurate theories on which to base more useful and valid predictions.

One might suspect that positive attitudes toward outgroups emerge in questionnaire data but not in real life. In fact, past applied research indicates that such attitudes occur regularly, although they receive far less research attention than do prejudice and hatred. For example, as early as 1967, Woodmansee and Cook found (unexpectedly at that time) that White participants reported instances of *ease of interracial contact* with African Americans. Patchen et al. (1976) found that a majority of White high school students believed that African American students exhibited each of a set of nine positive traits. Strikingly, the African American students in that study recognized the positive attitudes that White students held toward their group (e.g., White students believed that African Americans are friendly, helpful, and so on). Further, factor analyses indicated that the African Americans viewed the White students' positive attitudes as independent of their negative attitudes.

Taken together, these findings suggest that positive attitudes toward outgroups exist and are independent of negative attitudes—in the world as well as in the laboratory.

In summary, the ability to understand and predict positive orientations and behaviors toward outgroups can be markedly improved by recognizing and directly measuring positive attitudes toward those groups (Pittinsky et al., 2010). It remains crucial to measure negative attitudes, but our research indicates just out how problematic it is to infer positive attitudes from low scores on those measures.

The Allophilia Scale is a valid and reliable tool for measuring the multidimensional construct of positive attitudes toward outgroups. Including the Allophilia Scale in research will help us move beyond the constraints of the negative attitude literature and toward more comprehensive theories of behavior toward outgroups. If the goal of one's research is to understand hate crimes, then perhaps the study of negative attitudes would be sufficient. But if the goal is to understand when and why people step forward to help people in other groups, contribute to charities that benefit people in other groups, or support legislation and policies that benefit people in other groups—and perhaps even to promote these behaviors—the study of allophilia toward outgroups is most necessary.

REFERENCES

Bennett, C. (2001). Genres of research in multicultural education. *Review of Educational Research, 71,* 171–217. doi:10.3102/00346543071002171

Browne, M. W., & Cudeck, R. (1993). Alternative ways of assessing model fit. In K. A. Bollen & J. S. Long (Eds.), *Testing structural equation models* (pp. 136–162). Newbury Park, CA: Sage.

Cacioppo, J. T., & Berntson, G. G. (1994). Relationship between attitudes and evaluative space: A critical review, with emphasis on the separability of positive and negative substrates. *Psychological Review, 115,* 401–423.

Cacioppo, J. T., Gardner, W. L., & Berntson, G. G. (1997). Beyond bipolar conceptualizations and measures: The case of attitudes and evaluative space. *Personality and Social Psychology Review, 1,* 3–25. doi:10.1207/s15327957pspr0101_2

Cacioppo, J. T., Gardner, W. L., & Berntson, G. G. (1999). The affect system has parallel and integrative processing components: Form follows function. *Journal of Personality and Social Psychology, 76,* 839–855. doi:10.1037/0022-3514.76.5.839

Chen, M., & Bargh, J. A. (1999). Consequences of automatic evaluation: Immediate behavioral predispositions to approach or avoid the stimulus. *Personality and Social Psychology Bulletin, 25,* 215–224. doi:10.1177/0146167299025002007

Crandall, C. S., & Eshleman, A. (2003). A justification-suppression model of the expression and experience of prejudice. *Psychological Bulletin, 129*, 414–446. doi:10.1037/0033-2909.129.3.414

Czopp, A. M., & Monteith, M. J. (2006). Thinking well of African Americans: Measuring complimentary stereotypes and negative prejudice. *Basic and Applied Social Psychology, 28*, 233–250. doi:10.1207/s15324834basp2803_3

Devine, P. G. (2001). Implicit prejudice and stereotyping: How automatic are they? Introduction to the special section. *Journal of Personality and Social Psychology, 81*, 757–759. doi:10.1037/0022-3514.81.5.757

Dienstbier, R. A. (1970). Positive and negative prejudice: Interactions of prejudice with race and social desirability. *Journal of Personality, 38*, 198–215. doi:10.1111/j.1467-6494.1970.tb00004.x

Eisenstadt, D., Leippe, M. R., Stambush, M. A., Rauch, S. M., & Rivers, J. A. (2005). Dissonance and prejudice: Personal costs, choice, and change in attitudes and racial beliefs following counterattitudinal advocacy that benefits a minority. *Basic and Applied Social Psychology, 27*, 127–141. doi:10.1207/s15324834basp2702_4

Fiske, S. T., Xu, J., Cuddy, A. C., & Glick, P. (1999). (Dis)respecting and (dis)liking: Status and interdependence predict ambivalent stereotypes of competence and warmth. *Journal of Social Issues, 55*, 473–489. doi:10.1111/0022-4537.00128

Fletcher, G. J. O., Simpson, J. A., & Thomas, G. (2000). Ideals, perceptions, and evaluations in early relationship development. *Journal of Personality and Social Psychology, 79*, 933–940. doi:10.1037/0022-3514.79.6.933

Fredrickson, B. L. (1998). What good are positive emotions? *Review of General Psychology, 2*, 300–319. doi:10.1037/1089-2680.2.3.300

Fredrickson, B. L. (2001). The role of positive emotions in positive psychology: The broaden-and-build theory of positive emotions. *American Psychologist, 56*, 218–226. doi:10.1037/0003-066X.56.3.218

Gaertner, S. L., Dovidio, J. F., Rust, M. C., Nier, J. A., Banker, B. S., Ward, C. M., . . . Houlette, M. (1999). Reducing intergroup bias: Elements of intergroup cooperation. *Journal of Personality and Social Psychology, 76*, 388–402. doi:10.1037/0022-3514.76.3.388

Gaertner, S. L., Mann, J., Murrell, A., & Dovidio, J. F. (1989). Reducing intergroup bias: The benefits of recategorization. *Journal of Personality and Social Psychology, 57*, 239–249. doi:10.1037/0022-3514.57.2.239

Glick, P., & Fiske, S. T. (1996). The Ambivalent Sexism Inventory: Differentiating hostile and benevolent sexism. *Journal of Personality and Social Psychology, 70*, 491–512. doi:10.1037/0022-3514.70.3.491

Glick, P., Fiske, S. T., Mladinic, A., Saiz, J. L., Abrams, D., Masser, B., . . . López, W. L. (2000). Beyond prejudice as simple antipathy: Hostile and benevolent sexism across cultures. *Journal of Personality and Social Psychology, 79*, 763–775. doi:10.1037/0022-3514.79.5.763

Green, R. F., & Goldfried, M. R. (1965). On the bipolarity of semantic space. *Psychological Monographs*, *79*(6, Whole No. 599).

Gross, J. J., John, O. P., & Richards, J. M. (2000). The dissociation of emotion expression from emotion experience: A personality perspective. *Personality and Social Psychology Bulletin*, *26*, 712–726. doi:10.1177/0146167200268006

Henry, P. J., & Sears, D. O. (2002). The Symbolic Racism 2000 Scale. *Political Psychology*, *23*, 253–283. doi:10.1111/0162-895X.00281

Herr, P. M., & Page, C. M. (2004). Asymmetric association of liking and disliking judgments: So what's not to like? *Journal of Consumer Research*, *30*, 588–601. doi:10.1086/380291

Hu, L., & Bentler, P. M. (1999). Cutoff criteria for fit indexes in covariance structure analysis: Conventional criteria versus new alternatives. *Structural Equation Modeling*, *6*, 1–55. doi:10.1080/10705519909540118

Jordan, N. (1965). The "asymmetry" of "liking" and "disliking": A phenomenon meriting further reflection and research. *Public Opinion Quarterly*, *29*, 315–322. doi:10.1086/267327

Kaplan, K. J. (1972). On the ambivalence–indifference problem in attitude theory and measurement: A suggested modification of the semantic differential technique. *Psychological Bulletin*, *77*, 361–372. doi:10.1037/h0032590

Katz, D., & Stotland, E. (1959). A preliminary statement to a theory of attitude structure and change. In S. Koch (Ed.), *Psychology: A study of a science* (Vol. 3, pp. 423–475). New York, NY: McGraw-Hill.

Katz, I., & Hass, R. G. (1988). Racial ambivalence and American value conflict: Correlational and priming studies of dual cognitive structures. *Journal of Personality and Social Psychology*, *55*, 893–905. doi:10.1037/0022-3514.55.6.893

LeDoux, J. E. (1995). In search of an emotional system in the brain: Leaping from fear to emotion and consciousness. In M. S. Gazzaniga (Ed.), *The cognitive neurosciences* (pp. 1049–1061). Cambridge, MA: MIT Press.

Marsh, H. W., & Hau, K. T. (1996). Assessing goodness of fit: Is parsimony always desirable? *Journal of Experimental Education*, *64*, 364–390.

Marsh, H. W., & Hocevar, D. (1985). Application of confirmatory factor analysis to the study of self-concept: First- and higher order factor models and their invariance across groups. *Psychological Bulletin*, *97*, 562–582. doi:10.1037/0033-2909.97.3.562

McClanahan, K. K., Gold, J. A., Lenney, E., Ryckman, R. M., & Kulberg, G. E. (1990). Infatuation and attraction to a dissimilar other: Why is love blind? *Journal of Social Psychology*, *130*, 433–445.

McConahay, J. B. (1986). Modern racism, ambivalence, and the Modern Racism Scale. In J. F. Dovidio & S. L. Gaertner (Eds.), *Prejudice, discrimination, and racism* (pp. 91–125). Orlando, FL: Academic Press.

Neville, H. A., Lilly, R. L., Duran, G., Lee, R. M., & Browne, L. (2000). Construction and initial validation of the Color-Blind Racial Attitudes Scale (CoBRAS). *Journal of Counseling Psychology*, *47*, 59–70. doi:10.1037/0022-0167.47.1.59

Osgood, C. E., Suci, G. J., & Tannenbaum, P. H. (1957). *The measurement of meaning*. Urbana: University of Illinois Press.

Patchen, M., Hofmann, G., & Davidson, J. D. (1976). Interracial perceptions among high school students. *Sociometry, 39,* 341–354. doi:10.2307/3033499

Phillips, S. T., & Ziller, R. C. (1997). Toward a theory and measure of the nature of nonprejudice. *Journal of Personality and Social Psychology, 72,* 420–434. doi:10.1037/0022-3514.72.2.420

Pittinsky, T. L. (2009a). Allophilia: Moving beyond tolerance in the classroom. *Childhood Education, 85,* 212–215.

Pittinsky, T. L. (2009b). Look both ways. *Phi Delta Kappan, 90,* 363–364.

Pittinsky, T. L. (2010). A two-dimensional theory of intergroup leadership: The case of national diversity. *American Psychologist, 65,* 194–200. doi:10.1037/a0017329

Pittinsky, T. L., & Maruskin, L. (2008). Allophilia: Beyond tolerance. In S. J. Lopez (Ed.), *Positive psychology: Exploring the best in people* (pp. 141–148). Westport, CT: Praeger.

Pittinsky, T. L., & Montoya, R. M. (2009). Is valuing equality enough? Equality values, allophilia, and social policy support for multiracial individuals. *Journal of Social Issues, 65,* 151–163. doi:10.1111/j.1540-4560.2008.01592.x

Pittinsky, T. L., Montoya, R. M., Tropp, L. R., & Chen, A. (2007). How and when leader behavior affects intergroup liking: Affect, approval, and allophilia. In B. Mannix, M. Neale, & C. Anderson (Eds.), *Research on managing groups and teams: Affect & groups* (pp. 125–144). Oxford: Elsevier Science Press.

Pittinsky, T. L., Ratcliff, J. J., & Maruskin, L. A. (2008). *Coexistence in Israel: A national study*. Cambridge, MA: Harvard Kennedy School, Center for Public Leadership.

Pittinsky, T. L., Rosenthal, S. A., & Montoya, R. M. (2010). *Liking ≠ not disliking: The functional separability of positive and negative attitudes toward minority groups*. Manuscript submitted for publication.

Pittinsky, T. L., & Simon, S. (2007). Intergroup leadership. *Leadership Quarterly, 18,* 586–605. doi:10.1016/j.leaqua.2007.09.005

Rodin, M. J. (1978). Liking and disliking: Sketch of an alternative view. *Personality and Social Psychology Bulletin, 4,* 473–478. doi:10.1177/014616727800400324

Rosenberg, M. J., Hovland, C. I., McGuire, W. J., Abelson, R. P., & Brehm, J. W. (1960). *Attitude organization and change: An analysis of consistency among attitude components*. New Haven, CT: Yale University Press.

Schuman, H., & Harding, J. (1963). Sympathetic identification with the underdog. *Public Opinion Quarterly, 27,* 230–241. doi:10.1086/267163

Triandis, H. C. (1964). Exploratory factor analyses of the behavioral component of social attitudes. *Journal of Abnormal and Social Psychology, 68,* 420–430. doi:10.1037/h0043175

Watson, D., & Tellegen, A. (1985). Toward a consensual structure of mood. *Psychological Bulletin, 98,* 219–235. doi:10.1037/0033-2909.98.2.219

Woodmansee, J. J., & Cook, S. W. (1967). Dimensions of verbal racial attitudes: Their identification and measurement. *Journal of Personality and Social Psychology, 7,* 240–250. doi:10.1037/h0025078

Wright, S. C., & Taylor, D. M. (2003). The social psychology of cultural diversity: Social stereotyping, prejudice, and discrimination. In M. A. Hogg & J. Cooper (Eds.), *The Sage handbook of social psychology* (pp. 432–457). London, England: Sage.

II

MOTIVATIONS AND EXPECTATIONS ACROSS GROUP BOUNDARIES

3

UNDERSTANDING THE INTERGROUP FORECASTING ERROR

ROBYN K. MALLETT, DANA E. WAGNER, AND PATRICK R. HARRISON

Negative expectations based on social class nearly derailed one of literature's greatest love stories. In *Pride and Prejudice* (Austen, 1813/2002), outward appearances and unconfirmed hearsay initially led Elizabeth Bennet to believe that Mr. Darcy was an elitist aristocrat who would not deign to mingle with a woman of lesser social standing. It was not until the situation forced her into his company that he revealed his gracious and welcoming manner and she discovered that they shared much in common. As a result, the two overcame their negative first impressions and fell deeply in love.

Many people make the same mistake as Ms. Bennet made when imagining what it would be like to interact with someone from a different social group. In general, people are not very accurate when predicting their future feelings because they misconstrue the nature of upcoming events, apply inaccurate theories, overproject from their current feelings, and fail to anticipate the extent to which they have the psychological resources to cope with negative events (Wilson & Gilbert, 2003). All of these mistakes contribute to the discrepancy between our expectations of what it would feel like to interact with someone from a different social group and our actual experiences. The tendency to expect the worst from intergroup interactions, even though they often turn out better than anticipated, is termed the *intergroup forecasting error* (Mallett, Wilson, & Gilbert, 2008).

Mallett et al. (2008) tested the extent to which expectations about future intergroup interactions differed from reports of actual intergroup experiences. In a daily diary study, they found that both majority and minority group members expected more negative intergroup interactions than they actually experienced (Study 1). This was true across several social groups (e.g., race, age, gender, mental or physical disability, social status, sexual orientation, weight) and in a variety of domains (e.g., at school, shopping, socializing). In subsequent studies, they introduced participants to a person of a different race and randomly assigned half of the participants to report their expectations of what it would be like to have an 8-min getting-acquainted conversation with that person. The other half of the participants did not report expectations but instead actually engaged in the 8-min conversation and reported how they felt. Expectations of intergroup interactions were consistently more negative (and less accurate) than both expectations of same-race interactions in the same situation and actual experiences. Interestingly, although people expected intergroup interactions to go poorly, they tended to go quite well. In fact, Whites reported that interactions with a Black partner went just as well as interactions with a White partner.

One reason for the intergroup forecasting error is that when it comes to imagining how a stranger from a different social group will think, feel, and behave, people typically rely on stereotypes (Hebl, Tickle, & Heatherton, 2000). Stereotypes tend to be negative and contribute to negative expectations of intergroup relations. To be sure, there are times when minority and majority group members accurately pick up on cues that an intergroup interaction will not go well. Often, however, stereotypes create a negative expectation that undermines the quality of an interaction (Tropp, 2003; Word, Zanna, & Cooper, 1974). For example, when minority group members expect to be the target of prejudice, they report feeling a host of negative emotions (Swim, Hyers, Cohen, Fitzgerald, & Bylsma, 2003). Likewise, when majority group members believe their partner sees them as prejudiced, they leave intergroup interactions unhappy and cognitively drained (Butz & Plant, 2006; Plant & Butz, 2006; Richeson & Trawalter, 2005). Negative expectations and experiences reduce willingness to initiate contact with members of different social groups (Frey & Tropp, 2006; Mendoza-Denton, Downey, Purdie, Davis, & Pietrzak, 2002; Pinel, 1999; Plant & Devine, 2003; Shelton & Richeson, 2005; Shelton, Richeson & Salvatore, 2005).

We know that contact between different social groups reduces prejudice, especially when it creates the potential for friendship (Pettigrew & Tropp, 2000). Having interracial roommates and friends in college is typically associated with less bias and intergroup anxiety for Whites, Blacks, Asians, and

Latinos (Levin, Van Laar, & Sidanius, 2000; Shook & Fazio, 2008). Even people who are biased and fear rejection experience more comfort and less stress when they bond with someone from a different social group (Page-Gould, Mendoza-Denton, & Tropp, 2008). There is, however, a barrier to intergroup contact in everyday life. People fear being rejected or that the interaction will go poorly (Plant & Devine, 2003; Shelton & Richeson, 2005). We can potentially remove that barrier to intergroup contact if we discover ways to reduce the intergroup forecasting error.

Several factors impede accurate intergroup forecasts, including the reliance on stereotypes of one's partner, individual differences in sensitivity to group membership, and a failure to appreciate how the situation constrains one's experience (Dovidio, Kawakami, & Gaertner, 2002; Fazio, Jackson, Dunton, & Williams, 1995; Frey & Tropp, 2006; Pinel, 1999). If one person goes into an interaction expecting the worst while the other person approaches the same interaction hoping for the best, then the quality of the interaction can easily be compromised unless the individual with positive expectations can withstand some resistance from an initially negative partner. Next, we consider how addressing factors related to the partner, the self, and the situation can reduce the intergroup forecasting error.

THE INTERACTION PARTNER

Both majority and minority group members commit the intergroup forecasting error, but only when imagining what it would be like to interact with a partner from a different social group—predictions about what it would be like to interact with someone from the same social group are unaffected (Mallett et al., 2008). Simply being in the presence of an outgroup member increases categorization based on group membership, which leads people to perceive greater similarities between the self and people from their own social group and greater differences between the self and people from a different social group (Jones, 1990; Wilder, 1986). Every social group possesses attributes that influence the nature and intensity of how people expect to feel when interacting with a member of that group. In general, people expect to feel negatively toward a group that is perceived as capable of acting out negative intentions that threaten their safety or resources (Cottrell & Neuberg, 2005; Fiske, Cuddy, Glick, & Xu, 2002). The type of threat that one perceives determines the nature of one's emotional expectation. For example, the rich might expect to feel angry about requests from the poor if they perceive them as demands that threaten their resources, religious fundamentalists might expect to feel disgust if they thought moral contamination would result from interacting with atheists, and Whites would expect to feel afraid if they thought that Blacks wanted to threaten their physical safety.

Expectations are further shaped by *metastereotypes*, or what we think outgroup members believe about our group. Many times, metastereotypes lead people to overestimate the amount of tension and awkwardness they will experience during an intergroup interaction. Metastereotypes are activated when we anticipate being evaluated or perceive the potential for conflict with someone from a different social group (Vorauer, Main, & O'Connell, 1998). Majority group members worry that the interaction will not go well because their interaction partner will expect them to be racist, even if they behave in a nonbiased, friendly manner (Butz & Plant, 2006). Believing that someone from a different social group holds a negative stereotype of their group makes both minority and majority group members feel anxious, believe the other person is not interested in contact, and report little desire for contact (Mendez, Gomez, & Tropp, 2007). People do not report the same concerns when they expect the other person to hold a positive stereotype or when interacting with someone from their same social group (Mendez et al., 2007; Vorauer et al., 1998).

The intergroup forecasting error should be particularly likely to occur when one's interaction partner looks like a prototypical group member. People expect African Americans with strong Afrocentric features to possess more stereotypic traits and to behave more aggressively than those with weak Afrocentric features (Blair, Chapleau, & Judd, 2005). Therefore, cues such as facial features (e.g., shape of eyes, width of nose), clothing (e.g., Malcolm X shirt, rainbow pin), or mannerisms (e.g., dialect, gait) that highlight group membership activate stereotypes and trigger negative expectations. Yet because we are all members of multiple social groups, the category that initially captures our interaction partner's attention might not be the category that is accessible during the majority of the interaction (Macrae, Bodenhausen, & Milne, 1995). For example, in *Pride and Prejudice*, Mr. Darcy was a prototypical member of the aristocracy—exemplified in his mannerisms, dress, and speech. Accordingly, Ms. Bennet expected him to be aloof and reject her on the basis of her somewhat lower social standing. Contrary to expectations, gender, not social class, was the salient social category in many of their interactions. Given the fact that they were both single heterosexuals, the emphasis on gender led to an unexpectedly positive outcome.

Therefore, one way to reduce the intergroup forecasting error and increase the positivity of emotional expectations is to override the tendency to focus on group membership when imagining an intergroup interaction. In almost every case, two people interact for a reason—they are colleagues at work or they have mutual friends, similar interests, or a shared goal. Relying too heavily on stereotypes based on group membership can lead a person to overlook these commonalities and expect to share fewer similarities with a partner from a different social group, compared to a partner from the same social group. In reality, similarities often arise and smooth the social interaction. For example, both highly and less prejudiced Whites respond positively to a Black stranger when they believe they share similar attitudes with the person (Byrne & McGraw, 1964). Mallett and colleagues (2008) found support for this route to reducing the intergroup forecasting error when they encouraged people to consider small ways in which they were similar to someone from a different social group. As a result of considering, for example, a mutual preference for hardwood floors over carpet, their expectations changed to match their positive experiences. Of interest is that expectations were considerably more positive and more closely matched actual experiences after considering even trivial similarities—participants did not have to think about important ideological overlaps to override the influence of group membership.

THE SELF

Some people are especially attuned to group membership during social interactions and two individual differences likely enhance the intergroup forecasting error by highlighting cues of threat in the environment and potentially changing behavior during intergroup interactions. Specifically, sensitivity to race-based rejection and stigma consciousness increase attention to subliminal signs of threat in the environment, including facial expressions of contempt (Inzlicht, Kaiser, & Major, 2008) and evidence of rejection in the other person's behavior (Downey, Mougios, Ayduk, London, & Shoda, 2004). The fear of being viewed through a stereotypic lens also increases perceptions of subtle and overt discrimination (Pinel, 2004) and leads people to avoid outgroup members and stereotyped domains (Pinel, 1999). If intergroup interactions are unavoidable, sensitivity is associated with aggressive and inappropriate behavior, including devaluing the partner's contributions and dosing the partner with a large serving of hot sauce (Ayduk, Gyurak, & Luerssen, 2008). In *Pride and Prejudice*, Ms. Bennet's sensitivity to rejection on the basis of her social class and Mr. Darcy's unchecked bias against that class contributed to their rocky start. Their relationship could have permanently stalled if one or both parties had been unmotivated or unable to overcome that sensitivity and control their preexisting bias (see Butz & Plant, 2006; Mendoza-Denton et al., 2002; Pinel, 1999).

Mr. Darcy's initially judgmental reaction to Ms. Bennet's social standing illustrates how prejudice also enhances negative expectations and harms the quality of intergroup interactions. People who are highly prejudiced believe their partner will view them according to the group stereotype, and, as a result, they expect to feel anxious and wish to avoid intergroup contact (Ashburn-Nardo, Knowles, & Monteith, 2003; Dasgupta & Rivera, 2008; Vorauer et al., 1998). Bias is also related to less friendly (i.e., less smiling, eye contact) and more uncomfortable and biased behavior (i.e., asking racially stereotypic interview questions) toward outgroup members (Dovidio et al., 2002; Fazio et al., 1995). If the interaction partner responds in kind to these negative behaviors, then both parties will likely have an unpleasant encounter. Over time, greater expectations of being treated according to stereotypes are associated with lesser intergroup trust and fewer intergroup friendships (Mendoza-Denton et al., 2002; Shelton et al., 2005). In comparison, people who are low in prejudice tend to see more similarities between themselves and a person from a different social group, and this perception reduces the extent to which they expect to be seen through the lens of the negative stereotype of their group (Vorauer et al., 1998). Moreover, if those low in prejudice do not believe they conform to the group stereotype, they may avoid being influenced by the metastereotype of their group and anticipate positive emotions (Frey & Tropp, 2006).

Two individual differences, optimism and the internal motivation and ability to control prejudice, should reduce the intergroup forecasting error. Both of these individual differences increase the positivity of intergroup expectations as well as confidence in one's ability to have a successful intergroup interaction. Optimism broadens attention to positive cues in the environment and increases the perception that one is capable of dealing with a challenging situation (Segerstrom, 2001). Optimistic women and men exposed to sexism believe that they have sufficient resources to cope with the threat of discrimination, which allows them to protect their self-esteem and emotional well-being (Kaiser, Major, & McCoy, 2004). Positive expectations reduce anxiety and encourage contact, thereby increasing experience with intergroup interactions (Plant & Butz, 2006). Experience interacting with people from different social groups reduces the uncertainty surrounding future interactions by increasing knowledge about the other group and establishing norms and expectations for future interactions (Blair, Park, & Bachelor, 2003). As a result, one builds confidence in the ability to perform well during an intergroup encounter (Hyers & Swim, 1998; Stephan & Stephan, 1985).

People who are personally committed to upholding egalitarian values have an internal motivation to control biased behavior during intergroup interactions (Plant & Devine, 2003). Having an internal motivation to control prejudice, and believing that one can do so, is associated with positive intergroup expectations for both Whites and Blacks (Plant, 2004). Those who are internally motivated and practiced at controlling their nonverbal behavior do not exhibit biased behavior, even during threatening intergroup interactions (Dasgupta & Rivera, 2006; Fazio, 1990; Maddux, Barden, Brewer, &

Petty, 2005). Moreover, those who are internally motivated to control prejudice are dedicated to overcoming awkwardness and view even negative intergroup interactions as a feasible challenge. Those who are highly internally motivated succeed at intergroup interactions because they set positive, approach-related goals, spend more time interacting, and are friendlier with intergroup partners compared to those who lack this motivation (see Butz & Plant, this volume). Not only does this behavior enable the individual to express egalitarian values, it also results in a positive experience for the interaction partner.

Although many people are motivated to understand, belong, or present a nonprejudiced image during an intergroup interaction (Baumeister, 1998; Swim & Thomas, 2006), they often fail to anticipate the influence these goals exert on behavior. For example, if a majority group member wishes to present a nonprejudiced image, she may go out of her way to create a positive interaction by smiling and approaching a minority group member despite even a perceived reluctance on the other person's part. Similarly, if a minority group member wishes to be accepted by a majority group member, he may shift his attitudes and beliefs to align with those of his interaction partner (Sinclair, Huntsinger, Skorinko, & Hardin, 2005). Attempting to put one's best face forward during an interaction with a stranger improves the quality of the interaction for both parties; the person who is compensating feels good and the use of compensation increases perceptions of likeability, competence, and intelligence (Dunn, Biesanz, Human, & Finn, 2007; Mallett & Swim, 2005). Yet if one does not account for the fact that one's self or one's interaction partner might engage in these behaviors during the interaction, then one's expectations will likely be more negative than one's actual experiences.

THE SITUATION

Expectations of negative emotions are especially high in situations that highlight differences in group membership because they suggest the possibility of awkwardness or negative consequences for the self (Esses & Dovidio, 2002; Hebl et al., 2000; Mackie & Smith, 2002; Stephan & Stephan, 1985). Some situations clearly indicate that one will be perceived in terms of group membership and treated as either a perpetrator or target of prejudice. For example, contexts like jail, a ghetto, and a dark alley are perceived as more threatening than contexts like church, a classroom, or even a tornado, because they pair a stereotyped individual with a threatening situation (Maddux et al., 2005). Other contexts are more ambiguous, making it unclear whether one will be treated according to group membership (Crocker & Major, 1989).

When facing an ambiguous situation, factors such as demographics and personal base rates communicate the likelihood that the average person versus the self would have a negative experience (Marti, Bobier, & Baron, 2000). Expecting to be the only member of one's social group in a situation increases the amount of attention people expect to receive that is due to group membership, thereby increasing the negativity of expectations (Lord & Saenz, 1985). Perceiving that one has personally been the target of discrimination in the past increases the likelihood of expecting a similar outcome in the future (Stangor et al., 2003). Minority group members view certain behaviors as discriminatory, and observing these behaviors triggers negative expectations. For instance, African Americans report racism in the form of subtle behaviors, such as being stared or glared at, being the target of racial slurs, and receiving poor service in a store or restaurant (Swim et al., 2003), whereas women report sexism in the form of remarks regarding traditional social roles and sexually objectifying comments or behavior (Swim, Hyers, Cohen, & Ferguson, 2001). Some everyday experiences with discrimination are also seen as more prototypical than others. For example, women believe that the use of patronizing language is more likely a sign of prejudice than sexually objectifying comments (Swim, Mallett, Russo-Devosa, & Stangor, 2005). Although prototypical situations and behaviors provide a useful heuristic when developing expectations in an ambiguous situation, they can also create false positives whereby one inaccurately expects a negative experience.

One or both parties may also form inaccurate expectations if they fail to correctly estimate how much ability or effort is required to engage in compensation in that situation. *Compensation* is defined in many ways throughout the literature, but it can range from using a single simple strategy (e.g., smiling) to a more elaborately orchestrated effort (e.g., monitoring the direction of the conversation, inserting counterstereotypical comments, or asserting positive aspects of the self while smiling; Mallett & Swim, 2005). At times, one might anticipate having to work extremely hard to obtain a positive outcome but then be pleasantly surprised to find the interaction was relatively easy to negotiate. Alternatively, one could be caught off-guard by the awkwardness of an encounter and have to initiate a more elaborate form of compensation in the middle of the interaction. In both cases, expectations would diverge from one's actual experience. Interacting with a larger number of outgroup members in a variety of situations should provide a better basis on which to create expectations of what it will take to successfully compensate. Therefore, we expect that as both minority and majority group members increase their experience with intergroup contact, the accuracy of estimations regarding ability and effort needed to compensate should also increase.

Finally, intergroup expectations can diverge from experience because people cannot easily anticipate the complexity of future situations. The failure to account for situational constraints often causes people to overestimate dispositional and underestimate situational influences on their future experience (Wilson & Gilbert, 2003). Underestimating the positive influence of a situational feature such as task demands or social norms for politeness and overestimating the negative influence of a person's disposition can be especially dangerous because people assume that individuals from different social groups have more negative dispositions than individuals from one's own group (Jones, 1990). In *Pride and Prejudice*, Ms. Bennet spends a considerable amount of time with Mr. Darcy at the home of a mutual acquaintance while her sister Jane, also a guest, recovers there from a novelistically convenient illness. Mr. Darcy plays the role of a gracious and concerned host, ensuring that his previously aloof disposition will exert little influence on their interactions (see Mischel, 1984). After some initial resistance, Ms. Bennet reciprocates his pleasant demeanor. The two begin to discover commonalities and formed a lasting bond. It is unlikely that either character could have foreseen the positive outcome of their interaction because they initially failed to look beyond category membership and expected to feel more negatively toward each other than they actually did.

Reminding people that social situations are multifaceted and often constrain their behavior could lead them to form more accurate expectations of how they will feel in a future intergroup interaction. Such a reminder could work by encouraging people to focus on the self as an individual, rather than a group member, thereby reducing the salience of group membership. Thinking about the self as an individual increases expectations that the interaction partner will share one's view of the self, increases thoughts of similarity, and reduces reliance on stereotypes—all factors that increase the positivity of expectations (Frey & Tropp, 2006). Ms. Bennet expected to feel uncomfortable because the situation highlighted Mr. Darcy's social class, reminding her of their group differences and suggesting the potential for conflict. However, the situation at their friend's estate enforced norms for politeness that smoothed any impending awkwardness and led to the discovery of their similarities (i.e., a shared love of intellectual pursuits), allowing them both to overcome their initial misgivings. Thus, encouraging people to adopt a different focus, either by stepping forward to search for similarity or stepping back to appreciate the power of social norms, may adjust both expectations and experience. Doing so should reduce the tendency to avoid intergroup contact.

BRINGING EXPECTATIONS IN LINE WITH EXPERIENCE

Even if an interracial interaction goes better than expected, it can still produce anxiety, which reduces willingness to engage in future intergroup contact (Plant & Devine, 2003). Therefore, we must also consider ways of smoothing intergroup interaction along with improving expectations. Although Mallett and colleagues' (2008) "focusing on similarities" manipulation increased the positivity of intergroup expectations, it did not change the pleasantness of Whites' actual intergroup interactions. Thus, Mallett and Wilson (2010) investigated whether an intervention that increased people's expectations about the pleasantness of an interracial interaction would make an actual interaction more pleasant and less cognitively draining, thereby increasing willingness to form interracial friendships.

Research demonstrating an extended contact effect shows that simply observing a positive interaction between an ingroup and outgroup member can improve attitudes toward the outgroup (Wright, Aron, McLaughlin-Volpe, & Ropp, 1997). But seeing a positive intergroup interaction might not be sufficient to improve the pleasantness of a future intergroup interaction because people could see the positive example as an exception to the more general rule that intergroup friendships are difficult (Kunda & Oleson, 1995). Building on this research, Mallett and Wilson (2010) showed White college students a videotaped interview of two students at their university—one White, one Black—who had become friends despite having low expectations about the friendship to begin with. To reduce suspicion that the study was about race, the first two videos depicted White students talking about their 1st-year experiences (e.g., favorite class, toughest part of the transition to college) and friendships. The next two videos depicted one Black and one White student who were described as good friends. Both students mentioned that they did not expect to become friends and did not think they had much in common at first (e.g., the White student said, "I wasn't sure how much we would have in common . . . he didn't really seem like any of my old friends from home"). Both students also said that, to their surprise, they discovered that they had things in common, such as the same taste in books and similar senses of humor.

Mallett and Wilson (2010) went a step further by having some participants connect this story to their own experience, either by writing about a time when an interaction went "better than expected" (i.e., a time when "you didn't think that you could become friends with a person, but you were wrong for some reason") or a time when an interaction went "just as expected" (i.e., "you didn't think they could become friends with someone and were correct") or not writing. They predicted that the combination of seeing evidence of an intergroup friendship and connecting it to a time one's own experience was better than expected would improve White students' expectations about an interracial interaction, make them less nervous during that interaction, and make them more open to interracial friendships in the coming weeks. Participants who applied the "better than expected" story to their own lives not only had more accurate expectations of an interracial interaction, they also had a more positive interaction with a Black student they had never met.

Mallett and Wilson (2010) explored a potential mediator of these effects in the form of cognitive resources available to devote to the interaction. Positive expectations about the interactions should lead participants to feel relaxed and have more cognitive resources to devote to making the interaction go smoothly (Richeson & Trawalter, 2005). In support of this hypothesis, participants in the "better than expected" condition, who wrote about a time when their expectations were wrong, reported more accurate expectations about the interview and less nervousness during the interview than did participants in the other two conditions. Participant expectations also mediated the effects of writing on a measure of cognitive depletion, supporting the idea that writing about a personal experience similar to one seen in the interracial friendship videos improved expectations about an intergroup interaction, thereby freeing up cognitive resources.

A second study showed that changing people's expectations, beliefs, and attributions (e.g., Cohen, Garcia, Apfel, & Master, 2006; Wilson & Linville, 1982) gave them confidence about an interaction in the laboratory, and once this went well, people become even more confident and were more willing to initiate intergroup friendship outside of the laboratory. Specifically, participants who saw the interracial friendship videos and were in the "better than expected" writing condition showed a dramatic increase in the number of interracial friendships they formed in the next week. Self-reports of interracial friendships were confirmed by checking new friends added to the participant's Facebook profiles 2 weeks after the study. Thus, not only did the intervention increase the short-term positivity of an interracial interaction in the laboratory, it had long-term beneficial effects in people's everyday lives.

CONCLUSION

The novel *Pride and Prejudice* was originally titled *First Impressions*, Austen's theme being that the characters—like real people—often operated on uninformed assumptions about each other. Their reliance on stereotypes, their bias against people from a different social class, and their failure to appreciate the way that situations often constrain behavior created substantial barriers to developing a relationship. People commonly commit the same type of intergroup forecasting error today—anticipating the worst from intergroup interactions, even though they often turn out better than expected (Mallett et al., 2008). That is not to say that all intergroup contact goes well. Extreme prejudice against a group makes some people unwilling to engage in intergroup contact. Furthermore, a lack of motivation to create a positive interaction and an unwillingness to seek shared similarities can result in an awkward and unpleasant interaction. Many times, however, intergroup interactions go better than expected because our everyday interactions center on shared interests (e.g., work, sports, friends) and occur in highly scripted contexts (e.g., the office, a game, a party). Plus, many people truly desire more intergroup contact and, in many cases, the only thing holding them back is the potential sting of rejection.

Focusing on factors that contribute to more positive—and more accurate—expectations of intergroup contact signals a shift in the traditional approach of understanding the origin and nature of negative expectations. It is critical to continue identifying the roots of awkward intergroup experiences because doing so reveals opportunities for change. Yet, researchers often do not take the necessary steps to move from a problem focus to a solution focus. Research that investigates phenomena such as the intergroup forecasting error helps us to develop strategies that combat negative expectations and increase the frequency of positive intergroup contact. Considering how we can create positive expectations of challenging and worthwhile intergroup interactions has the potential to reveal relatively simple ways to put people on a more positive course to developing intergroup friendship.

Knowing that one was mistaken in the past about negative intergroup expectations should reduce the often-held belief that people from different social groups are simply uninterested in intergroup contact, thereby reducing one's fear of being rejected by members of such groups (Shelton & Richeson, 2005). Moreover, past success at negotiating interracial interactions should bolster people's confidence, thereby reducing the experience of anxiety during future interactions (Hyers & Swim, 1998). As a result, both majority and minority group members should be more willing to approach opportunities for intergroup contact and be more eager to attempt the formation of new intergroup friendships.

We know that under the right conditions intergroup contact decreases prejudice, yet little research attention has been devoted to uncovering ways to increase people's willingness to establish contact in the first place and, when such interactions do occur, to make them go smoothly. One way to promote intergroup contact is to convince people that their overly negative expectations about such interactions are often incorrect. We have isolated several ways to target these negative expectations: (a) reducing reliance on stereotypes of one's partner, (b) understanding individual differences in sensitivity to group membership, and (c) increasing the appreciation of how the situation constrains one's experience. Considering a time when interracial contact went better than expected was shown to smooth upcoming instances of interracial contact and pave the way for formation of future interracial friendships. Because each successful intergroup interaction builds on the previous one, it is imperative to strengthen people's confidence in their ability to present a positive image during intergroup interactions, and that confidence should then produce an increased willingness to form new friendships with members of other social groups in everyday life.

REFERENCES

Ashburn-Nardo, L., Knowles, M. L., & Monteith, M. J. (2003). Black Americans' implicit racial associations and their implications for intergroup judgment. *Social Cognition, 21*, 61–87. doi:10.1521/soco.21.1.61.21192

Austen, J. (2002). *Pride and prejudice*. New York, NY: Penguin Books. (Original work published 1813)

Ayduk, O., Gyurak, A., & Luerssen, A. (2008). Individual differences in the rejection–aggression link in the hot sauce paradigm: The case of rejection sensitivity. *Journal of Experimental Social Psychology, 44*, 775–782. doi:10.1016/j.jesp.2007.07.004

Baumeister, R. F. (1998). The self. In D. T. Gilbert, S. T. Fiske, & G. Lindzey (Eds.), *Handbook of Social Psychology* (4th ed., pp. 680–740). New York, NY: McGraw-Hill.

Blair, I. V., Chapleau, K. M., & Judd, C. M. (2005). The use of Afrocentric features as cues for judgment in the presence of diagnostic information. *European Journal of Social Psychology, 35*, 59–68. doi:10.1002/ejsp.232

Blair, I. V., Park, B., & Bachelor, J. (2003). Understanding intergroup anxiety: Are some people more anxious than others? *Group Processes & Intergroup Relations, 6*, 151–169. doi:10.1177/1368430203006002002

Butz, D. A., & Plant, E. A. (2006). Perceiving outgroup members as unresponsive: Implications for approach-related emotions, intentions, and behavior. *Journal of Personality and Social Psychology, 91*, 1066–1079. doi:10.1037/0022-3514.91.6.1066

Byrne, D., & McGraw, C. (1964). Interpersonal attraction towards Negroes. *Human Relations, 17*, 201–213. doi:10.1177/001872676401700301

Cohen, G. L., Garcia, J., Apfel, N., & Master, A. (2006, September 1). Reducing the racial achievement gap: A social-psychological intervention. *Science, 313*, 1307–1310. doi:10.1126/science.1128317

Cottrell, C. A., & Neuberg, S. L. (2005). Different emotional reactions to different groups: A sociofunctional threat-based approach to "prejudice." *Journal of Personality and Social Psychology, 88*, 770–789. doi:10.1037/0022-3514.88.5.770

Crocker, J., & Major, B. (1989). Social stigma and self-esteem: The self-protective properties of stigma. *Psychological Review, 96*, 608–630. doi:10.1037/0033-295X.96.4.608

Dasgupta, N., & Rivera, L. M. (2006). From automatic anti-gay prejudice to behavior: The moderating role of conscious beliefs about gender and behavioral control. *Journal of Personality and Social Psychology, 91*, 268–280. doi:10.1037/0022-3514.91.2.268

Dasgupta, N., & Rivera, L. M. (2008). When social context matters: The influence of long-term contact and short-term exposure to admired outgroup members on implicit attitudes and behavioral intentions. *Social Cognition, 26,* 112–123. doi:10.1521/soco.2008.26.1.112

Downey, G., Mougios, V., Ayduk, O., London, B. E., & Shoda, Y. (2004). Rejection sensitivity and the defensive motivational system: Insights from the startle response to rejection cues. *Psychological Science, 15,* 668–673. doi:10.1111/j.0956-7976.2004.00738.x

Dovidio, J. F., Kawakami, K., & Gaertner, S. L. (2002). Implicit and explicit prejudice and interracial interaction. *Journal of Personality and Social Psychology, 82,* 62–68. doi:10.1037/0022-3514.82.1.62

Dunn, E. W., Biesanz, J. C., Human, L. J., & Finn, S. (2007). Misunderstanding the affective consequences of everyday social interactions: The hidden benefits of putting one's best face forward. *Journal of Personality and Social Psychology, 92,* 990–1005. doi:10.1037/0022-3514.92.6.990

Esses, V. M., & Dovidio, J. F. (2002). The role of emotions in determining willingness to engage in intergroup contact. *Personality and Social Psychology Bulletin, 28,* 1202–1214. doi:10.1177/01461672022812006

Fazio, R. H. (1990). Illustrating the value of basic research. *Personality and Social Psychology Bulletin, 16,* 5–7. doi:10.1177/0146167290161001

Fazio, R. H., Jackson, J. R., Dunton, B. C., & Williams, C. J. (1995). Variability in automatic activation as an unobtrusive measure of racial attitudes: A bona fide pipeline? *Journal of Personality and Social Psychology, 69,* 1013–1027. doi:10.1037/0022-3514.69.6.1013

Fiske, S. T., Cuddy, A. J. C., Glick, P., & Xu, J. (2002). A model of (often mixed) stereotype content: Competence and warmth respectively follow from status and competition. *Journal of Personality and Social Psychology, 82,* 878–902. doi:10.1037/0022-3514.82.6.878

Frey, F. E., & Tropp, L. R. (2006). Being seen as individuals versus as group members: Extending research on metaperception to intergroup contexts. *Personality and Social Psychology Review, 10,* 265–280. doi:10.1207/s15327957pspr1003_5

Hebl, M., Tickle, J., & Heatherton, T. (2000). Awkward moments in interactions between nonstigmatized and stigmatized individuals. In R. E. Kleck, T. F. Heatherton, J. Hull, & M. Hebl (Eds.), *The social psychology of stigma* (pp. 275–306). New York, NY: Guilford.

Hyers, L. L., & Swim, J. K. (1998). A comparison of the experiences of dominant and minority group members during an intergroup encounter. *Group Processes & Intergroup Relations, 1,* 143–163. doi:10.1177/1368430298012003

Inzlicht, M., Kaiser, C. R., & Major, B. (2008). The face of chauvinism: How prejudice expectations shape perceptions of facial affect. *Journal of Experimental Social Psychology, 44,* 758–766. doi:10.1016/j.jesp.2007.06.004

Jones, E. E. (1990). *Interpersonal Perception.* New York, NY: Freeman.

Kaiser, C. R., Major, B., & McCoy, S. K. (2004). Expectations about the future and the emotional consequences of perceiving prejudice. *Personality and Social Psychology Bulletin, 30*, 173–184. doi:10.1177/0146167203259927

Kunda, Z., & Oleson, K. C. (1995). Maintaining stereotypes in the face of disconfirmation: Constructing grounds for subtyping deviants. *Journal of Personality and Social Psychology, 68*, 565–579. doi:10.1037/0022-3514.68.4.565

Levin, S., Van Laar, C., & Sidanius, J. (2000). The effects of ingroup and outgroup friendship on ethnic attitudes in college: A longitudinal study. *Group Processes and Intergroup Relations, 6*, 76–92.

Lord, C. G., & Saenz, D. (1985). Memory deficits and memory surfeits: Differential cognitive consequences of tokenism and tokens for observers. *Journal of Personality and Social Psychology, 49*, 918–926. doi:10.1037/0022-3514.49.4.918

Mackie, D. M., & Smith, E. R. (2002). Intergroup emotions: Prejudice reconceptualized as differentiated reactions to out-groups. In J. P. Forgas & K. D. Williams (Eds.), *The social self: Cognitive, interpersonal, and intergroup perspectives* (pp. 309–326). Philadelphia, PA: Psychology Press.

Macrae, C. N., Bodenhausen, G. V., & Milne, A. B. (1995). The dissection of selection in social perception: Inhibitory processes in social stereotyping. *Journal of Personality and Social Psychology, 69*, 397–407. doi:10.1037/0022-3514.69.3.397

Maddux, W. W., Barden, J., Brewer, M. B., & Petty, R. E. (2005). Saying no to negativity: The effects of context and motivation to control prejudice on automatic evaluative responses. *Journal of Experimental Social Psychology, 41*, 19–35. doi:10.1016/j.jesp.2004.05.002

Mallett, R. K., & Swim, J. K. (2005). Bring it on: Self-protective coping by targets of discrimination. *Motivation and Emotion, 29*, 411–441.

Mallett, R. K., & Wilson, T. D. (2010). Increasing positive intergroup contact. *Journal of Experimental Social Psychology, 46*, 382–387. doi:10.1016/j.jesp.2009.11.006

Mallett, R. K., Wilson, T. D., & Gilbert, D. T. (2008). Expect the unexpected: Failure to anticipate similarities leads to an intergroup forecasting error. *Journal of Personality and Social Psychology, 94*, 265–277. doi:10.1037/0022-3514.94.2.94.2.265

Marti, M. W., Bobier, D. M., & Baron, R. S. (2000). Right before our eyes: The failure to recognize non-prototypical forms of prejudice. *Group Processes & Intergroup Relations, 3*, 403–418. doi:10.1177/1368430200003004005

Méndez, E., Gomez, A., & Tropp, L. R. (2007). When metaperceptions are affected by intergroup processes. *International Journal of Psychology & Psychological Therapy, 7*, 237–250.

Mendoza-Denton, R., Downey, G., Purdie, V., Davis, A., & Pietrzak, J. (2002). Sensitivity to status-based rejection: Implications for African American students' college experience. *Journal of Personality and Social Psychology, 83*, 896–918. doi:10.1037/0022-3514.83.4.896

Mischel, W. (1984). On the predictability of behavior and the structure of personality. In R. A. Zucker, J. Aronoff, & A. I. Rabin (Eds.), *Personality and the prediction of behavior* (pp. 269–305). New York, NY: Academic Press.

Page-Gould, E., Mendoza-Denton, R., & Tropp, L. R. (2008). With a little help from my cross group friend: Reducing anxiety in intergroup contexts through cross-group friendship. *Journal of Personality and Social Psychology, 95,* 1080–1094. doi:10.1037/0022-3514.95.5.1080

Pettigrew, T. F., & Tropp, L. R. (2000). Does intergroup contact reduce prejudice? Recent meta-analytic findings. In S. Oskamp (Ed.), *Reducing prejudice and discrimination: The Claremont Symposium on Applied Social Psychology* (pp. 93–114). Mahwah, NJ: Erlbaum.

Plant, E. A. (2004). Responses to interracial interactions over time. *Personality and Social Psychology Bulletin, 30,* 1458–1471. doi:10.1177/0146167204264244

Plant, E. A., & Butz, D. A. (2006). The causes and consequences of an avoidance-focus for interracial interactions. *Personality and Social Psychology Bulletin, 32,* 833–846. doi:10.1177/0146167206287182

Plant, E. A., & Devine, P. G. (2003). The antecedents and implications of interethnic anxiety. *Personality and Social Psychology Bulletin, 29,* 790–801. doi:10.1177/0146167203029006011

Pinel, E. C. (1999). Stigma consciousness: The psychological legacy of social stereotypes. *Journal of Personality and Social Psychology, 76,* 114–128. doi:10.1037/0022-3514.76.1.114

Pinel, E. C. (2004). You're just saying that because I'm a woman: Stigma consciousness and attributions to discrimination. *Self and Identity, 3,* 39–51. doi:10.1080/13576500342000031

Richeson, J. A., & Trawalter, S. (2005). Why do interracial interactions impair executive function? A resource depletion account. *Journal of Personality and Social Psychology, 88,* 934–947. doi:10.1037/0022-3514.88.6.934

Segerstrom, S. C. (2001). Optimism and attentional bias for negative and positive stimuli. *Personality and Social Psychology Bulletin, 27,* 1334–1343. doi:10.1177/01461672012710009

Shelton, J. N., & Richeson, J. A. (2005). Pluralistic ignorance and intergroup contact. *Journal of Personality and Social Psychology, 88,* 91–107. doi:10.1037/0022-3514.88.1.91

Shelton, J. N., Richeson, J. A., & Salvatore, J. (2005). Expecting to be the target of prejudice: Implications for interethnic interactions. *Personality and Social Psychology Bulletin, 31,* 1189–1202. doi:10.1177/0146167205274894

Shook, N. J., & Fazio, R. H. (2008). Roommate relationships: A comparison of interracial and same-race living situations. *Group Processes & Intergroup Relations, 11,* 425–437. doi:10.1177/1368430208095398

Sinclair, S., Huntsinger, J., Skorinko, J., & Hardin, C. D. (2005). Social tuning of the self: Consequences for the self-evaluations of stereotype targets. *Journal of Personality and Social Psychology, 89,* 160–175. doi:10.1037/0022-3514.89.2.160

Stangor, C., Swim, J. K., Sechrist, G. B., DeCoster, J., Van Allen, K. L., & Ottenbreit, A. (2003). Ask, answer and announce: Three stages in perceiving and responding to discrimination. In W. Stroebe & M. Hewstone (Eds.), *European review of social psychology* (pp. 277–311). Hove, England: Psychology Press/Taylor & Francis.

Stephan, W. G., & Stephan, C. W. (1985). Intergroup anxiety. *Journal of Social Issues, 41*, 157–175. doi:10.1111/j.1540-4560.1985.tb01134.x

Swim, J. K., Hyers, L., Cohen, L. L., & Ferguson, M. J. (2001). Everyday sexism: Evidence for its incidence, nature, and psychological impact from three daily diary studies. *Journal of Social Issues, 57*, 31–53. doi:10.1111/0022-4537.00200

Swim, J. K., Hyers, L. L., Cohen, L. L., Fitzgerald, D. C., & Bylsma, W. H. (2003). African American college students' experiences with everyday racism: Characteristics of and responses to these incidents. *The Journal of Black Psychology, 29*, 38–67. doi:10.1177/0095798402239228

Swim, J. K., Mallett, R. K., Russo-Devosa, Y., & Stangor, C. (2005). Judgments of sexism. A comparison of the subtlety of sexism measures and sources of variability in judgments of sexism. *Psychology of Women Quarterly, 29*, 406–411. doi:10.1111/j.1471-6402.2005.00240.x

Swim, J. K., & Thomas, M. (2006). Responding to everyday discrimination: A synthesis of research on goal directed, self-regulatory coping behaviors. In S. Lavine & C. Vanx (Eds.), *The Claremont Symposium on Applied Social Psychology* (pp. 127–151). Mahwah, NJ: Erlbaum.

Tropp, L. R. (2003). The psychological impact of prejudice: Implications for intergroup contact. *Group Processes & Intergroup Relations, 6*, 131–149. doi:10.1177/1368430203006002001

Vorauer, J. D., Main, K. J., & O'Connell, G. B. (1998). How do individuals expect to be viewed by members of lower status groups? Content and implications of meta-stereotypes. *Journal of Personality and Social Psychology, 75*, 917–937. doi:10.1037/0022-3514.75.4.917

Wilder, D. A. (1986). Social categorization: Implications for creation and reduction of intergroup bias. In L. Berkowitz (Ed.), *Advances in experimental social psychology* (Vol. 19, pp. 293–355). San Diego, CA: Academic Press.

Wilson, T. D., & Gilbert, D. T. (2003). Affective forecasting. In M. P. Zanna (Ed.), *Advances in experimental social psychology* (Vol. 35, pp. 345–411). San Diego, CA: Academic Press.

Wilson, T. D., & Linville, P. W. (1982). Improving the academic performance of college freshmen: Attribution therapy revisited. *Journal of Personality and Social Psychology, 42*, 367–376. doi:10.1037/0022-3514.42.2.367

Word, C. O., Zanna, M. P., & Cooper, J. (1974). The nonverbal mediation of self-fulfilling prophecies in interracial interaction. *Journal of Experimental Social Psychology, 10*, 109–120. doi:10.1016/0022-1031(74)90059-6

Wright, S. C., Aron, A., McLaughlin-Volpe, T., & Ropp, S. A. (1997). The extended contact effect: Knowledge of cross-group friendships and prejudice. *Journal of Personality and Social Psychology, 73*, 73–90. doi:10.1037/0022-3514.73.1.73

4

APPROACHING VERSUS AVOIDING INTERGROUP CONTACT: THE ROLE OF EXPECTANCIES AND MOTIVATION

DAVID A. BUTZ AND E. ASHBY PLANT

Since the landmark 1954 *Brown v. Board of Education* decision outlawing segregation in the United States, decades of social science research have revealed that intergroup contact can have important social benefits (see Pettigrew & Tropp, 2006, 2008). Recently, researchers have begun to explore the psychological factors that contribute to the quality of intergroup interactions beyond traditional assessments of outgroup attitudes. Mounting evidence reveals that even though legislative and institutional changes have paved the way for more frequent relations between groups, many people continue to find intergroup interactions anxiety provoking and, if given the opportunity, choose to avoid them (e.g., Britt, Boniecki, Vescio, Biernat, & Brown, 1996; Plant, 2004; Plant & Butz, 2006; Plant & Devine, 2003; Stephan & Stephan, 1985). However, recent work has revealed that avoidant and even hostile responses to intergroup interactions are not necessarily expressions of outgroup antipathy but instead often reflect people's concerns that intergroup interactions will go poorly (e.g., Butz & Plant, 2006; Plant, 2004; Plant & Butz, 2006; Plant & Devine, 2003; Shelton & Richeson, 2005; Stephan & Stephan, 1985). Clarifying the specific obstacles to intergroup interactions is a vital step in uncovering how to improve these interactions. Importantly, research is also uncovering the motivational factors that help some people push past negative expectations regarding intergroup interactions and focus instead on effective routes to approaching positive intergroup contact (e.g., Plant & Devine, 2009).

When viewed alongside evidence supporting the positive effects of intergroup contact, findings regarding intergroup avoidance and hostility suggest that these negative responses may limit or even reverse the potential benefits of intergroup contact. We believe that promoting more frequent and harmonious relations between groups requires a deeper understanding of the factors that contribute to people's decisions to approach or avoid intergroup interactions, their experiences during intergroup interactions, and their interest in future intergroup contact. This chapter has two primary goals. First, we examine the implications of people's expectancies about the outcome of intergroup interactions for both negative approach-related responses, including anger and hostility, and avoidance-related responses, including anxiety and avoidant behavior. Second, we examine the factors that may lead people to overcome these negative responses and cultivate positive approach-oriented responses to intergroup interactions. Understanding the obstacles to positive intergroup interactions and knowing when people will work to overcome those obstacles will provide direction to interventions aimed at reducing intergroup conflict and building positive intergroup relations.

EXPECTANCIES AND INTERGROUP INTERACTIONS

Expectancies regarding the outcome of intergroup interactions are key in determining majority and minority group members' responses to these interactions (Butz & Plant, 2006; Devine, Evett, & Vasquez-Suson, 1996; Mallett, Wilson, & Gilbert, 2008; Plant & Devine, 2003; Shelton, 2003; see also Mallett, Wagner, & Harrison, this volume). For example, Plant and Devine (2003) demonstrated that White people's negative expectancies predicted their anxiety about interracial interactions, which in turn predicted the desire to avoid interracial interactions and their hostility concerning such interactions (see also Britt et al., 1996; Devine et al., 1996; Plant, 2004). Furthermore, White people who had negative expectancies and were highly anxious about an interaction with a Black person were more likely to choose to avoid the upcoming interracial interaction. There is also evidence that both racial majority and minority group members' negative expectancies about intergroup interactions may lead to less enjoyment of interactions (e.g., Shelton, 2003; Shelton, Richeson, & Salvatore, 2005; Tropp, 2003) and persistent avoidance of intergroup contact (e.g., Mendoza-Denton, Downey, Purdie, Davis, & Pietrzak, 2002; Plant, 2004; Shelton & Richeson, 2005). Together, these findings indicate that negative expectancies may contribute to the stress and anxiety that people experience in response to intergroup interactions, which may lead them to actively avoid such interactions.

Racial and ethnic diversity in the United States is projected to continue to increase steadily in the decades to come (U.S. Census Bureau, 2008), making complete avoidance of interracial or interethnic interactions difficult. We believe it is important to expand research to consider an anxious and avoidant pattern of response as one, but not the only, negative pattern of affective and behavioral response to intergroup interactions. In our previous work (Butz & Plant, 2006), we argued that a closer examination of the nature of people's expectancies about intergroup interactions sheds light on whether people will become anxious and avoid intergroup interactions or experience anger and the inclination to approach intergroup interactions with hostility. Thus, we argue that moving beyond a consideration of whether people generally expect positive or negative interactions to a more fine-grained consideration of the specific reasons for people to expect interactions to go poorly will clarify the sources of avoidance-related responses (e.g., anxiety) versus negative approach-related responses (e.g., anger, hostility) to interactions. Only by knowing the specific types of negative reactions that people have to intergroup contact and the sources of these reactions will we possess the necessary knowledge to develop effective interventions to improve intergroup relations.

Avoidance-Related Responses to Intergroup Interactions

In considering these issues, we draw on work from the social anxiety literature indicating that self-presentational concerns contribute to anxious and avoidant responses in social contexts more generally (Leary & Atherton, 1986; Schlenker & Leary, 1982). We propose that expectancies centered on one's ability to present oneself in a nonprejudiced manner (efficacy expectancies) determine anxious and avoidant responses to intergroup interactions (Butz & Plant, 2006; Plant & Butz, 2006). Specifically, people who perceive that they lack the efficacy to respond in a nonprejudiced manner become highly attuned to the possibility that they may convey a negative, and potentially prejudiced, impression in interactions. These concerns heighten anxiety and increase people's desire to avoid intergroup interactions.

Consistent with this possibility, we find that negative efficacy expectancies prior to an interracial interaction are associated with increased anxiety and desire to avoid the interaction (Butz & Plant, 2006). To examine whether negative self-efficacy expectancies cause anxiety and avoidance, we manipulated non-Black participants' efficacy expectancies for an upcoming interaction with a same-sex Black person (Plant & Butz, 2006, Study 1a). After completing a computer program ostensibly assessing their negativity toward Black people, participants received either negative, positive, or no efficacy feedback about their likely ability to respond in a nonprejudiced manner during the upcoming interaction. Participants who received the negative efficacy feedback reported more anxiety about the upcoming interaction and a heightened desire to avoid the interaction than the other participants. Responses in the positive and no feedback conditions did not significantly differ, which indicates that possessing negative efficacy has a stronger effect on avoidance responses than positive efficacy. It is hard to know whether the lack of impact of positive feedback is due to participants being less willing to believe they are more efficacious than they thought or not being as strongly influenced by positive efficacy as they are by negative efficacy. A subsequent study (Plant & Butz, 2006, Study 1b) demonstrated that it was the negative efficacy feedback regarding responses to interracial interactions and not negative feedback in general that heightened anxiety and avoidant intentions concerning an upcoming interracial interaction.

The fact that negative self-efficacy leads to a desire to avoid interracial interactions is particularly problematic because entering an interaction with a desire to avoid can have negative implications for the quality of the interaction (Plant & Butz, 2006, Study 2). Replicating our previous findings, non-Black participants who received negative compared to positive efficacy feedback reported heightened anxiety and a desire to avoid contact before interacting with a Black partner. They also reported having interactions of lesser quality, ended those interactions more quickly, and expressed an increased desire to avoid future interracial interactions (Plant & Butz, 2006, Study 2). Interestingly, the efficacy feedback also influenced the partner's perceptions of their behavior in the interaction. Confederate partners rated participants who received negative efficacy feedback as more anxious and avoidant during the interaction than participants who received the positive feedback. Moreover, confederate partners rated the interaction as less pleasant when participants were highly avoidance-focused. Together, these findings illustrate that negative efficacy expectancies and the resulting avoidance focus hold the potential to compromise the quality of intergroup interactions for all involved. We suspect that the resulting negative interactions may further exacerbate negative efficacy expectancies and heighten future avoidant responses. Thus, working to ease negative self-efficacy concerns may be key for improving intergroup contact for those who doubt their intergroup abilities.

Approach-Related Responses to Intergroup Interactions

In addition to being concerned about the impression they will convey in intergroup interactions, there is accumulating evidence that people are also concerned about how others will respond to them in interactions (e.g., Butz

& Plant, 2006; Frey & Tropp, 2006; Mendoza-Denton et al., 2002; Shelton, 2003; Shelton & Richeson, 2005; Shelton et al., 2005; Vorauer, Main, & O'Connell, 1998). For example, people may dread intergroup interactions because they believe that regardless of their own behavior, their interaction partner will respond negatively to them (termed *negative response expectancies*). Although people may expect others to respond negatively for a host of reasons, in our work we have focused on outgroup members' openness to intergroup contact–that is, whether they are perceived to be relatively interested or uninterested in engaging in intergroup contact. We argued that perceiving outgroup members as not open to contact (i.e., negative response expectancies) would lead people to perceive their partner as the primary source of tension in the interaction. As a result, people with negative response expectancies should direct their negative emotional and behavioral responses outward toward their interaction partner. Specifically, we proposed that instead of responding in an avoidant manner, perceiving outgroup members as not open to contact would lead to negative approach-related "attack" responses, including anger (Harmon-Jones, 2003), blaming one's partner for tension in an interaction, and other-directed antisocial behavior.

To examine the implications of negative response expectancies, Butz and Plant (2006) provided White participants with feedback regarding a cross-race (i.e., Black) or same-race (i.e., White) partner's openness to an upcoming interaction. Participants who received negative feedback indicating that their Black interaction partner was not open to the interaction reported increased anger about having to participate in the interaction. Furthermore, the negative feedback led to a readiness to blame their partner for tension in the interaction. An important finding was that receiving such feedback from a White interaction partner did not result in such anger and blame. These findings are consistent with work indicating that interracial interactions differ from same-race interactions because they heighten the potential of being viewed in terms of one's racial group membership and rejected on this basis (e.g., Frey & Tropp, 2006). Negative response expectancies in the context of interracial interactions may result in particularly intense negative reactions due to attributing an outgroup member's lack of openness to rejection based on one's racial group membership.

Subsequent work on response expectancies from the vantage point of both racial majority and minority group members provides further support for the negative approach-related implications of these expectancies. Both White and Black participants who received negative compared to positive feedback about a cross-race interaction partner's openness to an interaction responded with heightened anger and a tendency to blame their partners for any tension in the interaction (Butz & Plant, 2006, Study 1). Moreover, when viewing a photograph of their interaction partner, the White and Black participants who received the negative feedback evaluated their partner's photograph more negatively (i.e., they perceived that the person had an angry and hostile disposition) than participants who received positive or no feedback. It is worth noting that the positive feedback tended to result in less anger and blame but its effect was relatively weaker, and in many cases, nonsignificant.

Together, these results suggest that approaching an interaction with the expectation that one's partner is not open to the interaction may lead people to become angry, blame their partner, and view their partner through "expectancy-tinted lenses," perceiving anger and hostility in this person's demeanor and behavior. The tendency to externalize blame to one's partner and perceive anger and hostility in this person may in turn serve as a justification for responding to this person in an antisocial manner. An important finding was that the White and Black participants responded similarly to the response expectancy feedback. This finding is consistent with work highlighting the similarity in racial majority and minority group members' expectancies about outgroup members in interactions (e.g., Shelton & Richeson, 2005) and work noting the similarity in majority and minority group members' responses to interracial rejection (e.g., Mendes, Major, McCoy, & Blascovich, 2008).

A separate study (Butz & Plant, 2006, Study 2) revealed that White participants who received negative response expectancy feedback behaved in a more antisocial manner toward their Black partner than participants who received neutral feedback about their partners' more general social experiences. In this study, participants were given the opportunity to either help or hinder their partner's likely success on a "word-building task" in which the partner could earn money. Specifically, participants were in the position of selecting letters that their partner could use to form words on the word-building task. Participants who received the negative response expectancy feedback doled out less helpful, more difficult-to-use letters (e.g., Qs, Zs, and Xs) to their partners than did participants who had received neutral feedback. Additional analyses indicated that those participants were, in fact, aware that their partners would be angry with the letters allocated to them. These findings indicate that expecting that one's cross-race interaction partner is not open to interacting precipitates antisocial behavioral responses, which may in turn elicit anger and hostility from the partner.

In this work, simultaneous examination of expectancies for the self (negative efficacy) and one's interaction partner (response expectancies) indicates that they have independent effects on approach- and avoidance-related responses to interracial interactions. When considering one's partner, negative response expectancy feedback was a strong predictor of negative approach-related responses, including anger, hostility, and attributing blame to one's partner for tension in the interaction. However, this feedback did not predict avoidance-related responses such as anxiety and the desire to avoid the interracial interaction. In contrast, when considering one's self, negative efficacy expectancies for interracial interactions were associated with avoidant responses, including anxiety and avoidant intentions, but not with the negative approach-related responses.

Recently, we employed a similar approach to examine the differential role of efficacy and response expectancies in interethnic interactions among Whites, non-Hispanics, and Hispanic/Latinos (Plant, Butz, & Tartakovsky, 2008). Results of these studies indicate that negative efficacy and response expectancies tend to have approach- and avoidance-related implications for responses to these interethnic interactions that are similar to those for interracial interactions. Thus, we believe our work on expectancies may be applied beyond the context of interracial interactions to shed light on possible sources of approach- and avoidance-related responses in other intergroup contexts. It will be important in future work to examine whether these same types of expectancies have similar implications for different types of intergroup interactions (e.g., groups that differ in politics, nationality, sexual orientation).

Taken together, our previous work provides accumulating evidence in support of the differential implications of negative efficacy and response expectancies about intergroup interactions. Negative efficacy expectancies were associated with distinctly avoidance-related responses, whereas negative response expectancies resulted in distinctly negative approach-related responses. Thus, whereas people with negative efficacy expectancies become anxious and withdraw from intergroup interactions, people who enter interactions with negative response expectancies can experience a range of negative approach-related responses that lead to hostile and unpleasant interactions. This work clarifies the specific types of concerns that need to be addressed in order to ease negative expectations and encourage more positive intergroup relations. Improving expectations about intergroup contact may lead people to take the important step of initiating intergroup interactions. People may find that such interactions are "better than they expected," which may bolster their efficacy for responding in future interactions and their expectations about how others will respond to them (see Mallett et al., this volume). Thus, efforts to address people's initial apprehension and concerns about intergroup interactions may have far-reaching benefits for encouraging more frequent and positive intergroup interactions over time.

OVERCOMING NEGATIVE EXPECTANCIES

Although negative expectancies may precipitate negative approach- or avoidance-related patterns of responses, we believe it is not always the case that people will succumb to these negative expectancies and respond in an avoidant or antisocial manner. Indeed, there is evidence that negative expectancies hold the potential to precipitate positive behavior in interactions (see Shelton, 2003). These intriguing findings suggest that although some people may be burdened with negative expectancies about intergroup interactions, at the same time others may perceive the situation as one that can be overcome. When negative outcomes are anticipated in intergroup interactions, some individuals will interpret the situation not as threatening but instead as a challenge that requires effort and energy to overcome (for a review, see Trawalter, Richeson, & Shelton, 2009). Thus, we believe that some people will respond with positive approach-oriented responses in intergroup interactions even in the wake of negative expectancies.

Supporting this argument, Blascovich and colleagues (e.g., Blascovich & Mendes, 2000; Blascovich & Tomaka, 1996) and others (e.g., Lazarus, 1991) have argued that beyond considering people's initial appraisals about whether a situation is threatening, it is important to consider people's secondary appraisals about their resources for coping with the perceived threat. With this model, when one's personal resources for coping with a stressful situation are perceived to be insufficient to meet the demands posed by the situation, the response will be a "threat" response, characterized by anxiety, defeat, and withdrawal from the situation. In addition, an angry "fight" response is possible when people deflect blame to others for a stressful situation (see Mendes et al., 2008). In contrast, people who perceive that their personal resources for responding to a stressful situation outweigh the demands of the situation are likely to respond with a "challenge" response focused on "proving oneself" and striving for a positive resolution. Thus, those who perceive that their personal resources for responding to negative expectancies outweigh the demands of the situation are likely to respond in a positive approach-oriented manner, expending effort and energy to achieve positive outcomes in intergroup interactions.

An emerging body of work indicates that motivation may be an important resource for overcoming the consequences of negative expectancies. Many individuals are highly motivated to respond without prejudice in interracial interactions (see Crandall, Eshleman, & O'Brien, 2002; Dunton & Fazio, 1997; Plant & Devine, 1998). In considering the role of motivation in overcoming the consequences of negative expectancies, it is important to ascertain not only whether people are motivated to respond without prejudice but also what the source of their motivation may be. Plant and Devine (1998) demonstrated that people may be highly internally motivated to respond without prejudice and desire to respond in an egalitarian manner because responding with prejudice violates personally important nonprejudiced standards. People may also be highly externally motivated to respond without prejudice because of concerns that appearing prejudiced would precipitate social disapproval from others. Plant and Devine developed scales to tap into internal and external motivation to respond without prejudice and provided evidence of their reliability and validity. Participants' scores on these scales were found to be largely independent, indicating that people can be motivated to respond without prejudice primarily for internal reasons, primarily for external reasons, for both internal and external reasons, or for neither internal nor external reasons.

We believe that whether people respond to interracial interactions by feeling threatened or by feeling challenged depends on the source of their motivation to respond without prejudice. Specifically, we propose that internally motivated people are likely to view interracial interactions as a challenge because they perceive they have the personal resources to respond positively in interracial interactions and are personally dedicated to respond consistently with their egalitarian standards. In addition, we argue that internally motivated people actively work to overcome any perceived deficiency in their ability to convey an egalitarian impression in interracial interactions. To the degree that they perceive that outgroup members are not open to interacting with them (i.e., negative response expectancies), we posit that people who are internally motivated will work hard to treat outgroup members in a friendly manner and behave prosocially in hopes of changing the outgroup members' negative outlook on interracial interactions.

Supporting these ideas, research shows that possessing a strong internal motivation to respond without prejudice may be particularly beneficial for responding in a positive manner in intergroup interactions. Plant (2004) examined non-Black people's internal and external motivation to respond without prejudice and their expectancies, emotional reactions, and behavioral intentions regarding interactions with Black people. Participants who were higher in internal motivation to respond without prejudice reported more positive efficacy and response expectancies about interactions with Black people, as well as less anxiety and interest in avoiding future interactions with Black people, than participants lower in internal motivation. In contrast, participants who were higher in external motivation to respond without prejudice reported more negative efficacy and response expectancies and higher levels of anxiety and avoidance about interactions with Black people than participants lower in external motivation.

More recently Plant, Devine, and Peruche (in press) examined the influence of motivation to respond without prejudice on the goals people set for intergroup interactions and their behavior in these interactions. Highly internally motivated White participants reported goals for an interaction with a Black person that reflected positive, approach-oriented behavior (e.g., be friendly), whereas highly externally motivated participants reported goals focused on avoiding conveying a prejudiced impression (e.g., don't pry). Further, highly internally motivated participants spent more time interacting with a Black interaction partner and behaved in a friendlier manner in the interaction, which in turn increased their partner's enjoyment of the interaction as compared with that of partners of less internally motivated participants. Highly externally motivated participants reported engaging in more avoidant behavior in the interaction, and—ironically, given their concern about appearing prejudiced—they came across as more prejudiced to their Black interaction partner than less externally motivated participants.

Overall, the previous work demonstrates that possessing a strong internal motivation to respond without prejudice may result in generally positive approaches and responses to interracial interactions. In addition, we believe that people who are highly internally motivated to respond without prejudice will work to achieve positive outcomes in interactions, even when these interactions provoke anxiety or hostility. For example, Plant (2004) found that although participants who were anxious about interracial interactions tended to want to avoid them, internally motivated participants were not interested in avoiding such interactions even if they found them anxiety provoking. In related work, Butz and Plant (2010) assessed non-Black participants' motivation to respond without prejudice and provided them with either generally positive or negative feedback about the likely outcome of an upcoming interaction with a Black person. Consistent with previous work (e.g., Butz & Plant, 2006; Plant & Butz, 2006; Plant & Devine, 2003), instilling negative expectancies heightened anxiety and anger about the upcoming interracial interaction. However, regardless of whether participants received positive or negative feedback, internal motivation was consistently associated with more positive responses, such as feeling less angry about the interaction and having greater interest in strategies to improve the quality of interactions. Consistent with Plant's (2004) findings, external motivation had less positive implications for responses to the interaction. Regardless of the expectancy feedback they received, highly externally motivated participants reported more anxiety about the interaction than their less externally motivated counterparts.

Providing further support for the proposition that internally motivated people will work hard to improve interracial interactions even in the wake of negative expectancies, Butz and Plant (2005) supplied White participants with negative or neutral information about the openness of a Black interaction partner and then afforded them the opportunity to help or harm their interaction partner. Specifically, the participants were allowed to decide how much work to allocate to their partner versus themselves for an onerous Scantron-bubbling task. When participants were led to believe their partner was not open to the interaction, highly internally motivated participants exhibited more prosocial behavior (reflected in their taking more of the onerous task for themselves) than their less internally motivated counterparts. These results support the idea that in the wake of negative expectancies, people who are internally motivated to respond without prejudice engage in behaviors that hold promise for improving the quality of intergroup interactions.

To understand why highly internally motivated people are effective in overcoming the anxious and hostile responses that often result from negative expectancies, it is helpful to draw on self-determination theory (Deci & Ryan, 1985), which posits that greater internalization of a goal leads to greater success in responding consistently with that goal (see Butz & Plant, 2009; Devine, Plant, Amodio, Harmon-Jones, & Vance 2002). Specifically, we argue that people with a strong internal motivation to respond without prejudice have developed a highly internalized and autonomous means to regulate prejudice (see Butz & Plant, 2009; Moskowitz, Gollwitzer, Wasel, & Schaal, 1999). As a result of being able to regulate their prejudice efficiently and effectively, people who are highly internally motivated to respond without prejudice are likely to be relatively free of prejudice concerns in interracial interactions and comfortable in interracial contexts (Devine, Brodish, & Vance, 2005). Consistent with this possibility, highly internally motivated individuals experience relatively low levels of intergroup anxiety and behave in a positive manner in intergroup interactions (Plant et al., in press). In contrast, among externally motivated individuals for whom the goal of responding without prejudice is less internalized, interracial interactions may evoke anxiety and avoidance due to their relative inefficiency in controlling prejudice and the resulting concerns about the transparency of prejudice in interactions.

Consistent with these arguments, Plant and Devine (1998) demonstrated that highly internally motivated people attempt to regulate their prejudice both in public contexts (i.e., when their prejudice could be known to others) as well as in private contexts when reporting their prejudice anonymously. Their self-determined motivation to respond without prejudice leads them to attempt to control prejudice, even in the absence of social pressure to appear unprejudiced. Further, Devine et al. (2002) demonstrated that non-Black participants high in internal but low in external motivation to respond without prejudice (i.e., the most internalized) exhibited low levels of prejudice on explicit *and* difficult-to-control implicit measures of racial prejudice (see also Amodio, Devine, & Harmon-Jones, 2008). Their highly effective control of prejudice is underscored by recent work indicating that highly internalized (i.e., high internal, low external) individuals continue to effectively control prejudice even when executive function is impaired by cognitive busyness (Devine et al., 2002) or by alcohol intoxication (Schlauch, Lang, Plant, Christensen, & Donohue, 2009). The responses of participants who were highly externally motivated to respond without prejudice reflected a consistent pattern of failing to control prejudice on implicit measures of racial bias, including when executive function was impaired (Devine et al., 2002; Schlauch et al., 2009). In addition, although people who are primarily externally motivated (low internal, high external) may attempt to regulate prejudice in public contexts as a result of their fear of coming across to others as prejudiced (Plant & Devine, 1998), their success at initial attempts to control explicit prejudice tends to be followed by failure in subsequent attempts to regulate their prejudice (Hausmann & Ryan, 2004).

Highly internally motivated people's effective regulation of prejudice may provide insight into their positive responses even when interactions evoke concerns about responding with prejudice. Among people who are internally motivated to respond without prejudice, the expectation that one is likely to respond with prejudice in interactions may signal the need for self-regulatory efforts to control prejudice. Instead of retreating or withdrawing from intergroup contact because of concerns about communicating a prejudiced impression, those who are strongly internally motivated to respond without prejudice may instead engage in self-regulatory efforts to control prejudice.

To date, several empirical investigations provide support for this proposition. For example, when highly internally motivated participants envision deviating from their personally important nonprejudiced standards, their primary affective response is guilt (Plant & Devine, 1998), an emotional reaction recently implicated in the effective regulation of prejudice (Amodio, Devine, & Harmon-Jones, 2007). Across several studies Plant and Devine (2009) gave non-Black participants a chance to work on a computer program that they believed would reduce either their overt, detectable prejudice or subtle, undetectable prejudice for an upcoming interaction with a Black person. Participants who were high in internal and low in external motivation to respond without prejudice did not spend much time on the program unless they were provided with evidence indicating they had prejudice to be eliminated. When provided with evidence that they possessed prejudice, they exhibited extensive effort to eliminate the prejudice. It is not surprising that these participants worked hard on the program only when led to believe that they would respond with prejudice, given that they do not typically respond with prejudice and likely viewed the program as unnecessary unless provided with evidence to the contrary (Butz & Plant, 2009). Participants who were high in both internal and external motivation to respond without prejudice spent extensive time working on the program regardless of whether they were provided evidence of their own prejudice or whether they believed that the program would eliminate either detectable or undetectable prejudice. Such a response is consistent with a determination to eliminate all forms of prejudice and an appreciation that sometimes they respond with more racial bias than they wish they did.

In contrast, participants who were low in internal motivation but high in external motivation were interested in working on the program only if it would reduce detectable prejudice. Finally, those who were low in both internal and external motivation to respond without prejudice showed little interest in the prejudice-reduction program across conditions. These results support the idea that people who are highly internally motivated to respond without prejudice are likely to respond to expectations of harboring prejudice with efforts to control it, which may lead them to persist in interactions and achieve positive outcomes. People who are externally motivated to respond without prejudice will work to decrease their prejudice only if they believe others will be aware of it. People who are unmotivated to respond without prejudice (low in internal and external motivation) are unlikely to expend effort to decrease prejudice.

Taken together, these studies add to the growing literature on the role of expectancies and motivation in approach- and avoidance-related responses to intergroup interactions. Although negative expectancies may result in negative approach- or avoidance-related responses to intergroup interactions, such negative responses are not inevitable. People who are highly internally motivated to respond without prejudice effectively regulate prejudice and enter intergroup interactions with relatively positive expectancies about their ability to control prejudice and achieve positive outcomes. As a result, when faced with concerns about the impression they will convey or the openness of outgroup members to interactions, highly internally motivated people may appraise the situation as a "challenge," which may lead to self-regulatory efforts and positive approach-oriented goals and behavior in interactions (e.g., smiling, maintaining eye contact, trying to get to know their partner).

In contrast to internally motivated people, highly externally motivated individuals routinely fail at controlling prejudice (Devine et al., 2002) and are encumbered with negative expectancies about the outcomes of interracial interactions (Plant, 2004). As a result, when faced with the possibility that they may respond with prejudice in interactions, highly externally motivated individuals may respond in a threatened manner (i.e., with anxiety and avoidance). Furthermore, when faced with the possibility that outgroup members will not be open to interactions, externally motivated individuals may respond with anger and hostility rather than with prosocial efforts to change their partner's outlook. Although people who are high in both internal and external motivation to respond without prejudice are determined and work hard to regulate prejudice and convey positive impressions in interactions, in some situations their external motivation may result in failure to overcome the consequences of negative expectancies. In short, we believe a higher internal and lower external motivation to respond without prejudice is the optimal combination for overcoming the negative approach- or avoidance-related consequences of negative expectancies about intergroup interactions.

CONCLUSION

If we are to promote positive intergroup relations, it is critical to understand the obstacles that can interfere with positive intergroup contact. One goal for this chapter was to consider the specific and differing psychological barriers to positive intergroup relations in hopes of providing insight into how these hurdles can be overcome. A growing body of research indicates that the anxiety, tension, and hostility people experience prior to and during intergroup interactions comes from negative expectancies about such interactions. The current work demonstrates the importance of distinguishing between expectancies focused on one's ability to convey positive impressions and expectancies about the openness of outgroup members to interactions. Examining the specific nature of people's expectancies provides insight into whether they will respond in a distinctly avoidance-related or negative approach-related manner in interactions. By being able to identify the specific nature of people's concerns, we will be better suited to design effective and targeted interventions to improve people's expectancies and, hence, their responses during intergroup contact. The resulting positive contact may help to further improve expectancies and may lead to a self-perpetuating cycle of improved intergroup contact.

Another goal of the current work was to provide insight into the factors that may help people to avoid succumbing to the consequences of negative expectancies for intergroup contact. We demonstrated that people who are deeply motivated to respond without prejudice for internal, personal reasons set positive approach-oriented goals for interracial interactions and actively work to improve intergroup interactions, even when they are anxious or anticipate that the interaction is unlikely to go well. Thus, personal dedication to responding without prejudice may help people avoid the pitfalls resulting from negative expectancies for intergroup interactions and may result in more positive intergroup contact for all involved. Given the central role of internal motivation in overcoming the influence of negative expectancies on interactions, it is critical for future work to explore approaches to increase the personal importance that people place on responding without prejudice. Although one's level of internal motivation to respond without prejudice is typically assessed as a stable individual difference, contemporary perspectives emphasize that one's environment can dramatically impact personality (e.g., Mischel & Shoda, 1995). A number of approaches may heighten the personal importance of responding without prejudice. Appealing to people's egalitarian values and reflecting upon instances in which one's behavior in interracial interactions has not lived up to these values may strengthen people's internal motivation to respond without prejudice (e.g., Devine, Monteith, Zuwerink, & Elliot, 1991; Monteith, Devine, & Zuwerink, 1993). In an alternative approach, efforts to encourage empathy for racial outgroup members may solidify people's personal dedication to responding without prejudice. Although such possibilities await empirical confirmation, we are optimistic that instilling a strong internal motivation to respond without prejudice will encourage positive goals and behavior in intergroup interactions as well as resilience to the influence of negative expectancies on intergroup interactions.

REFERENCES

Amodio, D. M., Devine, P. G., & Harmon-Jones, E. (2007). A dynamic model of guilt: Implications for motivation and self-regulation in the context of prejudice. *Psychological Science, 18*, 524–530. doi:10.1111/j.1467-9280.2007.01933.x

Amodio, D. M., Devine, P. G., & Harmon-Jones, E. (2008). Individual differences in the regulation of intergroup bias: The role of conflict monitoring and neural signals for control. *Journal of Personality and Social Psychology, 94*, 60–74. doi:10.1037/0022-3514.94.1.60

Blascovich, J., & Mendes, W. B. (2000). Challenge and threat appraisals: The role of affective cues. In J. Forgas (Ed.), *Feeling and thinking: The role of affect in social cognition* (pp. 59–82). Paris, France: Cambridge University Press.

Blascovich, J., & Tomaka, J. (1996). The biopsychosocial model of arousal regulation. *Advances in Experimental Social Psychology, 28*, 1–51. doi:10.1016/S0065-2601(08)60235-X

Britt, T. W., Boniecki, K. A., Vescio, T. K., Biernat, M., & Brown, L. M. (1996). Intergroup anxiety: A person X situation approach. *Personality and Social Psychology Bulletin, 22*, 1177–1188. doi:10.1177/01461672962211008

Butz, D. A., & Plant, E. A. (2005, January). *Predicting prosocial behavior in interracial interactions: Motivations and expectations about outgroup members*. Poster presented at the annual meeting of the Society for Personality and Social Psychology, New Orleans, LA.

Butz, D. A., & Plant, E. A. (2006). Perceiving outgroup members as unresponsive: Implications for approach-related emotions, intentions, and behavior. *Journal of Personality and Social Psychology, 91*, 1066–1079. doi:10.1037/0022-3514.91.6.1066

Butz, D. A., & Plant, E. A. (2009). Prejudice control and interracial relations: The role of motivation to respond without prejudice. *Journal of Personality, 77*, 1311–1341. doi:10.1111/j.1467-6494.2009.00583.x

Butz, D. A., & Plant, E. A. (2010). [Expectations and motivations regarding interracial interactions]. Unpublished raw data.

Crandall, C. S., Eshleman, A., & O'Brien, L. (2002). Social norms and the expression and suppression of prejudice: The struggle for internalization. *Journal of Personality and Social Psychology, 82*, 359–378. doi:10.1037/0022-3514.82.3.359

Deci, E. L., & Ryan, R. M. (1985). *Intrinsic motivation and self-determination in human behavior*. New York, NY: Plenum Press.

Devine, P. G., Brodish, A. B., & Vance, S. L. (2005). Self-regulatory processes in interracial interactions. In J. P. Forgas, K. D. Williams, and S. M. Laham (Eds.), *Social motivation: Conscious and unconscious processes* (Sixth Sydney Symposium on Social Psychology) (pp. 249–273). New York, NY: Psychology Press.

Devine, P. G., Evett, S. R., & Vasquez-Suson, K. A. (1996). Exploring the interpersonal dynamics of interracial context. In R. M. Sorrentino & E. T. Higgins (Eds.), *Handbook of motivation and cognition: The interpersonal context* (Vol. 3, pp. 423–464). New York, NY: Guilford Press.

Devine, P. G., Monteith, M. J., Zuwerink, J. R., & Elliot, A. J. (1991). Prejudice with and without compunction. *Journal of Personality and Social Psychology, 60,* 817–830. doi:10.1037/0022-3514.60.6.817

Devine, P. G., Plant, E. A., Amodio, A. M., Harmon-Jones, E., & Vance, S. L. (2002). The regulation of implicit and explicit race bias: The role of motivations to respond without prejudice. *Journal of Personality and Social Psychology, 82,* 835–848. doi:10.1037/0022-3514.82.5.835

Dunton, B. C., & Fazio, R. H. (1997). An individual difference measure of motivation to control prejudiced reactions. *Personality and Social Psychology Bulletin, 23,* 316–326. doi:10.1177/0146167297233009

Frey, F. E., & Tropp, L. R. (2006). Being seen as individuals versus as group members: Extending research on metaperception to intergroup contexts. *Personality and Social Psychology Review, 10,* 265–280. doi:10.1207/s15327957pspr1003_5

Harmon-Jones, E. (2003). Anger and the behavioral approach system. *Personality and Individual Differences, 35,* 995–1005. doi:10.1016/S0191-8869(02)00313-6

Hausmann, L. R. M., & Ryan, C. S. (2004). Effects of external versus internal motivation to control prejudice on implicit prejudice: The mediating role of efforts to control prejudiced responses. *Basic and Applied Social Psychology, 26,* 215–225. doi:10.1207/s15324834basp2602&3_8

Lazarus, R. S. (1991). *Emotion and adaptation.* New York, NY: Oxford University Press.

Leary, M. R., & Atherton, S. C. (1986). Self-efficacy, social anxiety, and inhibition in interpersonal encounters. *Journal of Social and Clinical Psychology, 4,* 256–267.

Mallett, R. K., Wilson, T. D., & Gilbert, D. T. (2008). Expect the unexpected: Failure to anticipate similarities when predicting the quality of an intergroup interaction. *Journal of Personality and Social Psychology, 94,* 265–277. doi:10.1037/0022-3514.94.2.94.2.265

Mendes, W. B., Major, B., McCoy, S., & Blascovich, J. (2008). How attributional ambiguity shapes physiological and emotional responses to social rejection and acceptance. *Journal of Personality and Social Psychology, 94,* 278–291. doi:10.1037/0022-3514.94.2.278

Mendoza-Denton, R., Downey, G., Purdie, V. J., Davis, A., & Pietrzak, J. (2002). Sensitivity to status-based rejection: Implications for African-American students' college experience. *Journal of Personality and Social Psychology, 83*, 896–918. doi:10.1037/0022-3514.83.4.896

Mischel, W., & Shoda, Y. (1995). A cognitive–affective system theory of personality: Reconceptualizing situations, dispositions, dynamics, and invariance in personality structure. *Psychological Review, 102*, 246–268. doi:10.1037/0033-295X.102.2.246

Monteith, M. J., Devine, P. G., & Zuwerink, J. R. (1993). Self-directed versus other-directed affect as a consequence of prejudice-related discrepancies. *Journal of Personality and Social Psychology, 64*, 198–210. doi:10.1037/0022-3514.64.2.198

Moskowitz, G. B., Gollwitzer, P. M., Wasel, W., & Schaal, B. (1999). Preconscious control of stereotype activation through chronic egalitarian goals. *Journal of Personality and Social Psychology, 77*, 167–184. doi:10.1037/0022-3514.77.1.167

Pettigrew, T. F., & Tropp, L. R. (2006). A meta-analytic test of intergroup contact theory. *Journal of Personality and Social Psychology, 90*, 751–783. doi:10.1037/0022-3514.90.5.751

Pettigrew, T. F., & Tropp, L. R. (2008). How does intergroup contact reduce prejudice? Meta- analytic tests of three mediators. *European Journal of Social Psychology, 38*, 922–934. doi:10.1002/ejsp.504

Plant, E. A. (2004). Responses to interracial interactions over time. *Personality and Social Psychology Bulletin, 30*, 1458–1471. doi:10.1177/0146167204264244

Plant, E. A., & Butz, D. A. (2006). The causes and consequences of an avoidance-focus for interracial interactions. *Personality and Social Psychology Bulletin, 32*, 833–846. doi:10.1177/0146167206287182

Plant, E. A., Butz, D. A., & Tartakovsky, M. (2008). Interethnic interactions: Expectancies, emotions, and behavioral intentions. *Group Processes & Intergroup Relations, 11*, 555–574. doi:10.1177/1368430208095827

Plant, E. A., & Devine, P. G. (1998). Internal and external motivation to respond without prejudice. *Journal of Personality and Social Psychology, 75*, 811–832. doi:10.1037/0022-3514.75.3.811

Plant, E. A., & Devine, P. G. (2003). Antecedents and implications of interracial anxiety. *Personality and Social Psychology Bulletin, 29*, 790–801. doi:10.1177/0146167203029006011

Plant, E. A., & Devine, P. G. (2009). The active control of prejudice: Unpacking the intentions guiding control efforts. *Journal of Personality and Social Psychology, 96*, 640–652. doi:10.1037/a0012960

Plant, E. A., Devine, P. G., & Peruche, B. M. (in press). Regulatory concerns for interracial interactions: Approaching egalitarianism versus avoiding prejudice. *Personality and Social Psychology Bulletin*.

Schlauch, R. C., Lang, A. R., Plant, E. A., Christensen, R., & Donohue, K. F. (2009). The effect of alcohol on race-biased responding: The moderating role of internal and external motivations to respond without prejudice. *Journal of Studies on Alcohol and Drugs, 70*, 328–336.

Schlenker, B. R., & Leary, M. R. (1982). Social anxiety and self-presentation: A conceptualization and model. *Psychological Bulletin, 92*, 641–669. doi:10.1037/0033-2909.92.3.641

Shelton, J. N. (2003). Interpersonal concerns in social encounters between majority and minority group members. *Group Processes & Intergroup Relations, 6*, 171–185. doi:10.1177/1368430203006002003

Shelton, J. N., & Richeson, J. A. (2005). Intergroup contact and pluralistic ignorance. *Journal of Personality and Social Psychology, 88*, 91–107. doi:10.1037/0022-3514.88.1.91

Shelton, J. N., Richeson, J. A., & Salvatore, J. (2005). Expecting to be the target of prejudice: Implications for interethnic interactions. *Personality and Social Psychology Bulletin, 31*, 1189–1202. doi:10.1177/0146167205274894

Stephan, W. G., & Stephan, C. W. (1985). Intergroup anxiety. *Journal of Social Issues, 41*, 157–175. doi:10.1111/j.1540-4560.1985.tb01134.x

Trawalter, S., Richeson, J. A., & Shelton, J. N. (2009). Predicting behavior during interracial interactions: A stress and coping approach. *Personality and Social Psychology Review, 13*, 243–268. doi:10.1177/1088868309345850

Tropp, L. R. (2003). The psychological impact of prejudice: Implications for intergroup contact. *Group Processes & Intergroup Relations, 6*, 131–149. doi:10.1177/1368430203006002001

U.S. Census Bureau. (2008, August). *An older and more diverse nation by midcentury, Census Bureau Reports (CB08-123)*. Retrieved from http://www.census.gov/Press-Release/www/releases/archives/population/012496.html

Vorauer, J. D., Main, K. J., & O'Connell, G. B. (1998). How do individuals expect to be viewed by members of low status groups? Content and implications of meta-stereotypes. *Journal of Personality and Social Psychology, 75*, 917–937. doi:10.1037/0022-3514.75.4.917

5

FOCUSING BEYOND THE SELF: GOAL ORIENTATIONS IN INTERGROUP RELATIONS

KATYA MIGACHEVA, LINDA R. TROPP, AND JENNIFER CROCKER

Cross-group interactions create stress and anxiety (Blascovich, Mendes, Hunter, Lickel, & Kowai-Bell, 2001; Stephan & Stephan, 1985), motivating people to avoid intergroup contact (Butz & Plant, 2006; Plant & Devine, 2003). People often fear rejection by outgroup members (Frey & Tropp, 2006; Kramer & Messick, 1998; Shelton & Richeson, 2006), and they worry about whether others perceive them as prejudiced (Devine & Vasquez, 1998), whether they can meet the demands of the contact situation (Blascovich et al., 2001), and whether they can successfully navigate cross-group interactions (Butz & Plant, 2006; Plant & Butz, 2006; see also Butz & Plant, this volume).

We propose that the goals people have in cross-group interactions contribute to the discomfort they feel and that by shifting goals, people may not only reduce their discomfort and avoidance of cross-group interactions but may be better equipped to create positive relationships across group boundaries. We distinguish between two motivational systems underlying these goals: an *egosystem*, in which people focus on their own desires and needs; and an *ecosystem*, in which people recognize their connection to others. We then describe two sets of goals associated with each system and consider how a goals framework can inform strategies and interventions to improve relations between groups.

TWO MOTIVATIONAL SYSTEMS: ECOSYSTEM AND EGOSYSTEM ORIENTATIONS

A number of researchers have proposed that a fundamental problem in cross-race interactions involves perceived threats to desired self-images (Crocker & Garcia, 2006; Frey & Tropp, 2006; Shelton & Richeson, 2006; Steele, Spencer, & Aronson, 2002). For disadvantaged group members, cross-race interactions raise concerns about devaluation and being rejected (Crocker & Garcia, 2006; Shelton, Richeson, & Vorauer, 2006; Steele et al., 2002). For advantaged group members, cross-race interactions raise concerns about being seen as unfair and prejudiced or as unfairly benefiting from privileged status (Devine & Vasquez, 1998; Richeson & Shelton, 2007; Vorauer, 2006). Hence, cross-race interactions can threaten desired self-images for people on both sides. Driven by these fears, people typically approach cross-group interactions with a largely self-focused orientation, highly sensitive to possible threats to the social self (Vorauer, 2006; Vorauer & Kumhyr, 2001). Accordingly, research shows that people often respond more favorably toward outgroup members when concerns about the self are reduced (Fein, Hoshino-Browne, Davies, & Spencer, 2003; Goff, Steele, & Davies, 2008).

Thus, it appears that sensitivity to possible threat and discomfort in cross-group interactions may be reduced by shifting people's focus beyond the self and related concerns for their desired self-images. Crocker and her colleagues (Crocker, 2008; Crocker, Olivier, & Nuer, 2009) use an ecosystem as a metaphor for a perspective on human relationships in which the self is seen as part of a larger whole. People with an ecosystem orientation see themselves as connected to others, recognizing that their actions have consequences for others and can affect the ability of everyone to satisfy fundamental needs. It should be noted that an ecosystem orientation is not selfless, self-sacrificing, or self-disparaging; rather, in the ecosystem orientation, the self is seen as part of a larger context, and the needs of the self are as important as the needs of others.

Of course, people do not typically have an ecosystem orientation all, or even most, of the time. People instead tend to have a narrower perspective in which they focus on themselves and their own needs and desires, without thinking as much about those of others (Crocker, 2009). Within such an egosystem orientation, people focus on others only insofar as others can give or withhold social goods, such as approval, inclusion, or validation (Leary & Baumeister, 2000), or serve as a source of feedback about how one is viewed in the eyes of others (Tesser, 1988). Consequently, people with an egosystem orientation want to prove themselves, demonstrate their desired qualities, and validate their ability and worth.

Using ecosystem and egosystem orientations as a unifying framework, we describe two separate yet complementary perspectives on goals stemming from these orientations. One perspective distinguishes between compassionate and self-image goals (Crocker et al., 2008), and the other perspective adapts descriptions of learning and performance goals in achievement to the context of intergroup relations (Migacheva & Tropp, 2009). We summarize and explore points of convergence and divergence between these two approaches, and we discuss their utility for designing strategies to enhance people's intergroup experiences.

Self-Image and Compassionate Goals

Crocker and her colleagues have investigated the consequences of self-image and compassionate goals for interpersonal relationships. In one study, Crocker and Canevello (2008, Study 2) recruited 65 previously unacquainted roommate dyads, not selected on the basis of race, early in their first semester of college. Both roommates of each dyad completed pretest measures of relationship satisfaction and closeness. They then completed daily reports of their goals for the roommate relationship including support given and received, responsiveness, and competitive versus cooperative feelings. Participants rated how they wanted or tried to be with their roommate in the past day, using items to assess compassionate goals (e.g., "Be aware of the impact my behavior might have on my roommate's feelings"; $\alpha = .84$ at pretest, .93 at posttest) and self-image goals (e.g., "Avoid being blamed or criticized"; $\alpha = .80$ at pretest, .87 at posttest). After 21 days, participants again completed posttest measures of relationship satisfaction and closeness.

Without regard to the racial match or mismatch of the roommate dyads, initial analyses examined how self-image and compassionate goals predicted students' feelings when they were interacting with their roommates on subsequent days in lagged-day, multilevel modeling analyses (Crocker, Liu, & Canevello, 2008). Compassionate goals on one day predicted increased cooperative feelings the following day, which in turn predicted feeling more peaceful on the subsequent day. Self-image goals one day predicted increased competitive feelings the following day, which in turn predicted feeling more conflicted, confused, and fearful when interacting with roommates on the subsequent day. Participants' goals also interacted to predict change in their roommates' reports of support received and given: Participants with chronically high compassionate goals and chronically low self-image goals had roommates who reported receiving increased support and giving back increased support (Crocker & Canevello, 2008, Study 2).

This study was not originally designed to test the effects of self-image and compassionate goals in same-race and cross-race roommate relationships. However, about half of the roommate dyads were same-race dyads (mostly White–White), and half were cross-race dyads (mostly White–Asian or White–Black). Preliminary analyses of change in relationship quality in same-race compared with cross-race roommate dyads showed that, consistent with other recent work (e.g., Shook & Fazio, 2008a, 2008b), cross-race relationships started out less close and deteriorated over the first semester of college, relative to same-race roommate pairs. More important, over time, self-image goals predicted significantly larger drops (i.e., residual change) in closeness in cross-race than in same-race dyads, whereas compassionate goals predicted marginally greater increases in relationship satisfaction in cross-race compared with same-race dyads. These effects are particularly striking in light of the brief interval between pretest and posttest (23 days) and the heterogeneity of the cross-race dyads.

Thus, initial research suggests that self-image (egosystem) goals can undermine the quality of cross-group roommate relationships, whereas compassionate (ecosystem) goals can enhance relationship quality. These findings support other research showing that people worry about how others see them in cross-group interactions (Devine & Vasquez, 1998; Vorauer, 2006) and initially find cross-group interactions to be anxiety provoking (Page-Gould, Mendoza-Denton, & Tropp, 2008). Anxiety may be especially problematic in cross-group interactions because the nonverbal behaviors associated with anxiety are often interpreted as dislike (Dovidio, Kawakami, & Gaertner, 2002), which can disrupt the development of relationships across group boundaries (Tropp, 2008). However, approaching cross-group interactions with compassionate goals may attenuate the negative effects of self-image goals and reduce anxiety (Crocker & Canevello, 2008; Crocker, Canevello, Breines, & Flynn, 2010), thereby setting the stage for greater closeness and intimacy in cross-group relationships (Page-Gould et al., 2008).

Learning and Performance Goals in Intergroup Relations

A complementary approach views learning goals as a way to promote constructive cross-group interactions (Crocker & Garcia, 2006; Migacheva & Tropp, 2009). Achievement motivation researchers have compared two major categories of achievement goals: learning and performance. People with learning goals seek to obtain new information and knowledge, whereas people with performance goals seek to validate their own qualities and abilities (Grant & Dweck, 2003). Learning goals lead people to focus on growth and improvement (Elliott & Dweck, 1988), thereby reducing ego concerns (Dweck, 2000) and enhancing a range of positive outcomes, such as sustained intrinsic motivation and persistence (Grant & Dweck, 2003). Conversely, performance goals are largely ego-driven, in that people desire approval from others and seek to prove what they know (Nicholls, 1984); these tendencies in turn are associated with impaired performance, external motivation, and poor resilience to failure (Grant & Dweck, 2003).

When applied to the context of cross-group interactions, these conceptions of learning and performance goals mesh well with the ecosystem and egosystem motivational framework discussed previously. Learning goals reflect an ecosystem orientation to focus beyond oneself and view others as sources of knowledge and growth, whereas performance goals reflect an egosystem orientation to focus on evaluative concerns and self-presentation. As such, by adopting learning goals in cross-group interactions, people may be able to shift their focus away from evaluative concerns toward a focus on learning about and from their outgroup partners. We expect that such shifts help people to move beyond seeing outgroup members as sources of threat to viewing them as sources of knowledge and growth (Crocker & Garcia, 2006)—a change in viewpoint that should in turn promote greater motivation for, and less discomfort during, intergroup contact (see Ely & Thomas, 2001).

In an initial test of these ideas, 127 European American undergraduates completed surveys about their orientation toward learning (i.e. "I think I could learn a lot from . . . ") and their performance concerns (i.e., "I feel I would be misunderstood if I tried to interact with . . . ") in relation to contact with Asian Americans, African Americans, and Latino Americans. Responses to the learning and performance items were inversely correlated: A greater focus on learning was typically associated with less concern about being misunderstood by Asian Americans ($r = -.33$, $p < .001$), African Americans ($r = -.15$, $p < .10$), and Latino Americans ($r = -.24$, $p < .01$).

We also found that the learning and performance measures were correlated with additional items assessing interest in intergroup contact (i.e., "How interested are you in interacting with . . . ") and avoidance of intergroup contact (i.e., "I generally try to avoid interactions with . . . "). Learning goals positively correlated with interest in contact ($r = .52$, $.55$, and $.56$, in relation to Asian Americans, African Americans, and Latino Americans, respectively, $ps < .001$) and negatively correlated with contact avoidance ($r = -.38$, $-.29$, and $-.32$ in relation to Asian Americans, African Americans, and Latino Americans, respectively, $ps < .001$). By contrast, performance concerns related negatively to interest in contact with Asian Americans ($r = -.20$, $p < .05$), African Americans ($r = -.16$, $p < .10$), and Latino Americans ($r = -.25$, $p < .01$) and positively to avoidance of contact with Asian Americans ($r = .37$, $p < .001$), African Americans ($r = .27$, $p < .01$), and Latino Americans ($r = .39$, $p < .001$).

We obtained similar findings in a more recent survey of 111 European American and 152 African American students attending two different New York middle schools in racially homogeneous neighborhoods (Migacheva & Tropp, 2010). Regardless of their own race, children who reported being more curious about and interested in people of a different race (i.e., orientation toward learning) were more willing to form cross-group friendships and anticipated feeling more comfortable around people from other racial groups. At the same time, among European American children, concerns about how to act around people of a different race (i.e., concerns about performance) negatively related to their desire to form cross-group friendships and to their anticipated feelings of comfort during cross-group interactions.[1] Together, these findings suggest that an orientation toward learning may promote positive responses to intergroup contact, whereas concerns associated with the self and one's performance might inhibit such positive tendencies.

Experimental Evidence

Recent experimental research provides further evidence of the positive effects of learning goals in intergroup contexts (Goff et al., 2008; Migacheva & Tropp, 2009). For example, Goff et al. (2008) explored whether learning goals can alleviate participants' evaluative concerns in cross-group interactions. In two related studies, they instructed half of their European American participants to view an upcoming interaction with an African American or a European American partner as a learning experience and did not give any goal instructions to the other half. Those European American participants who did not receive learning-goal instructions created greater physical distance with an outgroup partner than with an ingroup partner. However, European American participants who received learning-goal instructions did not differ in their distancing patterns, regardless of the race of their partner. Goff et al. concluded that the learning-goal orientation led these participants to perceive their situation as less evaluative, thereby protecting them from stereotype threat concerns and reducing their need to distance themselves from the outgroup partner.

Building on Goff et al.'s (2008) initial support for the utility of learning goals in intergroup contexts, a recent experimental study (Migacheva & Tropp, 2009) extended this research in several important ways. First, Goff et al. (2008) manipulated only participants' learning goals and measured participants' evaluative concerns as a function of whether they did (or did not) receive learning-goal instructions. While showing the usefulness of learning goals in alleviating these concerns, such a design did not experimentally contrast them with the

---

[1]Unlike the results for European American children, African American children's concerns about how to act were not related either to their desire to form cross-group friendships or to how comfortable they reported feeling about interactions with people of other races. This divergence may have emerged because, by growing up in a largely White society, African American children are likely to have more intergroup contact experiences and therefore may be more accustomed to interactions with the White majority (see Blau & Schwartz, 1997).

potential effects of performance goals. Hence, we experimentally tested the effects of both learning- and performance-goal orientations on participants' experiences during cross-group interactions.

Further extending Goff et al.'s (2008) work, we also manipulated the racial sensitivity of the topic to be discussed during the interaction. Although discussing racially sensitive topics can be threatening (Tatum, 1992), it is conceivable that different goal orientations would be more or less effective in reducing such threat. This study allowed us to test the effects of goal orientations in a broad variety of interaction contexts, ranging from those that may be least threatening (e.g., race-neutral topic with a member of one's own racial ingroup) to most threatening (e.g., race-sensitive topic with a member of a racial outgroup).

Thus, we (Migacheva & Tropp, 2009) asked female European American participants to focus either on learning about their partner during their inter-action (i.e., "Focus on learning about your partner, her thoughts, ideas and opinions"), or on presenting themselves to their partner (i.e., "Focus on pre-senting yourself to your partner, your thoughts, ideas and opinions"). We then observed and coded participants' nonverbal behaviors during a short interaction with either a European American or an African American con-federate partner, when discussing a race-neutral (e.g., global warming) or a race-sensitive (e.g., racial profiling) topic. Behaviors such as eye contact, gaze aversion, and fidgeting were used to assess participants' affect toward outgroup partners, as well as their desire to avoid cross-group interactions (see Dovidio et al., 2002; Ickes, 1984; Mehrabian, 1972). Particularly among those discussing a race-sensitive topic with a cross-race partner, participants who were instructed to focus on learning maintained longer eye contact, averted their gaze less often, used fewer speech dysfluencies (e.g., "like," "umm"), and exhibited fewer fidgeting behaviors than those who were instructed to focus on how they present themselves to their partner. Together, these findings suggest that people who adopt learning goals may be less likely to exhibit discomfort during cross-group interactions than those who adopt performance goals.

The distinction between learning and performance goals in the achieve-ment literature provides a useful framework when applied to the context of intergroup relations. The parallel between these two domains seems rather clear: In both cases, performance and evaluative concerns generally lead to neg-ative achievement and intergroup outcomes, whereas focusing beyond the self, and specifically on learning, can lead to positive outcomes. Emerging research provides preliminary support for the effectiveness of learning goals in intergroup relations, whether defined as an orientation toward learning from experience (Goff et al., 2008) or toward acquiring knowledge about an outgroup member (Migacheva & Tropp, 2009). Thus, setting learning goals for cross-group interactions may be an effective tool for overcoming anxiety and threat even when discussing racially sensitive topics. Though more studies are necessary to enhance our understanding of how and why learning goals have these effects, these initial findings show promise for reducing people's anxieties and encouraging them to welcome future contact opportunities with outgroup members (see Plant & Devine, 2003; Stephan & Stephan, 1985).

TOWARD AN INTEGRATIVE MODEL OF GOAL ORIENTATIONS IN INTERGROUP CONTEXTS

Thus far, we have discussed two different sets of goals, which, we argue, stem from a broader distinction between eco- and egosystem motivations. Our exploration of ecosystem and egosystem motivations is a timely endeavor, echoing several related discussions in the recent literature. Social psychological research has increasingly paid attention to participants' regulatory focus during cross-group interactions (e.g., Trawalter & Richeson, 2006; Vorauer & Kumhyr, 2001), as well as to the expectations, orientations, and motivations with which people enter such interactions (e.g., Butz & Plant, this volume; Butz & Plant, 2006; Devine, Brodish, & Vance, 2005; Plant & Butz, 2006). Focusing beyond the self, such as concentrating on creating a positive experience (Trawalter & Richeson, 2006), being internally motivated to establish egalitarian relations (Plant & Devine, 2009), learning from the outgroup partner and the interaction experience (Goff et al., 2008; Migacheva & Tropp, 2009) or considering another's needs (Crocker, Liu, & Canavello, 2008) may all contribute to approaching cross-group interactions with an ecosystem orientation. Conversely, focusing on self-related concerns, such as monitoring one's own behavior and image (Vorauer & Turpie, 2004), avoiding expressions of prejudice (Devine et al., 2005), questioning one's efficacy and fearing rejection (Butz & Plant, 2006), may all contribute to avoiding cross-group interactions with an egosystem motivation.

In the present analysis, we examine two sets of goals—compassionate and self-image goals on the one hand, and learning and performance goals on the other—that we view as distinct yet complementary concepts that might help us better understand the structure of cross-group interactions. In our view, these goals basically differ in the degree to which the self is involved in the motivations for a cross-group interaction. Compassionate and learning goals tend to avert group members' focus from the self and evaluation (ecosystem orientation), whereas self-image and performance goals aim to protect and control one's desired image and monitor behavior (egosystem orientation). However, there are important differences within each set.

Compassionate Goals and Learning Goals

Compassionate goals focus on the needs of others; people who adopt these goals consider others' feelings and are motivated to care about others' well-being (Crocker & Canevello, 2008). When people are motivated by compassionate goals, they want to make sure they understand and meet the needs of the other, trusting that their own needs will be met. Learning goals, on the other hand, focus on the other as a source of knowledge or on the process of cross-group interaction itself, construing it as learning experience (Goff et al., 2008; Migacheva & Tropp, 2009). Thus, while learning and compassionate goals may both divert people's attention away from preoccupation with their own image, needs, and behaviors, they differ in the extent to which they emphasize the needs of the other.

Such qualitative differences between compassionate and learning goals may affect how these goals function in real-life contact situations between members of different groups. Whereas compassionate and learning goals may be either chronic or situational in nature, the focus on others' needs, more evident in compassionate goals, sets a higher bar for the motivation needed to adopt such a goal. For example, compassionate goals might take time to evolve, particularly in intergroup contexts of ongoing conflict or early stages of reconciliation; yet, once established, these goals may be more sustainable over time and likely to generalize to other intergroup situations. Conversely, although a well-developed learning-goal orientation may also require time to develop, its lesser focus on accommodating the needs of an outgroup member might make it more malleable and more readily induced in novel situations (see Ames, 1992). Still, while people with learning goals may be motivated to listen to others, they may not be as willing to extend themselves and take action to address their needs as would be those driven by compassionate goals.

Self-Image Goals and Performance Goals

Underlying the essence of both self-image and performance goals is a desired image, including how we wish to see ourselves and how we wish others to see us. These two goals likely work together to bolster, validate, and protect this image; however, each may have its own role in this process. In particular, a self-image goal orientation motivates people to focus on defining the image they wish to portray to others, whereas performance goals drive them to monitor and modify their behaviors in line with that image and in relation to their partner's responses and their beliefs about their efficacy and ability to do so. Given their conceptual relatedness, it may be difficult to operationally distinguish between these goals. But future research should further investigate whether self-image and performance goals function separately or cumulatively in predicting people's psychological and behavioral responses to cross-group interactions.

Caveats

Are Ecosystem and Egosystem Motivations Mutually Exclusive?

In describing ecosystem and egosystem motivations and in defining the goals we see as corresponding to each, we may give the impression that we view these orientations as mutually exclusive. But we believe such a perspective would overlook the complexity and dynamic nature of people's orientation systems and motivations, which may change as a function of situational factors, their relationships, and individual experiences (Crocker et al., 2008). Ecosystem and egosystem motivations may operate simultaneously, with one being relatively more dominant and providing stronger effects in one instance, and being latent and less pronounced in another instance. Consequently, it would also be naive to imagine that people possess only compassionate and learning goals, or only performance and self-image goals. Instead, people may approach cross-group interactions motivated both to validate their desired images and to understand the needs and perspectives of outgroup members, with one being more primary than the other.

One illustration of how both ecosystem and egosystem orientations may function simultaneously is provided by Vorauer and colleagues, who cautioned that attempts to take the perspective of an outgroup member may ironically trigger evaluations of how one or one's own group is viewed by the outgroup member; such evaluative concerns may in turn lead to outgroup derogation (for higher prejudice individuals; Vorauer & Sasaki, 2009) or complacency and decreased effort to communicate positive feelings toward outgroup members (for lower prejudice individuals; Vorauer, Martens, & Sasaki, 2009). More work is needed to understand the interplay between eco- and egosystem goals and how they affect intergroup outcomes both concomitantly and independently.

Are Compassion and Learning Always Indicative of a Focus Beyond the Self?

Generally, we have also discussed an ecosystem orientation as one in which people are focused beyond the self. However, we recognize that people may perform acts of compassion or show attempts to learn about members of another group to fulfill less than benevolent objectives: to gain trust, to get access to the resources, and/or to use the acquired information against them later. As has been proposed in the empathy–altruism debate (e.g., Batson, 1997; Cialdini, Brown, Lewis, Luce, & Neuberg, 1997), seemingly other-focused behaviors (e.g., learning, compassion, helping) might stem from self-focused motivations (e.g., personal gain, self-preservation). Thus, it is important to distinguish compassion and learning as *behaviors,* from compassion and learning as *motivations for behaviors.* In the case of less generous objectives, acquisition of knowledge and displays of compassion are behaviors that stem from self-serving motives. We hope, however, that when group members' behaviors are driven by compassion and learning motives, they will be likely to set constructive and positive objectives for cross-group interactions. The behavior-motivation distinction is also important for future investigations of how people interpret outgroup members' behaviors and what motivations they see behind them.

Are Self-Image and Performance Goals Inherently Selfish?

A related observation is that people who enter cross-group interactions with self-image or performance goals are not necessarily selfish. For example, people may adopt a performance goal to monitor and modify their behaviors during an interaction in order to make an outgroup partner feel welcome and included and/or to avoid hurting them with thoughtless remarks. Thus, while the description of these goals may initially seem negative, the resulting behaviors may in fact be pursued with the best of intentions.

It is also useful to remember that having an egosystem orientation is part of the human condition; it evolved as a means to cope with actual and perceived threats to survival. Under threat, our focus of attention narrows and physiological resources are mobilized to cope with the threat (Dickerson & Kemeny, 2004). Consequently, people may have the capacity to adopt an ecosystem orientation only in the absence of threat or when they care about something beyond the self strongly enough to counteract the stress response (e.g., see Butz & Plant, this volume).

Moreover, it is important to note that ecosystem and egosystem are broad orientations and that additional motivational processes may function within both of these systems. For example, research on self-regulation (e.g., Jonas, Sassenberg, & Scheepers, 2010) suggests that both ecosystem and egosystem goals could stem from a motivation to promote a desired outcome (e.g., to ensure that an interaction partner feels comfortable) or from a motivation to prevent an undesired outcome (e.g., to avoid hurting an interaction partner's feelings; see Plant & Devine, 2008). Emerging research has linked motivation to avoid a negative outcome (e.g., exhibiting racial bias) with increased cognitive depletion (Trawalter & Richeson, 2006), intergroup anxiety, and tendencies to withdraw from outgroup members (Plant & Butz, 2006; Plant & Devine, 2003), as well as with diminished enjoyment during cross-group interactions (Shelton, 2003; Vorauer & Turpie, 2004). Still, more research is needed to understand how and when attempts to promote positive outcomes and prevent negative outcomes may both stem from egosystem and ecosystem motivations.

IMPLICATIONS AND FUTURE RESEARCH

Our initial integration of these motivational perspectives lays important ground for further exploration of the nature and utility of goal setting in intergroup contexts. Although research on goals in intergroup relations is in its nascent stages, initial findings indicate that the goals people have for cross-group interactions can shape their own experiences and the experiences of their relationship partners in important ways. Because goals are to some degree malleable, they may provide a useful point of intervention to improve the nature of cross-group interactions.

Admittedly, introducing ecosystem motivations in intergroup contexts characterized by mistrust and spirals of violence may be challenging. When trust is lacking, group members are likely to doubt their adversaries' benevolent intentions (often with good reason) and are reluctant to make steps toward positive cross-group interactions themselves (Kramer & Messick, 1998; Nadler & Liviatan, 2006; Tropp, 2008). That being the case, if ecosystem motivations are important for positive contact, what can or should be done if such goals are not likely to emerge spontaneously? Future research on goal setting in intergroup contexts should therefore explore the challenges and conditions that would affect the ability of an ecosystem motivation to thrive.

Further examination of goals stemming from ecosystem motivation should also consider how they relate to other strategies that have been shown to enhance intergroup outcomes. For example, empathy and perspective taking might involve compassion (Crocker, 2008), seeing outgroup members as a source of knowledge (Migacheva & Tropp, 2009), or framing cross-group interactions as opportunities to gain valuable experience (e.g., Goff, et al., 2008). Alternatively, to counter potential negative effects of performance goals and self-image goals, we might remind people that they often anticipate experiences in cross-group interactions to be worse than they actually turn out to be (Mallett, Wilson, & Gilbert, 2008; see also Mallett, Wagner, & Harrison, this volume). We might also use self-affirmation as a tool to help people transcend the self (Crocker, Niiya, & Mischkowski, 2008).

Importantly, future studies should also examine how these sets of goals may have similar or divergent effects on the experiences of members of dominant and devalued groups. The expectations and concerns that group members bring into cross-group interactions are largely determined by their everyday experiences and differ between dominant and low-status group members (Devine & Vasquez, 1998; Shelton et al., 2006; Tropp, 2006). Thus, it is possible that different framings of goals may be needed to address the distinct motivations that different status groups bring to intergroup contexts (Shnabel, Nadler, Canetti-Nisim, & Ullrich, 2008).

CONCLUSION

People enter cross-group interactions not knowing what to expect and bearing multiple concerns about how they will be perceived and treated. These concerns negatively affect group members' experiences during cross-group interactions and often lead to the desire to avoid them. In this chapter, we have argued that one way to alleviate the discomfort raised by intergroup contexts is through fostering ecosystem motivations by setting goals that lead people to focus beyond the self (e.g., compassionate goals and learning goals). A growing number of studies provide evidence for the positive effects of these goals, indicating that this approach holds great promise for making cross-group interactions less stressful and thereby more constructive experiences.

REFERENCES

Ames, C. (1992). Classrooms: Goals, structures, and student motivation. *Journal of Educational Psychology, 84*, 261–271. doi:10.1037/0022-0663.84.3.261

Batson, C. D. (1997). Self-other merging and the empathy–altruism hypothesis: Reply to Neuberg et al. (1997). *Journal of Personality and Social Psychology, 73*, 517–522. doi:10.1037/0022-3514.73.3.517

Blascovich, J., Mendes, W. B., Hunter, S. B., Lickel, B., & Kowai-Bell, N. (2001). Perceiver threat in social interactions with stigmatized others. *Journal of Personality and Social Psychology, 80*, 253–267. doi:10.1037/0022-3514.80.2.253

Blau, P., & Schwartz, J. (1997). *Crosscutting social circles: Testing a macrostructural theory of intergroup relations*. New Brunswick, NJ: Transaction.

Butz, D. A., & Plant, A. E. (2006). Perceiving outgroup members as unresponsive: Implications for approach-related emotions, intentions, and behavior. *Journal of Personality and Social Psychology, 91*, 1066–1079. doi:10.1037/0022-3514.91.6.1066

Cialdini, R. B., Brown, S. L., Lewis, B. P., Luce, C., & Neuberg, S. L. (1997). Reinterpreting the empathy-altruism relationship: When one into one equals oneness. *Journal of Personality and Social Psychology, 73*, 481–494. doi:10.1037/0022-3514.73.3.481

Crocker, J. (2008). From egosystem to ecosystem: Implications for learning, relationships, and well-being. In H. A. Wayment & J. J. Brauer (Eds.), *Transcending self-interest: Psychological explorations of the quiet ego* (pp. 63–72). Washington, DC: American Psychological Association. doi:10.1037/11771-006

Crocker, J., & Canevello, A. (2008). Creating and undermining social support in communal relationships: The role of compassionate and self-image goals. *Journal of Personality and Social Psychology, 95*, 555–575. doi:10.1037/0022-3514.95.3.555

Crocker, J., Canevello, A., Breines, J. G., & Flynn, H. (2010). Interpersonal goals and change in anxiety and dysphoria in first-semester college students: The role of compassionate and self-image goals. *Journal of Personality and Social Psychology*, 98, 1009–1024. doi:10.1037/a0019400

Crocker, J., & Garcia, J. A. (2006). Stigma and the social basis of the self: A synthesis. In S. Levin & C. Van Laar (Eds.), *Stigma and group inequality: Social psychological perspectives* (pp. 287–308). Mahwah, NJ: Erlbaum.

Crocker, J., Garcia, J., & Nuer, N. (2008). From egosystem to ecosystem in intergroup interactions: Implications for intergroup reconciliation. In A. Nadler, T. Malloy, & J. D. Fisher (Eds.), *The social psychology of intergroup reconciliation* (pp. 171–194). New York, NY: Oxford University Press.

Crocker, J., Liu, M. Y., & Canevello, A. (2008). *Interpersonal goals, zero-sum relationship views, and relationship affect.* Unpublished manuscript.

Crocker, J., Niiya, Y., & Mischkowski, D. (2008). Why does writing about important values reduce defensiveness? The role of positive, other-directed feelings. *Psychological Science*, 19, 740–747. doi:10.1111/j.1467-9280.2008.02150.x

Crocker, J., Olivier, M.-A., & Nuer, N. (2009). Self-image goals and compassionate goals: Costs and benefits. *Self and Identity*, 8, 251–269. doi:10.1080/15298860802505160

Dickerson, S. S., & Kemeny, M. E. (2004). Acute stressors and cortisol responses: A theoretical integration and synthesis of laboratory research. *Psychological Bulletin*, 130, 355–391. doi:10.1037/0033-2909.130.3.355

Devine, P. G., Brodish, A. B., & Vance, S. L. (2005). Self-regulatory processes in interracial interactions: The role of internal and external motivation to respond without prejudice. In J. P. Forgas, K. D. Williams, & S. M. Laham (Eds.), *Social motivation: Conscious and unconscious processes* (pp. 249–273). New York, NY: Cambridge University Press.

Devine, P. G., & Vasquez, K. A. (1998). The rocky road to positive intergroup relations. In J. L. Eberhardt & S. T. Fiske (Eds.), *Confronting racism: The problem and the response* (pp. 234–262). Thousand Oaks, CA: Sage.

Dovidio, J. F., Kawakami, K., & Gaertner, S. (2002). Implicit and explicit prejudice and interracial interaction. *Journal of Personality and Social Psychology*, 82, 62–68. doi:10.1037/0022-3514.82.1.62

Dweck, C. S. (2000). *Self-theories: Their role in motivation, personality, and development.* Philadelphia, PA: Psychology Press.

Elliott, E. S., & Dweck, C. S. (1988). Goals: An approach to motivation and achievement. *Journal of Personality and Social Psychology*, 54, 5–12. doi:10.1037/0022-3514.54.1.5

Ely, R. J., & Thomas, D. A. (2001). Cultural diversity at work: The effects of diversity perspectives on work group processes and outcomes. *Administrative Science Quarterly*, 46, 229–273. doi:10.2307/2667087

Fein, S., Hoshino-Browne, E., Davies, P. G., & Spencer, S. J. (2003). Self-image maintenance goals and sociocultural norms in motivated social perception. In S. J.

Spencer & S. Fein (Eds.), *The Ontario Symposium: Vol. 9. Motivated social perception* (pp. 21–44). Mahwah, NJ: Erlbaum.

Frey, F. E., & Tropp, L. R. (2006). Being seen as individuals versus as group members: Extending research on metaperception to intergroup context. *Personality and Social Psychology Review, 10,* 265–280. doi:10.1207/s15327957pspr1003_5

Grant, H., & Dweck, C. S. (2003). Clarifying achievement goals and their impact. *Journal of Personality and Social Psychology, 85,* 541–553. doi:10.1037/0022-3514. 85.3.541

Goff, P. A., Steele, C., & Davies, P. (2008). The space between us: Stereotype threat and distance in interracial contexts. *Journal of Personality and Social Psychology, 94,* 91–107. doi:10.1037/0022-3514.94.1.91

Ickes, W. (1984). Compositions in black and white: Determinants of interaction in interracial dyads. *Journal of Personality and Social Psychology, 47,* 330–341. doi:10.1037/0022-3514.47.2.330

Jonas, K., Sassenberg, K., & Scheepers, D. (2010). Self-regulation within and between groups. *Group Processes & Intergroup Relations, 13,* 131–136. doi:10.1177/1368430 209359982

Kramer, R. M., & Messick, D. M. (1998). Getting by with a little help from our enemies: Collective paranoia and its role in intergroup relations. In C. Sedikides & J. Schopler (Eds.), *Intergroup cognition and intergroup behavior* (pp. 233–255). Mahwah, NJ: Erlbaum.

Leary, M. R., & Baumeister, R. F. (2000). The nature and function of self-esteem: Sociometer theory. In M. Zanna (Ed.), *Advances in experimental social psychology* (Vol. 32, pp. 1–62). San Diego, CA: Academic Press.

Mallett, R. K., Wilson, T. D., & Gilbert, D. T. (2008). Expect the unexpected: Failure to anticipate similarities leads to an intergroup forecasting error. *Journal of Personality and Social Psychology, 94,* 265–277. doi:10.1037/0022-3514.94.2.94. 2.265

Mehrabian, A. (1972). *Nonverbal communication.* Oxford, England: Aldine-Atherton.

Migacheva, K., & Tropp, L. R. (2009). *The effects of learning and performance goals on psychological and behavioral responses to intergroup contact.* Manuscript submitted for publication.

Migacheva, K., & Tropp, L. R. (2010). *Improving intergroup contact: How learning and performance goals affect contact outcomes in real-life settings.* Manuscript in preparation.

Nadler, A., & Liviatan, I. (2006). Intergroup reconciliation: Effects of adversary's expressions of empathy, responsibility, and recipients' trust. *Personality and Social Psychology Bulletin, 32,* 459–470. doi:10.1177/0146167205276431

Nicholls, J. G. (1984). Achievement motivation: Conceptions of ability, subjective experience, task choice, and performance. *Psychological Review, 91,* 328–346. doi:10.1037/0033-295X.91.3.328

Page-Gould, E., Mendoza-Denton, R., & Tropp, L. (2008). With a little help from my cross-group friend: Reducing anxiety in intergroup contexts through cross-group friendship. *Journal of Personality and Social Psychology, 95*, 1080–1094. doi:10.1037/0022-3514.95.5.1080

Plant, E. A., & Butz, D. A. (2006). The causes and consequences of an avoidance-focus for interracial interactions. *Personality and Social Psychology Bulletin, 32*, 833–846. doi:10.1177/0146167206287182

Plant, E. A., & Devine, P. G. (2003). The antecedents and implications of interracial anxiety. *Personality and Social Psychology Bulletin, 29*, 790–801. doi:10.1177/0146167203029006011

Plant, E. A., & Devine, P. G. (2008). Interracial interactions: Approach and avoidance. In A. J. Elliot (Ed.), *Handbook of approach and avoidance motivation* (pp. 571–584). New York, NY: Psychology Press.

Plant, E. A., & Devine, P. (2009). The active control of prejudice: Unpacking the intentions guiding control efforts. *Journal of Personality and Social Psychology, 96*, 640–652. doi:10.1037/a0012960

Richeson, J. A., & Shelton, J. N. (2007). Negotiating interracial interactions: Costs, consequences, and possibilities. *Current Directions in Psychological Science, 16*, 316–320. doi:10.1111/j.1467-8721.2007.00528.x

Shelton, J. (2003). Interpersonal concerns in social encounters between majority and minority group members. *Group Processes & Intergroup Relations, 6*, 171–185.

Shelton, J. N., & Richeson, J. A. (2006). Interracial interactions: A relational approach. In M. P. Zanna (Ed.), *Advances in experimental social psychology* (Vol. 38, pp. 121–181). San Diego, CA: Elsevier Academic Press.

Shelton, J., Richeson, J., & Vorauer, J. (2006). Threatened identities and interethnic interactions. *European Review of Social Psychology, 17*, 321–358. doi:10.1080/10463280601095240

Shnabel, N., Nadler, A., Canetti-Nisim, D., & Ullrich, J. (2008). The role of acceptance and empowerment in promoting reconciliation from the perspective of the needs-based model. *Social Issues and Policy Review, 2*, 159–186. doi:10.1111/j.1751-2409.2008.00014.x

Shook, N., & Fazio, R. (2008a). Interracial roommate relationships: An experimental field test of the contact hypothesis. *Psychological Science, 19*, 717–723. doi:10.1111/j.1467-9280.2008.02147.x

Shook, N. J., & Fazio, R. (2008b). Roommate relationships: A comparison of interracial and same-race living situations. *Group Processes & Intergroup Relations, 11*, 425–437. doi:10.1177/1368430208095398

Steele, C. M., Spencer, S. J., & Aronson, J. (2002). Contending with group image: The psychology of stereotype and social identity threat. In M. P. Zanna (Ed.), *Advances in experimental social psychology* (Vol. 34, pp. 379–440). San Diego, CA: Academic Press.

Stephan, W. G., & Stephan, C. W. (1985). Intergroup anxiety. *Journal of Social Issues, 41*, 157–175. doi:10.1111/j.1540-4560.1985.tb01134.x

Tatum, B. (1992). Talking about race, learning about racism: The application of racial identity development theory in the classroom. *Harvard Educational Review, 62*, 1–24.

Tesser, A. (1988). Toward a self-evaluation maintenance model of social behavior. In L. Berkowitz (Ed.), *Advances in experimental social psychology* (Vol. 21, pp. 181–227). New York, NY: Academic Press.

Trawalter, S., & Richeson, J. (2006). Regulatory focus and executive function after interracial interactions. *Journal of Experimental Social Psychology, 42*, 406–412. doi:10.1016/j.jesp.2005.05.008

Tropp, L. R. (2006). Stigma and intergroup contact among members of minority and majority status groups. In S. Levin & C. Van Laar (Eds.), *Stigma and group inequality: Social psychological perspectives* (pp. 171–191). Mahwah, NJ: Erlbaum.

Tropp, L. (2008). The role of trust in intergroup contact: Its significance and implications for improving relations between groups. In U. Wagner, L. Tropp, G. Finchilescu, & C. Tredoux (Eds.), *Improving intergroup relations: Building on the legacy of Thomas F. Pettigrew* (pp. 91–106). Malden, MA: Blackwell. doi:10.1002/9781444303117

Vorauer, J. D. (2006). An Information search model of evaluative concerns in intergroup interaction. *Psychological Review, 113*, 862–886. doi:10.1037/0033-295X.113.4.862

Vorauer, J., & Kumhyr, S. (2001). Is this about you or me? Self- versus other-directed judgments and feelings in response to intergroup interaction. *Personality and Social Psychology Bulletin, 27*, 706–719. doi:10.1177/0146167201276006

Vorauer, J. D., Martens, V., & Sasaki, S. (2009). When trying to understand detracts from trying to behave: Effects of perspective taking in intergroup interaction. *Journal of Personality and Social Psychology, 96*, 811–827. doi:10.1037/a0013411

Vorauer, J. D., & Sasaki, S. J. (2009). Helpful only in the abstract? Ironic effects of empathy in intergroup interaction. *Psychological Science, 20*, 191–197. doi:10.1111/j.1467-9280.2009.02265.x

Vorauer, J. D., & Turpie, C. A. (2004). Disruptive effects of vigilance on dominant group members' treatment of outgroup members: Choking versus shining under pressure. *Journal of Personality and Social Psychology, 87*, 384–399. doi:10.1037/0022-3514.87.3.384

III

CLOSENESS AND INCLUSION IN CROSS-GROUP RELATIONSHIPS

6

CROSS-GROUP FRIENDSHIPS: HOW INTERPERSONAL CONNECTIONS ENCOURAGE POSITIVE INTERGROUP ATTITUDES

KRISTIN DAVIES, STEPHEN C. WRIGHT, AND ARTHUR ARON

Among the various types of intergroup contact, cross-group friendship is unique in its ability to promote positive intergroup attitudes. The interpersonal processes underlying interactions between cross-group friends (e.g., including the other in the self [IOS] and affective processes) serve as strong psychological mechanisms for producing positive intergroup attitude change. Moreover, observing cross-group friendships can serve as an additional and vicarious means by which individuals interact with outgroup members; our work examining "extended" intergroup contact suggests that the mere knowledge of a close relationship between an ingroup and outgroup member is sufficient to improve intergroup attitudes. Furthermore, recent research suggests that individuals can become motivated to interact with outgroup members because doing so offers an opportunity for self-expansion; their different group membership is viewed as potentially self-expanding and thus attractive. In this chapter, we review these topics, focusing primarily on our own research, and provide an overview of the ways in which cross-group friendships are likely to encourage positive shifts in intergroup attitudes.

A BRIEF HISTORY OF FRIENDSHIP CONTACT

Gordon Allport's intergroup contact hypothesis (1954), which has been credited with being the first clearly articulated framework for intergroup contact, identified four key conditions of cross-group contact necessary for improved intergroup attitudes: equal status, common goals, intergroup cooperation, and support of authorities, law, or customs. Several early studies served as important starting points for understanding the relationship between close, meaningful contact situations and intergroup attitudes (e.g., Harlan, 1942; Kelly, Ferson, & Holtzman, 1958; Segal, 1965), but it was not until much later that the underlying psychology of cross-group friendship was examined in greater detail and the especially potent impact of interpersonal closeness fully explored.

Recent reviews of the literature suggest that friendship can have a stronger positive impact on intergroup attitudes than more casual forms of contact (e.g., Davies, Tropp, Aron, Pettigrew, & Wright, 2010; Pettigrew, 1997; Pettigrew & Tropp, 2006). It has also been proposed that friendship contact may have the capacity not only to reduce prejudice but to move intergroup attitudes beyond tolerance and toward compassionate love (Brody, Wright, Aron, & McLaughlin-Volpe, 2008). In addition, cross-group friendships are more likely than casual forms of contact to have a broader generalized impact, in terms both of improving the contact partners' attitudes toward other outgroups not involved in the contact and of improving the attitudes of other individuals not involved in the contact. Using a large multinational European survey, Pettigrew (1997) found that cross-group friendships, more so than acquaintanceships, were associated with more positive attitudes toward multiple outgroups—even groups not involved in the cross-group interaction. Furthermore, research investigating the extended contact hypothesis (i.e., knowledge of an ingroup member's cross-group relationship) suggests that a cross-group friendship can improve the attitudes of individuals not directly involved in the cross-group interaction (Wright, Aron, & Brody, 2008; Wright, Aron, McLaughlin-Volpe, & Ropp, 1997).

POTENTIAL MECHANISMS BY WHICH CROSS-GROUP FRIENDSHIPS PRODUCE CHANGE IN INTERGROUP ATTITUDES

In sum, substantial research supports the claim that close interpersonal relationships such as cross-group friendships are especially effective for improving intergroup attitudes. But what makes friendship contact more effective than other forms of contact? In this section, we highlight several mechanisms that can explain how cross-group friendship improves intergroup attitudes.

We begin by presenting our own accounts rooted in the self-expansion model (Aron & Aron, 1986, 1996). This is followed by an examination of several other explanatory mechanisms that may also be relevant to the context of cross-group friendship: building affective bonds, self-disclosure, trust, anxiety, and empathy. It is important to note from the onset that, although we will discuss these mechanisms individually, it is unlikely that they are mutually exclusive; rather, it is almost certain that they operate in conjunction with one another, both simultaneously and interactively.

Self-Expansion, Inclusion of the Other in Self, and Inclusion of the Outgroup in Self

Our own theorizing about the processes by which feelings about an individual outgroup member generalize to the outgroup as a whole leans heavily on aspects of Aron and Aron's (1986, 1996) self-expansion model. There are two main premises of the self-expansion model. The first premise is that individuals wish to expand their own sense of self-efficacy (i.e., their perceived potential to accomplish goals) and are motivated by a desire to experience the positive affect resulting from this "expansion" of the self. To promote self-expansion, people seek opportunities to acquire new or enhance their existing material and social resources, perspectives, and identities (see Aron, Norman, & Aron, 1998), and the rapid acquisition of these resources often produces a feeling of aroused positive affect. The second key premise of the model is that, although self-expansion can be accomplished by a variety of strategies, one key strategy is the forming of close relations with other people, gaining access to the resources, perspectives, and identities of the other through a process of including the IOS. When people become close, cognitive representations of the self and the close other increasingly overlap. That is, as one forms a meaningful relationship with another, the resources, perspectives, and identities of the other are increasingly experienced as also belonging to the self.

The idea that interpersonal closeness involves (and is even defined by) increasing self-other overlap has received support from a variety of studies (for reviews, see Aron, McLaughlin-Volpe, Mashek, Lewandowski, Wright, & Aron, 2004; and Aron, Mashek, & Aron, 2004), including findings from reaction-time procedures showing that people are typically slower in identifying traits as being true or false of the self, when those traits differ between the self and a close other, than they are in responding regarding traits that are shared by self and a close other. This pattern was predicted on the basis of the idea that if a close other is part of "me," then there is some interference when evaluating a trait of "me" as true or false if it is not similarly true or false of the close other. This effect is not found for traits that are different or similar between the self and a nonclose other (e.g., Aron, Aron, Tudor, & Nelson, 1991; Aron & Fraley, 1999). IOS theory further posits that, as individuals become closer and the boundary between "self" and "other" becomes less clear, one's positive regard for the self becomes increasingly applied to the other, and the other is increasingly treated like self.

Applying this line of logic to cross-group friendships, we theorized that when a member of an outgroup is included in the self and that person's outgroup membership is made salient, the other's identification with the outgroup and *the outgroup itself* can *also* become part of the self (Wright et al., 1997; Wright, Brody, & Aron, 2005; Brody et al., 2008). Work on the inclusion of the ingroup in the self suggests that, like individuals, groups can also be included in the self (Tropp & Wright, 2001; see also Otten, 2002; Smith, Coats, & Walling, 1999). Thus, when one becomes close to an outgroup member, aspects of the outgroup member's own identity, including his or her group membership, may also be included in the self.

This model of inclusion of the outgroup in the self provides a potential answer to the critical question of how feelings for an individual outgroup member come to generalize to the entire outgroup. A psychological connection to the outgroup is forged through the close friend such that one comes to view and treat the outgroup as one would view and treat the self. In other words, we hypothesize that when one includes the outgroup in the self, the positive regard and concern for one's welfare that is usually reserved for the self is extended to the outgroup. Thus, cross-group friendships should influence one's relationship with the outgroup in ways that go well beyond the usual reduction in prejudice that has been the focus of intergroup contact research. Instead, the inclusion of the outgroup should engender deep positive regard, including feelings of warmth, obligation, admiration, and compassion for the outgroup and its members and motivation to protect, advance, and benefit them.

We have conducted a number of studies that lend support for the roles of IOS and including the outgroup in the self (IOGS) in the development of positive intergroup attitudes. For instance, in research by McLaughlin-Volpe, Aron, Wright, and Reis (2002), respondents reported their general attitudes toward three target outgroups, and they reported their levels of closeness felt toward members of these same three target outgroups using the IOS Scale (Aron, Aron, & Smollan, 1992). The IOS Scale is a single-item measure that displays seven pairs of increasingly overlapping circles, with one circle representing the self and the other circle representing a target other. The respondent is asked to choose the pair of circles that best represents his or her relationship with the target other. Results indicated that participants with fewer close friends in a given outgroup tended to have more negative overall attitudes toward that outgroup. Furthermore, high levels of closeness (more self/other overlap) with one's closest friend in a given outgroup *predicted* more positive attitudes for the outgroup. In a follow-up study conducted in the context of rival universities, McLaughlin-Volpe and colleagues (2002) found a significant positive relationship between inclusion of an outgroup member in the self and a positive attitude for the outgroup that remained significant even after controlling for the quantity of contact (i.e., number of cross-group interactions). Additional analyses revealed a significant quantity of contact by closeness interaction, such that when closeness (i.e., IOS) to an outgroup interaction partner was high, more interactions were associated with more positive attitudes toward the outgroup, but when closeness to the interaction partner was low, more interactions were associated with less positive attitudes.

In work with students in a service learning program (i.e., university course work combined with working in a social service agency), Brody (2003) found that the more contact students had with a member of the outgroup during the program, the more positive their attitudes toward that outgroup at the end of the program. Important, however, was that a measure of the degree to which the outgroup other was included in the self mediated the relationship between the amount of contact and positive attitudes.

We have also used laboratory procedures to test the link between close interpersonal contact and intergroup attitudes. Wright and colleagues (2009) randomly paired White women with either a cross-group (Asian-American or Latina) or a same-group (White) female partner. The partners met four times over an 8-week period and engaged in a series of friendship-building activities, including the "fast-friends procedure" (Aron, Melinat, Aron, Vallone, & Bator, 1997), to reflect the process of self-sharing and trust that develops over time in a naturally developing friendship. Although closeness among cross-group pairings developed somewhat more slowly than in same-group pairings, levels of closeness were equal among both types of pairings at the end of the final meeting. Of greater importance was the finding that White participants who had an outgroup (i.e., Asian or Latina) activity partner had significantly more positive intergroup attitudes than did those who had an ingroup partner. Furthermore, compared with those making a same-group friend, those making an outgroup friend reported lower feelings of intergroup anxiety, much stronger rejection of "antiminority" policies (e.g., bans on affirmative action, tightening of immigration rules), and cut significantly less money from the Latino/Chicano Student Association and the Asian & Pacific Islander Student Alliance budgets in a budget-cutting task.

We have also applied the fast-friends procedure to study the impact of cross-group friendships in two real-world contexts: higher education and police–community relations (Davies, Aron, Wright, Brody, & McLaughlin-Volpe, 2007). At a large U.S. state university with substantial ethnic diversity, several hundred new university freshmen were recruited in a mandatory weekly orientation class. One week prior to the friendship intervention, attitudes toward four target ethnic groups (African Americans, Asians, Latino/as, and Whites) were assessed online using a feeling thermometer as part of a general freshman survey (a context unrelated to our experiment). Immediately following the intervention, participants answered questions about liking and IOS toward their partner and their feelings toward the target ethnic groups. As part of a regular freshman survey, 4 weeks later and again 12 weeks later, feeling thermometer ratings of attitudes toward the four ethnic groups were assessed online. Initial analyses of the responses of White participants showed that, compared with those who had a White (ingroup) partner, White students paired with a member of any of the three target outgroups (African American, Asian, or Latino/a) reported significantly greater feelings of warmth for that outgroup 4 weeks postintervention, and, in addition, the scores themselves were not merely around the scale midpoint, indicating tolerance, but were much closer to the high end of the scale, indicating attitudes that were clearly positive. Furthermore, reported liking for the partner, as well as inclusion of the outgroup partner in the self on the day of the activity, was positively associated with warmth for the partner's group 4 weeks postintervention. Liking for the partner reported on the day of the intervention was also positively related to warmth for the partner's group 12 weeks postintervention.

In the context of police–community relations (Eberhardt, Aron, Davies, Wright, & Bergsieker, 2007), we recruited 34 community members or "citizens" attending a "Citizen's Police Academy" in Northern California. Civilians voluntarily attend classes that teach them about their local police department, and police partners from the department volunteer to complete intervention activities with community members. After 14 community members and 14 police officers were paired together (all cross-group pairs), they underwent the fast-friends procedure as well as other activities designed to encourage further bonding (e.g., discussing something in common, discussing group memberships in a positive light). We randomly selected citizens who were in a police academy course but did not undergo the intervention to serve as a control group. Consistent with our earlier experimental findings, community participants completing the friendship-building activities with a police partner had significantly more admiration for local police and police in general) than did control group participants ($n = 20$), as assessed in a survey 5 weeks later in a context seemingly not related to the study. Furthermore, closeness felt to the partner, measured with the IOS Scale on the activity day, significantly predicted attitudes at the end of the academy course, even after controlling for pre-academy-course attitudes.

Combined evidence from these cross-sectional, laboratory, and intervention studies provides strong support for the effectiveness of cross-group friendships in producing positive intergroup attitudes, and it also supports the important mediating role of inclusion of the other in the self. Inclusion of the outgroup other in the self predicted subsequent attitudes toward the outgroup. Those who showed the most inclusion of the outgroup other in the self also tended to show the most positive attitude change as a result of the cross-group friendship. This process of inclusion of the other in the self appears to play a critical role in translating positive feelings for the individual to positive attitudes toward the group as a whole, and the resulting attitudes typically demonstrate changes that go well beyond the reduction of prejudice, often reaching the extremely positive range on many of our measures.

Furthermore, it is important to note that these data support the proposition that these effects and the mechanisms that underlie them can be used in real-life settings. Our intervention research appears to show clear benefits of building meaningful, personal, cross-group connections in contexts where improved intergroup relations could have a meaningful impact on the lives of the participants. So, in summary, we believe that the processes of IOS and IOGS, emerging out of the larger self-expansion model play important roles in building positive pathways and encouraging not only reduction in prejudice but also the development of much stronger positive connections across group boundaries.

Additional Potential Mechanisms

In a very influential review, Pettigrew (1998) described four potential processes through which attitudes toward the outgroup can improve: learning about the outgroup, changing behavior, forming affective ties, and engaging in "deprovincialization" (i.e., rethinking ingroup norms and customs). While undoubtedly playing key roles in more casual forms of intergroup contact, these mechanisms may also be important in explaining the effects of close, intimate contact (for a full discussion, see Wright et al., 2005). The general idea is that many of the processes thought to mediate the contact–attitude relationship may be particularly potent when the contact involves interpersonal closeness on an affective level—more potent than when the contact is casual or less meaningful in nature.

Pettigrew (1997, 1998) contended that as an individual becomes close to an outgroup member, emotional bonds are developed, and this affection for the outgroup member generalizes to the entire outgroup. Likewise, in their review of intergroup emotions, Paolini, Hewstone, Voci, Harwood, and Cairns (2006) identified "affect generalization" as a key process in prejudice reduction. Regarding empirical work, we recently conducted a meta-analysis of friendship contact and positive intergroup attitudes (Davies, Tropp, Aron, Pettigrew, & Wright, 2010) and found that some of the strongest effect sizes emerged for affective interpersonal processes such as closeness. However, to say that positive affect "generalizes" to the outgroup as a whole does not provide an explanation for how or why this generalization occurs. We believe our previously discussed mechanism of inclusion of the outgroup in the self provides precisely what is missing here. Positive affect is transferred from the self to the close other *because* the other is included in the self, and positive affect is transferred from the self to the outgroup *because* the outgroup comes to be included in the self as well. So, while we agree entirely with these other researchers that positive affective ties play a critical role in reducing prejudice, we see these positive affective ties as a byproduct of another more essential process—the inclusion of others and outgroups in the self.

Self-disclosure has also been proposed as a critical mediating process that results from contact and leads to more positive attitudes toward the outgroup (see Davies et al., 2008). Self-disclosure plays a primary role in friendship formation, and self-disclosure between cross-group partners is likely to encourage trust and reduce anxiety, in turn allowing one to process group-related information more accurately, reducing reliance on stereotypes (Miller, 2002). Research by Turner, Hewstone, and Voci (2007) further suggests that self-disclosure in cross-group friendships may generate improvements in intergroup attitudes by creating empathy, trust for the outgroup, and beliefs in the importance of cross-group contact (see also Swart, Turner, Hewstone, & Voci, this volume). Some of our own work, described in the previous section of this chapter, employs the fast-friends procedure and generates closeness through the process of gradual mutual self-disclosure (Aron et al., 1997). Page-Gould, Mendoza-Denton, and Tropp (2008) have also conducted recent experimental work suggesting that self-disclosure can make situations of cross-group contact more comfortable and thus potentially more influential (see also Page-Gould & Mendoza-Denton, this volume).

In addition, the trust that grows in intimate cross-group friendships is more likely than more casual forms of contact to generate positive intergroup attitudes. Trust has been long identified in the interpersonal literature as a key factor in the process of developing closeness to another individual (e.g., Rempel, Holmes, & Zanna, 1985), and it has recently been highlighted in discussions of intergroup contact and intergroup relations (Miller, 2002; see also Nadler & Shnabel, this volume). Also, cognitive empathy (i.e., understanding of perspective) has been found to encourage stronger perceptions of ingroup–outgroup similarity (Stephan & Finlay, 1999), discourage the use of outgroup stereotypes (Galinsky & Moskowitz, 2000), and reduce intergroup anxiety (Aberson & Haag, 2007). Finally, emotional empathy (i.e., understanding of emotions) for an outgroup member has been linked to intimate cross-group interactions (Pettigrew, 1997, 1998). Empirical work has begun to find that both kinds of empathy are involved in encouraging positive attitudes toward the outgroup as a whole (Batson et al., 1997; Vescio, Sechrist, & Paolucci, 2003).

It appears that many of the proposed mechanisms that help to account for the positive effects of contact on intergroup attitudes are more likely to emerge when that contact involves the development of a close friendship. Friendship is associated with strong affective ties, increasing self-disclosure, trust, and empathy. The transfer of these feelings and perspectives from the individual outgroup member to the larger outgroup may well account in part for the improvements in intergroup attitudes.

EXTENDED CONTACT AND CROSS-GROUP FRIENDSHIPS

An additional and unique avenue by which cross-group friendship affects intergroup attitudes is via "extended" contact with outgroup members. The extended contact hypothesis (Wright, Aron, et al., 1997; Wright, Aron, & Brody, 2008) proposes that the mere knowledge that an ingroup member has a close relationship with an outgroup member can lead to more positive intergroup attitudes. To the extent that such an effect occurs, it has very promising implications for social change, in part because it provides an additional route by which one's attitude toward an outgroup may change. In a cross-group friendship, group membership is more likely to be salient to observers who are less acquainted with the individuating features of a person than to participants in an interaction. Further, observing an ingroup–outgroup friendship involving others should not evoke the interaction anxiety and other negative emotions for the observer that actual participation in intergroup contact might. In addition, the extended contact hypothesis proposes a means by which widespread reductions in prejudice could occur without everyone having to have outgroup friendships themselves.

We have identified several mechanisms that likely underlie the effectiveness of extended contact: reductions in intergroup anxiety, normative processes (i.e., ingroup and outgroup exemplars for cross-group relations), and, finally, inclusion of the other in the self. First, extended contact may encourage reductions in intergroup anxiety. Comfortable interaction demonstrated by the ingroup friend may serve to reduce fears and negative expectations in the observer, leading to a more positive impression of the outgroup and perhaps even to actual positive interactions with the outgroup that would permit direct contact effects to operate. Regarding ingroup norms, social identity and self-categorization theorists have proposed that members of the relevant ingroup can provide information about how group members understand the situation and how a group member should respond. Along similar lines, the observation of friendly behaviors of an outgroup member interacting with an ingroup member may serve as a basis for modification of a negative prototypic image (or stereotype) of the outgroup. Thus, perceived norms for how one is supposed to interact with outgroup members and how outgroup members typically behave toward the ingroup may come to be altered via extended contact.

Finally, we hypothesize a central role for Aron and Aron's (1986, 1996) IOS mechanisms, as described earlier. When applied to the context of a direct cross-group friendship, this process allows for the possibility that the group membership of one's outgroup friend may be included, to some extent, in one's self-concept. Therefore, if one has a close relationship with an ingroup member who in turn has a cross-group friendship, one includes the outgroup in the self through extended (or vicarious) contact with the outgroup. The outgroup identity is included in the outgroup member's self, which because of their cross-group friendship is included in the ingroup friend's self, which therefore becomes included in one's own self because of the direct relationship with the ingroup member. This has been referred to as the "friend of a friend" effect (Wright et al., 2008).

We have also hypothesized that this process can happen even if the ingroup member is not known personally to the observer. As the ingroup is included in the self (e.g., Tropp & Wright, 2001), one also includes the unfamiliar ingroup member in the self because of that person's shared group membership. To the extent that the relationship between this ingroup member and the outgroup member is viewed as positive and intimate (i.e., perceived overlap between the ingroup and outgroup member), this outgroup should be included in one's self via the connection to the ingroup member (see also Page-Gould & Mendoza-Denton, this volume).

Several studies provided initial evidence for the extended contact hypothesis (Wright, Aron, et al., 1997). A first study found that White participants who knew an ingroup friend who had an outgroup friend felt significantly more positive affect toward the outgroup, even after controlling for the respondent's own direct friendships with outgroup members. Furthermore, the greater the number of known cross-group friendships, the lower the participant's prejudice, even after controlling for one's own firsthand cross-group friendships. Results from a second study replicated the initial results with another sample of White participants and also in a minority sample of Latino participants. Two additional experimental studies addressed the issue of causality, showing that participants reported a more positive view of the opposing group after having heard from an ingroup member about a friendly interaction he or she had with a member of the opposing group. Reductions in ingroup favoritism, both in money allocation and in a general evaluation of the groups, were observed. A fourth study, using a modified minimal group paradigm, assigned participants to one of two experimental groups based on what they believed to be their performance in a series of estimation tasks. They then observed a member of their ingroup and a member of the outgroup (confederates) interacting. The actor's relationship appeared either as one of close friends, strangers, or disliked acquaintances through the use of verbal and nonverbal cues (e.g., "close friends" hugged each other upon meeting). Seeing an interaction between cross-group friends led to more positive evaluations of the outgroup than seeing an interaction with a cross-group stranger or a disliked acquaintance.

In addition to the studies noted above, we have investigated a number of proposed mediators of this effect. For example, we (Wright, Davies, & Sanders, 2007) examined heterosexuals' attitudes toward gays and lesbians in conjunction with extended contact and norm beliefs. Heterosexual participants who knew ingroup members with gay friends, compared with those who knew of no such friendships, were more likely to believe that heterosexuals generally accepted gay relationships and that heterosexuals generally had positive feelings about gay men. Furthermore, the degree of one's belief in positive ingroup norms partially accounted for the positive impact of extended contact on outgroup attitudes.

Additionally, two recent experiments employed a minimal group paradigm to investigate several parts of the transitive inclusion of the outgroup in the self mechanism. The first (Kiu, Wright, & Toews, 2007) tested the importance of three proposed links in the transitive process: the inclusion of the ingroup in the self, the inclusion of the ingroup member in the ingroup, and the inclusion of the outgroup in the outgroup members. Participants were led to believe that they were highly prototypical members of their group, and they were told that they would interact with another participant. First, however, they watched a recorded interaction from a previous session that was actually a scripted demonstration of a close cross-group friendship. To manipulate the degree of overlap between actors and their relevant ingroups, participants were given the actor's "score" on a survey indicating how well the actor fit her ingroup profile. Participants then completed a measure of ingroup identification and (dependent) measures of inclusion of the outgroup in the self, anxiety about further cross-group interaction, and general evaluations of the outgroup. Results indicated that observing cross-group friendship can most effectively improve intergroup attitudes and reduce intergroup anxiety for high ingroup-identifiers when they believe that there is strong overlap between the ingroup member and the ingroup as well as between the outgroup member and the outgroup.

In a second study, participants who were assigned to an "underestimator" group observed, through a one-way mirror, another underestimator interacting with an overestimator. Again, the behavior of the partners in the interaction led observes to believe they were either "close friends, "strangers," or a "disliked acquaintance." A second manipulation varied the degree of personal closeness between the participants and the ingroup member whom they observed in the cross-group interaction. To accomplish this, friends were recruited in pairs (but then separated) and one individual was randomly selected to act as a confederate and enact the appropriate relationship with the staff confederate. (In the "ingroup stranger" condition, both individuals watched unknown ingroup and outgroup members.) Observing a cross-group interaction produced the most positive attitudes toward the outgroup when the interaction was friendly and when the ingroup member was a personal friend. Attitudes toward the outgroup were less positive when the ingroup friend was involved in a neutral cross-group interaction, and attitudes were *least* positive when the ingroup friend was involved in a hostile cross-group interaction. When the ingroup member was a stranger rather than a known friend, attitudes toward the outgroup were less influenced by the type of cross-group interaction.

In summary, a range of research findings suggest that the extended contact effect may be a successful and unique method to improve intergroup attitudes. We should note that, in addition to our own work, several studies by other researchers have also found support for the utility of extended intergroup contact (e.g., Turner, Hewstone, Voci, & Vonofakou, 2008; for a review, see Crisp & Turner, 2009). The premise that even the mere knowledge of a cross-group relationship can have a positive influence on one's perspective of an outgroup has important implications for real-world improvements in intergroup relations. Extended contact is an especially promising method for promoting positive intergroup relations, because it is not likely to invoke intergroup anxiety and also because it suggests the possibility of widespread attitude improvements, given its vicarious nature.

SELF-EXPANSION AND THE DESIRE FOR CROSS-GROUP FRIENDSHIPS

One potential concern with this focus on cross-group friendships as the key to more positive intergroup attitudes is that cross-group friendships may seem hard to produce and thus unlikely to happen. Indeed, there is a large literature in social psychology and considerable popular discussion about all the many reasons why we should ignore, avoid, fear, dislike, and even persecute members of other groups. However, we believe that the self-expansion model (Aron & Aron, 1986) provides reason for some optimism. The model proposes that people actively seek opportunities for self-expansion and that one strategy to do so involves including the resources, perspectives, and identities of others by forming close relationships (i.e., IOS; e.g., Aron, Norman, & Aron, 1998). Combining this claim with evidence that outgroups can be included in the self (i.e., IOGS) leads to the prediction that people may, at times, find outgroup members to be particularly attractive potential friends. In other words, based on this model, we propose that people sometimes *actively seek out* interactions with members of outgroups because of their difference from the self (see Wright, Aron, & Tropp, 2002). Outgroup members often appear to be quite different from the current self and thus we may sometimes find them to be especially attractive potential friends for what is perceived to be a maximal self-expansion experience. Thus, individuals who are seeking a way to self-expand may be motivated to interact with people who differ from them because these individuals offer greater opportunity for self-expansion.

We have completed several studies that lend initial empirical support for self-expansion motives in intergroup relations. First, in a longitudinal study of Australian university students, McLaughlin-Volpe and Wright (2002) had participants fill out questionnaires on four occasions over the first 6 weeks of the semester. Among items about new experiences and "self-change" were requests for the initials of any new friends that they had recently made. At the end of the study they provided demographic information about their new friends and then rated the degree to which these friends differed on a variety of dimensions. Results indicate that making friends with a "very different" individual was indeed considered to be a self-expanding experience by participants, as indicated by later self-change ratings, including new self-domains and greater feelings of social self-efficacy. Furthermore, how different the friends seemed was positively related to continuing changes in the self-concept over time.

Similarly, Davies (2009), in a online survey of cross-group friendship, asked participants who described both cross-race and same-race friendships to rate how much they considered their friend to be "a unique individual different from my other friends," as well as their degree of belief that the relationship would last well into the future. A significant positive association between perceived friend uniqueness and optimistic beliefs about the future of the friendship emerged among both cross-race and same-race friendship participants. In other words, the more strongly people believed that their friend was unique and that the friendship was different from other relationships, the greater confidence they had that the friendship would be a lasting one. Interestingly, however, this correlation was significantly stronger among those describing a cross-race friendship than those describing a same-race friendship. These findings support the contention that cross-group friendships provide opportunities that are considered to be valuable, likely due to the possibility for self-expansion via the unique nature of the relationship. Individuals are likely to be motivated to maintain such fruitful opportunities, and so the more unique the friend is considered to be, the more one perceives that the friendship will thrive.

Finally, experimental work by Wright, McLaughlin-Volpe, and Brody (2004) suggests that fluctuations in the need for self-expansion can influence the desire for the opportunity to develop a cross-group friendship. Undergraduate students first completed a short self-description followed by what they believed was a personality test. Students in the high self-expansion need condition were then told that their personality test indicated that their life was predictable and stagnant and that they therefore may not be adequately equipped to meet potential upcoming challenges. By contrast, students in the low self-expansion need condition were told that the test indicated that they had recently experienced considerable psychological change and that they were somewhat overwhelmed. After receiving the "personality" feedback, participants were made to believe that they would next interact with other (same-gender) participants in other cubicles of the lab. They were told that they must first rate their interest in meeting these individuals, and they received descriptions of individuals who included two Whites, two Chinese, and two Latinos/as. In line with predictions, compared with participants in the low self-expansion motivation condition, those who received the high self-expansion motivation feedback generally showed greater interest in having friendly interactions with others, the greatest interest being for members of other ethnic groups.

So perhaps the outlook for cross-group friendships need not be so grim. It appears that at times we can be highly motivated to interact with and get to know members of the outgroup and that, when we do, we experience a particularly strong feeling of positive self-change. When outgroup members offer a chance for self-expansion, we may well seek them out. Thus, our first task in improving intergroup attitudes may not be to convince reluctant participants to try to interact with outgroup members but, rather, to seek to remove barriers that prevent interested participants from making friends across group lines. While similar, this second perspective presents from a much more optimistic view.

BEYOND FRIENDSHIPS: OTHER CONTEXTS OF CLOSE CROSS-GROUP RELATIONSHIPS

In addition to friendships, some research investigating close, meaningful cross-group relationships has examined the functioning of romantic partners and families. A longitudinal study by Levin, Taylor, and Caudle (2007) investigated the dating behaviors of university students. Controlling for precollege attitudes and background variables, this research showed that those dating outside of their ethnic group during the first 3 years of college were less likely to report ingroup bias and intergroup anxiety at the end of their senior year. Furthermore, family relationships have also been studied as a potential context for meaningful cross-group contact that could potentially improve intergroup attitudes. For example, in a study of grandchildren, Soliz and Harwood (2003) found that greater levels of communication satisfaction and relationship involvement with grandparents was associated with more positive perceptions of traits and conversations with older adults in general. In addition, recent work by Soliz, Thorson, and Rittenour (2009), although focusing on the internal functioning of multiethnic families, discussed the potential importance of the intergroup nature of these family relationships and called for future research to investigate their likely impact on larger intergroup attitudes. To summarize, in addition to cross-group friendships, other intimate cross-group relationships such as romantic partnerships and families provide additional contexts by which positive cross-group connections are likely to form and may therefore provide unique insights concerning the relationship between interpersonal processes and intergroup attitudes.

CONCLUSION

In sum, the information we have reviewed in this chapter highlights the benefits of intimate cross-group friendships. First, cross-group friendships are likely not only to reduce ingroup bias and build feelings of intergroup tolerance but can even encourage extremely favorable and positive emotions toward the outgroup. Cross-group friendships can promote positive intergroup attitudes directly via interpersonal processes with an outgroup member (e.g., inclusion of other in self, affect, self-disclosure), and indirectly through "extended" contact with outgroup members via the cross-group relationships of one's ingroup friends. In addition, work investigating self-expansion suggests that cross-group friendships serve an additional role relating to one's identity and self-value; they provide an opportunity for the broadening of one's sense of self. Thus, under the right circumstances, people may demonstrate a genuine interest in forming friendships across group lines. In addition, although friendship has been the focus of the majority of research on close cross-group contact, we share with several other researchers the view that other meaningful relationships, such as romantic relationships and family relationships, also represent contexts in which close and especially intimate contact with outgroup members may produce the kind of self–outgroup connections that can be the basis not merely for prejudice reduction but for the building of truly positive intergroup attitudes and actions.

It should be noted that the current overview is not meant to suggest that meaningful personal relationships always develop from cross-group interactions or even that they always have a positive impact on intergroup attitudes. Intergroup anxiety (e.g., Stephan & Stephan, 1985) and the phenomenon of subtyping (i.e., seeing the outgroup member as an "exception"; Allport, 1954;

Rothbart & John, 1985) are potential barriers to the development of more positive intergroup attitudes. Taken as a whole, however, research investigating the mechanisms underlying friendship resulting from contact suggests that the interpersonal processes inherent in these close relationships are often quite valuable in promoting positive intergroup relations.

These findings underscore the importance of assessing these interpersonal factors whenever possible in research, as greater knowledge of these mechanisms will help scientists to gain a more accurate overview of the friendship contact process, allowing for more effective future real-world applications. For example, our fast-friends procedure has already shown promise in real-world settings. This is most clearly demonstrated in our work with cross-racial partners in university settings and with police/community relations. Furthermore, recent work investigating self-expansion as a motivation for cross-group contact suggests that people may be more open to such interactions if they can easily see the potential self-expanding benefits. These two sets of findings might be combined to facilitate, for example, community outreach programs. Efforts to encourage people to participate in interventions involving the fast-friends procedure may include an advertising campaign that describes the self-expansion experienced by participants in cross-group friendships. Similarly, our research shows that observing cross-group friendships (extended contact) led not only to direct changes in attitudes but also to changes in the belief that these kinds of relationships are accepted and even valued by the ingroup. Thus, advertising the existence and benefits of a cross-group friendship could also serve to inform people that positive cross-group relationships do exist and perhaps encourage direct participation in opportunities to form one's own cross-group relationship.

Finally, procedures like these that create an opportunity for members of differing groups to connect may engender other important intergroup emotions and actions such as trust, forgiveness, reconciliation (see González, Manzi, & Noor; Nadler & Shnabel; and Swart, Turner, Hewstone, & Voci, this volume), and perhaps even direct action to support positive social change on behalf of the outgroup (e.g., Iyer & Leach, 2010). In other words, our research supports not only the theoretical significance of self-expansion motives and the inclusion of outgroup members (and consequently the outgroup as a whole) in understanding how positive attitudes can be generalized from a single outgroup friend to the outgroup as a whole, the interventions we have piloted also provide encouraging evidence that this knowledge can be used to create positive intergroup perspectives in a real-world context. Future research should continue to investigate the practical applications of these interventions, while more basic research should consider a wider range of positive psychological and behavioral outcomes that continues to take us beyond the usual focus on prejudice reduction and tolerance.

REFERENCES

Aberson, C. L., & Haag, S. C. (2007). Contact, perspective taking, and anxiety as predictors of stereotype endorsement, explicit attitudes, and implicit attitudes. *Group Processes & Intergroup Relations, 10,* 179–201. doi:10.1177/1368430207074726

Allport, G. W. (1954). *The nature of prejudice.* Reading, MA: Addison-Wesley.

Aron, A., & Aron, E. N. (1986). *Love and the expansion of self: Understanding attraction and satisfaction.* Washington, DC: Hemisphere.

Aron, A., & Aron, E. N. (1996). Self and self-expansion in relationships. In G. J. O. Fletcher & J. Fitness (Eds.), *Knowledge structures in close relationships: A social psychological approach* (pp. 325–344). Mahwah, NJ: Erlbaum.

Aron, A., Aron, E. N., & Smollan, D. (1992). Inclusion of Other in the Self Scale and the structure of interpersonal closeness. *Journal of Personality and Social Psychology, 63,* 596–612. doi:10.1037/0022-3514.63.4.596

Aron, A., Aron, E. N., Tudor, M., & Nelson, G. (1991). Close relationships as including other in the self. *Journal of Personality and Social Psychology, 60,* 241–253. doi:10.1037/0022-3514.60.2.241

Aron, A., & Fraley, B. (1999). Relationship closeness as including other in the self: Cognitive underpinnings and measures. *Social Cognition, 17,* 140–160.

Aron, A., Mashek, D., & Aron, E. (2004). Closeness as including other in the self. In D. J. Mashek & A. Aron (Eds.), *Handbook of closeness and intimacy* (pp. 27–41). Mahwah, NJ: Erlbaum.

Aron, A., McLaughlin-Volpe, T., Mashek, D., Lewandowski, G., Wright, S. C., & Aron, E. (2004). Including others in the self. *European Review of Social Psychology, 15,* 101–132.

Aron, A., Melinat, E., Aron, E. N., Vallone, R., & Bator, R. (1997). The experimental generation of interpersonal closeness: A procedure and some preliminary findings. *Personality and Social Psychology Bulletin, 23,* 363–377. doi:10.1177/0146167297234003

Aron, A., Norman, C. C., & Aron, E. N. (1998). The self-expansion model and motivation. *Representative Research in Social Psychology, 22,* 1–13.

Batson, C. D., Polycarpou, M. P., Harmon-Jones, E., Imhoff, H. J., Mitchener, E. C., Bednar, L. L., . . . Highberger, L. (1997). Empathy and attitudes: Can feeling for a member of a stigmatized group improve feelings toward the group? *Journal of Personality and Social Psychology, 72,* 105–118. doi:10.1037/0022-3514.72.1.105

Brody, S. M. (2003). *Serving a higher purpose: How service-learning leads to improved intergroup relations.* Unpublished doctoral dissertation, University of California, Santa Cruz.

Brody, S. M., Wright, S. C., Aron, A.,, & McLaughlin-Volpe, T. (2008). *Compassionate love for individuals outside one's social group.* Manuscript in preparation.

Crisp, R. J., & Turner, R. N. (2009). Can imagined interactions produce positive perceptions? Reducing prejudice through simulated social contact. *American Psychologist, 64*, 231–240. doi:10.1037/a0014718

Davies, K. M. (2009). *Identifying key themes in cross-group friendship formation*. Unpublished doctoral dissertation, Stony Brook University, Stony Brook, NY.

Davies, K. M., Aron, A., Wright, S. C., Brody, S., & McLaughlin-Volpe, T. (2007). *The fast-friends project: Some initial results of an intergroup contact intervention*. Manuscript in preparation.

Davies, K. M., Tropp, L. R., Aron, A., Pettigrew, T. F. & Wright, S. C. (2010). *Cross-group friendships and intergroup attitudes: A meta-analytic review*. Manuscript under review.

Eberhardt, J. L., Aron, A., Davies, K., Wright, S. C., & Bergsieker, H. B. (2007). A *social–psychological intervention to improve community relations with police: Initial results*. Manuscript in preparation.

Galinsky, A. D., & Moskowitz, G. B. (2000). Perspective-taking: Decreasing stereotype expression, stereotype accessibility, and in-group favoritism. *Journal of Personality and Social Psychology, 78*, 708–724. doi:10.1037/0022-3514.78.4.708

Harlan, H. H. (1942). Some factors affecting attitude toward Jews. *American Sociological Review, 7*, 816–827. doi:10.2307/2085406

Iyer, A., & Leach, C. W. (2010). Helping disadvantaged out-groups challenge unjust inequality: The role of group-based emotions. In S. Stürmer & M. Snyder (Eds.), *The psychology of prosocial behavior: Group processes, intergroup relations, and helping* (pp. 337–353). Hoboken, NJ: Wiley-Blackwell.

Kelly, J. G., Ferson, J. E., & Holtzman, W. H. (1958). The measurement of attitudes toward the Negro in the South. *Journal of Social Psychology, 48*, 305–317.

Kiu, L., Wright, S. C., & Toews, M. (2007, January). *The extended contact effect: The influence of group typicality on intergroup attitudes*. Paper presented at the Annual Meeting of the Society for Personality and Social Psychology, Memphis, TN.

Levin, S., Taylor, P. L., & Caudle, E. (2007). Interethnic and interracial dating in college: A longitudinal study. *Journal of Social and Personal Relationships, 24*, 323–341. doi:10.1177/0265407507077225

McLaughlin-Volpe, T., Aron, A., Wright, S. C., & Reis, H. T. (2002). *Intergroup social interactions and intergroup prejudice: Quantity versus quality*. Unpublished manuscript.

McLaughlin-Volpe, T., & Wright, S. C. (2002, June). *The hidden rewards of cross-group friendship: Self-expansion across group membership*. Paper presented at the meeting of the European Association of Experimental Social Psychology, San Sebastian, Spain.

Miller, N. (2002). Personalization and the promise of contact theory. *Journal of Social Issues, 58*, 387–410. doi:10.1111/1540-4560.00267

Otten, S. (2002). "Me" and "us" or "us" and "them"?—The self as heuristic for defining novel ingroups. In W. Stroebe & M. Hewstone (Eds.), *European*

Review of Social Psychology (Vol. 13, pp. 1–33). Philadelphia, PA: Psychology Press.

Page-Gould, E., Mendoza-Denton, R., & Tropp, L. R. (2008). With a little help from my cross-group friend: Reducing anxiety in intergroup contexts through cross-group friendship. *Journal of Personality and Social Psychology, 95,* 1080–1094. doi:10.1037/0022-3514.95.5.1080

Paolini, S., Hewstone, M., Voci, A., Harwood, J., & Cairns, E. (2006). Intergroup contact and the promotion of intergroup harmony: The influence of intergroup emotions. In R. Brown & D. Capozza, D. (Eds.), *Social identities: Motivational, emotional and cultural influences.* (pp. 209–238). Hove, England: Taylor & Francis.

Pettigrew, T. F. (1997). Generalized intergroup contact effects on prejudice. *Personality and Social Psychology Bulletin, 23,* 173–185. doi:10.1177/0146167297232006

Pettigrew, T. F. (1998). Intergroup contact theory. *Annual Review of Psychology, 49,* 65–85. doi:10.1146/annurev.psych.49.1.65

Pettigrew, T. F., & Tropp, L. (2006). A meta-analytic test of intergroup contact theory. *Journal of Personality and Social Psychology, 90,* 751–783. doi:10.1037/0022-3514.90.5.751

Rempel, J. K., Holmes, J. G., & Zanna, M. P. (1985). Trust in close relationships. *Journal of Personality and Social Psychology, 49,* 95–112. doi:10.1037/0022-3514.49.1.95

Rothbart, M., & John, O. P. (1985). Social categorization and behavioral episodes: A cognitive analysis of the effects of intergroup contact. *Journal of Social Issues, 41,* 81–104. doi:10.1111/j.1540-4560.1985.tb01130.x

Segal, B. E. (1965). Contact, compliance, and distance among Jewish and non-Jewish undergraduates. *Social Problems, 13,* 66–74. doi:10.1525/sp.1965.13.1.03a00060

Smith, E. R., Coats, S., & Walling, D. (1999). Overlapping mental representations of self, in-group, and partner: Further response time evidence and a connectionist model. *Personality and Social Psychology Bulletin, 25,* 873–882. doi:10.1177/0146167299025007009

Soliz, J., & Harwood, J. (2003). Perceptions of communication in a family relationship and the reduction of intergroup prejudice. *Journal of Applied Communication Research, 31,* 320–345. doi:10.1080/1369681032000132582

Soliz, J., Thorson, A. R., & Rittenour, C. E. (2009). Communicative correlates of satisfaction, family identity, and group salience in multiracial/ethnic families. *Journal of Marriage and the Family, 71,* 819–832. doi:10.1111/j.1741-3737.2009.00637.x

Stephan, W. G., & Finlay, K. (1999). The role of empathy in improving intergroup relations. *Journal of Social Issues, 55,* 729–743. doi:10.1111/0022-4537.00144

Stephan, W. G., & Stephan, C. (1985). Intergroup anxiety. *Journal of Social Issues, 41,* 157–175. doi:10.1111/j.1540-4560.1985.tb01134.x

Tropp, L. R., & Wright, S. C. (2001). Ingroup identification as the inclusion of ingroup in the self. *Personality and Social Psychology Bulletin, 27,* 585–600. doi:10.1177/0146167201275007

Turner, R. N., Hewstone, M., & Voci, A. (2007). Reducing explicit and implicit out-group prejudice via direct and extended contact: The mediating role of self-disclosure and intergroup anxiety. *Journal of Personality and Social Psychology, 93,* 369–388. doi:10.1037/0022-3514.93.3.369

Turner, R. N., Hewstone, M., Voci, A., & Vonofakou, C. (2008). A test of the extended intergroup contact hypothesis: The mediating role of intergroup anxiety, perceived ingroup and outgroup norms, and inclusion of the outgroup in the self. *Journal of Personality and Social Psychology, 95,* 843–860.

Vescio, T. K., Sechrist, G. B., & Paolucci, M. P. (2003). Perspective taking and prejudice reduction: The mediational role of empathy arousal and situational attributions. *European Journal of Social Psychology, 33,* 455–472. doi:10.1002/ejsp.163

Wright, S. C., Aron, A., & Brody, S. M. (2008). Extended contact and including others in the self: Building on the Allport/Pettigrew legacy. In U. Wagner, L.R. Tropp, G. Finchilescu,& C. Tredoux (Eds.), *Improving intergroup relations: Building on the legacy of Thomas F. Pettigrew* (pp. 143–159). Malden, MA: Blackwell.

Wright, S. C., Aron, A., McLaughlin-Volpe, T., & Ropp, S. A. (1997). The extended contact effect: Knowledge of cross-group friendships and prejudice. *Journal of Personality and Social Psychology, 73,* 73–90. doi:10.1037/0022-3514.73.1.73

Wright, S. C., Aron, A., & Tropp, L. R. (2002). Including others (and groups) in the self: Self-expansion and intergroup relations. In J. P. Forgas & K. D. Williams (Eds.), *The social self: Cognitive, interpersonal and intergroup perspectives* (pp. 343–363). Philadelphia, PA: Psychology Press.

Wright, S. C., Brody, S. A., & Aron, A. (2005). Intergroup contact: Still our best hope for reducing prejudice. In C. S. Crandall & M. Schaller (Eds.), *The social psychology of prejudice: Historical perspectives* (pp. 115–142). Seattle, WA: Lewinian Press.

Wright, S. C., Davies, K., & Sanders, L. (2007) *Direct and extended contact effects on attitudes toward lesbians and gay men: Testing mechanisms.* Unpublished manuscript.

Wright, S. C., McLaughlin-Volpe, T., & Brody, S. M. (2004). *Seeking and finding an expanded "me" outside my ingroup: Outgroup friends and self change.* Paper presented at the Annual Meeting of the Society for Personality and Social Psychology, Austin, TX.

Wright, S. C., Van der Zande, C. C., Tropp, L. R., Ropp, S. A., Zanna, M. P., Aron, A., & Young, K. (2009). *Friendship and cross-group contact effects: An experimental test.* Manuscript in preparation.

7

FRIENDSHIP AND SOCIAL INTERACTION WITH OUTGROUP MEMBERS

ELIZABETH PAGE-GOULD AND RODOLFO MENDOZA-DENTON

A large body of research in intergroup relations has found that contact—or social interaction—between people from different social groups reduces prejudice toward those groups (e.g., Allport, 1954; Pettigrew & Tropp, 2006). Meanwhile, other research has established anxiety and threat as the basic response to intergroup interaction (Dovidio, Kawakami, & Gaertner, 2002; Mendes, Blascovich, Lickel, & Hunter, 2002; Stephan & Stephan, 1985). This propensity to experience anxiety while interacting with outgroup members—termed *intergroup anxiety*—feeds prejudice (Paolini, Hewstone, Voci, Harwood, & Cairns, 2006; Pettigrew & Tropp, 2008) and avoidance of contact experiences (Paolini, Hewstone, Cairns, & Voci, 2004; Plant & Devine, 2003). Therefore, in order for contact to improve intergroup attitudes, the anxiety experienced during intergroup interactions must be overcome.

Prejudice is associated with anxiety during intergroup interactions and avoidance of outgroup members (Dovidio et al., 2002; Stephan & Stephan, 1985). An ironic aspect of prejudice in modern society is that some individuals hold two conflicting attitudes: They explicitly value egalitarianism while having implicit intergroup attitudes that are nonegalitarian. This discrepancy between intergroup values and attitudes is termed *aversive racism* (Dovidio & Gaertner, 2004; Gaertner & Dovidio, 1986). Gaertner and

139

Dovidio (this volume) describe and extend this classic theory, emphasizing how relatively strong ingroup favoritism may characterize aversive racism. They suggest that because aversive racists are focused on not appearing prejudiced, discriminatory behavior in aversive racists may be expressed mostly as ingroup favoritism. This new perspective may help explain why many people still exhibit racial homophily (see Tropp & Mallett, this volume) when choosing the people that they interact with and befriend. Heightened concerns about appearing prejudiced may lead individuals to avoid intergroup interactions (Butz & Plant, this volume), and a heightened degree of ingroup favoritism may lead aversive racists to lean toward potential friends and romantic partners of their own race.

Aversive racists may avoid social interactions with outgroup members because these interactions hold the potential for them to behave in a manner that may be dissonant with their egalitarian values (Dovidio et al., 2002). Although the ultimate desire of aversive racists is to be nonprejudiced, intergroup contact cannot help aversive racists if they avoid that contact altogether. However, desire for intergroup interaction increases if an outgroup member is seen as similar to the self (Mallett, Wagner, & Harrison, this volume). As such, it seems likely that associating outgroup members with the self is a promising pathway toward positive intergroup relations, in a way that does not conflict with aversive racists' tendency towards ingroup favoritism.

In this chapter, we review experimental work suggesting that if people can form close relationships across group boundaries, their experiences with and attitudes toward outgroup members will generally improve. We focus specifically on the role of close cross-group friendships in improving contact experiences among prejudiced individuals and on how these relationships can be facilitated among biased individuals who would otherwise avoid them. Complementing the ideas of Mallett et al. (this volume), we then describe research suggesting that cross-group friendship affects intergroup interactions because cross-group closeness leads to a process whereby the group membership of another person becomes a part of one's own self-concept. Finally, we discuss the role of cross-group friendship in facilitating a sense of belonging in institutions that have traditionally restricted access to members of devalued or low-status groups.

EFFECTS OF CROSS-GROUP FRIENDSHIP ON INTERGROUP ATTITUDES AND EXPERIENCES

Ample survey research has associated cross-group friendship with less intergroup anxiety and prejudice (e.g., Levin, van Laar, & Sidanius, 2003; Paolini et al., 2004; Pettigrew & Tropp, 2000, 2006 [footnote 4]). However, the direction of causality has been difficult to determine, because while cross-group friendship may reduce intergroup anxiety and prejudice, it is just as likely that people who are already comfortable interacting with outgroup members are more likely to form friendships with them (Binder et al., 2009). For this reason, multiple independent labs have recently employed experimental methods to determine whether cross-group friendship has causal effects on intergroup attitudes and experiences (Akinola & Mendes, 2008; Davies, Aron, Wright, & McLaughlin-Volpe, 2007; Mendoza-Denton & Page-Gould, 2008; Page-Gould, Mendoza-Denton, Alegre, & Siy, 2010; Page-Gould, Mendoza-Denton, & Tropp, 2008; Paolini, 2005; Wright, Aron, & Tropp, 2002). Wright and colleagues (Wright & van der Zande, 1999; Wright et al., 2002) reported data showing that making a new cross-ethnic friend in the lab improved a breadth of intergroup outcomes for White students: They reported less intergroup anxiety and racial bias and advocated allocating more resources to ethnic minority student organizations.

Moreover, it appears that cross-group friendship is most beneficial for the prejudiced individuals who, as we pointed out, are most likely to avoid such friendships (Akinola & Mendes, 2008; Page-Gould et al., 2008). Over the course of 5 weeks, Page-Gould and colleagues (2008) created friendships between same-group and cross-group pairs in the laboratory using an expanded version of the fast-friends procedure (Aron, Melinat, Aron, Vallone, & Bator, 1997). This procedure guides the study participants through a series of questions designed to increase self-disclosure, with the effect that the participants subsequently feel closer to each other. We expected that participants who were highly prejudiced would experience the greatest benefits from cross-group friendship. We measured changes in cortisol—a hormone released by the adrenal gland in response to environmental stressors—over the course of the study. We found that participants who were high in implicit prejudice at the outset of the study exhibited increases in cortisol during the first cross-group friendship meeting, suggesting that they were physiologically threatened by the friendly interaction with an outgroup member. By comparison, implicitly prejudiced participants who were paired with a same-group friendship partner and all low-prejudice participants exhibited decreases in cortisol during the first friendship meeting. However, by the second friendship meeting, the hormonal stress responses of implicitly prejudiced participants in the cross-group condition had attenuated, such that their cortisol responses were no longer distinguishable from those of low-prejudice participants. This trend was carried through the final friendship meeting. These findings suggest that intergroup-related stress can be abated early in the development of cross-group friendship, and they add balance to a literature stressing the difficulty and anxiety associated with initial cross-group interactions.

Following the final friendship meeting, we followed participants' daily social interactions for 10 days to examine how frequently they sought out social interactions with outgroup members. After making a new cross-group friend, participants who were high in implicit prejudice self-initiated more daily social interactions with ethnic outgroup members. Moreover, all participants reported less anxiety in the diverse environment if they had made a cross-group friend in the lab. Thus, in addition to the effects at the level of the dyad (the study participants themselves), we observed effects that may translate more broadly to decreased intergroup avoidance and anxiety.

Emerging work suggests that the development of a new cross-group friend shifts implicit prejudice among initially prejudiced individuals. Akinola and Mendes (2008) similarly induced friendship between same-race and cross-race pairs of Black and White participants in the laboratory using a multisession version of the fast-friends procedure. After each friendship meeting, participants completed a measure of implicit prejudice as measured by the Implicit Associations Test (Greenwald, McGhee, & Schwartz, 1998)—the degree to which one associates particular ethnic groups with the concepts of "good" and "bad." They observed progressive decreases in implicit prejudice after each laboratory friendship meeting, suggesting that becoming close with an outgroup member decreases the strength of negative associations with the new friend's social group. This is an important finding given that implicit associations are responses that cannot be consciously controlled (Greenwald et al., 1998), yet are indeed malleable (Dasgupta & Greenwald, 2001).

Taken together, this work demonstrates the power of cross-group friendship for improving intergroup relations. A nice feature of this research is that it has been conducted among both majority and minority groups, allowing us to view cross-group friendship as being beneficial for the intergroup attitudes and expectations of minority- and majority-group members alike. People who formed cross-group friends in the laboratory showed improvements in their experiences with and attitudes toward outgroup members. These effects were specific to people who were prejudiced prior to the formation of a new cross-group friendship—in other words, people who are most likely to avoid and be anxious during intergroup interactions.

ASSOCIATING OUTGROUPS WITH THE SELF

Given the findings noted thus far, an important secondary question emerges: *How* do cross-group friendships improve intergroup relations? As friendship is fundamentally a form of interpersonal closeness, it is possible that intergroup benefits of cross-group friendship emerge from basic processes of interpersonal closeness. Drawing on self-expansion theory described in more detail elsewhere (see Davies, Wright, & Aron, this volume), we tested the possibility that people with close cross-group friends have better intergroup interactions because they grow to include qualities and characteristics of friends from outgroups into their own self-concepts (Aron, Aron, Tudor, & Nelson, 1991; Aron & McLaughlin-Volpe, 2001). This association of the self with the characteristics of close others has been referred to as "inclusion of other in the self" (Aron & Aron, 1996) and "self-other overlap" (Kenworthy, Turner, Hewstone, & Voci, 2005), with the terms reflecting a contextual association between a close other and the self. In the context of a close cross-group relationship, the group membership of each friend is a collective characteristic that is not shared between them. Self-expansion theorists argue that outgroups may also be associated with the self to the extent that one feels close to outgroup members (Aron & McLaughlin-Volpe, 2001; Aron et al., 2004; Wright et al., 2002; 2005). This idea has received initial empirical support through work demonstrating that the effects of cross-group friendship are mediated through self-reports of including a cross-group friend in the self (Turner, Hewstone, Voci, & Vonofakou, 2008).

We extended this work in two main ways: (a) We examined how deeply the association between outgroups and the self is encoded among people with cross-group friends and (b) we experimentally tested whether cross-group friendship causes a heightened association between the self and outgroups. We did so by measuring the speed with which participants could classify a cross-ethnic friend's ethnicity as non-self-descriptive as a function of how close they felt to that friend (Page-Gould et al., 2010). Consistent with the logic of the self-expansion model, we reasoned that a longer reaction time to categorize the outgroup as nondescriptive of the self would imply a stronger association between that outgroup and the self. In other words, if I am a member of Group A and am asked if I am a member of Group B, the answer is, of course, "No." Nevertheless, to the degree that a member of Group A associates the self with Group B, we expected this association to interfere with, and thus slow, that person's classification of Group B as non-self-descriptive.

Participants first completed a social network questionnaire that allowed us to determine whether they had any outgroup members in their social network and how close they felt to them. Later in the study, participants completed a reaction-time task in which they were presented with a personality trait in the middle of a computer screen and were asked to categorize each trait as descriptive, by pressing a button labeled *Me*, or nondescriptive, by pressing a button labeled *Not Me*. Labels of ethnic groups (e.g., Asian, Black, White) were randomly interspersed with the personality trait stimuli. Each trial consisted of a single stimulus trait or ethnic group, and each stimulus was presented randomly three times across all the trials. As hypothesized, we found a strong positive correlation between closeness with cross-group friends and the time it took participants to categorize a friend's ethnic group as non-self-descriptive. This finding implies that the closer participants felt to their cross-group friends, the more they identified with the ethnicities of their friends.

Consistent with past theorizing (Aron & McLaughlin-Volpe, 2001; Wright et al., 2002), these data suggest that cross-group friendship involves an inclusion of an outgroup in the self-concept. Given that ingroup identification involves including the ingroup in the self-concept (Tropp & Wright, 2001; Wright et al., 2002), these data suggest that close cross-group friendship involves identification with an outgroup. When these findings are considered together with the work described in earlier chapters, there is mounting evidence that associating an outgroup with the self may lead to improved expectations for upcoming intergroup interactions (Gaertner & Dovidio; Mallett et al., this volume).

We hypothesized, then, that cross-group friendship should facilitate positive intergroup interactions through an increased sense of similarity between oneself and novel outgroup members—a potentially powerful pathway to positive intergroup relations. We further reasoned that if cross-group friendship causes an association between the self and an outgroup member to develop, then this association should be facilitated or inhibited to the degree that a cross-group friend is accessible in working memory. To test this idea, we used a novel experimental paradigm that manipulates the cognitive accessibility of a cross-group friend.

ACCESSIBILITY OF CROSS-GROUP FRIENDSHIP

In this section, we describe data suggesting that cross-group friendship facilitates smooth intergroup interactions through the mechanism of associating outgroups with the self. However, we wanted to address two additional questions that remained unanswered. First, is the mere presence of an outgroup member within one's social network sufficient for improving contact experiences with novel outgroup members? There is some reason to doubt that cross-group friendships always improve contact experiences (Damico, Bell-Nathaniel, & Green, 1981), particularly when someone has only a few cross-group friends with whom they are not very close. Second, does cross-group friendship improve social interactions with outgroup members whom the perceiver has never met before? For cross-group friendship to play a role in the development of inclusive, diverse communities, positive intergroup attitudes about one's cross-group friend must generalize to outgroup strangers from the larger community. There is some initial support for the idea that positive feelings about a cross-group friend generalizes from a single outgroup member to outgroup members on the whole (Levin et al., 2003; Page-Gould et al., 2008; Paolini et al., 2004; Pettigrew & Tropp, 2006; Wright et al., 2002), and we sought to test this idea directly.

Page-Gould and colleagues (2010) suggested that the benefits of cross-group friendship are present to the extent that a cross-group friend is readily brought to mind when engaging in an interaction with a novel member of a cross-group friend's social group. Social-cognitive research on interpersonal relationships has demonstrated that concepts of close others are activated when a new person is similar to a close other in some way (Andersen & Berk, 1998). Research on the transference of a significant other's characteristics to new individuals indicates that even subtle similarities between a new person and a significant other can trigger increases in significant-other salience (Chen, Anderson, & Hinkley, 1999). With a characteristic encoded as deeply as race (Cosmides, Tooby, & Kurzban, 2003), it is likely that new individuals of the same race as a cross-race friend activate the concept of that friend. It is thus possible that the accessibility of a cross-group friend may be a more proximal predictor of positive intergroup interactions than whether or not one has an outgroup member in one's social network.

Across two studies, we manipulated the accessibility of a close cross-group or same-group friend and observed improvements in intergroup interactions. For these studies, we focused on individuals who already had a very close cross-group friend (specifically, a person of another ethnicity whom the participants rated as a 6 or a 7 on a 7-point Likert scale of closeness). Participants who had at least one very close same-group and cross-group friend along this criterion were invited to the lab, and the names of their same-group and cross-group friends were stored for use as idiographic stimuli. To manipulate the accessibility of a cross-group friendship, participants were randomly assigned to describe either their same-group or cross-group friend in detail, identified only by the friend's name.

In the first study, we were interested in whether participants who had just described their cross-ethnic friend in detail would have better expectations for interactions with novel outgroup members. Expectations for intergroup interaction may play a key role in intergroup anxiety and avoidance, as people tend to predict intergroup interactions will be less enjoyable than these interactions actually are (Mallett, Wilson, & Gilbert, 2008; Park, 2009). After describing either a close cross-group or same-group friend in detail, participants took the reaction-time task that measured associations between the self and ethnic outgroups described earlier, and then imagined themselves in a vignette that depicted a social interaction with an outgroup member that they had just met. After imagining themselves in the story and writing briefly what they would say to the interaction partner, they rated how much they would enjoy the social interaction. Consistent with our hypotheses, participants who had just described a cross-group friend in detail reported that they would enjoy the interaction more than participants who had just described a close same-group friend. In addition, participants who had just described a close cross-group friend took longer to classify that friend's ethnic group as non-self-descriptive compared with the participants who had described a same-group friend in detail. Moreover, associations of the self with a close friend's group partially explained the relationship between describing a close cross-group friend in detail and better expectations for a social interaction with an unfamiliar outgroup member. Again, consistent with Mallett et al. (this volume), a sense of similarity with an outgroup member increased desire for intergroup interaction. Our study builds on this work by demonstrating that the accessibility of a cross-group friend enhances the perceived association between oneself and an outgroup, and in turn this improves expectations for intergroup interactions.

As a next step, we tested whether these effects would apply to a real interaction with an unfamiliar outgroup member. As with the first study, only individuals who had both a very close cross-group friend and same-group friend were recruited. Participants were scheduled for lab sessions in cross-ethnic stranger pairs, but they did not know that they would be interacting with another participant until halfway through the lab session. The participants were randomly assigned to describe their same-group or cross-group friend in detail when they arrived at the lab, and then they completed the reaction-time task measuring associations between ethnic outgroups and the self. Next, participants were introduced to each other, and—after confirming that they were indeed strangers—were left together for a 20-min, unstructured social interaction. They were only told that their goal was to "get to know each other" during the interaction.

At the beginning and end of the social interaction, we collected saliva samples so that we could assess hormonal responses to the novel intergroup interaction. We hypothesized that participants who had just described a cross-group friend prior to the social interaction with an unfamiliar outgroup member would evidence more adaptive hormonal responses to the social interaction than participants who had just described a same-group friend. From the saliva samples, we measured two hormones, cortisol and dehydroepiandrosterone-sulphate (DHEA-S), to gain a measure of anabolic balance (the ratio of DHEA-S to cortisol). Anabolic balance is so named because DHEA-S is an anabolic hormone that builds muscle tissue and facilitates growth, whereas cortisol is a catabolic hormone that breaks down muscle tissue and halts bodily processes to quickly muster energy. Anabolic balance is associated with physiological resilience and health (Epel, McEwen, & Ickovics, 1998) because it protects the body against the tissue damage caused by cortisol and predicts recovery from the stress response.

Supporting our hypotheses, participants who had just described a close cross-group friend prior to interacting with a novel outgroup member responded to the social interaction with greater increases in anabolic balance than participants who had just described a close same-group friend. Once again, participants who had just described their close cross-group friend in detail took longer to classify that friend's ethnic group as non-self-descriptive, and these reaction times fully mediated the effects of the friendship prime on anabolic balance during the novel intergroup interaction. As all participants in these two studies had a very close cross-group friend, these studies suggest that benefits of cross-group friendship are not solely predicated on the presence versus the absence of such friends in one's network. Rather, the intergroup benefits of cross-group friendship appear to be contingent on how readily that friend is activated when in the presence of a novel outgroup member.

Altogether, the research described here demonstrates that cross-group friendship causally improves intergroup contact experiences, and this is explained through a heightened association between an outgroup and the self. The benefits of cross-group friendship can even apply to social interactions with outgroup members whom one has never met before. However, even among individuals with close cross-group friends, their experiences with novel outgroup members are facilitated only to the extent that their cross-group friend is accessible in mind. It is important to remember that one does not need an experimental procedure that brings cross-group friends to mind for the benefits of cross-group friendship to occur. As we mentioned earlier, group membership is often a salient feature of the strangers that we meet, and this salient feature is often powerful enough to bring to mind friends who belong to that same group. As Willie Nelson reminds us in "Always on My Mind" (Christopher, James, & Thompson, 1972), our closest, most significant others are *chronically accessible*. It is likely that if a cross-group friendship is very close, there may be no need of contextual cues for the effects of cross-group friendship to exert positive effects.

SPREADING THE BENEFITS OF CROSS-GROUP FRIENDSHIP

An additional question remains: How can cross-group friendships be encouraged? We have shown that the people who benefit the most from cross-group friendships are the least likely people to form them, so why would these friendships ever develop? While creating friendships in vitro provides a possible outlet for stimulating cross-group friendships, this process taxes both time and money and is not readily applicable to real-world contexts. Luckily, there are at least two exciting prospects for increasing interest in cross-ethnic bonds in vivo, which we discuss in detail next.

Indirect Cross-Group Friendship

An intriguing line of work focuses on the benefits of indirect cross-group friendship (Cameron, Rutland, & Brown, 2007; Cameron, Rutland, Brown, & Douch, 2006; Wright, Aron, McLaughlin-Volpe, & Ropp, 1997), which has been described elsewhere in the literature as the *extended contact effect* (see, e.g., Davies et al., this volume).[1] A person has an indirect cross-group friendship when, beyond any cross-group friends he or she may have, that person is aware that at least one same-group friend has a cross-group friend. The theory of indirect friendship was informed by studies of racial integration of previously all-White neighborhoods and housing projects (Deutsch & Collins, 1951; Hamilton & Bishop, 1976), where improved racial attitudes were observed even among Whites who had no direct contact with their Black neighbors. A laboratory test of the effects of indirect friendship (Wright et al., 1997) adapted the minimal groups paradigm (Tajfel, 1970) to incorporate a manipulation of knowledge of an ingroup member's cross-group friendship. Participants who witnessed an ingroup member exhibit hostile or neutral behavior toward an outgroup member exhibited many classic aspects of intergroup competition (Tajfel & Turner, 1979), such as attributing less positive affect toward the outgroup and allocating fewer resources to that group. However, participants who witnessed an ingroup member behaving in a friendly way toward an outgroup member ascribed more positive affect to the other team and distributed resources more equitably between the two teams. This provided experimental evidence that the knowledge of an ingroup member's cross-group friendship can improve intergroup attitudes and behaviors.

This effect of indirect friendship has now been replicated both among groups that experience more subtle forms of intergroup conflict (Turner et al., 2008) and groups with high levels of violent conflict, like Protestants and Catholics in Northern Ireland (Paolini et al., 2004). Turner and colleagues (2008) further demonstrated that indirect friendship decreases intergroup anxiety and prejudice through a heightened inclusion of the cross-group friend's group in the self. Their work also showed that indirect friendship decreases prejudice through changes in perceived ingroup and outgroup norms and decreases in intergroup anxiety. Thus, it appears that indirect friendship

---

[1]We use the term *indirect contact effect* to describe the phenomenon described elsewhere as the *extended contact effect*. We intend these two terms to be interpreted as interchangeable synonyms. However, we choose to use the term *indirect contact effect* in this chapter to follow the terminology used by traditional contact theorists (cf. Paolini et al., 2004; Pettigrew, 2008; Pettigrew, Christ, Wagner, & Stellmacher, 2007). Moreover, we prefer this term because it emphasizes the point that intergroup contact affects intergroup attitudes even when actual, direct intergroup contact is absent.

improves intergroup experience through a similar sense of identification with an outgroup that has been found for direct friendship effects.

These findings are exciting from the perspective of how contact experiences can be improved at a broad societal level. They suggest that not everyone needs to form a cross-group friendship in order to improve contact experiences with outgroup members; the mere knowledge of an ingroup member's cross-group friend is sufficient for improving intergroup attitudes. This knowledge may be key for individuals who have no opportunity to forge intergroup relationships or for whom prejudiced attitudes lead to intergroup avoidance. From an intervention standpoint, then, cross-group friendships could be formed in the lab or through social programs, and the benefits of these efforts could spread by encouraging participants in these programs to mention their new cross-group friendships to other ingroup members. Exciting research conducted among Catholic and Protestant community members in Northern Ireland has demonstrated that both direct and indirect cross-group friendships improve intergroup attitudes, even among groups that have a strong history of violence (Paolini et al., 2004). Altogether, the work reviewed in this section speaks to the power of cross-group friendships to build positive intergroup relations, both between friends and among other ingroup members, as well.

Conceptions of Race

Still, some people might be less responsive to the benefits of indirect intergroup friendship because of the way they conceptualize race. A series of compelling studies (Williams & Eberhardt, 2008) suggests that people who view race as biologically based (as opposed to being largely a social construction) are more accepting of racial disparities in the United States and less engaged by media depictions of growing racial inequality. This concept is similar to recent work demonstrating that essentialist versus constructivist lay theories of race affect how information about social groups is encoded, represented, and applied (Hong, Chao, & No, 2009). Relevant to our discussion, Williams and Eberhardt (2008) found that people who view race as biologically based have fewer cross-group friends. However, this view can be changed. Participants were randomly assigned to read one of two fake articles from a magazine, Gene, that either depicted race as a physical feature that can be determined by looking at one's DNA or a physical feature that is not detectable at the genetic level. Participants who read the article describing race as a nongenetic property showed more interest in friendships with racial outgroup members than did participants who were randomly assigned to read an article describing race as genetically determined.

The studies of Williams and Eberhardt (2008) suggest an important role that the media can play in increasing intergroup friendships. Since the mapping of the human genome (Venter et al., 2001), there has been little support for the previously assumed genetic distinctiveness of racial groups (e.g., Cho, 2006; Foster & Sharp, 2004; Royal & Dunston, 2004). Therefore, it is ethical—if not ethically necessitated—for media campaigns to focus on educating the population about the lack of support for racial "groups." The work of Williams and Eberhardt (2008) suggests that such a media focus would increase interracial friendliness while simultaneously decreasing people's acceptance of racial inequality.

Taken together, research on indirect friendship and conceptions of race present pathways for facilitating cross-group friendship among prejudiced individuals. Media messages that educate the public on social construction of racial groups may encourage cross-group friendship formation. If only a single member of a social network is affected by these messages, the prejudice-reducing effects of indirect friendship will nonetheless spread. These two lines of research suggest peripheral routes to cross-group friendship that may be most effective for prejudiced individuals.

APPLICABILITY OF INTERPERSONAL RELATIONSHIPS TO INSTITUTIONAL ADJUSTMENT

In addition to intergroup benefits at the individual level, cross-group friendship can also provide possible benefits at the societal level by improving inclusivity within higher education. Rev. Dr. Martin Luther King Jr. (1964) noted that "it is precisely because education is the road to equality and citizenship that it has been made more elusive for Negroes than many other rights" (p. 12). In the half-century since the Supreme Court's 1954 ruling in *Brown vs. Board of Education*, U.S. schools have attempted to facilitate intergroup contact and reduce racial disparities in education through integration. While these structural changes have covaried with rapid increases in the proportions of racial minorities attaining degrees in higher education (U.S. Census Bureau, 2007), a more insidious legacy of racial inequality has remained. In the context of universities that historically discriminated against non-White students in their admission practices, some minority-race students are left to wonder whether they are equally valued members of the campus community or are only grudgingly tolerated (Bowen & Bok, 2000).

Feeling alienated from the campus community can impact academic success. Specifically, students who are sensitive to social rejection based on their race (*RS-race*; Mendoza-Denton et al., 2002) have additional hurdles to success in institutions of higher education that historically discriminated against their group. RS-race among minority-race students leads to feelings of estrangement from the university, avoidance of professors and other academic resources, and declining GPA over the college years. Universities that have a history of discriminatory practices are culturally associated with majority groups and majority group members (Bowen & Bok, 2000). We therefore reasoned that close relationships with majority-group peers should buffer at-risk students from the negative effects of RS-race by extinguishing learned associations between majority-group members, institutions associated with the majority group, and social rejection (Mendoza-Denton, Page-Gould, & Pietrzak, 2006).

We tested this hypothesis directly across two studies that combined longitudinal field research with experimental data (Mendoza-Denton & Page-Gould, 2008). The first study examined the effects of the natural development of friendship with White students among incoming Black freshmen at a historically White research university. The results of this study indicated that, near the end of college, students who were initially high in RS-race (assessed prior to the start of college) and had made few or no White friends during their 1st year reported significantly decreased satisfaction with the university and less sense of belonging with the university community. However, students who were high in RS-race and made more White friends at the beginning of college were buffered—they were as satisfied and felt as much a part of the university at the end of college as Black students who were low in RS-race. It is important to note that we controlled for the participants' number of Black friends in these analyses, which means that the beneficial relationship between cross-group friendship and institutional belonging did not come at the cost of same-group friendship.

Although these longitudinal findings provided evidence that the development of cross-group friendship chronologically preceded changes in institutional adjustment, experimental data were still needed to distinguish the impact of making new majority-group friends from individual characteristics of high-RS-race students who chose to form these friendships in the first place. Furthermore, as we examined the experiences of only Black students, we did not explicitly test the hypothesis that these effects were unique to minority-race students in historically all-White universities.

To address these issues, we included questions regarding institutional satisfaction after the final friendship meeting of the previously described Page-Gould et al. (2008) study. Latino/a participants who scored high on RS-race prior to the friendship manipulation were less satisfied at a historically White public research university than their low RS-race counterparts at the end of the study if they had been assigned to make a same-group friend. However, the formation of a cross-group friendship in the laboratory predicted similarly high levels of institutional satisfaction among both low- and high-RS-race Latino/a students.

This effect was moderated by ethnicity, as White students who were concerned about rejection on the basis of their race were equally satisfied at the university as White students who scored low on the RS-race scale (Mendoza-Denton & Page-Gould, 2008). This particular finding is expected because White students do not have as much reason to doubt their acceptance as a function of their race as do students of racial minority backgrounds (e.g., see Purdie-Vaughns & Walton, this volume). However, our hypothesis for institutional identification is more general than describing institutional belonging among minority-race students. Take, for example, the context of a historically all-Black university: In this context, friendships with Black students should improve the institutional outcomes of White students, but friendships with White students should be irrelevant to the institutional identification of Black students. Our work embraces the more general viewpoint that developing cross-group friendship enhances institutional identification when that friendship is formed with members of outgroups that are associated with the institution, and this phenomenon should apply across varying manifestations of institution–outgroup associations.

In sum, these studies demonstrate that cross-group friendship improves institutional adjustment among individuals who have reasons to question their acceptance in institutions of higher education. Again, these data show that cross-group friendship is most beneficial for individuals who feel threatened by outgroup members and alienated from institutions associated with an outgroup. Given that minority-race students who are low in RS-race feel greater institutional belonging and have increasing GPA over time (Mendoza-Denton et al., 2002), it is important to identify factors that facilitate these positive outcomes for all students in higher education. Moreover, in the first study described in this section, we controlled for students' development of same-group friendship, which implies that the benefits of cross-group friendship do not come at the cost of friendships with ingroup members. The institutional benefits of cross-group friendship provide a method through which students can not only coexist but interrelate.

SAME-GROUP FRIENDSHIP

We have been discussing the benefits of cross-group friendship for people who are vulnerable to intergroup alienation. In such a discussion, a question invariably arises of how same-group friendship plays into intergroup relations. Throughout the studies we have described here, same-group friendship has played a nuanced role in intergroup experience. When we manipulated the accessibility of same-group and cross-group friendships (Page-Gould et al., 2010), participants who were primed with a same-group friend had a weaker association between the outgroup and the self and exhibited more aversive stress responses during an intergroup interaction. This was the case despite the fact that they had a very close cross-group friend. However, when examining the impact of cross-group friendship on institutional adjustment (Mendoza-Denton & Page-Gould, 2008), cross-group friendship affected institutional well-being independently of same-group friendship. Furthermore, the work on indirect friendship (e.g., Wright et al., 1997) emphasizes that same-group friends play a pivotal role in improved intergroup attitudes if the same-group friends have cross-group friends.

These studies imply that same-group friendship does not need to be sacrificed for the benefits of cross-group friendship to be realized. In fact, the benefits of cross-group friendship may be spread efficiently through a social network of same-group friends through indirect friendship processes. However, when meeting with an unfamiliar outgroup member, people who have close cross-group friends will have smoother intergroup interactions only to the degree that their cross-group friend is cognitively accessible. In this latter case, a salient same-group friend will not facilitate positive contact experiences. Altogether, same-group friendship does not diminish the benefits of cross-group friendship—in the case of indirect friendship, it spreads the intergroup value of any given cross-group friendship to many people—but only an accessible cross-group friend will ensure positive contact experiences with novel outgroup members.

CONCLUSION

In this chapter, we have reviewed recent experimental work on cross-group friendship. This research converges to show that cross-group friendship causally affects intergroup experience at both the interpersonal and institutional levels. Moreover, cross-group friendship holds the most benefits for people who are at risk for alienation in diverse contexts. While at once inspiring, the distinct benefits of cross-group friendship for individuals who are prejudiced or anxiously expect prejudice simultaneously present a conundrum of how these relationships can be fostered in everyday life. We reviewed work showing that interracial friendliness can be increased through media portrayals of the foundation of racial differences, and that the benefits of cross-group friendship spread throughout one's social network even in the absence of direct cross-group friendship.

The most exciting component of the work described here and in other chapters (e.g., Davies et al.; Mallett et al., this volume) is the clear path that cross-group friendship paves toward positive intergroup relations. Martin Luther King's "I Have a Dream" speech (see Tropp & Mallett, this volume) identified the goal that children of different races would one day play together. Cross-group friendship is the manifestation of that image. Altogether, it appears that cross-group friendships hold benefits for multiple spheres of life, from improved social interactions with outgroup members to a greater sense of inclusion and satisfaction in marginalizing performance environments. In an increasingly diverse social environment, cross-group friendships may play an important role in fostering unified, tolerant societies.

REFERENCES

Akinola, M., & Mendes, W. B. (2008, January). Vigilance and intergroup interactions. In J. Richeson & S. Neuberg (Chairs), *Taking a relational approach to intergroup contact: When stigmatized and non-stigmatized group members' experiences diverge and converge*. Symposium conducted at the annual scientific meeting of the Society for Personality and Social Psychology, Albuquerque, NM.

Allport, G. W. (1954). *The nature of prejudice*. Reading, MA: Addison-Wesley.

Andersen, S. M., & Berk, M. S. (1998). The social–cognitive model of transference: Experiencing past relationships in the present. *Current Directions in Psychological Science, 7*, 109–115. doi:10.1111/1467-8721.ep10774744

Aron, A., & Aron, E. N. (1996). Self and self-expansion in relationships. In G. J. O. Fletcher & J. Fitness (Eds.), *Knowledge structures in close relationships: A social psychological approach* (pp. 325–344). Mahwah, NJ: Erlbaum.

Aron, A., Aron, E. N., Tudor, M., & Nelson, G. (1991). Close relationships as including other in self. *Journal of Personality and Social Psychology, 80*, 253–267.

Aron, A., & McLaughlin-Volpe, T. (2001). Including others in the self: Extensions to own and partner's group memberships. In C. Sedikides & M. B. Brewer (Eds.), *Individual self, relational self, and collective self: Partners, opponents, or strangers?* (pp. 89–109). Philadelphia, PA: Psychology Press.

Aron, A., McLaughlin-Volpe, T., Mashek, D., Lewandowski, G., Wright, S. C., & Aron, E. N. (2004). Including others in the self. *European Review of Social Psychology, 15*, 101–132. doi:10.1080/10463280440000008

Aron, A., Melinat, E., Aron, E. N., Vallone, R., & Bator, R. (1997). The experimental generation of interpersonal closeness: A procedure and some preliminary findings. *Personality and Social Psychology Bulletin, 23*, 363–377. doi:10.1177/0146167297234003

Binder, J., Zagefka, H., Brown, R., Funke, F., Kessler, T., Mummendey, A., . . . Leyens, J.-P. (2009). Does contact reduce prejudice or does prejudice reduce contact? A longitudinal test of the contact hypothesis in three European countries. *Journal of Personality and Social Psychology, 96*, 843–856. doi:10.1037/a0013470

Bowen, W. G., & Bok, D. (2000). *The shape of the river: Long-term consequences of considering race in college and university admissions*. Princeton, NJ: Princeton University Press.

Cameron, L., Rutland, A., & Brown, R. (2007). Promoting children's positive intergroup attitudes towards stigmatized groups: Extended contact and multiple classification skills training. *International Journal of Behavioral Development, 31,* 454–466. doi:10.1177/0165025407081474

Cameron, L., Rutland, A., Brown, R. J., & Douch, R. (2006). Changing children's intergroup attitudes towards refugees: Testing different models of extended contact. *Child Development, 77,* 1208–1219. doi:10.1111/j.1467-8624.2006.00929.x

Chen, S., Anderson, S. M., & Hinkley, K. (1999). Triggering transference: Examining the role of applicability in the activation and use of significant-other representations in social perception. *Social Cognition, 17,* 332–365.

Cho, M. K. (2006). Racial and ethnic categories in biomedical research: There is no baby in the bathwater. *Journal of Law, Medicine & Ethics, 34,* 497–499. doi:10.1111/j.1748-720X.2006.00061.x

Christopher, J., James, M., & Thompson, W. C. (1972). Always on my mind (recorded by Willie Nelson). On *Always on my mind* [CD]. New York, NY: Columbia Records.

Cosmides, L., Tooby, J., & Kurzban, R. (2003). Perceptions of race. *Trends in Cognitive Sciences, 7,* 173–179. doi:10.1016/S1364-6613(03)00057-3

Damico, S. B., Bell-Nathaniel, A., & Green, C. (1981). Effects of school organizational structure on interracial friendships in middle schools. *Journal of Educational Research, 74,* 388–393.

Dasgupta, N., & Greenwald, A. G. (2001). On the malleability of automatic attitudes: Combating automatic prejudice with images of admired and disliked individuals. *Journal of Personality and Social Psychology, 81,* 800–814. doi:10.1037/0022-3514.81.5.800

Davies, K. M., Aron, A., Wright, S. C., & McLaughlin-Volpe, T. (2007, January). *The Stony Brook Intergroup Fast Friends Project: Some initial results.* Poster presented at the annual meeting of the Society for Personality and Social Psychology, Memphis, TN.

Deutsch, M., & Collins, M. (1951). *Interracial housing: A psychological evaluation of a social experiment.* Minneapolis: University of Minnesota Press.

Dovidio, J. F., & Gaertner, S. L. (2004). Aversive racism. In M. P. Zanna (Ed.), *Advances in experimental social psychology* (pp. 1–52). San Diego, CA: Academic Press.

Dovidio, J. F., Kawakami, K., & Gaertner, S. L. (2002). Implicit and explicit prejudice and interracial interaction. *Journal of Personality and Social Psychology, 82,* 62–68. doi:10.1037/0022-3514.82.1.62

Epel, E. S., McEwen, B. S., & Ickovics, J. R. (1998). Embodying psychological thriving: Physical thriving in response to stress. (Thriving: Broadening the paradigm beyond illness to health). *Journal of Social Issues, 54,* 302–313.

Foster, M. W., & Sharp, R. R. (2004). Beyond race: Towards a whole-genome perspective on human populations. *Nature Reviews Genetics, 5,* 790–796. doi:10.1038/nrg1452

Gaertner, S. L., & Dovidio, J. F. (1986). The aversive form of racism. In J. F. Dovidio & S. L. Gaertner (Eds.), *Prejudice, discrimination, and racism* (pp. 61–89). Orlando, FL: Academic Press.

Greenwald, A. G., McGhee, D. E., & Schwartz, J. L. K. (1998). Measuring individual differences in implicit cognition: The Implicit Associations Test. *Journal of Personality and Social Psychology, 74*, 1464–1480. doi:10.1037/0022-3514.74.6.1464

Hamilton, D. L., & Bishop, G. D. (1976). Attitudinal and behavioral effects of initial integration of White suburban neighborhoods. *Journal of Social Issues, 32*, 47–67. doi:10.1111/j.1540-4560.1976.tb02494.x

Hong, Y., Chao, M. M., & No, S. (2009). Dynamic interracial/intercultural processes: The role of lay theories of race. *Journal of Personality, 77*, 1283–1310.

Kenworthy, J. B., Turner, R. N., Hewstone, M., & Voci, A. (2005). Intergroup contact: When does it work, and why? In J. Dovidio, P. Glick, & L. Rudman (Eds.), *On the nature of prejudice: 50 years after Allport* (pp. 278–292). Malden, MA: Blackwell. doi:10.1002/9780470773963.ch17

King., M. L., Jr. (1964). Education and equality. *Equity & Excellence in Education, 2*, 12–13.

Levin, S., van Laar, C. Y., & Sidanius, J. H. (2003). The effects of ingroup and outgroup friendships on ethnic attitudes in college: A longitudinal study. *Group Processes & Intergroup Relations, 6*, 76–92. doi:10.1177/1368430203006001013

Mallett, R. K., Wilson, T. D., & Gilbert, D. T. (2008). Expect the unexpected: Failure to anticipate similarities leads to an intergroup forecasting error. *Journal of Personality and Social Psychology, 94*, 265–277. doi:10.1037/0022-3514.94.2.94.2.265

Mendes, W. B., Blascovich, J., Lickel, B., & Hunter, S. (2002). Challenge and threat during social interactions with White and Black men. *Personality and Social Psychology Bulletin, 28*, 939–952.

Mendoza-Denton, R., Downey, G., Purdie, V. J., Davis, A., & Pietrzak, J. (2002). Sensitivity to status-based rejection: Implications for African American students' college experience. *Journal of Personality and Social Psychology, 83*, 896–918. doi:10.1037/0022-3514.83.4.896

Mendoza-Denton, R., & Page-Gould, E. (2008). Can cross-group friendships influence minority students' well being at historically White universities? *Psychological Science, 19*, 933–939. doi:10.1111/j.1467-9280.2008.02179.x

Mendoza-Denton, R., Page-Gould, E., & Pietrzak, J. (2006). Mechanisms for coping with status–based rejection expectations. In S. Levin & C. Van Laar (Eds.), *Stigma and group inequality: Social psychological perspectives* (pp. 151–169). Mahwah, NJ: Erlbaum.

Page-Gould, E., Mendoza-Denton, R., Alegre, J. M., & Siy, J. O. (2010). Understanding the impact of cross-group friendship on interactions with novel outgroup members. *Journal of Personality and Social Psychology, 98*, 775–793. doi:10.1037/a0017880

Page-Gould, E., Mendoza-Denton, R., & Tropp, L. R. (2008). With a little help from my cross-group friend: Reducing anxiety in intergroup contexts through cross-group friendship. *Journal of Personality and Social Psychology, 95,* 1080–1094. doi:10.1037/0022-3514.95.5.1080

Paolini, S. (2005, July). *Direct and indirect friendship between ingroup and outgroup members: A combined, multi-session, and experimental test of their effects and mediators.* Paper presented at the general meeting of the European Association of Experimental Social Psychology, Wurzburg, Germany.

Paolini, S., Hewstone, M., Cairns, E., & Voci, A. (2004). Effects of direct and indirect cross-group friendships on judgments of Catholics and Protestants in Northern Ireland: The mediating role of an anxiety-reduction mechanism. *Personality and Social Psychology Bulletin, 30,* 770–786. doi:10.1177/0146167203262848

Paolini, S., Hewstone, M., Voci, A., Harwood, J., & Cairns, E. (2006). Intergroup contact and the promotion of intergroup harmony: The influence of intergroup emotions. In R. Brown & D. Capozza (Eds.). *Social identities: Motivational, emotional, and cultural influences* (pp. 209–238). New York, NY: Psychology Press.

Park, S. H. (2009). *Prediction processes in intergroup interaction.* Unpublished doctoral dissertation, University of California, Berkeley.

Pettigrew, T. F., & Tropp, L. R. (2000). Does intergroup contact reduce prejudice? Recent meta-analytic findings. In S. Oskamp (Ed.), *Reducing prejudice and discrimination: Social psychological perspectives* (pp. 93–114). Mahwah, NJ: Erlbaum.

Pettigrew, T. F., & Tropp, L. R. (2006). A meta-analytic test of intergroup contact theory. *Journal of Personality and Social Psychology, 90,* 751–783. doi:10.1037/0022-3514.90.5.751

Pettigrew, T. F., & Tropp, L. R. (2008). How does intergroup contact reduce prejudice? Meta-analytic tests of three mediators. *European Journal of Social Psychology, 38,* 922–934. doi:10.1002/ejsp.504

Plant, E. A., & Devine, P. G. (2003). The antecedents and implications of interracial anxiety. *Personality and Social Psychology Bulletin, 29,* 790–801. doi:10.1177/0146167203029006011

Royal, C. D., & Dunston, G. M. (2004). Changing the paradigm from "race" to human genome variation. *Nature Genetics, 36,* S5–S7. doi:10.1038/ng1454

Stephan, W. G., & Stephan, C. W. (1985). Intergroup anxiety. *Journal of Social Issues, 41,* 157–175. doi:10.1111/j.1540-4560.1985.tb01134.x

Tajfel, H. (1970). Experiments in intergroup discrimination. *Scientific American, 223,* 96–102. doi:10.1038/scientificamerican1170-96

Tajfel, H., & Turner, J. C. (1979). An integrative theory of intergroup conflict. In W. G. Austin & S. Worchel (Eds.), *The social psychology of intergroup relations* (pp. 33–47). Monterey, CA: Brooks/Cole.

Tropp, L. R., & Wright, S. C. (2001). Ingroup identification as inclusion of ingroup in the self. *Personality and Social Psychology Bulletin, 27,* 585–600. doi:10.1177/0146167201275007

Turner, R. N., Hewstone, M., Voci, A., & Vonofakou, C. (2008). A test of the extended intergroup contact hypothesis: The mediating role of intergroup anxiety, perceived ingroup and outgroup norms, and inclusion of the outgroup in the self. *Journal of Personality and Social Psychology, 95,* 843–860. doi:10.1037/a0011434

U.S. Census Bureau. Current Population Survey. (2007). *Educational attainment: Table A-2, Percent of people 25 years and over who have completed high school or college, by race, Hispanic origin and sex: Selected years 1940 to 2007* [Data file]. Retrieved from http://www.census.gov/population/socdemo/education/cps2007/tabA-2.csv

Venter, J. C., Adams, M. D., Myers, E. W., Li, P. W., Mural, R. J., Sutton, G. G., . . . Zhu, X. (2001, February 16). The sequence of the human genome. *Science, 291,* 1304–1351. doi:10.1126/science.1058040

Williams, M. J., & Eberhardt, J. L. (2008). Biological conceptions of race and the motivation to cross racial boundaries. *Journal of Personality and Social Psychology, 94,* 1033–1047. doi:10.1037/0022-3514.94.6.1033

Wright, S. C., Aron, A., McLaughlin-Volpe, T., & Ropp, S. A. (1997). The extended contact effect: Knowledge of cross–group friendships and prejudice. *Journal of Personality and Social Psychology, 73,* 73–90. doi:10.1037/0022-3514.73.1.73

Wright, S. C., Aron, A., & Tropp, L. R. (2002). Including others (and groups) in the self: Self-expansion and intergroup relations. In J. P. Forgas & K. D. Williams (Eds.), *The social self: Cognitive, interpersonal and intergroup perspectives* (pp. 343–363). Philadelphia, PA: Psychology Press.

Wright, S. C., Brody, S. M. & Aron, A. (2005). Intergroup contact: Still our best hope for improving intergroup relations. In C. S. Crandall & M. Schaller (Eds.). *Social psychology of prejudice: Historical and contemporary issues* (pp. 115–142). Seattle, WA: Lewinian Press.

Wright, S. C., & van der Zande, C. C. (1999, October). *Bicultural friends: When cross-group friendships cause improved intergroup attitudes.* Paper presented at the annual meeting of the Society for Experimental Social Psychology, St. Louis, MO.

8

IS MULTICULTURALISM BAD FOR AFRICAN AMERICANS? REDEFINING INCLUSION THROUGH THE LENS OF IDENTITY SAFETY

VALERIE PURDIE-VAUGHNS AND GREGORY M. WALTON

In the late 1990s, Susan Okin wrote a withering critique of multiculturalism in her essay "Is Multiculturalism Bad for Women?" that sparked a lively debate about the claims racial minority groups make to acknowledge their existence and whether they clash with norms of gender equality (Okin, 1999). Inspired by her title and critique, we believe social psychologists could benefit from a critical analysis of multiculturalism as it relates to racial minorities in the United States, specifically African Americans. Although our arguments apply to multiple groups in the United States, we focus on African Americans because their full inclusion in mainstream institutions has been historically contentious (Glazer, 1997; Olson, 2001). Moreover, architects of multiculturalism often judge the effectiveness of multicultural policies by the degree to which African Americans are effectively incorporated into a given institution (Glazer, 1997).

Multiculturalism refers to the general notion that group differences should be the basis for mutual respect and that these differences should be valued. Typically, multiculturalism stands in contrast to so-called color blindness, the idea that people are universally similar and that group differences should be minimized (Plaut, 2002). By no means do we plan to offer a critique of multiculturalism as severe as Okin did in her article. Much good has come from multiculturalism, and African Americans have benefited from institutional policies and practices in which diversity is valued, endorsed, and supported (Carbado & Gulati, 2004; McHugh, Nettles, & Gottfredson, 1993). Yet, because multiculturalism explicitly acknowledges and values the centrality of group identity for people from diverse backgrounds (Glazer, 1997; Markus, Steele, & Steele, 2000; Plaut, 2002; Tropp & Bianchi, 2006), and because it tends to be contrasted with color-blind ideologies that deemphasize group identity (Markus et al., 2000), it is tempting to conclude that multiculturalism is unequivocally good for African Americans and color blindness is unequivocally bad.

We aim to shift conversations away from the multiculturalism/color blindness dichotomy toward a third approach to diversity—what we and others have termed *identity safety* (Davies, Spencer, & Steele, 2005; Markus, Steele, & Steele, 2000; Purdie-Vaughns, Steele, Davies, Ditlmann, & Crosby, 2008; Steele, Spencer, & Aronson, 2002; Walton & Cohen, 2007). Like multiculturalism, identity safety explicitly acknowledges that diversity can be a source of value. But it also emphasizes that people from different social groups and backgrounds can experience the same social contexts in similar ways but that various barriers in mainstream institutions can also prevent them from doing so (Markus et al., 2000; Steele et al., 2002). In many school and corporate settings, people from different social groups contend with different *identity contingencies*—that is, ways in which their experiences differ as a consequence of numeric underrepresentation, social hierarchies, explicit and unintended discrimination, and stereotypes (Purdie-Vaughns et al., 2008). The goal of identity safety is to systematically identify the identity contingencies unique to each social group in a given setting and to mitigate the ways in which identity contingencies undermine some people's experiences. We argue that identity safety is a viable alternative to both multiculturalism and color-blind ideologies and review findings from several research studies that demonstrate its utility.

SETTING THE STAGE: MULTICULTURALISM AND IDENTITY SAFETY IN MAINSTREAM SETTINGS

The term *multiculturalism* is traditionally used by scholars to stress the importance of cultural diversity, the recognition of diverse ethnic, racial, and cultural groups, and the explicit valuing of this diversity in mainstream settings (Markus et al., 2000; Plaut, 2002; Wolsko, Park, Judd, & Wittenbrink, 2000). Theories of multiculturalism prioritize cultural groups (as opposed to individuals) as the cornerstone with which a person's identity is constructed, shaped, and constituted (Kymlicka, 1999; Verkuyten & Martinovic, 2006). Importantly, a cultural group can be based on any number of identities, such as age, socioeconomic status, race, ethnicity, religion, sexual orientation, geography, and physical or psychological ability.

Multiculturalism is not merely a theory. It serves as a framework for policies and practices, a set of normative beliefs, and a guiding ideology about how people should behave in diverse settings (Gerteis & Hartmann, 2007). Multicultural education, for example, is designed not only to broaden students' educational base but also to foster self-esteem and positive intergroup relations by emphasizing respect for people from diverse backgrounds (McHugh et al., 1993). Accordingly, multiculturalism in educational settings can take the form of diversity-related initiatives, such as ethnic studies majors and sponsored minority-targeted orientations, events, and tutoring programs. These initiatives may also involve sanctioning of professors and students who violate or disrespect multicultural norms, as well as creating admissions practices that consider diversity as one of many factors (Glazer, 1997).

In corporate settings, multiculturalism highlights the benefits of a diverse workforce and recognizes employee differences as a source of strength (Stevens, Plaut, & Sanchez-Burks, 2008). Organizations can use several strategies to achieve and effectively manage diversity in the workplace. For instance, "diversity days" may be organized to celebrate the cultures of different employees, and diversity trainings may target managerial stereotyping and increase cultural awareness (Stevens et al., 2008). Such multiculturalist approaches often necessitate the creation of diversity manager positions, diversity committees and task forces, affinity groups, networking programs, and mentoring programs—most of which are designed to reduce the social isolation felt by female and ethnic minority employees (Dobbin & Kalev, 2007; Thomas & Kanji, 2004).

By contrast, identity safety emphasizes that people from different social groups and backgrounds have the potential to experience the same social contexts in similar ways and that doing so is an ideal that organizations should strive for (Markus et al., 2000; Steele et al., 2002). Identity safety also acknowledges that people from different social groups bring different perspectives, values, and experiences to mainstream institutions. Consistent with multiculturalism, in identity safety, this heterogeneity is seen as a source of strength and value. But identity safety also presumes that within-group variability is as meaningful as between-group variability. Consequently, in identity safety, people should be perceived, treated, and evaluated primarily as individuals.

In positing the idea that people from different backgrounds have the potential to experience a social context in the same way, identity safety also posits that various barriers can prevent people from doing so. People's experiences may differ significantly as a function of their social-group background (e.g., Steele, 1997; Steele et al., 2002). This difference in experience occurs because people from different social groups simply perceive settings from different perspectives. In a given situation, different people may contend with different *identity contingencies*.

A key goal of identity safety is to mitigate the ways in which identity contingencies can undermine some people's experiences in mainstream settings relative to others. Consequently, in an ideal setting, people's experiences and outcomes would be determined primarily by their individual interests and aptitudes, and where their group identity is relevant, it would be a source of advantage and value, not disadvantage and threat. We call such environments *identity safe*. Importantly, to reduce negative identity contingences, it is effective neither to essentialize group identity and differences, as is risked by multiculturalism, nor to ignore the reality of group identity, as is risked by color blindness. Instead, what is required is a theory-based, empirical assessment of the ways in which each group identity can potentially undermine people's experiences and of effective strategies to mitigate such identity contingencies.

Both multicultural and identity safety frameworks have the potential to be most effective in modern pluralistic societies in which underlying assumptions about ethnic, cultural, and religious groups include the notion that each group deserves equal recognition, representation, and treatment in a given mainstream institution (e.g., corporation, school, or government institution; Brubaker, 1992). They also have the potential to be effective in societies where cultural, religious, and ethnic group memberships are distinct from political membership and distinct from citizenship (Brubaker, 1992; e.g., although African Americans tend to vote for the Democratic Party, there is no policy or explicit rule that racial identity is tied to the Democratic Party). Indeed, acknowledging and valuing the distinctiveness of outgroups are best considered long after conflicts have subsided and both advantaged and disadvantaged groups have come to share common goals of fostering social cooperation. We emphasize that in the absence of these conditions, other policies and frameworks that focus on reducing conflict between groups, incrementally building trust (see Swart, Turner, Hewstone, & Voci, this volume) and establishing forgiveness (see González, Manzi, & Noor, this volume) might be more applicable than either multicultural or identity-safety frameworks.

Yet, identity safety is a paradigm shift relative to multiculturalism, just as the iPhone is a paradigm shift from the more pedestrian cell phone. Identity safety is an *empowerment* framework in that it seeks to identify the unique identity-based concerns that each disadvantaged group contends with and tailors intervention toward addressing those concerns. In this sense, the power and potential of identity safety lie in its ability to move beyond formulaic equal representation of all groups at all times, as multicultural frameworks emphasize. Visual symbols and cultural representations of multiculturalism—rainbows with stripes that are the same size, colorful interlocking hands, ethnic minority dolls of different hues orbiting the a globe, and the like—amusingly depict a type of stubborn equal recognition that identity safety attempts to avoid. In this sense identity safety is akin to Nadler and Shnabel's needs-based model of reconciliation, a socioemotional approach to reconciliation that assumes that the nature of injury to a group's identity differs for advantaged and disadvantaged groups because they arise in different contexts (see Nadler & Shnabel, this volume).

IS MULTICULTURALISM BAD FOR AFRICAN AMERICANS?

Research on attitudes toward multiculturalism has yielded two main findings that provide the background for the rest of this chapter. First, multiculturalism appeals more to minority group members, such as African Americans, than to majority group members, such as White Americans (Lambert & Taylor, 1988). Indeed, minority group members prefer multiculturalist ideologies over assimilationist ideologies, such as color blindness (Brug & Verkuyten, 2007; Ryan, Hunt, Weible, Peterson, & Casas, 2007; Verkuyten, 2005). Second, opposition to multicultural ideologies is typically limited to Whites (Haidt, Rosenberg, & Hom, 2003; James, Brief, Dietz, & Cohen, 2001). Presumably, White youth are socialized to perceive that making racial distinctions of any kind is wrong and thus, as adults, display more favorable attitudes toward and feel more comfortable with color-blind ideologies (Bonilla-Silva, 2006). Given evidence that African Americans view multiculturalism more favorably than Whites, it is often simply assumed that multiculturalism is "good" for African Americans. We think this assumption requires a more critical and nuanced analysis.

Another issue involves disconnects between multicultural ideals and their implementation "on the ground." While theoretical advances offer important guidance for how multicultural initiatives should be implemented, multicultural policies, programs, and practices often fall short of these ideals (Glazer, 1997; Olson, 2001; Stevens et al., 2008). Consider the University of Wisconsin's attempt to illustrate its diverse enrollment by digitally embedding an African American student in an otherwise all-White crowd of Wisconsin football fans on the cover of a university brochure (Durhams, 2000). As this example illustrates, representations of diversity and multiculturalism may be ill-conceived or misguided and in some instances may do more harm than good (Roediger, 2005). Moreover, the discrepancy between African Americans' attitudes and lived experiences with respect to multiculturalism may lead them to hold favorable attitudes in the abstract yet be skeptical of its implementation

(Tropp & Bianchi, 2006). Thus, rather than evaluate all forms of multiculturalism favorably and equally, we propose to ask instead about the identity-based concerns African Americans have in mainstream settings and whether multiculturalism attenuates or aggravates those concerns.

In this chapter, our aim is to interrogate the assumption that because multiculturalism acknowledges the centrality of group identity, it is good for African Americans. We do this by highlighting four primary limitations of multiculturalism as a guiding ideology about diversity in mainstream American organizations. First, multiculturalism may enhance stereotyping and subtyping. Second, multiculturalism may aggravate the experience of intersectional invisibility (Purdie-Vaughns & Eibach, 2008). Third, multiculturalism often fails to explicitly challenge racial inequality. Fourth, in some respects there are inconsistencies between multiculturalism and the on-the-ground strategies African Americans use to achieve racial equality.

Limitations of Multiculturalism

The Risk of Stereotyping and Subtyping

One limitation of multiculturalism is comically illustrated by an episode of the TV series *The Office* (Novak & Kwapis, 2005), in which the office manager organizes "Diversity Day." Each employee has to tape to his or her own forehead a randomly assigned index card that assigns him or her a racial identity. The employees cannot see their own cards and hence do not know which identity they have "taken on." Employees are then asked to interact with their coworkers in such a way that their coworkers will guess the race written on their own card. As the African American man slaps a "Black" card on his own forehead, the office manager, in an effort to display his diversity prowess, engages the office worker in a conversation about collard greens, a stereotypically African American food, and one that this particular employee does not eat.

Just as this episode illustrates how identity can be unnaturally and uncomfortably highlighted, multicultural policies and practices may place people at risk of being uncomfortably categorized. By describing and categorizing cultural differences, multiculturalism, by definition, defines groups. And while categorization can be affirming if it advances an inclusive multicultural agenda, it can also result in stereotyping (Ryan et al., 2007; Wolsko et al., 2000). Indeed, not only can multiculturalism inadvertently lead people to categorize others, but it can also produce and construct identity by making assumptions about what constitutes the contours of that group and how members of that group should behave (Carbado, Fisk, & Gulati, 2008). Accordingly, multiculturalism may lead people to perceive outgroup members who are in some sense prototypical members of their constituent groups as more representative of that group than people who are nonprototypical members (just as people perceive a robin as more of a bird than an ostrich is).

Take, for instance, a search committee's goal of increasing the representation of African American faculty on a college campus. Committee members' assumptions about how different demographic and personal attributes define racial identity—such as the relative importance of physiological attributes (e.g., skin color) versus ideas or perspectives (e.g., the study of civil rights; Jackson, Stone, & Alvarez, 1993)—may determine the kind of African American they seek out. If a search committee views race as a demographic attribute, they may unwittingly recruit African American faculty who physiologically look Black without consideration for personal attributes. Or if the committee views race as a constellation of ideas and perspectives, the committee might be more apt to recruit African American faculty who adhere to what they perceive to be African American perspectives (e.g., Langston Hughes scholar). As a consequence of such hiring decisions, the university could end up enhancing the representation of African American faculty while simultaneously engaging in discrimination—hiring only those African American faculty who conform to a particular set of identity-relevant attributes. How people operationalize their commitment to multiculturalism may thus shape the kinds of people they value in a setting.

In our view, much more work is needed to examine how multiculturalism interacts with people's lay theories about race to affect their attitudes toward and perceptions of racial and ethnic minorities. However, some recent research is consistent with our claims. For example, an experiment by Gutierrez and Unzueta (2010) showed that people exposed to a multicultural ideology preferred stereotypic Black targets (e.g., those who had interests in basketball or hip-hop) *more* than counterstereotypic Black targets (e.g., those who had interests in surfing or country dancing). By contrast, people exposed to a color-blind ideology preferred the counterstereotypic target more. These results illustrate how people link diversity ideologies to people's individual attributes. They are also consistent with our broader argument that multiculturalism can lead people to engage in stereotyping by highlighting prototypical outgroup members.

Aggravating the Experience of Intersectional Invisibility

A second limitation of multiculturalism is that it may reinforce or aggravate the invisibility of people with multiple subordinate group identities. *Intersectional invisibility* refers to the general failure of people to fully recognize individuals with intersecting identities as members of their constituent groups (Purdie-Vaughns & Eibach, 2008). People who have multiple subordinate group identities (e.g., Black women, Black gay men, White lesbians) tend to be defined as nonprototypical members of both groups to which they belong.

Because these individuals do not fit the prototype of either identity group, and because multiculturalism attunes people to prototypical aspects more than nonprototypical aspects (Carbado et al., 2008; Gutierrez & Unzueta, 2010), multiculturalism may cause people with multiple subordinate group identities to be marginalized in comparison with more prototypical members of their constituent groups.

The problem of intersectional invisibility is clearly illustrated in a case study about IBM's diversity initiatives (Thomas & Kanji, 2004). In 1995, IBM launched an ambitious initiative designed to increase the retention and promotion of employees from underrepresented groups. To accomplish this goal, IBM created eight executive-level task forces to broadly represent ethnic, gender, and sexual identities. By every benchmark, this diversity initiative was innovative: It was ambitious—encompassing the entire company; it was inclusive—employees of all ranks were invited to participate; and it was endorsed by executives at the highest levels of IBM (Thomas & Kanji, 2004).

The problem was that each employee was invited to affiliate with only *one* of the eight groups: Asian, Black, gay and lesbian, Hispanic, Native American, people with disabilities, White men, and women. From the perspective of an intersectional person, the dilemma is clear. An African American gay man, for instance, must decide whether to affiliate with the Black group, whose mission was to focus on improving the institutional culture for African American employees through partnering with senior and junior African American executives, or with the gay and lesbian group, whose mission was to secure domestic partner benefits. Either way, the African American gay man will miss meaningful opportunities relevant to his life and career and will be less visible to an entire group of constituents than would be a more prototypical African American man or White gay man.

Although intersectional invisibility can certainly occur in the absence of multicultural policies and practices, initiatives born out of multiculturalism may exacerbate the experience. African American feminist scholars have long connected the rise of multiculturalism with the deepened invisibility of African American women in historical and contemporary feminist movements (Crenshaw, 1991; Davis, 1981; Purdie-Vaughns & Eibach, 2008). Some might claim in exasperation that at least multiculturalism is preferable to no ideology at all. We certainly agree. But two points are worth noting. First, people grossly underestimate the number of people who possess intersectional subordinate group identities. Consequently, multicultural ideologies that intend to recognize, describe, and acknowledge cultural differences may privilege some identities and marginalize many others. Second, the challenges associated with multiculturalism and multiple identities highlight the need for a guiding ideology that can account for the dynamic and situated nature of identity across different settings. We return to this issue at the end of the chapter.

Failure to Explicitly Interrogate Structural Inequality

A third limitation of multiculturalism centers on the relationship between recognizing racial differences and combating structural inequality between groups. Despite their educational, occupational, and political gains, African Americans continue to face gross disparities relative to Whites in wealth, home ownership, employment, educational attainment, and health outcomes (Hochschild, 1995). Multicultural frameworks tend to emphasize acknowledging and valuing cultural differences. But it remains unclear whether such frameworks explicitly address structural inequality in more fundamental ways (Andersen, 1999; Glazer, 1997; Olson, 2001).

Sociologist Margaret Andersen (1999) coined the term *diversity without oppression* to describe how multiculturalism fails to address the ways in which racial differences structure social life. She argues that multiculturalism is situated outside of the context of systemic inequality and thus that people who advocate for multiculturalism shift attention away from race and racism toward an amorphous dialogue of "cultural difference" (Andersen, 1999). Critics of multicultural curricula advance similar arguments, claiming that such curricula can diminish or mystify deep structural inequalities, especially with respect to race, by emphasizing cultural recognition instead (Glazer, 1997). In this sense, multiculturalism may serve as a moral credential (Monin & Miller, 2001) that allows members of privileged groups to downplay or dismiss structural inequalities because they feel they have recognized and valued minority cultural groups.

Social scientific evidence supports the idea that multiculturalism can obscure power and structural inequality. Majority group members tend to think of multiculturalism as a descriptive term to signal heterogeneity without implied power relations (Bell & Hartmann, 2007). They also tend to conceptualize culture as cosmetic or as peripheral to the true self (Plaut, 2002). Furthermore, when asked to explicitly contextualize racial inequality within the context of multiculturalism, majority group members' responses range from confusion to irritation (Bell & Hartmann, 2007).

One potential consequence of diversity without oppression is that it can lead to an intriguing variation of color blindness. Advocates of multiculturalism may divorce laws, policies, and accountability practices that have traditionally been central to achieving racial equality—affirmative action, reducing racial achievement gaps, eradicating racial profiling and racial stereotyping—from their broader agenda. Multiculturalism can then become a set of ideologies, practices, and policies through which people acknowledge cultural differences, but these differences are severed from meaningful action aimed at achieving racial equality.

Inconsistencies Between Multiculturalism and How African Americans Attempt to Achieve Racial Equality

A fourth limitation is that whereas African Americans typically prefer multicultural ideologies over color-blind ones (Ryan et al., 2007), they often cope with the possibility of being stigmatized in daily life by using egalitarian, individualist, and color-blind strategies. Legal scholar Richard Ford (2002) observed the following about African Americans during the Civil Rights era: "Some of the most passionate advocates of color blindness, strong racial integration, and even assimilation were people of color who truly believed in the moral justice and pragmatic necessity of these goals" (p. 32). Recent empirical research suggests that African Americans continue to combat racism with egalitarian and individualistic strategies.

For African Americans, the primary goal in most mainstream institutions is to combat stigmatization and achieve racial equality. Sociologist Michèle Lamont (Lamont & Aksartova, 2002; Lamont & Fleming, 2005) has found that both elite and working-class African Americans seek to achieve this goal by highlighting their intelligence and competence in the workplace in an effort to demonstrate that racial stereotypes do not apply to them and/or that such stereotypes are unfounded. Whereas working-class African Americans employ individualistic rhetorical strategies that the elite do not—such as color-blind religious themes (e.g., "We are all Children of God"; Lamont & Aksartova, 2002, p. 31)—both working-class and elite African Americans draw on themes of economic egalitarianism (e.g., "money makes us equal"; Lamont & Aksartova, 2002, p. 34), individualism, and personal competence as rhetorical strategies to resist stigmatization.

African Americans also tend to draw on commonalities between people, as highlighted in sociologist Elijah Anderson's (1999) research on corporate executives. Anderson outlined the archetype of the successful African American corporate executive: one who feels a strong need to personally believe that his or her presence in the organization is not due to race but is due to excellence and accomplishments in business. Accordingly, African American corporate executives, particularly those who have successfully integrated themselves into the corporate culture, publicly embrace the meritocratic norms of the company and explicitly project the appearance of color blindness. This produces, Anderson argued, a color-blind self-presentation style in the workplace:

> In management, in the various and sundry issues of the corporate world, members of the periphery [e.g., African American corporate executives]

like to appear colorblind, indicating that race plays a limited role in their understanding of the social world, but they display some ambivalence in this regard . . . It is with such ambivalences and reservations that, on a social basis [African American corporate executives] tend to fraternize with both blacks and whites, often believing they are making little distinction on the basis of skin color, but yet doing so all the while. It is within this context, from this benchmark, that they project a kind of cosmopolitanism ideal." (pp. 12–13)

Similarly, Barack Obama, the first African American president of the United States, frequently emphasizes how we can reduce racial polarization by focusing on common interests among racial groups (see also Eibach & Purdie-Vaughns, 2009). For instance, he has suggested that African Americans can gain more widespread support for the cause of racial justice by "binding our particular grievances . . . to the larger aspirations of all Americans" (Obama, 2008, p. 264) and that we can "pursue our individual dreams, yet still come together as a single American family" (Obama, 2008, pp. 102–103). Such common interest frames promote a color-blind view of society, downplay group differences and encourage people to focus on shared objectives (see also Gaertner & Dovidio, this volume).

Why might African Americans, from the working class to the White House, express and enact color-blind rhetorical strategies, when color blindness may at times disadvantage their group? Color blindness may be an ideology that denies the existence of White privilege and obscures racial inequalities, but it is also an ideology that can be used to advocate for racial equality and race-neutral treatment (Purdie-Vaughns et al., 2008). When it provides a means to promote fair treatment, African Americans may ironically prefer this form of color blindness over multiculturalism. This reasoning is not without its challenges, namely, the psychic struggle that accompanies enacting color blindness in the workplace (Anderson, 1999) or disambiguating which form of color blindness is at play, a process that consumes cognitive resources (Purdie-Vaughns et al., 2008). Nevertheless, multiculturalism in which group identities are highlighted and celebrated may not provide African Americans the same means to contend with race and racial identity in mainstream settings.

TOWARD A MODEL OF IDENTITY SAFETY

In general, at their best, we assume that diversity ideologies like multiculturalism and color blindness represent different means toward achieving a common goal: equal opportunity and inclusion in mainstream settings for people from all social groups. But neither ideology promotes this goal in a nonproblematic way. Multiculturalism risks reifying social categories—by treating people as members of a group first and as individuals second. Color blindness can deny the reality of people's group identities and the power of these identities to shape the experiences and outcomes of people from minority groups. Insofar as people wish to be perceived and treated as individuals rather than as group ambassadors, it is important to highlight their individual experiences while still acknowledging the importance of group identity. We believe that identity safety attempts to achieve this balance by acknowledging the *individual* experiences of members of minority groups while nevertheless recognizing how group identity affects these experiences.

In what follows, we outline two approaches to achieving identity safety in mainstream institutions. One approach focuses on identifying features of a given environment that give rise to negative identity contingencies. The other focuses on securing a felt sense of social belonging in settings where negative identity contingencies exist.

Achieving Identity Safety

Identifying Cues in the Setting That Trigger Threat

One way to make a setting identity safe is to identify what it is about the environment that conveys a risk of devaluation and alter those aspects of the setting. Because stigmatized group members' concerns are tied to specific settings, such group members draw information from features or cues in those settings that hold relevance for their group's status. Therefore, identifying features or cues in the setting that explicitly or implicitly convey devaluation and then objectively changing them should alter the psychological experience of members of a given group.

To test this process, we (Purdie-Vaughns et al., 2008) first identified two cues that African Americans use to discern the value accorded their racial identity in corporate workplaces: (a) the number of other minority group members and (b) the stated diversity philosophy of the organization—that is, whether the setting stresses color blindness or the principle of valuing diversity. African American professionals received brochures delivered from a corporate booth at a job fair designed to appear authentic. Minority representation in the organization (high or low) was experimentally manipulated via the number of "minority consultants" depicted in the brochure. Diversity philosophy (color blindness or valuing diversity) was presented in the form of a quotation from the company president. After exposure to these cues, we elicited open-ended judgments from African American professionals about the kinds of concerns and positive experiences they expected to face in the company's workplace. These judgments were coded for the degree to which they focused on identity contingencies relevant to African American professionals' racial identity. We also assessed institutional trust and motivation.

Our results revealed that these cues, though seemingly subtle, had powerful effects on African American professionals. These professionals anticipated that the corporation would value minorities, and they reported a high level of trust and anticipated a high sense of belonging in all conditions but one. In the condition in which they were exposed to two devaluing cues—a low minority representation and a color-blind diversity philosophy—African American professionals' motivation and institutional trust plummeted. Moreover, they reported more threatening and fewer affirming identity contingencies in this condition. Additional experiments showed that these effects were not found among White professionals, as their group identity is not at risk in corporate settings. They are thus less attentive to such cues.

Other studies reveal differences in the kinds of cues to which members of different groups attend. Female professionals, for instance, report concerns about gender power dynamics and, accordingly, attend to cues such as gender representation (high or low) and communication styles (competitive or relational) in corporate settings (Grewal, 2007). Gay men and lesbians face their own identity-relevant concerns. They must decide whether to conceal or reveal this aspect of their identity. Accordingly, gay men in corporate settings are attentive to social intimacy cues (i.e., interactions that require detailed knowledge of others) and are attentive to situations that require social intimacy disclosures (e.g., "What do you like to do in your spare time?"; Sedlovskaya & Purdie-Vaughns, 2009). Taken together, the research we have summarized thus far illuminates the promise of one approach to increasing identity safety: reducing identity-related threats embedded in a given setting.

Securing a Felt Sense of Belonging

Another example of a strategy to reduce identity contingences is an intervention to secure people's sense of social belonging (Walton & Cohen, 2007). This intervention begins with the premise that an important consequence of being underrepresented and negatively stereotyped in a setting is to feel uncertain about social belonging—about whether others will include and value one in that setting. As a consequence of this uncertainty, people may perceive even commonplace negative events in school settings—like critical feedback from an instructor or social rejection from a peer—as evidence that they do not belong in school. This interpretation may sap people's motivation to work hard in the setting. This is a type of identity contingency—it arises because, in light of underrepresentation and negative stereotypes, negative social events carry a more threatening meaning to some students than to others.

To reduce this form of identity contingency in academic contexts and to create an identity-safe academic environment, the social belonging intervention conveys to students that negative social events and feelings of non-belonging are common for all students in a new academic setting but that these negative experiences dissipate with time and eventually most students come to feel at home. This message conveys to underrepresented students that such experiences are not specific to them or to their social group and are not diagnostic of their actual belonging or that of their group. The treatment is thus intended to buttress underrepresented students' sense of belonging and motivation in the face of negative social events.

An initial test of the intervention included a sample of African American and White American 1st-year college students attending an elite university. Students read the results of a survey of ethnically diverse upper-year students at their school. The survey indicated that negative social events and feelings of nonbelonging are normal in the transition to college and dissipate with time. The materials were designed to lead students to attribute such events to the difficulty of the transition to college, rather than to a lack of belonging on their part or on the part of their racial group. In the control condition, students learned how the social-political attitudes of students change over time, controlling for the provision of normative information and for the representation of growth over time in college.

For White students, who have little cause to doubt their belonging in school, the treatment had little effect. However, the treatment had many benefits for African American students. In the week following its delivery, the treatment buffered African American students' academic motivation against negative social events. In the control condition, African American students' motivation dropped precipitously on socially adverse days; in the treatment condition, their motivation stayed high even on adverse days. Notably, the treatment did not reduce African American students' experience of social adversity. In both conditions, African American students experienced similar levels of social adversity. Instead, it changed the meaning of adversity so that it no longer conveyed a global lack of belonging in the school environment.

The treatment also increased African American students' self-reported engagement in behaviors that promote academic success, such as e-mailing with professors. Moreover, in the next semester, African American students in the treatment group earned grades that were one third of a grade point higher than those of students in the control group (Walton & Cohen, 2007). Subsequent analyses tracked students' academic outcomes over the following 3 years of college through senior year. The treatment effect continued to boost African American students' grades over this period. A second, independent cohort of students replicated this long-term gain in grades. Although important questions remain about the mechanisms by which this treatment works, one possibility is that it led African American students to experience and perceive the academic environment as welcoming and inclusive of people like them—to experience it as identity safe.

Although methodologically different from the research on cues described earlier, research on the social belonging intervention shares the notion that reducing the experience of identity-related threats rooted in a setting may improve the experiences of members of underrepresented groups.

More broadly, by identifying group members' identity-relevant concerns and aspects of settings that convey information about their identity value, one can circumvent several of the limitations associated with multiculturalism described earlier. For instance, identity safety is not associated with a guiding ideology about prototypical behaviors and strategies a group should employ. An identity-safety approach offers the possibility that group identity matters, but architects of identity-safe approaches, such as policymakers, systematically determine *if, how,* and *when* in each setting. Such a strategy obviates stereotyping and subtyping of both prototypical and intersectional group members. Furthermore, identity safety draws explicit attention to institutional transformation—that is, to key aspects of settings that require change to remove systemic sources of inequality. Identity safety has systemic inequality at its core and celebrating group membership at its periphery. Thus, it would be difficult to water down identity safety into "identity safety without oppression," as can occur with multiculturalism.

CONCLUSION

In recent years, there has been a growing need to shift the focus in thinking about intergroup relations from reducing conflict to optimizing intergroup relations; in short, there has been a call for positive intergroup relations. One aim of this chapter was to critically assess multiculturalism. We believe that a serious consideration of positive intergroup relations requires a critique of current frameworks and policies that aim to optimize contact between disadvantaged and advantaged group members. Furthermore, we introduced identity-safety theory as part of a new dialogue about how to improve the *individual* experiences of members of minority groups, nevertheless recognizing how group identity affects these experiences. Our research suggests that relatively simple but theory-based strategies can enhance historically marginalized group members' experience and achievement in mainstream settings while reducing threats based on group identity.

Two insights from identity-safety theory and research offer starting points for real-world intervention. First, organizations should begin to move away from diversity programs that lump all individuals with a specific identity together, because such programs exacerbate the tendency for individuals to be perceived exclusively through the lens of their group. Second, organizations aiming for positive intergroup relations should move away from programs with formulaic identity groups because different groups face unique identity-based concerns in the same social context. The future of programs and policies that embrace cultural differences lies in identifying identity-related threats relevant to each group and how they affect people's experiences in each specific setting. While this may seem hopelessly abstract, every day companies use research about how students learn to design flexible learning programs that accommodate a diversity of learning styles and abilities among students. Just as educators are rethinking one-size-fits-all approaches to education, so must we rethink one-identity-fits-all multicultural programs. Given these insights, reducing identity-related threats that are rooted in the setting may be the most effective intervention to move toward positive intergroup relations.

Ultimately, the benefits of any diversity ideology, whether it is color blindness, multiculturalism, or identity safety, relies on the care with which it is implemented and the degree of institutional scaffolding that accompanies it. It will take more than new theories to fully include historically marginalized groups in mainstream settings. Lasting change requires widespread institutional movements driven by sustained activism that challenges systemic inequality and discourages people from becoming complacent as progress is made toward ensuring that all people can thrive in mainstream school and work environments.

REFERENCES

Andersen, M. L. (1999). The fiction of "diversity" without oppression. In R. H. Tai & M. L. Kenyatta (Eds.), *Critical ethnicity: Countering the waves of identity politics* (pp. 5–20). Oxford, England: Rowman & Littlefield.

Anderson, E. (1999) The social situation of the Black executive: Black and White identities in the corporate world. M. Lamont (Ed.), *The cultural territories of race: Black and White boundaries* (pp. 3–29). Chicago, IL: University of Chicago Press.

Bell, J. M., & Hartmann, D. (2007). Diversity in everyday discourse: The cultural ambiguities and consequences of happy talk. *American Sociological Review, 72,* 895–914. doi:10.1177/000312240707200603

Bonilla-Silva, E. (2006). *Racism without racists.* Lanham, MA: Rowman & Littlefield.

Brubaker, R. (1992). *Citizenship and nationhood in France and Germany.* Cambridge, MA: Harvard University Press.

Brug, P., & Verkuyten, M. (2007). Dealing with cultural diversity: The endorsement of societal models among ethnic minority and majority youth in the Netherlands. *Youth & Society, 39*(1), 112–131. doi:10.1177/0044118X06297074

Carbado, D., Fisk, C., & Gulati, M. (2008). After inclusion. *Annual Review of Law and Social Science, 4,* 83–102. doi:10.1146/annurev.lawsocsci.4.110707.172323

Carbado, D. W., & Gulati, M. (2004). Race to the top of the corporate ladder: What minorities do when they get there. *Washington and Lee Law Review, 61,* 1645–1694.

Crenshaw, K. (1991). Mapping the margins: Intersectionality, identity politics, and violence against women of color. *Stanford Law Review, 43,* 1241–1299. doi:10.2307/1229039

Davies, P. G., Spencer, S. J., & Steele, C. M. (2005). Clearing the air: Identity safety moderates the effects of stereotype threat on women's leadership aspirations. *Journal of Personality and Social Psychology, 88,* 276–287. doi:10.1037/0022-3514.88.2.276

Davies, P. G., Steele, C. M., & Markus, H. R. (2008). A nation challenged: The impact of foreign threat on America's tolerance for diversity. *Journal of Personality and Social Psychology, 95,* 308–318. doi:10.1037/0022-3514.95.2.308

Davis, A. Y. (1981). *Women, race, & class.* New York, NY: Random House.

Dobbin, F., & Kalev, A. (2007). The architecture of inclusion: Evidence from corporate diversity programs. *Harvard Journal of Law & Gender, 30,* 279–302.

Durhams, S. (2000, September 20). University of Madison doctors photo. *The Milwaukee Journal Sentinel,* p. 1A.

Eibach, R. & Purdie-Vaughns, V. (2009). Change we can believe in? Barack Obama's framing of strategies for bridging racial divisions. *Du Bois Review: Social Science Research on Race,* 137–151.

Ford, R. T. (2002). Beyond difference: A reluctant critique of legal identity politics. In W. Brown & J. E. Halley (Eds.), *Left legalism/left critique* (pp. 38–79). Durham, NC: Duke University Press.

Glazer, N. (1997). *We are all multiculturalists now.* Cambridge, MA: Harvard University Press.

Gerteis, J. H., & Hartmann, D. R. (2007). *The multiple meanings of diversity: How Americans express its possibilities and problems.* Paper presented at the annual meeting of the American Sociological Association, New York, NY.

Grewal, D. (2007). *Take charge or be a team player? The effects of leadership style and gender representation on women's perceptions of the workplace.* Unpublished doctoral dissertation, Yale University, New Haven, CT.

Gutierrez, A. S., & Unzueta, M. M. (2010). The effect of interethnic ideologies on the likability of stereotypic vs. counterstereotypic targets. *Journal of Experimental Social Psychology, 46,* 775–784. doi:10.1016/j.jesp.2010.03.010

Haidt, J., Rosenberg, E., & Hom, H. (2003). Differentiating diversities: Moral diversity is not like other kinds. *Journal of Applied Social Psychology, 33,* 1–36. doi:10.1111/j.1559-1816.2003.tb02071.x

Hochschild, J. L. (1995). *Facing up to the American dream: Race, class, and the soul of the nation.* Princeton, NJ: Princeton University Press.

Jackson, S. E., Stone, V. K., & Alvarez, E. B. (1993). Socialization amidst diversity: The impact of demographics on work team oldtimers and newcomers. In L. L. Cummings & B. M. Staw (Eds.), *Research in organizational behavior* (pp. 45–109). Greenwich, CT: JAI Press.

James, E. H., Brief, A. P., Dietz, J., & Cohen, R. R. (2001). Prejudice matters: Understanding the reactions of whites to affirmative action programs targeted to benefit blacks. *Journal of Applied Psychology, 86,* 1120–1128. doi:10.1037/0021-9010.86.6.1120

Kymlicka, W. (1999). Liberal complacencies. In J. Cohen, M. Howard, & M. C. Nussbaum (Eds.), *Is multiculturalism bad for women?* (pp. 31–34). Princeton, NJ: Princeton University Press.

Lambert, W. E., & Taylor, D. M. (1988). Assimilation versus multiculturalism: The views of urban Americans. *Sociological Forum, 3*(1), 72–88. doi:10.1007/BF01115124

Lamont, M., & Aksartova, S. (2002). Ordinary cosmopolitanisms: Strategies for bridging racial boundaries among working-class men. *Theory, Culture & Society, 19*(4), 1–25.

Lamont, M., & Fleming, C. M. (2005). Everyday antiracism: Competence and religion in the cultural repertoire of the African American elite. *Du Bois Review: Social Science Research on Race, 2*(1), 29–43. doi:10.1017/S1742058X05050046

Markus, H. R., Steele, C. M., & Steele, D. M. (2000). Colorblindness as a barrier to inclusion: Assimilation and nonimmigrant minorities. *Daedalus, 129*(4), 233–259.

McHugh, B., Nettles, S. M., & Gottfredson, G. D. (1993). *Meeting the challenges of multicultural education: Second report from the evaluation of Pittsburgh's multicultural education center* (No. 42). Baltimore, MD: Johns Hopkins University Center for Research.

Monin, B., & Miller, D. T. (2001). Moral credentials and the expression of prejudice. *Journal of Personality and Social Psychology, 81,* 33–43. doi:10.1037/0022-3514.81.1.33

Novak, B. J. (Writer), & Kwapis, K. (Director). (2005). Diversity day [Television series episode]. In G. Daniels, R. Gervais, H. Klein, S. Merchant, & B. Silverman (Producers), *The office.* Los Angeles, CA: NBC Universal Television Studios.

Obama, B. (2008). *Change we can believe in: Barack Obama's plan to renew America's promise.* New York, NY: Three Rivers Press.

Okin, S. M. (1999). Is multiculturalism bad for women? In J. Cohen, M. Howard, & M. C. Nussbaum (Eds.), *Is multiculturalism bad for women?* (pp. 7–26). Princeton, NJ: Princeton University Press.

Olson, J. (2001). The limits of colorblind and multicultural personhood. *Stanford Agora: An Online Journal of Legal Perspectives, 2*(1). Retrieved from http://agora.stanford.edu/agora/libArticles2/agora2v1.pdf

Plaut, V. C. (2002). Cultural models of diversity: The psychology of difference and inclusion. In R. Shweder, M. Minow, & H. R. Markus (Eds.), *Engaging cultural differences: The multicultural challenge in liberal democracies* (pp. 365–395). New York, NY: Russell Sage Foundation.

Purdie-Vaughns, V., & Eibach, R. P. (2008). Intersectional invisibility: The distinctive advantages and disadvantages of multiple subordinate-group identities. *Sex Roles, 59*(5–6), 377–391. doi:10.1007/s11199-008-9424-4

Purdie-Vaughns, V., Steele, C. M., Davies, P. G., Ditlmann, R., & Crosby, J. R. (2008). Social identity contingencies: How diversity cues signal threat or safety for African Americans in mainstream institutions. *Journal of Personality and Social Psychology, 94*, 615–630. doi:10.1037/0022-3514.94.4.615

Roediger, D. (2005). What's wrong with these pictures? Race, narratives of admission, and the liberal self-representations of historically white colleges and universities. *Journal of Law and Policy, 18*, 203–222.

Ryan, C. S., Hunt, J. S., Weible, J. A., Peterson, C. R., & Casas, J. F. (2007). Multicultural and colorblind ideology, stereotypes, and ethnocentrism among Black and White Americans. *Group Processes & Intergroup Relations, 10*, 617–637. doi:10.1177/1368430207084105

Sedlovskaya, A., & Purdie-Vaughns, V. (2009). *Social intimacy cues and identity threat among people with concealable stigmas*. Manuscript submitted for publication.

Steele, C. M. (1997). A threat in the air: How stereotypes shape intellectual identity and performance. *American Psychologist, 52*, 613–629. doi:10.1037/0003-066X.52.6.613

Steele, C. M., Spencer, S., & Aronson, J. (2002). Contending with images of one's group: The psychology of stereotype and social identity threat. *Advances in Experimental Social Psychology, 34*, 379–440. doi:10.1016/S0065-2601(02)80009-0

Stevens, F. G., Plaut, V. C., & Sanchez-Burks, J. (2008). Unlocking the benefits of diversity: All-inclusive multiculturalism and positive organizational change. *Journal of Applied Behavioral Science, 44*(1), 116–133. doi:10.1177/0021886308314460

Thomas, D. A., & Kanji, A. (2004). IBM's diversity strategy: Bridging the workplace and the marketplace. *Harvard Business School Case 405-044*. Boston, MA: Harvard Business School.

Tropp, L. R., & Bianchi, R. A. (2006). Valuing diversity and interest in intergroup contact. *Journal of Social Issues, 62*, 533–551. doi:10.1111/j.1540-4560.2006.00472.x

Verkuyten, M. (2005). Ethnic group identification and group evaluation among minority and majority groups: Testing the multiculturalism hypothesis. *Journal of Personality and Social Psychology, 88*, 121–138. doi:10.1037/0022-3514.88.1.121

Verkuyten, M., & Martinovic, B. (2006). Understanding multicultural attitudes: The role of group status, identification, friendships, and justifying ideologies. *International Journal of Intercultural Relations, 30*(1), 1–18. doi:10.1016/j.ijintrel.2005.05.015

Walton, G. M., & Cohen, G. L. (2007). A question of belonging: Race, social fit, and achievement. *Journal of Personality and Social Psychology, 92*, 82–96. doi:10.1037/0022-3514.92.1.82

Wolsko, C., Park, B., Judd, C. M., & Wittenbrink, B. (2000). Framing interethnic ideology: Effects of multicultural and color-blind perspectives on judgments of groups and individuals. *Journal of Personality and Social Psychology, 78*, 635–654. doi:10.1037/0022-3514.78.4.635

IV

APPLICATIONS TO POSTCONFLICT RECONCILIATION

9

ACHIEVING FORGIVENESS AND TRUST IN POSTCONFLICT SOCIETIES: THE IMPORTANCE OF SELF-DISCLOSURE AND EMPATHY

HERMANN SWART, RHIANNON TURNER, MILES HEWSTONE, AND ALBERTO VOCI

You never really understand a person until you consider things from his point of view—until you climb into his skin and walk around in it.
—Atticus Finch in Harper Lee's *To Kill a Mockingbird*

Outgroups often continue to elicit negative cognitive, affective, and/or behavioral reactions in postconflict societies, long after the conflict has ended. The challenge of achieving positive intergroup relations and reconciliation within postconflict societies is often typified by the need to encourage outgroup forgiveness and build outgroup trust, over and above mere liking, between groups that were previously in conflict. Positive intergroup contact experiences have been consistently associated with reduced prejudice (for reviews, see Brown & Hewstone, 2005; Pettigrew & Tropp, 2006). The evidence is encouraging in that it suggests that intergroup contact—specifically, cross-group friendship—is capable of simultaneously reducing the negative factors associated with outgroup prejudice and augmenting the positive factors associated with more positive intergroup relations (Pettigrew, 1997, 1998).

In this chapter, we consider the importance of self-disclosure and empathy for promoting the development of outgroup forgiveness and trust in postconflict societies. This focus on intergroup forgiveness and trust is deliberate,

We acknowledge the support of the Rhodes Trust, which funded Hermann Swart's doctoral studies at Oxford University, Oxford, England, during which much of the research reported here was undertaken.

acknowledging that each embodies a distinctly more positive orientation between groups in postconflict societies than does mere tolerance. Our emphasis on two positive behaviors and experiences that could be encouraged to promote these positive outcomes deviates from the more traditional preoccupation with specifying what negative intergroup behaviors should be limited, reduced, or inhibited to minimize group-based prejudice. We discuss self-disclosure, empathy, forgiveness, and trust in the context of cross-group friendships, although we do not intend to focus on the role of friendships per se in promoting positive intergroup relations (see Davies, Wright, & Aron; Page-Gould & Mendoza-Denton, this volume).

Most, but not all, of the research that we present in this chapter was undertaken in the postconflict societies of Northern Ireland and South Africa. Notwithstanding some important differences, these two contexts share notable parallels to each other and to other postconflict societies around the world, including persistent segregation, a lack of cross-group friendships, and generally negative outgroup attitudes (e.g., Gibson, 2004; Hofmeyr, 2006; Hughes & Donnelly, 2001; Robinson, 2003; Turner et al., 2010). We use our research in these two postconflict societies to illustrate and discuss the importance of positive intergroup contact and the roles of outgroup forgiveness and trust for fostering positive intergroup relations within postconflict societies in general.

Below, we discuss the importance of reciprocal self-disclosure and empathy for promoting positive intergroup relations in postconflict societies, specifically outgroup forgiveness and trust. In our discussion on empathy, we distinguish between cognitive empathic responding, in the form of perspective taking, and affective empathic responding, in the form of affective empathy (Duan & Hill, 1996). This is followed by a closer look at two particular contact outcomes associated with more positive intergroup relations, namely, outgroup forgiveness and outgroup trust. We then discuss some policy implications of our research and conclude with some suggestions for future research. First, we take a brief look at the context within which the operation of reciprocal self-disclosure and empathy will be discussed, namely, that of cross-group friendships (for a detailed discussion of the role of friendships in promoting positive intergroup relations, see Davies et al.; Page-Gould & Mendoza-Denton, this volume).

CROSS-GROUP FRIENDSHIPS AND POSITIVE INTERGROUP RELATIONS

Although the focus on cross-group friendship as a potent dimension of intergroup contact is relatively recent (e.g., Pettigrew, 1997, 1998; Pettigrew & Tropp, 2006; Turner, Hewstone, Voci, Paolini, & Christ, 2007), creating contact that is "intimate" or has "acquaintance potential" has long been recognized as a means of generating positive intergroup relations (e.g., Allport, 1954; Amir, 1969). The efficacy of this form of intergroup contact was confirmed by Pettigrew and Tropp's (2006) meta-analysis, which reported a significantly stronger negative mean relationship between intergroup contact and outgroup prejudice in the 154 tests that included cross-group friendships as the measure of contact (mean $r = -.25$) than in the 1,211 tests that did not (mean $r = -.21$). This significant difference in the effects of these two types of contact on prejudice may be largely attributed to the fact that cross-group friendships generally embody greater *quality* of contact than casual, intergroup contact experiences (e.g., Allport, 1954; Pettigrew, 1997, 1998). Thus, cross-group friendships provide a powerful context within which the important processes of reciprocal self-disclosure and empathy might operate.

Cross-group friendships are generally considered to involve three of Allport's (1954) optimal contact conditions: equal status, common interests and goals, and cooperation. Such contact generally occurs over an extended period of time, involving frequent high-quality contacts (Pettigrew, 1997, 1998; Pettigrew & Tropp, 2006), serving as a particularly positive form of intergroup contact that by its very nature encourages more positive interactions with members of the outgroup. Pettigrew (1998) suggested four mechanisms that drive the relationship between cross-group friendships and positive intergroup relations: increased learning about the outgroup; reappraisal of ingroup norms relating to intergroup contacts; change in behavior toward other outgroup members in general; and the generation of affective ties within the dyadic relationship, which include both the reduction of negative affect and the augmentation of positive affect.

Meta-analytic evidence suggests that the benefits of positive intergroup contact experiences are capable of extending from the outgroup exemplar to the outgroup as a whole, and also to other outgroups not involved in the original contact setting (Pettigrew & Tropp, 2006). Furthermore, ingroup members who witness or become aware of such positive interactions between a fellow ingroup member and an outgroup friend are likely to develop more positive attitudes toward the outgroup in general and toward ingroup–outgroup relations in particular, an effect known as the *extended contact effect* (e.g., Turner, Hewstone, Voci, & Vonofakou, 2008; Wright, Aron, McLaughlin-Volpe, & Ropp, 1997). Cross-group friendships, therefore, not only encourage more positive intergroup relations in a direct manner among those ingroup members with outgroup friends but also likely encourage more positive intergroup relations in an indirect manner via the extended contact effect.

An additional benefit of cross-group friendships for positive intergroup relations is that individuals with outgroup friends from one outgroup generally also have outgroup friends from other outgroups (e.g., Levin, Van Laar, & Sidanius, 2003; Pettigrew, 1997). This apparent generalized positive orientation toward outgroups that is associated with having outgroup friends may be the result of selection bias, whereby less prejudiced individuals are more likely to have outgroup friends from a range of outgroups. And while this causal pathway from low prejudice to cross-group friendships certainly operates in some instances, there is overwhelming evidence in the contact literature in support of the causal pathway from cross-group friendships to reduced prejudice (see Pettigrew & Tropp, 2006). We recently undertook a three-wave longitudinal study within the postconflict society of South Africa (Swart, Hewstone, Christ, & Voci, 2010a), the results of which illustrate the value of cross-group friendships as a context within which to explore the promotion of positive intergroup relations. To appreciate the significance of this study, it is necessary to provide a brief overview of intergroup relations in South Africa.

The South African population has traditionally been divided into four broad (and often contested) categories: White, Black (African), Colored (of mixed racial heritage), and Indian (of Asian descent). The country's history is dominated by accounts of intergroup conflict (no more so than that of the 40 years of legislated racial discrimination and racial segregation—a period known as Apartheid—that ended in 1990). Since the advent of democratic rule in South Africa in 1994, the political power has shifted from White South Africans to Black South Africans, although White South Africans continue to enjoy a socioeconomic advantage over Black and Colored South Africans. The traditionally intermediate, or marginalized, status of Colored South Africans has remained relatively unchanged, and they continue to occupy an arguably lower group status than that of majority-status White South Africans. Despite complete desegregation, intergroup contact remains limited in South Africa, and such contact is often characterized by a sense of discomfort and mistrust (e.g., Durrheim & Dixon, 2005; Gibson, 2004).

In our three-wave longitudinal study, we explored the mediators between cross-group friendships and positive outgroup attitudes, perceptions of outgroup variability, and negative behavioral action tendencies—the desire to engage in negative behaviors against the outgroup (Wright et al., 1997)— as affective, cognitive, and behavioral outcomes of prejudice (Swart et al., 2010a). We considered two potential affective mediators: *intergroup anxiety*, which is the anxiety that may be experienced when anticipating future intergroup encounters (Stephan & Stephan, 1985), and *affective empathy*, which is the affective component of the broad empathic response (Duan & Hill, 1996). We collected three waves of survey data over a 12-month period from Colored South African high school students between 14 and 16 years old ($N = 465$). Cross-group friendships with White South Africans at Time 1 were negatively associated with intergroup anxiety and positively associated with affective empathy at Time 2. Intergroup anxiety at Time 2 was negatively associated with perceived outgroup variability at Time 3.

Affective empathy was positively associated with positive outgroup attitudes and perceived outgroup variability and negatively associated with negative behavioral action tendencies at Time 3. In other words, these findings suggest (among other things) that those participants who had White South African friends were more likely to experience empathy toward White South Africans and were more likely to develop positive outgroup attitudes toward White South Africans in general over time.

In summary, cross-group friendships offer an important context within which to explore the positive processes that promote more constructive, positive intergroup relations in postconflict societies. That said, we recognize that developing cross-group friendships in these societies is particularly challenging. One reason for this is that the pervasive segregation that is a common feature of postconflict societies limits opportunities for the positive intergroup contact experiences that would stimulate friendship development. Opportunity for contact with the outgroup is positively associated with cross-group friendship development and is essentially a prerequisite for it (e.g., Turner et al., 2007; Wagner, van Dick, Pettigrew, & Christ, 2003).

RECIPROCAL SELF-DISCLOSURE

We now turn our attention toward reciprocal self-disclosure as an important mechanism operating in close, high-quality interpersonal relationships. *Self-disclosure* is the voluntary presentation of intimate or personal information to another person (Miller, 2002). As an important aspect of interpersonal relationships, facilitating mutual trust (Petty & Mirels, 1981), and the development of personalized relationships, self-disclosure is considered a friendship-developing mechanism (Pettigrew, 1997, 1998). Self-disclosures made early on in the development of any interpersonal relationship (be they across groups or not) are generally characterized by content that relates more to the self as an individual. Within cross-group friendships in particular, these predominantly personalized self-disclosures may develop over time as the emotional and psychological bonds between friends strengthen, so that they come to include more group-related content, in which thoughts and attitudes about group differences or intergroup relations are shared. In this way, reciprocal self-disclosure allows for the acquisition of knowledge about the outgroup and the sharing of knowledge about the ingroup. It also facilitates a more in-depth understanding of the outgroup through increased perspective taking and subsequent feelings of empathy for the outgroup, both of which are important for the development of positive intergroup relations.

Self-disclosure provides individuals with the means of controlling how others see them; through self-disclosure they are able to communicate to others how they see and understand themselves and the world around them. Often, such self-disclosures reveal previously unknown similarities between individuals, heightening interpersonal attraction and increasing the perceived self–other overlap between individuals (Aron, Aron, & Smollan, 1992; Aron et al., 2004). Aron et al. (1992) showed that individuals spontaneously feel a close self–other overlap with individuals they consider to be close to them, such as friends and family. As the self expands to include the other, thoughts about the other become more selflike (Aron & McLaughlin-Volpe, 2001; see also Davies et al., this volume). Being the recipient of the self-disclosures of another not only increases the interpersonal attraction felt toward the self-discloser, but it also increases the likelihood of reciprocating this self-disclosure (Berg & Wright-Buckley, 1988). Within the context of high-quality intergroup contacts, self-disclosure similarly plays a central role in the development of close, cross-group interpersonal relationships such as friendships (Pettigrew, 1998).

When ingroup and outgroup members interact with one another and engage in reciprocal self-disclosure, it provides an opportunity for increased learning about, and understanding for, the respective outgroup member and the outgroup culture. Thus, in the same way that self-disclosure gives individuals control over how others see them on an interpersonal level, it also gives them control over how others view them as an outgroup member and how others view the outgroup as a whole. With increased interpersonal attraction and self–other overlap between cross-group friends, the outgroup friend becomes viewed as more similar to the self (Aron & McLaughlin-Volpe, 2001), accompanied by an increase in the affection felt toward the outgroup friend and an increased appreciation for the well-being of the outgroup friend (Batson et al., 1997; Batson, Turk, Shaw, & Klein, 1995; Finlay & Stephan, 2000). The self–other overlap experienced with the outgroup friend eventually extends to include a self–other overlap with the outgroup as a whole (Aron & McLaughlin-Volpe, 2001). Thus, attitudes held toward the outgroup become more positive, including increased trustworthiness and a greater willingness to cooperate with the outgroup.

Self-disclosure is also able to improve outgroup attitudes by tapping into the affective components that underlie intergroup relations. Meta-analytic evidence suggests that although outgroup knowledge significantly mediates the negative relationship between intergroup contact and prejudice, affective variables such as the empathic response and intergroup anxiety are more prominent mediators of the contact-prejudice relationship than is outgroup knowledge (Pettigrew & Tropp, 2008). Self-disclosure is capable of both inducing positive affect (or what is referred to as *allophilia*; see Pittinsky, Rosenthal, & Montoya, this volume), such as empathy, and reducing negative affect, such as intergroup anxiety (Turner, Hewstone, & Voci, 2007; Turner, Hewstone, Voci, Paolini, & Christ, 2007).

Turner, Hewstone, and Voci (2007, Study 4) undertook a cross-sectional study among White British undergraduate students ($N = 142$), exploring the relationships among cross-group friendships, self-disclosure with outgroup members, empathy toward the outgroup, and outgroup attitudes. Those participants reporting that they had cross-group friendships with South Asians also reported engaging in more reciprocal self-disclosure with South Asians and experiencing greater empathy toward South Asians. These participants were more likely to value positive intergroup relations with South Asians and were more likely to report having positive attitudes toward South Asians, including trust. This positive relationship between self-disclosure and empathy is not at all surprising, given the preceding discussion of how self-disclosure encourages an increased perception of self–other overlap. As described in the following section, experiencing empathy with another, being able to put oneself into the "shoes' of another individual or "climb into another's skin," can be considered one particular manifestation of the increased self–other overlap found in close interpersonal relationships (Aron et al., 2004).

In summary, then, reciprocal self-disclosure is an important friendship-developing and trust-building mechanism (Pettigrew, 1998). Though such reciprocal self-disclosure may include either individual-level information (i.e., information relating to the individual, such as hobbies and interests), group-level information (i.e., information relating to group customs or history, such as religious festivals or a group's history of being victims of oppression), or both, individual-level reciprocal self-disclosure may be more important in encouraging the development of interpersonal attraction and facilitating trust (Miller, 2002) than group-level self-disclosure. The danger of entering into group-level self-disclosure too early in the initial interactions is that it may evoke negative responses, such as intergroup anxiety, that would lower the perceived quality of the contact experience (Brown & Hewstone, 2005). It is important to bear in mind that self-disclosure not only *builds* trust, it also *requires* trust if the self-disclosures are to reach particularly personal depths such as the volunteering of sensitive, personal information or, of particular relevance to postconflict societies, volunteering group-level disclosures. Reciprocal self-disclosure is instrumental in giving ingroup members an "inside view" into the world of their cross-group friend and the outgroup as a whole, partly through increased outgroup knowledge and, more importantly, through the generation of cognitive and affective empathy, to which we now turn.

EMPATHY

The *empathic response* is one particular positive affective response that typically results from the reciprocal self-disclosure associated with close interpersonal relationships (e.g., Turner, Hewstone, & Voci, 2007). Davis (1994) described the empathic response in both cognitive and affective terms as "the ability to engage in the cognitive process of adopting another's psychological point of view, and the capacity to experience affective reactions to the observed experience of others" (p. 45). Duan and Hill (1996) described the cognitive and affective dimensions of the empathic response as perspective taking and affective empathy, respectively. *Perspective taking* concerns the ability to "see," or cognitively understand, the world from another's point of view. *Affective empathy*, on the other hand, concerns the ability to experience vicariously the affective reaction of another.

These two forms of empathic responding have both been associated with a host of positive outcomes in interpersonal relationships, including more positive evaluative judgments of others, increased situational attributions for the behaviors of others, increased concern for the well-being of others, increased motivation to engage in altruistic behaviors, a sense of injustice or anger in response to discrimination, a common humanity, less stereotyping, and reduced prejudice (e.g., Batson et al., 1995, 1997; Davis, 1994; Finlay & Stephan, 2000; Galinsky & Moskowitz, 2000). These positive outcomes are often capable of lasting well after the initial empathic response has dissipated (Batson et al., 1995) and, important for the prospect of positive intergroup relations, are capable of generalizing from the interpersonal, cross-group friendships to the outgroup as a whole and even to other outgroups not involved in the contact situation (Galinsky & Moskowitz, 2000).

In one of our earliest studies on the importance of empathy in intergroup relations, Voci and Hewstone (2003) undertook in Italy a series of studies in which they explored Italians' attitudes toward immigrants. Across all three studies, including independent samples of Italian adults and Italian factory workers, Voci and Hewstone (2003) found intergroup contact with immigrants to be positively associated with empathy for immigrants, which in turn was positively associated with outgroup attitudes toward immigrants and negatively associated with subtle prejudice against immigrants. Empathy has recently emerged as a significant mediator of the contact–prejudice relationship in postconflict societies such as Northern Ireland (e.g., Myers, Hewstone, & Cairns, 2009b) and South Africa (e.g., Swart et al., 2010a; Swart, Hewstone, Christ, & Voci, 2010b).

Batson et al. (1997) suggested that perspective taking and affective empathy can be related to one another in a three-step model describing how empathic responding might improve outgroup attitudes. In the first step, the ingroup friend imagines how the outgroup friend is affected by his or her situation, gaining some perspective on how the outgroup friend experiences the world by putting on the outgroup friend's "shoes," so to speak. This first step might be prompted during or after receiving self-disclosed information from the outgroup friend. This cognitive empathic response, or perspective taking, then results in an affective empathic response (Batson et al., 1997).

In the second step, this affective empathic response is followed by an increased valuing of the well-being of the outgroup friend. This may be due to an increase in perceived self–other overlap (Aron et al., 1992, 2004; Aron & McLaughlin-Volpe, 2001). The increased sense of similarity or overlap between the in- and outgroup friend encourages the thoughts related to the outgroup friend to become more self-like, increasing perspective taking (Galinsky & Moskowitz, 2000). In the process, a greater number of attributes used to describe the self or the ingroup are attributed to the outgroup friend (Aron & McLaughlin-Volpe, 2001; Brown & Hewstone, 2005). Thus, the benefits usually reserved for the ingroup and the self are now extended to the outgroup friend. These benefits include an increased complexity with which the outgroup friend is viewed as an individual, given that the self is generally considered to be multifaceted and complex (Davis, 1994; Miller, 2002), increased trust of the outgroup friend (e.g., Turner, Hewstone, & Voci, 2007), and a greater concern for the well-being of the outgroup friend (Aron & McLaughlin-Volpe, 2001; Batson et al., 1997).

In the third step of Batson et al.'s (1997) model, the heightened valuing of the well-being of the outgroup friend generalizes to the entire outgroup. Furthermore, the ingroup friend develops a more complex view of the outgroup as a whole, perceiving the outgroup in a more complex manner, such as comprising many varied and complex individuals. This inhibits the reliance on stereotypes for processing group-related information (Aron & McLaughlin-Volpe, 2001; see also Aberson & Haag, 2007). As the outgroup is viewed and understood in more empathic, human terms, it should generate a greater willingness among the ingroup to forgive the outgroup for the wrongs of the past (see Hewstone et al., in press).

TOWARD POSITIVE INTERGROUP RELATIONS: FORGIVENESS AND TRUST

In the preceding sections, we have discussed the importance of two positive processes, reciprocal self-disclosure and empathy, that operate within the context of cross-group friendships and are capable of improving intergroup relations. We now turn to two particular outcomes of positive intergroup contact associated with more positive intergroup relations: outgroup forgiveness and outgroup trust. We also highlight some of our most recent research undertaken in Northern Ireland and South Africa, exploring how intergroup contact might encourage both outgroup forgiveness and outgroup trust in postconflict societies.

Forgiveness

Memories of past events and conflicts often endure into the present in the collective memory of both victims and perpetrators living in postconflict societies, and such memories play an important role in fueling existing conflicts or rekindling old conflicts (Cairns & Roe, 2003). Cycles of aggression and revenge play a central role in the enduring nature of intergroup conflict (Nadler & Saguy, 2004), partly because the experience of victimization limits the willingness of individuals to forgive the perceived perpetrators for past wrongs (see Hewstone, Cairns, Voci, Hamberger, & Niens, 2006; Hewstone et al., 2004). Forgiveness offers one means through which these cycles may be broken (Nadler & Saguy, 2004) in that it allows victims and perpetrators to assimilate the past in a manner that does not provoke further violence (Boleyn-Fitzgerald, 2002; Hewstone et al., in press; see also Nadler & Shnabel, this volume).

Conceptualizations of forgiveness in the psychological literature include the release of anger (Boleyn-Fitzgerald, 2002) and the giving up of the right to revenge (Cloke, 1993). Definitions such as these have been corroborated in exploratory research using focus groups in conflict settings such as Northern Ireland (McLernon, Cairns, & Hewstone, 2002). The concept of intergroup forgiveness is gaining momentum as an essential psychological aspect of intergroup reconciliation in postconflict societies, stimulating the recent research on intergroup forgiveness in Northern Ireland (e.g., Hewstone et al., 2006; McLernon et al., 2002) and South Africa (e.g., Gibson & Gouws, 1999; Swart, Dixon, & Kagee, 2009). While forgiveness will not solve intergroup conflict in and of itself, at the very least it provides an opportunity for postconflict reconciliation (Hewstone et al., in press). It offers postconflict societies hope for the future as it orients groups toward a shared future, as opposed to continuously recycling the past in the form of reprisals and counter-reprisals. This, in turn, holds distinct benefits in the form of improved mental health within postconflict societies. Recent evidence from Northern Ireland suggests that group-level forgiveness is negatively associated with the development of mild psychiatric conditions (Myers, Hewstone, & Cairns, 2009a). Unfortunately, forgiveness, as a complex prosocial transformation that can be powerfully healing, reconciling, and future-oriented, is volitional and cannot be prescribed or forced (Hewstone et al., in press). To do so would in all likelihood add to the cycle of violence rather than diminish it. One intervention that is considered capable of encouraging an increased willingness to forgive the outgroup is positive intergroup contact.

Positive intergroup contact experiences, particularly those that encourage the development of cross-group friendships (Pettigrew, 1997, 1998), have been shown to predict a greater willingness to forgive the outgroup (e.g., Swart et al., 2009; Tam et al., 2007). From our most recent survey research with college students, representative national samples, and opportunity community samples among Protestants and Catholics in Northern Ireland (e.g., Myers, Hewstone, & Cairns, 2009b) and among Black South Africans (Swart et al., 2009), the relationship between intergroup contact and outgroup forgiveness appears to be mediated by an increase in perspective taking (Myers et al., 2009b) and affective empathy (Swart et al., 2009) toward the outgroup. Myers et al. (2009b) explored the simultaneous effects of perspective taking and affective empathy as mediators of the relationship between cross-group friendships and outgroup forgiveness and outgroup trust. Cross-group friendships were positively associated with both perspective taking and affective empathy, which in turn were positively associated with outgroup forgiveness and outgroup trust.

A number of other important findings related to the relationship between intergroup contact and outgroup forgiveness have also emerged from our research program. Space limitations permit mention of only some of these, briefly, but for more details see Hewstone et al. (2004, 2006, in press), Myers et al. (2009a), and Tam et al. (2007). Important correlates of outgroup forgiveness include (a) reduced anger-related emotions, (b) collective guilt, and (c) outgroup trust. Thus, a willingness to forgive the outgroup is an important step in overcoming some of the psychological barriers toward positive intergroup relations discussed in Butz and Plant (this volume). Conversely, greater ingroup identification and infrahumanization of the outgroup (see Leyens et al., 2000) discourage outgroup forgiveness.

Together, these studies highlight the mechanisms that discourage outgroup forgiveness, namely, negative emotions, strong ingroup identification, and infrahumanizing the outgroup. However, they also support the importance of positive intergroup contact experiences as a means of mitigating these limiting factors and augmenting those positive mechanisms that encourage outgroup forgiveness and reconciliation, such as perspective taking and affective empathy. Outgroup forgiveness has also been associated with another indicator of positive intergroup relations, namely, outgroup trust (Hewstone et al., 2004, 2006), to which we now turn.

Trust

Mutual trust is an essential ingredient of any interpersonal relationship. Such mutual trust is often gradually established as the intimacy and self–other overlap between individuals increases (Aron & McLaughlin-Volpe, 2001; Davies et al., this volume). As proposed by self-expansion theory, ingroup members who exhibit strong ingroup identification share a close self–other overlap with fellow ingroup members, often resulting in ingroup bias (Aron & McLaughlin-Volpe, 2001). One of the ways in which this ingroup bias is expressed is the perception of fellow ingroup members as trustworthy and outgroup members as untrustworthy.

Distrust often plays a central role in maintaining intergroup conflict (Dovidio, Gaertner, Kawakami, & Hodson, 2002). Establishing outgroup trust therefore forms an essential part of strategies and policies aimed not only at deescalating intergroup conflict but also at developing positive intergroup relations once the conflict has passed. Outgroup trust can be defined as a positive expectation about the intentions and behavior of an outgroup toward the ingroup (Lewicki, McAllister, & Bies, 1998) and is accompanied by the implicit expectation that this vulnerability to the intentions of the outgroup will not be abused or exploited by the outgroup (Dovidio et al., 2002). Given that outgroup trust requires ingroup members to make themselves vulnerable to the intentions of the outgroup, while outgroup attitudes do not, outgroup trust might be regarded as distinct from one's outgroup attitudes (Tam, Hewstone, Kenworthy, & Cairns, 2009) and far more difficult to achieve than outgroup liking (Hewstone et al., 2008).

One particular reason why outgroup trust may be more difficult to achieve than outgroup liking is that more effort is often required to establish trust than is required to destroy it. Where it may require multiple positive encounters, or "trustworthy" behaviors, to build trust, it often requires only one "untrustworthy" act or betrayal to arouse distrust that is very resistant to change (Rothbart & Park, 1986). For this reason, the outgroup distrust stemming from a history of intergroup conflict often remains evident in postconflict societies long after the conflict itself has ended (e.g., Gibson, 2004).

Successfully establishing outgroup trust holds numerous benefits for intergroup relations. Trust is generally associated with the facilitation of a number of mutually beneficial outcomes (see Kramer & Carnevale, 2001). Creating and maintaining mutual trust is essential for the establishment of positive intergroup relations because, as a process, trust building is capable of replacing suspicion, fear, and anger with benevolence and cooperation (Lewicki & Wiethoff, 2000). It might be appropriate here to distinguish briefly between two forms of trust described by Lewicki and Wiethoff, namely, *calculus-based trust* and *identification-based trust*. Calculus-based trust is generally nonintimate and task-oriented, whereas identification-based trust is often more intimate in nature, relying on a greater understanding and appreciation of the two parties' needs. Calculus-based trust is often witnessed in the early stages of intimate, personal relationships, whereas identification-based trust comes to the fore in relationships characterized by greater closeness.

Promoting mutual trust within postconflict societies requires that the parties involved engage in the psychological process of reconciliation (Tam et al., 2008). Intergroup contact may provide a means for achieving this (Hewstone et al., 2008; see also Tropp, 2008). As discussed earlier, the development of cross-group friendships is facilitated by reciprocal self-disclosure, perspective taking, and affective empathy. Self-disclosure, as the voluntary sharing of personal information, by its very nature requires a certain degree of trust in the person with whom this personal information is being shared (Petty & Mirels, 1981). While initial self-disclosures between individuals who are only beginning to get to know one another are bound to be relatively superficial, requiring minimal trust, these self-disclosures will become more intimate as the interpersonal relationship develops, requiring increasingly more trust. These self-disclosures allow group members to predict the future behavior of others, which is an important ingredient for the building of trust (Kerr, Stattin, & Trost, 1999)—specifically, identification-based trust (Lewicki & Wiethoff, 2000)—and encourages more positive outgroup attitudes. As will be recalled from our earlier discussion on self-disclosure, Turner, Hewstone, and Voci, (2007, Study 4) found that outgroup trust played an important role in mediating the relationship between self-disclosure in cross-group friendships and positive outgroup attitudes among White British undergraduate students and their interactions with South Asians in Britain.

In Northern Ireland, our recent research on outgroup trust among Protestants and Catholics has provided strong evidence that (a) both direct and indirect intergroup contact are positively associated with outgroup trust (e.g., Myers et al., 2009b; Tam et al., 2009), (b) affective empathy and perspective taking are important mediators of the relationship between cross-group friendships and outgroup trust (e.g., Myers et al., 2009b), and (c) outgroup trust is positively associated with positive behavioral action tendencies toward the outgroup (e.g., Tam et al., 2009). Furthermore, Tam et al. (2009) found that outgroup trust mediated the relationship between direct and extended intergroup contact and behavioral action tendencies toward the outgroup, while outgroup attitudes only marginally mediated direct contact effects and failed to mediate extended contact effects. These results suggest that building outgroup trust may be more important for the achievement of positive intergroup relations than simply pursuing outgroup liking.

Factors that discourage outgroup trust include strong ingroup identification (Myers et al., 2009b) and intergroup anxiety. Swart and Hewstone (2009) undertook a cross-sectional study among White and Colored South African high school students, exploring the relationship between cross-group friendships, intergroup anxiety, and outgroup trust. Cross-group friendships were positively associated with outgroup trust, and this relationship was mediated by a reduction in intergroup anxiety. Thus, cross-group friendships were associated with reduced intergroup anxiety, which in turn was associated with outgroup trust.

Moving from calculus-based trust toward identification-based trust in postconflict societies is important for encouraging positive intergroup relations. It allows suspicion and distrust of the outgroup, which is often characterized by self-imposed segregation or negative behaviors toward the outgroup, to be replaced with a greater willingness to engage with the outgroup in a cooperative, constructive manner (Kramer & Carnevale, 2001; Lewicki & Wiethoff, 2000). Frequent high-quality intergroup contacts have the potential to encourage outgroup trust through both self-disclosure and cognitive and affective empathy for the outgroup. It is, however, important to acknowledge that at this stage of our research program, the cross-sectional nature of most of the data we have presented here prevents us from drawing unequivocal causal conclusions about the nature of the various interrelationships we have described. So, for example, while the data support our hypothesis that positive intergroup contact promotes outgroup trust, it is also likely that greater outgroup trust will encourage greater intergroup contact. Longitudinal data are needed to better explore these causal relationships.

POLICY IMPLICATIONS

As we have described, positive intergroup contact experiences are capable of bringing about more than just prejudice reduction; such experiences often encourage greater outgroup forgiveness and assist in building outgroup trust. Here, cross-group friendships may play a particularly important role, especially as they have been shown to encourage greater reciprocal self-disclosure, perspective taking, and affective empathy. Unfortunately, however, it is often the case that postconflict societies remain characterized by continued segregation, where cross-group friendships are the exception rather than the rule.

Initiatives and policies aimed at fostering more positive intergroup relations should pay particular attention to creating more opportunities for regular, high-quality contacts that possess acquaintance potential. In time such high-quality contacts will encourage the development of cross-group friendships (Davies et al., this volume). These contact-driven intergroup initiatives should be structured so as to encourage reciprocal self-disclosure, as this has been associated with increased perspective taking and affective empathy. Together, high-quality intergroup contact experiences that encourage the development of cross-group acquaintances and friendships, reciprocal self-disclosure, and increased empathic responding to the outgroup member and the outgroup as a whole should encourage greater outgroup forgiveness and outgroup trust. This is suggested by our research findings reported above. It is important to emphasize that these benefits are unlikely to result from single, isolated contact experiences. Instead, multiple, varied opportunities for positive contact experiences should be created that will encourage outgroup forgiveness and build outgroup trust.

CONCLUSION

The absence of outgroup forgiveness and the presence of outgroup distrust often characterize intergroup relations in postconflict societies. Achieving forgiveness and trust within postconflict societies is made all the more challenging in the face of continued segregation and a lack of cross-group relationships common in these societies. Intergroup contact serves as one means of encouraging positive intergroup relations. Positive intergroup contact experiences have consistently been associated with a reduction in outgroup prejudice (Pettigrew & Tropp, 2006). Furthermore, our recent survey research in real-world postconflict settings provides strong support for the efficacy of intergroup contact in increasing outgroup forgiveness and building outgroup trust.

We have found that both direct intergroup contact and extended intergroup contact are associated with indicators of positive intergroup relations (e.g., Swart et al., 2010a, 2010b; Tam et al., 2009; Tausch, Hewstone, Schmid, Cairns, & Hughes, 2009). We have also identified reciprocal self-disclosure, perspective taking, and affective empathy as positive mediators of the relationship between intergroup contact, on the one hand, and outgroup forgiveness and outgroup trust, on the other hand (e.g., Hewstone et al., 2004, 2006; Myers et al., 2009b; Turner, Hewstone, & Voci, 2007).

The identification of these (and other) positive processes that promote the kind of positive intergroup relations that go beyond mere tolerance marks an important shift in the focus of social psychological research in intergroup relations. Findings such as those reported earlier in this chapter could be incorporated within reconciliation initiatives in postconflict societies. So, for example, such initiatives could be built around multiple, varied opportunities for positive intergroup contact experiences that give members of different groups the opportunity to learn and socialize together. These opportunities are essential for encouraging outgroup forgiveness and building outgroup trust. Specifically, such interventions should encourage reciprocal self-disclosure, affective empathy, and perspective taking, while also reducing anxiety about interacting with the outgroup. With this focus, reconciliation initiatives can strive to go beyond achieving tolerance between groups previously in conflict, toward promoting the kind of positive intergroup relations that are characterized by constructive intergroup interactions.

Further research on the positive processes that could encourage more positive intergroup relations in postconflict societies is needed. Although our recent research in Northern Ireland and South Africa has broadened our understanding of the processes underlying the relationship between positive intergroup contact and both outgroup forgiveness and outgroup trust, it comprises mostly cross-sectional survey data. Despite numerous replications and the fact that the findings we presented in this chapter were derived from the best-fitting model that was in each case superior to theoretically plausible alternatives, we recommend that future research explore the causal relationship between intergroup contact, affective and cognitive mediators, and outgroup forgiveness and outgroup trust using both experimental and longitudinal research. Such studies will deepen our understanding of the causal processes that drive the relationship between intergroup contact, outgroup forgiveness, and outgroup trust, and they will increase our confidence in the mediating processes highlighted in this chapter.

REFERENCES

Aberson, C. L., & Haag, S. C. (2007). Contact, perspective taking, and anxiety as predictors of stereotype endorsement, explicit attitudes, and implicit attitudes. *Group Processes & Intergroup Relations, 10,* 179–201. doi:10.1177/1368430207074726

Allport, G. (1954). *The nature of prejudice.* Cambridge, MA: Perseus Books.

Amir, Y. (1969). Contact hypothesis in ethnic relations. *Psychological Bulletin, 71,* 319–342. doi:10.1037/h0027352

Aron, A., Aron, E. N., & Smollan, D. (1992). Inclusion of other in the self scale and the structure of interpersonal closeness. *Journal of Personality and Social Psychology, 63,* 596–612. doi:10.1037/0022-3514.63.4.596

Aron, A., & McLaughlin-Volpe, T. (2001). Including others in the self: Extensions to own and partner's group memberships. In C. Sedikides & M. B. Brewer (Eds.), *Individual self, relational self, collective self* (pp. 89–108). Ann Arbor, MI: Psychology Press.

Aron, A., McLaughlin-Volpe, T., Mashek, D., Lewandowski, G., Wright, S. C., & Aron, E. N. (2004). Including others in the self. *European Review of Social Psychology, 15,* 101–132. doi:10.1080/10463280440000008

Batson, C. D., Polycarpou, M. P., Harmon-Jones, E., Imhoff, H. J., Mitchener, E. C., Bednar, L. L., . . . Highberger, L. (1997). Empathy and attitudes: Can feeling for a member of a stigmatized group improve feelings toward the group? *Journal of Personality and Social Psychology, 72,* 105–118. doi:10.1037/0022-3514.72.1.105

Batson, C. D., Turk, C. L., Shaw, L. L., & Klein, T. R. (1995). Information function of empathic emotion: Learning that we value the other's welfare. *Journal of Personality and Social Psychology, 68,* 300–313. doi:10.1037/0022-3514.68.6.1042

Berg, J. H., & Wright-Buckley, C. (1988). Effects of racial similarity and interviewer intimacy in a peer counseling analogue. *Journal of Counseling Psychology, 35,* 377–384. doi:10.1037/0022-0167.35.4.377

Boleyn-Fitzgerald, P. (2002). What should "forgiveness" mean? *Journal of Value Inquiry, 36,* 483–498. doi:10.1023/A:1021929531830

Brown, R., & Hewstone, M. (2005). An integrative theory of intergroup contact. *Advances in Experimental Social Psychology, 37,* 255–343. doi:10.1016/S0065-2601(05)37005-5

Cairns, E., & Roe, M. (Eds.). (2003). *The role of memory in ethnic conflict.* Basingstoke, England: Palgrave/Macmillan.

Cloke, K. (1993). Revenge, forgiveness and the magic of mediation. *Mediation Quarterly, 11,* 67–78. doi:10.1002/crq.3900110108

Davis, M. H. (1994). *Empathy: A social psychological approach.* Madison, WI: Brown & Benchmark.

Dovidio, J. F., Gaertner, S. L., Kawakami, K., & Hodson, G. (2002). Why can't we just get along? Interpersonal biases and interracial distrust. *Cultural Diversity & Ethnic Minority Psychology, 8,* 88–102. doi:10.1037/1099-9809.8.2.88

Duan, C., & Hill, C. E. (1996). The current state of empathy research. *Journal of Counseling Psychology, 43,* 261–274. doi:10.1037/0022-0167.43.3.261

Durrheim, K., & Dixon, J. (2005). *Racial encounter: The social psychology of contact and desegregation.* London, England: Routledge.

Finlay, K. A., & Stephan, W. G. (2000). Improving intergroup relations: The effects of empathy on racial attitudes. *Journal of Applied Social Psychology, 30,* 1720–1737. doi:10.1111/j.1559-1816.2000.tb02464.x

Galinsky, A. D., & Moskowitz, G. B. (2000). Perspective-taking: Decreasing stereotype expression, stereotype accessibility, and in-group favoritism. *Journal of Personality and Social Psychology, 78,* 708–724. doi:10.1037/0022-3514.78.4.708

Gibson, J. L. (2004). *Overcoming apartheid: Can truth reconcile a divided nation?* New York, NY: Russell Sage Foundation.

Gibson, J. L., & Gouws, A. G. (1999). Truth and reconciliation in South Africa: Attributions of blame and the struggle over apartheid. *American Political Science Review, 93,* 501–517. doi:10.2307/2585571

Hewstone, M., Kenworthy, J. B., Cairns, E., Tausch, N., Hughes, J., Tam, T., . . . & Pinder, C. (2008). Stepping stones to reconciliation in Northern Ireland: Intergroup contact, forgiveness and trust. In A. Nadler, T. Malloy, & J. D. Fisher (Eds.), *The social psychology of inter-group reconciliation* (pp. 199–226). Oxford, England: Oxford University Press. doi:10.1093/acprof:oso/9780195300314.003.0010

Hewstone, M., Cairns, E., Voci, A., Hamberger, J., & Niens, U. (2006). Intergroup contact, forgiveness, and experience of "The Troubles" in Northern Ireland. *Journal of Social Issues, 62,* 99–120. doi:10.1111/j.1540-4560.2006.00441.x

Hewstone, M., Cairns, E., Voci, A., McLernon, F., Niens, U., & Noor, M. (2004). Intergroup forgiveness and guilt in Northern Ireland: Social psychological dimensions of "The Troubles." In N. R. Branscombe & B. Doosje (Eds.), *Collective guilt: International perspectives* (pp. 193–215). Cambridge, England: Cambridge University Press.

Hewstone, M., Maslen, H., Cairns, E., Tam, T., Myers, E., & Lloyd, H. (in press). Intergroup forgiveness and apology: Psychological research and philosophical considerations. In C.A. Lewis, M.B., Rogers, K.M., Loewenthal, R., Amlot, M., Cinnirella, & H. Ansari (Eds.), *Aspects of terrorism and martyrdom: Dying for good, dying for God*. Lampeter, England: Edwin Mellen Press.

Hofmeyr, J. H. (2006). *Report of the sixth round of the South African Reconciliation Barometer Survey*. Retrieved from http://www.ijr.org.za/politicalanalysis/reconcbar/copy_of_sixthroundreportfinal/view

Hughes, J., & Donnelly, C. (2001). *Ten years of social attitudes to community relations in Northern Ireland*. Department of Psychology, University of Ulster, Jordanstown, Ireland. Manuscript in preparation.

Kerr, M., Stattin, H., & Trost, K. (1999). To know you is to trust you: Parents' trust is rooted in child disclosure of information. *Journal of Adolescence, 22,* 737–752. doi:10.1006/jado.1999.0266

Kramer, R. M., & Carnevale, P. J. (2001). Trust and intergroup negotiation. In R. Brown & S. Gaertner (Eds.), *Blackwell handbook of social psychology: Intergroup processes* (pp. 431–450). Malden, MA: Blackwell.

Lee, H. (1960). *To kill a mockingbird*. New York, NY: Lippincott.

Levin, S., Van Laar, C., & Sidanius, J. (2003). The effects of ingroup and outgroup friendships on ethnic attitudes in college: A longitudinal study. *Group Processes & Intergroup Relations, 6,* 76–92. doi:10.1177/1368430203006001013

Lewicki, R. J., McAllister, D. J., & Bies, R. J. (1998). Trust and distrust: New relationships and realities. *Academy of Management Review, 23,* 438–458. doi:10.2307/259288

Lewicki, R. J., & Wiethoff, C. (2000). Trust, trust development, and trust repair. In M. Deutsch & P. T. Coleman (Eds.), *The handbook of conflict resolution: Theory and practice* (pp. 86–107). San Francisco, CA: Jossey-Bass.

Leyens, J.-P., Paladino, P. M., Rodriguez, R. T., Vaes, J., Demoulin, S., Rodriguez, A. P., & Gaunt, R. (2000). The emotional side of prejudice: The attribution of secondary emotions to ingroups and outgroups. *Personality and Social Psychology Review, 4,* 186–197. doi:10.1207/S15327957PSPR0402_06

McLernon, F., Cairns, E., & Hewstone, M. (2002). Views on forgiveness in Northern Ireland. *Peace Review: A Journal of Social Justice, 14,* 285–290.

Miller, N. (2002). Personalization and the promise of contact theory. *Journal of Social Issues, 58,* 387–410. doi:10.1111/1540-4560.00267

Myers, E., Hewstone, M., & Cairns, E. (2009a). Impact of conflict on mental health in Northern Ireland: The mediating role of intergroup forgiveness and collective guilt. *Political Psychology, 30,* 269–290.

Myers, E., Hewstone, M., & Cairns, E. (2009b). *Predictors and mediators of intergroup forgiveness and outgroup trust in Northern Ireland*. Unpublished manuscript. University of Oxford, Oxford, England.

Nadler, A., & Saguy, T. (2004). Reconciliation between nations: Overcoming emotional deterrents to ending conflicts between groups. In H. Langholz & C. E. Stout (Eds.), *The psychology of diplomacy* (pp.29–46). New York, NY: Praeger.

Pettigrew, T. F. (1997). Generalized intergroup contact effects on prejudice. *Personality and Social Psychology Bulletin, 23*, 173–185. doi:10.1177/0146167297232006

Pettigrew, T. F. (1998). Intergroup contact theory. *Annual Review of Psychology, 49*, 65–85. doi:10.1146/annurev.psych.49.1.65

Pettigrew, T. F., & Tropp, L. R. (2006). A meta-analytic test of intergroup contact theory. *Journal of Personality and Social Psychology, 90*, 751–783. doi:10.1037/0022-3514.90.5.751

Pettigrew, T. F., & Tropp, L. R. (2008). How does intergroup contact reduce prejudice? Meta-analytic tests of three mediators. *European Journal of Social Psychology, 38*, 922–934. doi:10.1002/ejsp.504

Petty, R. E., & Mirels, H. L. (1981). Intimacy and scarcity of self-disclosure: Effects on interpersonal attraction for males and females. *Personality and Social Psychology Bulletin, 7*, 493–503. doi:10.1177/014616728173020

Robinson, G. (2003, March 5). *Northern Irish communities drifting apart—UU report.* Retrieved from http://www.ulst.ac.uk/news/releases/2003/725.html

Rothbart, M., & Park, B. (1986). On the confirmability and disconfirmability of trait concepts. *Journal of Personality and Social Psychology, 50*, 131–142. doi:10.1037/0022-3514.50.1.131

Stephan, W. G., & Stephan, C. W. (1985). Intergroup anxiety. *Journal of Social Issues, 41*, 157–175. doi:10.1111/j.1540-4560.1985.tb01134.x

Swart, H., Dixon, D., & Kagee, A. (2010). *Intergroup contact, empathy, and the willingness to forgive White South Africans: A cross-sectional study amongst Black South Africans.* Manuscript in preparation.

Swart, H., & Hewstone, M. (2010). *Intergroup trust in South Africa.* Manuscript in preparation.

Swart, H., Hewstone, M., Christ, O., & Voci, A. (2010a). *Affective mediators of intergroup contact: A longitudinal analysis in South Africa.* Manuscript submitted for publication.

Swart, H., Hewstone, M., Christ, O., & Voci, A. (2010b). The impact of cross-group friendships in South Africa: Affective mediators and multi-group comparisons. *Journal of Social Issues, 66*, 309–333. doi:10.1111/j.1540-4560.2010.01647.x

Tam, T., Hewstone, M., Cairns, E., Tausch, N., Maio, G., & Kenworthy, J. (2007). The impact of intergroup emotions on forgiveness in Northern Ireland. *Group Processes & Intergroup Relations, 10*, 119–136. doi:10.1177/1368430207071345

Tam, T., Hewstone, M., Kenworthy, J., & Cairns, E. (2009). Intergroup trust in Northern Ireland. *Personality and Social Psychology Bulletin, 35*, 45–59. doi:10.1177/0146167208325004

Tam, T., Hewstone, M., Kenworthy, J., Cairns, E., Marinetti, C., Geddes, L., & Parkinson, B. (2008). Postconflict reconciliation: Intergroup forgiveness, trust, and implicit biases in Northern Ireland. *Journal of Social Issues, 64*, 303–320. doi:10.1111/j.1540-4560.2008.00563.x

Tausch, N., Hewstone, M., Schmid, K., Cairns, E., & Hughes, J. (2010). *Exploring the impact of extended contact: Longitudinal impact on direct contact, and moderation by relationship closeness.* Manuscript in preparation.

Tropp, L. R. (2008). The role of trust in intergroup contact: Its significance and implications for improving relations between groups. In U. Wagner, L. R. Tropp, G. Finchilescu, & C. Tredoux (Eds.), *Improving intergroup relations: Building on the legacy of Thomas F. Pettigrew* (pp. 91–106). Malden, MA: Blackwell. doi:10.1002/9781444303117.ch7

Turner, R. N., Hewstone, M., Swart, H., Tam, T., Myers, E., & Tausch, N. (2010). Promoting intergroup trust among adolescents and young adults. In K. Rotenberg (Ed.), *Interpersonal trust during childhood and adolescence* (pp. 295–321). Cambridge, England: Cambridge University Press.

Turner, R. N., Hewstone, M., & Voci, A. (2007). Reducing explicit and implicit outgroup prejudice via direct and extended contact: The mediating role of self-disclosure and intergroup anxiety. *Journal of Personality and Social Psychology, 93,* 369–388. doi:10.1037/0022-3514.93.3.369

Turner, R. N., Hewstone, M., Voci, A., Paolini, S., & Christ, O. (2007). Reducing prejudice via direct and extended cross-group friendship. In W. Stroebe & M. Hewstone (Eds.), *European Review of Social Psychology* (Vol. 18, pp. 212–255). Hove, England: Psychology Press.

Turner, R. N., Hewstone, M., Voci, A., & Vonofakou, C. (2008). A test of the extended intergroup contact hypothesis: The mediating role of intergroup anxiety, perceived ingroup and outgroup norms, and inclusion of the outgroup in the self. *Journal of Personality and Social Psychology, 95,* 843–860. doi:10.1037/a0011434

Voci, A., & Hewstone, M. (2003, August). *Contact and prejudice reduction in the Italian context: The impact of empathy, perspective taking, and group salience.* Paper presented at the meeting of the Society for Experimental Social Psychology, Boston, MA.

Wagner, U., van Dick, R., Pettigrew, T. F., & Christ, O. (2003). Ethnic prejudice in East and West Germany: The explanatory power of intergroup contact. *Group Processes & Intergroup Relations, 6,* 22–36. doi:10.1177/1368430203006001010

Wright, S. C., Aron, A., McLaughlin-Volpe, T., & Ropp, S. A. (1997). The extended contact effect: Knowledge of cross-group friendships and prejudice. *Journal of Personality and Social Psychology, 73,* 73–90. doi:10.1037/0022-3514.73.1.73

10

PROMOTING INTERGROUP RECONCILIATION IN CONFLICTS INVOLVING DIRECT OR STRUCTURAL VIOLENCE: IMPLICATIONS OF THE NEEDS-BASED MODEL

ARIE NADLER AND NURIT SHNABEL

Intergroup conflict has been a dominant theme in social psychology since its emergence as an independent field of study during the first half of the 20th century. The dramatic social upheavals that have occurred since then, such as World War II, the Cold War, and the feminist and civil rights movements, have driven the theoretical and research concerns in this field. Primary among these have been attempts to identify the roots of intergroup conflicts and find ways to resolve them (Jones, 1998). For the most part, this research focused on the reduction of negative intergroup phenomena such as violent conflict, prejudice, and discrimination. In recent years, however, there has been a growing awareness—manifested in the present volume—that just as the prevention of illness is not equal to the promotion of good health, the reduction of "negative" phenomena in intergroup relations is not equal to the promotion of positive phenomena. Consistent with this understanding, this chapter presents a social psychological perspective on reconciliation, which requires "healing" impaired intergroup relations (Staub, Pearlman, Gubin, & Hagengimana, 2005) and thus goes beyond conflict settlement and conflict resolution, which focus on the cessation of conflict (see Kelman, 2008). The chapter addresses reconciliation processes between adversarial groups in two different kinds of intergroup conflicts: those involving direct violence and those involving structural violence.

THE STUDY OF INTERGROUP CONFLICT IN CONTEXTS OF DIRECT AND STRUCTURAL VIOLENCE: TWO SOCIAL PSYCHOLOGICAL TRADITIONS

In an influential distinction, Galtung differentiated between conflicts characterized by *direct violence* and those characterized by *structural violence* (1969). Conflicts of direct violence involve episodic, intentional, and explicit acts of aggression by members of rival groups. Death, destruction, and extreme humiliation typify such disputes, of which open war is a pinnacle example. In conflicts that involve structural violence, injury to the outgroup takes the form of prejudice, discrimination, and social disadvantage. Structural violence is committed via the manner in which social institutions are arranged, rather than by the deliberate actions of particular group members (Christie, Tint, Wagner, & Winter, 2008). For example, development decisions that make residents of poor areas vulnerable to environmental hazards or workplace policies that penalize employees for time spent caring for their family members may exemplify structural violence because they cause disproportionate harm to minorities or women.

Although not explicitly stated, the distinction between direct and structural violence has steered two traditions in the social psychological study of intergroup conflict. The first research tradition, which has focused on overt violence, employs cases of extreme intergroup aggression to assess and refine the social psychological understanding of group conflict. These include contexts such as the Rwandan genocide (e.g., Staub, 2008), the Balkan wars (e.g., Čehajić, Brown, & Castano, 2008) and the conflict in the Middle East (e.g., Kelman, 1999). The second tradition, which has focused on structural violence, has been conceptualized and carried out mainly in North America, a world region characterized by entrenched structural violence but where direct intergroup violence is now relatively rare. This research tradition is embodied in copious social research on racism and sexism and ways to reduce them (Fiske, 1998).

Despite the distinction between these two research traditions in the forms of social harm they probe, both have recently undergone a similar shift in theoretical emphasis, reflected in the present volume. Rather than attending mainly to the *prevention* of aggression between groups (e.g., by reducing violence or prejudice), there is a growing interest in *promoting* positive forms of group contact and relations, such as forgiveness (e.g., Philpot & Hornsey, 2008) and allophilia—positive attitudes toward groups other than one's own (e.g., Pittinsky, Rosenthal, & Montoya, this volume). The growing interest in reconciliation—a concept that has only recently entered the scientific discourse (Nadler, Malloy, & Fisher, 2008; Rouhana, 2004)—is part of this trend because, as mentioned, it relates to healing relations between former adversaries rather than merely hastening the cessation of violence. Thus, in addition to the absence of prejudice or discrimination, a reconciled social reality is characterized by positive intergroup phenomena such as mutual respect and an appreciation of the positive qualities of each group and its contribution to society as a whole.

In this chapter, we discuss the meaning of reconciliation and reasons for current interest in this concept. Although the notion of reconciliation has grown out of the research tradition that focuses on direct violence, it is also applicable to contexts of structural violence. Thus, for the sake of simplicity and parsimony, we use the term *reconciliation* in relation to both contexts. We then present the needs-based model of reconciliation, which has guided our own work in the area, and describe studies supporting this model in contexts of direct and structural violence. We conclude by discussing the implications of our approach and highlighting issues that remain to be addressed.

RECONCILIATION AND ITS INSTRUMENTAL AND SOCIOEMOTIONAL ROUTES

For several decades, scientific discourse on conflict and its resolution has been dominated by the so-called realist approach (Scheff, 1994), which views conflict essentially as the outcome of disputes between parties over scarce resources and conflict resolution as the achievement of an agreed formula for dividing such resources (e.g., Campbell, 1965). In contrast, the reconciliation approach views conflict resolution more holistically, as a process of dismantling the residual emotional barriers that remain from conflict (e.g., feelings of victimhood and guilt), so as to foster more harmonious relations (Nadler et al., 2008). If these barriers continue to exist, they will make agreement on the division of resources more difficult. Moreover, even if such an agreement had been reached, as long as these barriers had not been dismantled the conflict may flare up again.

The growing interest in reconciliation within social psychology can be traced to developments both outside and within the field. Within the larger societal context, there is a growing awareness of the need to address the emotional consequences of conflict. This awareness has found expression in the establishment of truth commissions in different postconflict regions, such as South Africa and Guatemala (Hughes, Scabas, & Thakur, 2007), and in public apologies by national and community leaders seeking to heal intergroup relations through expressing regret for the pain and suffering inflicted by their group in the past (Blatz, Schumann, & Ross, 2009). Examples of these apologies are Pope John Paul's apology in 2000 to the Jewish people for the role of the Catholic Church in 2 millennia of anti-Semitic persecution and Tony Blair's 2006 expression of sorrow for the role of Britain in the slave trade during the 17th and 18th centuries.

Within our field, recent work has documented how the emotional consequences of intergroup aggression, such as trauma and humiliation, may inhibit the resolution of conflicts or ignite their reemergence after their seeming close (e.g., Lindner, 2006). This research is consistent with the observation that the emotional consequences of conflict continue to influence intergroup relations long after open violence has abated (e.g., Scheper-Hughes & Bourgois, 2004). Moreover, the shift from a view of conflict resolution as synonymous with resource reallocation to an emphasis on the emotional consequences of conflict is compatible with the growing attention to emotional constructs in social psychological research and theory on intergroup relations (e.g., collective guilt, Branscombe & Doosje, 2004; collective victimhood, Noor, Brown, & Prentice, 2008; intergroup forgiveness, González, Manzi, & Noor, this volume).

We suggest that the emotional barriers to reconciliation fall into two main clusters: One cluster relates to issues of intergroup trust, and the other relates to matters of the ingroup's identity. At the center of the first cluster are feelings and perceptions that concern the other party and one's relationship with it. The pivotal issue here is the degree to which one feels that the members of the other group wish the ingroup well and act accordingly. At the center of the second cluster are feelings and perceptions that relate to the adequacy and worth of the ingroup's identity. These may include feelings and perceptions of collective guilt on the one hand or the feelings of collective powerlessness that are associated with viewing the ingroup as the victim of an outgroup's aggression or oppression. This distinction between a focus on intergroup relations and the identities of each of the groups is in line with Kelman's suggestion that the end of intergroup conflict can be facilitated by changing the quality of intergroup *relations*, or by changing aspects of the *identities* of the involved parties (Kelman, 2008). In line with Kelman's theorizing, we have distinguished between two corollary types of reconciliation: *instrumental reconciliation*, which aims to effect positive change in intergroup relations by restoring trust and promoting benevolent feelings among adversaries; and *socioemotional reconciliation*, which aims to reduce the threats posed to the parties' identities (see also Rouhana, 2004). An example of socioemotional reconciliation is when identity threat associated with the perception that one's group is held responsible for wrongdoings is ameliorated by an expression of forgiveness from one's adversary.

The chapters in the present volume provide examples of these two different components of intergroup reconciliation, that is, the restoration of trust and positive intergroup relations on one hand, and the restoration of groups' positive identities on the other hand. Chapters by Davies, Wright, and Aron; Page-Gould and Mendoza-Denton; and Swart, Turner, Hewstone, and Voci center on the effects of significant contact across group boundaries on the improvement intergroup relations and the enhancement of intergroup trust; the present chapter, as well as Chapters by Butz and Plant, Purdie-Vaughns and Walton, and González et al., focus on different threats posed to the identities of groups in a conflict and on socioemotional processes that ameliorate these threats and provide identity safety, such as intergroup forgiveness. It should be noted, however, that these two processes of reconciliation, instrumental and socioemotional, are not purely distinct, and the separation between them is made for sake of conceptual clarity. For example, past research noted that the effects of socioemotional processes such as apologies for past wrongdoings are dependent on the level of trust that one has in the adversary (Nadler & Liviatan, 2006), and Swart et al. in the present volume show that contact across group boundaries affects willingness to forgive the outgroup for past wrongdoings. Thus, instrumental and socioemotional reconciliation are distinct yet interdependent processes.

THE INSTRUMENTAL ROUTE TO RECONCILIATION: "MENDING" BROKEN RELATIONSHIPS BY RESTORING INTERGROUP TRUST

Scholars warn that trust is often the first casualty of conflict and that, as long as relations are strained by intense distrust, a conflict is not likely to end (Deutsch, 2008). When groups feel that they cannot trust their adversary, even positive gestures become imbued with negative meanings. An illustration of this is the finding by Nadler and Liviatan (2006) that Israelis who distrusted Palestinians had worse perceptions of Palestinians and were less willing to reconcile with them if they read an apology by a Palestinian leader than if they had not read the apology. In contrast, Israelis who were relatively trusting of Palestinians were more willing to reconcile after they read such an apology. Thus, not only is trust important to hastening the cessation of hostilities, but its absence may upend the intended consequences of well-meaning concessions.

How can trust between parties that are involved in conflicts of direct violence be restored? Research on intergroup relations shows that this trust can be achieved via a sequence of positive and reciprocal acts that convince adversaries that the other side no longer harbors malevolent intentions. The graduated and reciprocated initiatives in tension reduction (GRIT) proposal developed by Osgood (1962) as a way to reduce Cold War–era distrust between the United States and the Soviet Union, which stresses the importance of reciprocal "confidence building measures" for trust building between adversaries, represented such a process in international relations. It advocated an exchange of incrementally more meaningful acts of goodwill with the aim of increasing adversaries' mutual trust. The basic ingredient of this approach to intergroup reconciliation that is applicable to intergroup relations within societies is the steadily growing belief in the trustworthiness of the adversary, which emanates from repeated and reciprocal steps toward cooperation. These exchanges advance goals that are instrumental for both parties, such as public health, and exemplify *instrumental reconciliation* (Nadler, 2002).

The instrumental route to reconciliation is relevant in contexts of both direct and structural violence. In contexts of *direct intergroup violence*, many peace-building efforts that pave the transition from enmity to peace are based on this logic. For example, the architects of the 1993 Oslo agreement between Israelis and Palestinians reasoned that, after years of protracted conflict associated with many episodes of direct violence, the transition to peace must be ushered by an interim period of trust building. The plan was to precede negotiations on the thorny issues that divided the parties, such as land, by a 5-year period in which the parties would cooperate on shared problems having instrumental value, such as economic development, thereby gradually learning to trust each other (Maoz, Shikaki, & Rothstein, 2002).

In intergroup relations characterized by structural violence, the instrumental route to reconciliation is used to move beyond prejudice and discrimination to equality and cooperation. A dominant framework in this approach has been the contact hypothesis (Allport, 1954), which has produced voluminous research in the social sciences. This approach is consistent with our conception of instrumental reconciliation as the product of sustained, cooperative, and meaningful contact between members of opposing groups. When sociocultural shifts make prejudice and discrimination unconscionable to both advantaged and disadvantaged groups, reducing its existence becomes a common instrumental goal, as both groups may be interested in smoothing their relations, preventing further societal unrest, and reaching a new, more equal, status quo.

Research on the contact hypothesis increasingly demonstrates that the benefits of contact are attributable to psychological processes that go beyond the "cold" dimension of goal-oriented cooperation. Indeed, warm feelings and cross-group friendship shepherd constructive changes in intergroup relations (Brown & Hewstone, 2005; Pettigrew & Tropp, 2006; Tropp & Pettigrew, 2005). Moreover, increased trust was found to mediate the link between positive intergroup contact, such as occurs in affectively meaningful cross-group friendships, and reduced prejudice (Swart et al., this volume). Apparently, group members generalize the greater trust they feel toward the outgroup member with whom they have friendly relations to the outgroup in general, thus generating greater willingness to engage with the outgroup in a constructive manner (Tropp, 2008). It is important to note, however, that in contexts of both direct and structural violence, instrumental reconciliation focuses on effecting current, pragmatic change in intergroup relations. It has a lesser focus on the emotional consequences of past suffering and humiliation for each of the parties' identities.

SOCIOEMOTIONAL RECONCILIATION: THE PERSPECTIVE OF THE NEEDS-BASED MODEL ON REMOVING THREATS TO GROUPS' IDENTITIES

The second route to reconciliation consists of redressing these threats to adversaries' identities caused by the suffering of direct violence and the long-term oppression of structural violence. As we will explain, because this process involves changing the social identities of the involved parties by satisfying their emotional needs, we have labeled it *socioemotional reconciliation*. It describes how the removal of the threats posed to the identities of victimized–disadvantaged groups as well as perpetrating–advantaged groups restores their sense of worthy identity and promotes their willingness to reconcile with each other. The needs-based model accounts for this process and assumes that the nature of the injury to identity differs for victims and perpetrators (Nadler & Liviatan, 2004; Nadler & Shnabel, 2008; Shnabel, Nadler, Ullrich, Dovidio, & Carmi, 2009) and for disadvantaged versus advantaged groups (Shnabel, Nadler, Dovidio, & Ullrich, 2010).

The Needs-Based Model in Contexts of Direct Violence

Acts of direct violence pose different types of identity threats for victims and aggressors. Victims, by definition, are harmed by acts over which they have little power or control. According to the needs-based model, victimizing experiences threaten group members' sense of themselves as human beings who have agency and equal worth. Although perpetrators have more power than victims, their identities are also imperiled by the perpetration of violence, in the form of threats to their image as morally worthy human beings. When wrongdoing is exposed, perpetrators risk accusations of guilt and exclusion from the moral community to which they belong (Tavuchis, 1991). Because the threats to the identities of victims and perpetrators are not symmetrical, they give rise to different needs in each group. For victims, identity threat brings about an enhanced need for power. For perpetrators, identity threat enhances their need to regain social acceptance from relevant others. Satisfying these needs restores the victims' sense of power and the perpetrators' moral image.

The restoration of their impaired dimensions of identity can be met unilaterally by the victim and the perpetrator, though not necessarily by constructive means. Victims may restore their sense of power by taking revenge, while perpetrators may reduce threat to their moral image by using exonerating cognitions to legitimize their actions, by belittling the painful consequences of their actions, or by psychologically distancing themselves or even dehumanizing their victims (Nadler & Shnabel, 2008). Obviously, these unilateral methods of restoring deficits in social power and moral image will likely fuel rather than quell intergroup conflict (Lindner, 2006).

More constructively, the restoration of impaired identity dimensions can also be achieved through reciprocal interactions. Specifically, the needs-based model considers socioemotional reconciliation to be a process of *social exchange* in which victims' need for empowerment is satisfied by the perpetrator and perpetrators' need for acceptance is satisfied by the victim. A primary illustration of this social exchange is the apology–forgiveness cycle, which, if successful, can alter the conflictual reality between two adversaries (Tavuchis, 1991). By apologizing and taking responsibility for past wrongdoing, perpetrators put their fate in the hands of victims, who have the power to grant or withhold forgiveness. This is an empowering experience for victims (Gobodo-Madikizela, 2003). At the same time, granting forgiveness to the perpetrator removes the aforementioned threat to the perpetrator's moral image (Gobodo-Madikizela, 2003). Thus, our model suggests that a process of reciprocal need satisfaction removes threats to victims' and perpetrators' identities and produces a greater willingness for reconciliation. We have labeled this approach the *needs-based model of reconciliation* because it bases socioemotional reconciliation on the satisfaction of victims' and perpetrators' needs (Nadler & Shnabel, 2008; Shnabel & Nadler, 2008). This process is described in Figure 10.1.

We examined the model's predictions in two intergroup contexts: relations between Israeli Jews and German nationals and between Israeli Jews and Israeli Arabs. Although the two contexts differ on central dimensions (e.g., the history of one includes genocide, whereas the other constitutes an ongoing intergroup conflict within the Israeli society), they were both framed in the experiments as representing direct violence. In the study on Jewish–German relations, the element of direct violence was made salient by reminding participants of the Holocaust. In the study on relations between Israeli Arabs and Israeli Jews, the element of direct violence was made salient by reminding participants of the Kefar Kasem killings of 1956, in which the Israeli border patrol killed 43 unarmed Arab civilians who had broken a curfew restriction.

The significance of coevaluating these two contexts is that the same group (i.e., Israeli Jews) represents the victimized group in the first context and the perpetrating group in the second. This allowed us to assess the assertion that receiving messages expressing either acceptance or empowerment from the outgroup differentially affects victims' and perpetrators' willingness

Social Role

	Victim	*Perpetrator*
Threatened Identity Dimension:	Sense of power	Moral image
	↓	↓
Enhanced Need for:	Empowerment	Acceptance
	↓	↓
Restored Identity Dimension:	Sense of power	Moral image
	↓	↓
Resulting in:	Increased willingness to reconcile	

Figure 10.1. The needs-based model of reconciliation. From "A Needs-Based Model of Reconciliation: Satisfying the Differential Emotional Needs of Victim and Perpetrator as a Key to Promoting Reconciliation," by N. Shnabel and A. Nadler, 2008, *Journal of Personality and Social Psychology, 94,* p. 118. Copyright 2008 by the American Psychological Association.

to reconcile in isolation from sociocultural variations between actual victim–perpetrator dyads. Thus, in the context of Jewish–German relations, Jews, as members of the victimized group, were expected to be readier to reconcile after receiving a message of empowerment from a German representative, whereas German participants, as members of the perpetrating group, were expected to be readier to reconcile following a message of acceptance from a Jewish representative. In the Arab–Jewish context, Israeli Jews, as members of the perpetrating group, were expected to be readier to reconcile following a message of acceptance from an Arab representative, whereas Arab participants would be readier to reconcile following a message of empowerment from a Jewish representative. Our findings supported these predictions (see Shnabel et al., 2009).

The Needs-Based Model in Contexts of Structural Violence

As a step toward integrating the research traditions of direct violence and structural violence, we examined the applicability of the needs-based model to the latter context as well. This examination sought to answer three questions: (a) whether members of disadvantaged groups suffer threats to their sense of agency and power and whether members of advantaged groups suffer threats to their moral image; (b) whether these threats deepen needs for empowerment and acceptance, respectively; and (c) whether intergroup relations could be improved with a social exchange interaction in which the disadvantaged group's need for empowerment is satisfied by the advantaged group and the advantaged group's need for acceptance is satisfied by the disadvantaged group.

The first question touches on a fundamental distinction between conflicts of direct and structural violence. In conflicts of direct violence, the suffering inflicted on victims is salient, and thus threats to victims' and perpetrator's identities are almost constantly present. In contexts of structural violence, social identity theory tells us that as long as status relations are perceived as legitimate and stable (i.e., secure), no identity threat is likely to occur (Tajfel & Turner, 1986), and members of both groups are likely to view social inequality as normative and justified (Jost & Hunyady, 2005). However, when status relations are perceived as illegitimate and unstable (i.e., insecure), members of disadvantaged groups will view equality as attainable and therefore experience their relative powerlessness as threatening to their ingroup identity (Tajfel & Turner, 1986). Similarly, when the legitimacy of privilege is questioned, allegations of exploitation and injustice will embody potent threats to the moral identity of the advantaged group (Leach, Snider, & Iyer, 2002). This suggests an affirmative, but conditional, answer to the first question: Advantaged groups are likely to experience a threat to their moral image, and disadvantaged groups are likely to experience a threat to their sense of power, but only when status relations are insecure.

The second question is whether these threats to sense of power and moral image translate into increased needs for empowerment and acceptance by the disadvantaged and advantaged groups, respectively. Research suggests an affirmative answer. Members of disadvantaged groups typically approach encounters with the advantaged group with the goal of gaining power and changing the status quo toward intergroup equality. Members of advantaged groups are more cautious not to "upset the applecart" and seek social harmony and mutual acceptance between members of the two groups so as to alleviate their unease about their relative privilege (Dovidio, Saguy, & Shnabel, 2009). More directly, Shelton, Richeson, and Vorauer (2006) suggested that advantaged groups seek to be *liked* by disadvantaged groups, whereas disadvantaged groups seek *respect* from members of their outgroup. Although not entirely identical, these concepts correspond to acceptance and empowerment, suggesting that the logic underlying the needs-based model in explicitly violent conflicts is applicable to structurally violent conflicts.

This brings us to the third question: whether the reciprocal satisfaction of needs for empowerment and acceptance benefits intergroup relations. To answer this question, it should be noted that, because of their different nature, the means to promote reconciliation in contexts of structural and direct violence are different. Because structural violence reflects the existence of an unequal and discriminatory social structure, ending it requires equality and social justice. In comparison, reducing direct violence requires lessening or eliminating the likelihood of future overt violent episodes. These two aspects of peacemaking have been labeled as *positive peacemaking* and *negative peacemaking,* respectively (Christie et al., 2008). The different meanings of reconciliation in either setting should be expressed in different behaviors. In conflicts involving direct violence, reconciliation should be expressed in willingness to mend ruptured relations and to foster greater intergroup closeness (e.g., participation in joint activities), which will lessen the possibility of future direct intergroup violence. In conflicts involving structural violence, reconciliation should be expressed in the advantaged group's commitment to achieving intergroup equality and its willingness to relinquish privileges that obstruct that goal.

We recently tested these hypotheses among participants who belonged to either a prestigious or less prestigious university (Shnabel et al., 2010). Participants were told that the selection committee of a prestigious university had repeatedly discriminated against students from a less prestigious university in selecting candidates for admission to a competitive program of study. Students from both universities had applied to the program, which exists only in the prestigious university. However, students from the less prestigious university were categorically excluded from consideration, regardless of their individual merit. Framing the scenario as one of repeated discrimination by the advantaged group against the less advantaged group in access to a resource that both groups desired but only the advantaged group had control over rendered the experimental setting as one of structural violence.

Once given this information, both groups received an accepting, empowering, or neutral message from the outgroup. Afterward, the orientation of both groups toward the other side was assessed, and members of the advantaged group rated their willingness to invest in efforts to end discrimination against students from the outgroup. The willingness of the disadvantaged group to work against discrimination was not measured because it reflects struggling for their own cause rather than for the benefit of the other group or the relations with it. In other words, it was not assumed to be indicative of a positive outgroup orientation.

As expected, members of the disadvantaged group who received an empowering message from the outgroup expressed a more positive orientation toward the outgroup's members (e.g., a more favorable attitude and a willingness for cooperative interaction) than did those who received the accepting or neutral message. This was particularly true when members of the disadvantaged group had perceived the discrimination to be intentional, possibly reflecting the more acute emotional consequences of a deliberate versus unintended wrong. The finding that a message of acceptance did not have a similar positive effect on the social orientation of members of the disadvantaged group indicates that expressions of social acceptance, even if well-intentioned, are not enough to satisfy the needs of victimized groups. Disadvantaged group members desire social change and greater intergroup equality; therefore, they have a greater need for empowerment than for empathy (see Saguy, Tausch, Dovidio, & Pratto, 2009). Moreover, expressions of empathy and social acceptance are sometimes used by advantaged groups as a rhetorical tool to avoid the real problem of changing an existing social structure of inequality (Shnabel, Nadler, Canetti-Nisim, & Ullrich, 2008). Benevolent sexism (Glick & Fiske, 1996) serves as an example of such rhetoric.

The picture regarding members of the advantaged group was more complex. Consistent with the predictions of the needs-based model, a message of acceptance increased the positive orientation of advantaged group members toward the outgroup, which in turn led to greater willingness to work against discrimination. Apparently, a message of acceptance from the disadvantaged group alleviated the threat to advantaged group members' moral image, increasing their feelings of solidarity with the disadvantaged group while implying that, as members of a moral community, they should be sensitive to others' distress (Nadler & Liviatan, 2004). Thus, it encouraged their readiness to oppose discrimination, despite the cost to their relative social advantage.

The empowering message also improved the orientation of advantaged group members toward the outgroup, apparently because it satisfied their wish to maintain their superior status (Tajfel & Turner, 1986). However, this positive change in orientation failed to translate into an increased willingness to work to end intergroup discrimination. Instead, the empowering message, which reminded advantaged group members of their influence and ability, reinforced their perception that the status quo was legitimate and undermined their willingness to act for greater equality.

From a broader perspective, these findings tell us that, in the context of structural violence, the specific elements included in intergroup reciprocal messages are highly important, as even objectively positive messages may fail to promote reconciliation if they do not address the unique emotional needs of advantaged and disadvantaged groups. Specifically, messages that legitimize the advantaged group's position will bolster the view that structural violence is acceptable and justified. When this legitimization comes from the disadvantaged group itself—as was the case in the empowering message condition of our experiment—its capacity to sanction structural violence is particularly great because it absolves the advantaged group of the sense of guilt that would otherwise taint the benefit of an unearned advantage. Thus, such messages provide the advantaged group with the rationale for doing nothing to change the system of structural violence from which it benefits. The finding that only an empowering message had a positive effect on the social orientation of members of the disadvantaged group tells us that apologetic messages directed at the disadvantaged group may be regarded by them as manipulative ploys intended to placate them rather than a genuine expression of remorse and commitment for a future that is free of structural violence. The results of previous research suggest that this is especially likely when there is low trust in the outgroup; without trust, conciliatory messages from one's adversary do not have positive effects on willingness for reconciliation (Nadler & Liviatan, 2006).

ALTERNATIVE WAYS TO REMOVE THREATS TO IDENTITY AND THE AMBIGUITY OF THE VICTIM–PERPETRATOR DISTINCTION

The findings above provided empirical and theoretical support for the needs-based model in both directly and structurally violent contexts. Yet, the implications of these findings are limited because the source of the message that satisfied the emotional needs of the ingroup was the adversarial outgroup and the distinction between the social roles of victimized–disadvantaged group vs. perpetrating–advantaged group was unambiguous. To gain a more comprehensive picture on the processes of socioemotional reconciliation that are described by the needs-based model we consider (a) whether there are alternative modes of need satisfaction located outside the conflict dyad and (b) the implications of ambiguity in the victim–perpetrator and the disadvantaged–advantaged distinction for the process of socioemotional reconciliation.

Satisfaction of Needs Outside the Victim–Perpetrator Dyad

Instead of the unilateral (e.g., revenge or dehumanization) or reciprocal (e.g., the apology–forgiveness cycle) routes we described above, needs can also be satisfied when an authoritative third party (e.g., an opinion leader or international tribunal) acts as the source of empowerment or acceptance. Such a third party may denounce the injustice suffered by victims of direct or structural violence, punish the perpetrators, or demand social change, thereby increasing the victimized groups' relative power and influence. Perpetrators' need for acceptance may be satisfied when an authoritative third party sanctions direct or structural violence as understandable in a given context (e.g., violence that is carried out in self-defense or social privileges that have a legitimate basis). It remains for future research to determine whether such need satisfaction from a third party increases adversaries' readiness for reconciliation to the same degree or in the same manner as the reciprocal satisfaction of needs as described by the needs-based model.

Ambiguity of the Distinction Between Social Roles

For the sake of conceptual clarity, the needs-based model assumes a clear distinction between victim and perpetrator. Yet, in many directly violent intergroup conflicts, this distinction is ambiguous, with both parties viewing themselves as victims (Noor et al., 2008). Being a victim has psychological gains. It absolves actors from the need to examine their own responsibility for violence and grants them the legitimacy to be preoccupied with their own wounds and with their adversary's guilt for having caused them. Leaving the relative safety of victimhood by admitting responsibility for past wrongdoing is hazardous (Tavuchis, 1991). The party that decides to "go first" (e.g., by apologizing to the other group) risks an indelible stain of guilt and a correspondingly permanent debt to the adversary. This wariness about going first may be reduced if actors know in advance that their admission of responsibility will be met with a willingness to understand and forgive. This knowledge will shield the repentant party from sole culpability and moral ostracism. In contexts of structural violence, the advantaged group may be similarly concerned about the consequences of admitting to the existence of discrimination and prejudice. Although in contexts of structural violence there is usually consensus as to which party is the advantaged and which the disadvantaged, members of the advantaged group may nevertheless avoid acknowledging inequality because they fear that the disadvantaged group will use this admission to pursue demands they oppose or dislike.

How can these difficulties be dealt with? In explicitly violent conflicts, the trap of double victimhood can be bypassed when both parties are encouraged to view themselves simultaneously as victims and perpetrators of past transgressions. In this case the admission of wrongdoing by one party needs to be reciprocated by a similar admission by the other. This cannot occur when there is a clear consensus as to which side perpetrated the wrongdoing (e.g., the Holocaust, the Apartheid regime). In such cases, issues of responsibility, guilt, and justice are commonly addressed by institutional mechanisms such as war tribunals or truth commissions. In a similar manner, in contexts of structural violence, greater clarity about the reactions of the disadvantaged group to an admission of responsibility by the advantaged group may allay the advantaged group's fears and promote socioemotional reconciliation. Finally, it should be reemphasized that unless such admissions of responsibility are accompanied by concrete acts to promote equality, they may be interpreted as ploys to maintain the status quo and consequently increase rather than decrease intergroup tension.

CONCLUSIONS AND IMPLICATIONS

This chapter has differentiated instrumental reconciliation and socioemotional reconciliation as two distinct yet interdependent processes that promote positive intergroup relations and has examined the operation and implications of these processes in contexts of both direct and structural violence. It should be emphasized that structural and direct intergroup violence should not be viewed as mutually exclusive phenomena (Galtung, 1996). First, many structurally violent conflicts are born of a history of direct violence (e.g., slavery forerunning a history of racial inequality in the United States). Thus, groups become subservient to other groups because they have been subdued by force into a lower social position. Second, the structural violence of routine and continuous discrimination is often dotted with episodes of direct and intentional violence, such as police brutality. This means that a given intergroup conflict can be experienced as both structurally and directly violent, depending on the situation and even on its psychological construal, which explains why—at least to some extent—common processes, dynamics, and variables seem to operate in both contexts.

One particular aspect that both types of contexts have in common is that in both of them the reduction of negative intergroup phenomena (i.e., the cessation of direct or structural violence) is not equivalent to the promotion of positive intergroup phenomena (i.e., the restoration of trustworthy relations between and positive identities of the involved groups). Our chapter's concern with the positive phenomenon of intergroup reconciliation follows a broader shift in the study of intergroup relations, from conflict prevention to promoting harmonious relations between adversarial groups.

Although some of our review addressed processes of instrumental reconciliation, its main focus was on the needs-based model, which has been developed to examine processes of socioemotional reconciliation. The model was originally formulated to explain the emotional needs of groups involved in conflicts of direct violence, but the present chapter suggested that it can also be applied to conflicts of structural violence. We have underscored the need for an active removal of identity threats that are experienced by victimized–disadvantaged and perpetrator–advantaged groups in a way that is consistent with the principles of the needs-based model of reconciliation. We hope this chapter has contributed to this volume's endeavor to theoretically and empirically identify the factors that may realize the goal of fostering positive intergroup relations in different kinds of intergroup conflicts.

REFERENCES

Allport, G. W. (1954). *The nature of prejudice.* Reading, MA: Addison-Wesley.

Blatz, C. W., Schumann, K., & Ross, M. (2009). Government apologies for historical injustices. *Political Psychology, 30,* 219–241. doi:10.1111/j.1467-9221. 2008.00689.x

Branscombe, N. R., & Doosje, B. (Eds.). (2004). *Collective guilt: International perspectives.* Cambridge, England: Cambridge University Press.

Brown, R., & Hewstone, M. (2005). An integrative theory of intergroup contact. In M. P. Zanna (Ed.), *Advances in experimental social psychology* (pp. 255–343). San Diego, CA: Academic Press.

Campbell, D. T. (1965). Ethnocentric and other altruistic motives. In D. Levine (Ed.), *Nebraska Symposium on Motivation* (pp. 283–311). Lincoln: University of Nebraska Press.

Čehajić, R., Brown, R., & Castano, E. (2008). Forgive and forget? Antecedents and consequences of intergroup forgiveness in Bosnia and Herzegovina. *Political Psychology, 29,* 351–367. doi:10.1111/j.1467-9221.2008.00634.x

Christie, D. J., Tint, B. S., Wagner, R. V., & Winter, D. D. (2008). Peace psychology for a peaceful world. *American Psychologist, 63,* 540–552. doi:10.1037/0003-066X.63.6.540

Deutsch, M. (2008). Reconciliation after destructive intergroup conflict. In A. Nadler, T. Malloy, & J. D. Fisher (Eds.), *Social psychology of intergroup reconciliation* (471–487). New York, NY: Oxford University Press. doi:10.1093/acprof:oso/ 9780195300314.003.0021

Dovidio, J. F., Saguy, T., & Shnabel, N. (2009). Cooperation and conflict within groups: Bridging intragroup and intergroup processes. *Journal of Social Issues, 65,* 429–449. doi:10.1111/j.1540-4560.2009.01607.x

Fiske, S. T. (1998). Prejudice, stereotypes and discrimination. In D. T. Gilbert, S. T. Fiske, & G. Lindzey (Eds.), *The handbook of social psychology* (4th ed., pp. 3–58). New York, NY: Oxford University Press.

Galtung, J. (1969). Violence, peace and peace research. *Journal of Peace Research, 3,* 176–191.

Galtung, J. (1996). *Peace by peaceful means: Peace and conflict, development and civilization.* London, England: Sage.

Glick, P., & Fiske, S. T. (1996). The Ambivalent Sexism Inventory: Differentiating hostile and benevolent sexism. *Journal of Personality and Social Psychology, 70,* 491–512. doi:10.1037/0022-3514.70.3.491

Gobodo-Madikizela, P. (2003). *A human being died that night: A South African woman confronts the legacy of apartheid.* New York, NY: Houghton-Mifflin.

Hughes, E., Scabas, W. A., & Thakur, R. (Eds.). (2007). *Atrocities and international accountability: Beyond transitional justice.* New York, NY: United Nations University.

Jones, E. E. (1998). Major developments in five decades of social psychology. In D. T. Gilbert, S. T. Fiske, & G. Lindzey (Eds.), *The handbook of social psychology* (4th ed., pp. 3–57). New York, NY: Oxford University Press.

Jost, J. T., & Hunyady, O. (2005). Antecedents and consequences of system justification ideologies. *Current Directions in Psychological Science, 14,* 260–265. doi:10.1111/j.0963-7214.2005.00377.x

Kelman, H. C. (1999). The interdependence of Israeli and Palestinian national identities: The role of the other in existential conflicts. *Journal of Social Issues, 55,* 581–600. doi:10.1111/0022-4537.00134

Kelman, H. C. (2008). Reconciliation from a social–psychological perspective. In A. Nadler, T. Malloy, & J. D. Fisher (Eds.), *Social psychology of intergroup reconciliation* (pp. 15–33). New York, NY: Oxford University Press. doi:10.1093/acprof:oso/9780195300314.003.0002

Leach, C. W., Snider, S. L., & Iyer, A. (2002). "Poisoning the conscience of the fortunate": The experience of relative advantage and support for social equality. In I. Walker & H. J. Smith (Eds.), *Relative deprivation: Specification, development and integration* (pp. 136–163). New York, NY: Cambridge University Press.

Lindner, E. (2006). *Making enemies: Humiliation and international conflict.* London, England: Greenwood Press.

Maoz, M., Shikaki, H., & Rothstein, R. L. (Eds.). (2002). *The Israeli–Palestinian peace process: Oslo and the lessons of failure: Perspectives, predicaments and prospects.* Sussex, England: Academic Press.

Nadler, A. (2002). Post resolution processes: Instrumental and socio-emotional routes to reconciliation. In G. Salomon & B. Nevo (Eds.), *Peace education: The concept, principles, and practices around the world* (127–143). Mahwah, NJ: Erlbaum.

Nadler, A., & Liviatan, I. (2004). Inter-group reconciliation processes in Israel: Theoretical analysis and empirical findings. In N. R. Branscombe & B. Doosje (Eds.), *Collective guilt: International perspectives* (pp.216–235). New York, NY: Cambridge University Press.

Nadler, A., & Liviatan, I. (2006). Intergroup reconciliation: Effects of adversary's expressions of empathy, responsibility, and recipients' trust. *Personality and Social Psychology Bulletin, 32,* 459–470. doi:10.1177/0146167205276431

Nadler, A., Malloy, T., & Fisher, J. D. (2008). Intergroup reconciliation: Dimensions and themes. In A. Nadler, T. Malloy, & J. D. Fisher (Eds.), *Social psychology of intergroup reconciliation* (pp. 3–12). New York, NY: Oxford University Press. doi:10.1093/acprof:oso/9780195300314.003.0001

Nadler, A., & Shnabel, N. (2008). Intergroup reconciliation: The instrumental and socio-emotional paths and the need-based model of socio-emotional reconciliation. In A. Nadler, T. Malloy, & J. D. Fisher (Eds.), *Social psychology of intergroup reconciliation* (pp. 37–57). New York, NY: Oxford University Press. doi:10.1093/acprof:oso/9780195300314.003.0003

Noor, M., Brown, R., & Prentice, G. (2008). Prospects for intergroup reconciliation: Social psychological predictors of intergroup forgiveness and reparation in

Northern Ireland and Chile. In A. Nadler, T. Malloy, & J. D. Fisher (Eds.), *The social psychology of intergroup reconciliation* (pp. 97–115). New York, NY: Oxford University Press. doi:10.1093/acprof:oso/9780195300314.003.0006

Osgood, C. E. (1962). *An alternative to war or surrender*. Urbana: University of Illinois Press.

Pettigrew, T. F., & Tropp, L. R. (2006). A meta-analytic test of intergroup contact theory. *Journal of Personality and Social Psychology, 90*, 751–783. doi:10.1037/0022-3514.90.5.751

Philpot, C. R., & Hornsey, M. J. (2008). What happens when groups say sorry: The effect of intergroup apologies on their recipients. *Personality and Social Psychology Bulletin, 34*, 474–487. doi:10.1177/0146167207311283

Rouhana, N. N. (2004). Group identity and power asymmetry in reconciliation processes: The Israeli–Palestinian case. *Peace and Conflict, 10*, 33–52. doi:10.1207/s15327949pac1001_3

Saguy, T., Tausch, N., Dovidio, J. F., & Pratto, F. (2009). The irony of harmony: Intergroup contact can produce false expectations for equality. *Psychological Science, 20*, 114–121. doi:10.1111/j.1467-9280.2008.02261.x

Scheff, T. J. (1994). *Bloody revenge: Emotions, nationalism and war*. Boulder, CO: Westview Press.

Scheper-Hughes, N., & Bourgois, P. (Eds.). (2004). *Violence in war and peace: An anthology*. Oxford, England: Blackwell.

Shelton, J. N., Richeson, J. A., & Vorauer, J. D. (2006). Threatened identities and interethnic interactions. In W. Stroebe & M. Hewstone (Eds.), *European review of social psychology* (Vol. 17, pp. 321–358). New York, NY: Psychology Press.

Shnabel, N., & Nadler, A. (2008). A needs-based model of reconciliation: Satisfying the differential emotional needs of victim and perpetrator as a key to promoting reconciliation. *Journal of Personality and Social Psychology, 94*, 116–132. doi:10.1037/0022-3514.94.1.116

Shnabel, N., Nadler, A., Canetti-Nisim, D., & Ullrich, J. (2008). The role of acceptance and empowerment from the perspective of the needs-based model. *Social Issues and Policy Review, 2*, 159–186. doi:10.1111/j.1751-2409.2008.00014.x

Shnabel, N., Nadler, A., Dovidio, J., & Ullrich, J. (2010). *The effects of receiving messages of empowerment and acceptance from the outgroup on high and low status group members' positive intergroup orientation and willingness to act for changing the status-quo*. Unpublished manuscript.

Shnabel, N., Nadler, A., Ullrich, J., Dovidio, J. F., & Carmi, D. (2009). Promoting reconciliation through the satisfaction of the emotional needs of victimized and perpetrating group members: The needs-based model of reconciliation. *Personality and Social Psychology Bulletin, 35*, 1021–1030. doi:10.1177/0146167209336610

Staub, E. (2008). Promoting reconciliation after genocide and mass killing in Rwanda and other post-conflict settings: Understanding the roots of violence, healing, shared history, and general principles. In A. Nadler, T. Malloy, & J. D. Fisher

(Eds.), *The social psychology of intergroup reconciliation* (395–423). New York, NY: Oxford University Press. doi:10.1093/acprof:oso/9780195300314.003.0018

Staub, E., Pearlman, L. A., Gubin, A., & Hagengimana, A. (2005). Healing, reconciliation, forgiving and the prevention of violence after genocide or mass killing: An intervention and its experimental evaluation in Rwanda. *Journal of Social and Clinical Psychology, 24*, 297–334.

Tajfel, H., & Turner, J. C. (1986). The social identity theory of intergroup behavior. In W. G. Austin & S. Worchel (Eds.), *The social psychology of intergroup relations* (pp. 7–24). Chicago, IL: Nelson-Hall.

Tavuchis, N. (1991). *Mea culpa: A sociology of apology and reconciliation*. Stanford, CA: Stanford University Press.

Tropp, L. R. (2008). The role of trust in intergroup contact: Its significance for improving relations between groups. In U. Wagner, L. R. Tropp, G. Finchilescu, & C. Tredoux (Eds.), *Improving intergroup relations: Building on the legacy of Thomas F. Pettigrew* (pp. 91–106). Oxford, England: Blackwell. doi:10.1002/9781444303117.ch7

Tropp, L. R., & Pettigrew, T. F. (2005). Differential relationships between intergroup contact and affective and cognitive indicators of prejudice. *Personality and Social Psychology Bulletin, 31*, 1145–1158. doi:10.1177/0146167205274854

11

INTERGROUP FORGIVENESS AND REPARATION IN CHILE: THE ROLE OF IDENTITY AND INTERGROUP EMOTIONS

ROBERTO GONZÁLEZ, JORGE MANZI, AND MASI NOOR

Over the past 50 years, social psychology has prioritized the study of intergroup prejudice and conflict (Allport, 1954; Brewer, 1999; Brown, 1995; Hewstone, Rubin, & Willis, 2002). Our discipline now has numerous models to explain how intergroup conflict is created, maintained, and reduced (Ashmore, Jussim, & Wilder, 2001). By contrast, our understanding about how to actively promote positive outcomes within intergroup relations is less well developed. Studying the psychological processes of such positive outcomes is important because it could provide new insights for planning real-life interventions aimed at improving intergroup relations rather than simply reducing prejudice and conflict between groups (Brown, González, Zagefka, Manzi, & Čehajić, 2008; Noor, Brown, Lewis, González, & Manzi, 2008; Tam, Hewstone, Kenworthy, & Cairns, 2009; Wohl & Branscombe, 2005). This chapter contributes to this goal by presenting a novel theoretical framework examining the role of intergroup emotions and social identities in predicting intergroup forgiveness and reparation attitudes. In so doing, we review the research we have conducted on intergroup emotions, forgiveness, and reparation in the post-Pinochet era in Chile.

THE CHILEAN POLITICAL CONTEXT

Unlike most intergroup contexts addressed in this book, which are based on racial or ethnic tensions, the strongest sources of conflict and division in Chilean society have been political or ideological identities. In fact, Chile experienced strong political tensions from the end of the 1950s until the military coup in 1973. During those years, three political blocs (right-wing, center, and left-wing) alternated in power. These blocs represented antagonistic ideological views, which translated into political tension, threat, and polarization. As a result, political violence increased during the second half of the 1960s and reached its peak in 1972–1973, before the military coup against Socialist president Salvador Allende.

Political violence became systematic during the military regime, especially following the creation of repressive organizations, such as the National Intelligence Directorate. These organizations were involved in many forms of systematic human rights violations (e.g., torture, executions, kidnappings), mainly against groups who were opposed to the military regime and identified with the political left. The political right supported the military regime and was consequently perceived as responsible for the cited human rights abuses. This perception was a permanent source of conflict in Chilean politics and remains so even now, 20 years after the return of democracy.

As soon as the country returned to democracy in 1990, the newly elected president, Christian Democrat Patricio Aylwin, appointed a Truth and Reconciliation Commission with the mandate of documenting human rights violations during the military regime. After a year of investigation and hearings, the commission delivered a report that represented the first official recognition of the magnitude of these atrocities. Reparation laws and institutions followed (1991–1997) as a way of providing economic, educational, and symbolic compensation for the suffering of victims and their relatives (Lira, 2009).

Naturally, these initiatives of reconciliation, and those that followed, have sparked a series of important and challenging questions for Chilean society. Among the many questions raised, two have been particularly pertinent to such initiatives: How can people be encouraged to let go of past wrongs and focus on a positive future? What are valid and acceptable ways of providing symbolic and other forms of reparations for the victim groups? To address these major issues from a social psychological perspective, we have developed a theoretical model in which we point out that because these types of issues are common to most other postconflict settings, our model is likely to offer general utility beyond the Chilean context.

KEY ASPECTS OF RECONCILIATION: INTERGROUP FORGIVENESS AND REPARATION

Intergroup forgiveness and reparation are usually introduced as necessary conditions to overcome past troubles (Bar-Tal, 2000; Staub, 2000). Even though they both represent positive reactions that can lead to a reduction in intergroup tensions, they are distinct constructs.

Forgiveness is an important and complex concept that was originally studied in the interpersonal context (Exline, Worthington, Hill, & McCullough, 2003). It has been described as a positive disposition that inhibits the release of anger and reduces the desire to retaliate (Enright & Zell, 1989). Forgiveness may be fostered through reestablishing connections with those associated with the offence, promoting positive emotions such as empathy and trust (Nadler, 2002; see also Swart, Turner, Hewstone, & Voci, this volume) and the expectation of reaching a positive future (Nadler & Saguy, 2003).

Although our understanding of intergroup forgiveness may be usefully informed by the interpersonal forgiveness literature, there may be qualitative differences between forgiveness at the two levels (Hewstone et al., 2004; Noor, Brown, Lewis, et al., 2008). Indeed, when talking about intergroup forgiveness we are not necessarily dealing with direct exchanges between victims and offenders but with people who identify with groups with different roles in the conflict and who experience emotions such as forgiveness as members of their groups (Wohl & Branscombe, 2005).

As Noor, Brown, Lewis, et al. (2008) have suggested, intergroup forgiveness may entail (a) clarity regarding each group's role in and responsibility for the conflict, (b) generosity in absolving the outgroup from the "total blame," (c) leaving past grievances behind, and (d) ultimately finding closure for a past hostile intergroup relationship (see also Nadler & Saguy, 2003). Thus, forgiveness offers both victims and perpetrators a unique way of reintegrating into postconflict society in which intergroup relations are transformed from hostility to mutual understanding and reconciliation (Nadler, 2002).

Reparation, on the other hand, has its roots in psychology and law. Both disciplines document the tendency to compensate past damage or wrongdoing through a number of symbolic or real actions. Research on equity, aggression, and guilt demonstrates that once people become aware of their wrongdoing, they typically offer positive compensation and other forms of prosocial behavior to those harmed (Barkan, 2000; Roccas, Klar, & Liviatan, 2004). Recent studies addressing the relationship between reparation and emotions at the group level show that people who identify with groups involved in collective misdeeds are likely to support reparation, particularly when they feel collectively guilty (Brown et al. 2008; Doosje, Branscombe, Spears, & Manstead,

1998). Thus, reparation can be predicted by intergroup emotions associated with the wrongdoing.

Assuming that intergroup conflicts can involve asymmetry in pain and suffering, it is expected that the willingness to forgive or make reparations will vary as a function of the role that the groups played in the conflict (i.e., perpetrator or victim; see also Nadler & Shnabel, this volume). In particular, Manzi and González (2007) observed that forgiveness and reparation were positively correlated only in the case of the group associated with perpetrating past political repression (the right-wing group); in the group associated with past victimization (the left-wing group), forgiveness and reparation were not correlated. This pattern of results may reflect the differential nature and implications of forgiveness and reparation for groups with different roles in the conflict. Forgiveness has a clear intergroup focus: It represents the extent to which groups in conflict are willing to put behind them the ill feelings regarding the opposing group. In contrast, reparation focuses on the victims, their needs and suffering. As a whole, it seems clear that both forgiveness and reparation are central constructs to examine when dealing with reconciliation processes.

GENERAL FRAMEWORK

Our general framework focuses on group identity and intergroup emotions, which we expect to be associated with intergroup forgiveness and reparation in the Chilean and other postconflict contexts. By focusing on these factors, we highlight the importance of bringing together social representations of the aggregate (identification at the group and superordinate level) and emotional dimensions (e.g., intergroup anger, trust, empathy, guilt, shame). In Figure 11.1, we provide a theoretical framework to explain

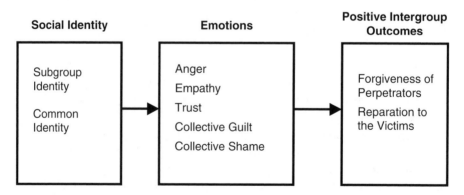

Figure 11.1. General framework to predict positive intergroup attitudes after group conflicts.

how social identity, both at the group and superordinate level, can differently predict forgiveness and willingness to compensate the victims. We hypothesize that these associations will be mediated by several intergroup emotions.

By *group identity*, we refer to a distinctive and salient representation of the group. In this context, it refers to people's identification with their ingroup involved in the conflict (i.e., political identity; Tajfel & Turner, 1986). *Superordinate identity*, on the other hand, represents a more inclusive representation of the aggregate that usually includes a broader definition of group boundaries (see Gaertner & Dovidio, this volume). At that level, both ingroup and outgroup members are conceived of as sharing the same common identity (i.e., national identity). However, as is discussed later, depending on the level of categorization that group members activate (the ingroup or superordinate level), the nature of the relationship between identity and outcomes such as intergroup forgiveness and reparation should vary. Overall, embracing a superordinate identity will foster intergroup forgiveness and willingness to repair intergroup relations, whereas identification with the ingroup is expected to be negatively associated with them.

Assuming that the conflict caused harm to ingroup and outgroup members (Ashmore, Jussim, & Wilder, 2001; Bar-Tal, 2000), anger is likely to emerge on all sides. The presence of anger is expected to prevent people involved in the conflict from forgiving, making reparations, and ultimately reconciling with the outgroup. However, a number of other group-based emotions might produce the opposite pattern; for example, intergroup emotions such as empathy, trust, guilt, and shame can promote forgiveness toward the perpetrators and a willingness to offer reparation to the victims. Assuming further that the conflict involves two parties, we expect both groups to exhibit these emotions. However, the intensity of each emotion might vary depending on which group was the victim or the perpetrator in the conflict (Manzi & González, 2007). These ideas are in line with Nadler and Shnabel's (this volume) concept of *instrumental reconciliation*, which recognizes the central role that intergroup trust plays in changing the nature of the relationship between the groups involved in the conflict. Swart et al. (this volume) also argue about the important function that empathy plays in predicting forgiveness. Altogether, this growing body of evidence suggests the need for considering intergroup emotions when dealing with the process of reconciliation, forgiveness, and reparation.

Specifically, we propose different relationships among identity representations, intergroup emotions, and attitudes, depending on the role that groups play in the conflict. Indeed, intergroup conflicts can be characterized as either symmetrical or asymmetrical. The former clearly involves the recognition that both groups inflicted mutual harm on each other. That is, at some level, they were perpetrators as well as victims of harm. Asymmetrical conflicts, on the other hand, imply that there is an identifiable boundary between the perpetrator and victim groups in terms of their misdeeds and suffering. Recent research indicates that different intergroup needs may arise in asymmetrical conflicts (Ashmore, Jussim, & Wilder, 2001; McAuley, McGlynn & Tonge, 2008; Shnabel & Nadler, 2008). Often the victim groups will seek to restore their power and control that were diminished by their victim role in the conflict. This need is met through the validation of their victimhood experiences and demands for reparation. By contrast, the perpetrator group will highlight their need for social acceptance and inclusion into the human moral community, both of which may be under threat because of the atrocities carried out on behalf of their group (Shnabel, Nadler, Ullrich, Dovidio, & Carmi, 2009). As we address later, such asymmetry in conflict will moderate the predictions derived from the framework.

GROUP AND SUPERORDINATE IDENTITIES

We now describe the central role that group and superordinate identities play in predicting intergroup forgiveness and reparation attitudes. In our framework, we focus on two different levels of group identification. The first one concerns the specific ingroup identity that is involved in the conflict (i.e., being a member of the left- or right-wing group). Most intergroup conflicts are driven by the threat to this identity and perceived competition with other identity groups, both of which typically predict negative intergroup attitudes (Stephan & Stephan, 2000). Group members can also identify with superordinate categories in which both ingroup and outgroup members may be included (i.e., Chileans). Being a member of such an inclusive category might foster positive intergroup attitudes (Gaertner & Dovidio, 2000; Noor, Brown, Lewis, et al., 2008). In this section, we discuss how both types of identification function in predicting intergroup emotions and positive intergroup attitudes such as forgiveness and willingness to make reparations.

Group Identity

As described by social identity theory (SIT), the self can be conceptualized on a continuum ranging from the self as a separate individual to the self as part of a social group (Tajfel & Turner, 1986). Based on this assumption, social identity derives from people's knowledge of their membership in a social group. The basic prediction of SIT is that social groups will attempt to differentiate themselves from each other through social comparisons.

Under the assumption that most intergroup conflicts activate emotions, behavior, and attitudes, the extent to which individuals identify with a group involved in the conflict should influence group members' disposition to forgive or make reparations to outgroup members. Moreover, the consideration to forgive and willingness to make reparations to the outgroup may also confront each group with issues involving disloyalty toward one's ingroup, and particularly toward those ingroup members who bore huge costs for actively pursuing the ingroup's goals (Marques, Abrams, & Serodio, 2001). Thus, in this context and according to our framework, the more strongly ingroup members identify with their ingroup, the less they will be willing to forgive the outgroup.

Moreover, depending on the role that each group played in the conflict (i.e., being a victim or perpetrator), a different pattern of relationships should emerge when predicting reparation to the victims. For those who perceive their group as being the victims, we expect a positive link between group identity and support for reparation. On the other hand, we expect a negative relationship between these two variables among members of the perpetrator group: The more they identify with their ingroup, the less willing they will be to make reparations to the victims.

Common Ingroup Identity

The common ingroup identity model (CIIM) offers an important extension to understanding how group identities may influence intergroup forgiveness and reparation between conflicting groups (Gaertner & Dovidio, 2000). It asserts that to improve intergroup relations, strategies should attempt to recategorize the groups so that ingroup and outgroup identities become subsumed within a more inclusive superordinate category. In this way, prior outgroup members will be perceived as belonging to a common ingroup, and, hence, some of the cognitive and motivational processes that initially contributed to ingroup bias will be redirected toward the development of a more positive intergroup relationship.

An extensive research program has demonstrated that bias is reduced when recategorization, either in its simple (one-group) or complex (dual-identity) form, is promoted (Gaertner & Dovidio, 2000; González & Brown, 2003, 2006; González et al., 2008). In the present research program, we sought to examine the relationship between identification with a common ingroup identity (i.e., Chileans) and both intergroup forgiveness and willingness to make reparations to victims. Specifically, our framework (see Figure 11.1) proposes that the more ingroup and outgroup members (left- and right-wingers) identify with a common ingroup identity (Chile), the more they will be willing to forgive and make reparations to the victims.

INTERGROUP EMOTIONS ASSOCIATED
WITH FORGIVENESS AND REPARATION

Previous research has suggested a number of potential antecedents of reparation, forgiveness, and other positive forms of conflict resolution in intergroup contexts (Noor, Brown, Lewis, et al., 2008; Noor, Brown, & Prentice, 2008). Considering the emotional impact that the conflict and its traumatic events produce in all parties, emotions are expected to have a prominent role in promoting or inhibiting the willingness to forgive and make reparations. For example, people who identify with a victimized group may feel angry for the atrocities caused by the perpetrator group. This anger will, in turn, inhibit the willingness to forgive the outgroup. Therefore, we expect emotions to mediate between social identity and the willingness to make reparations or forgive.

We address the roles of five intergroup emotions: anger, guilt, shame, trust, and empathy. The selection of these emotions was based on the attention they have received in the intergroup conflict literature (Mackie & Smith, 2002). Considering the positive or negative valence of these emotions, we predict a systematic pattern of relationships between them and the two levels of identity: The more people identify with their ingroup, the more they will experience negative emotions (e.g., anger) toward the outgroup and the less they will experience positive feelings (e.g., trust). The opposite pattern is hypothesized for the common identity, in which the outgroup becomes included in the same category with the ingroup (see Figure 11.1). In the following pages, we describe these emotions and develop hypotheses about their relationships with forgiveness and willingness to repair. Due to the asymmetric nature of the Chilean conflict, in some cases, different hypotheses are generated for the left-wing and right-wing groups.

Intergroup Anger

Conflicts that are motivated by intergroup hate often spark and leave behind a long-lasting tendency to experience anger. Anger can also result from the way that groups in conflict tend to interpret outgroup behavior, generally attributing the other group's negative actions to internal characteristics. In contexts of social conflict, intergroup anger is perpetuated through the collective memories of the conflicting groups, even years after the hostilities have stopped (Bar-Tal, 2000). Moreover, Butz and Plant (this volume) have shown that negative expectancies about an outgroup provoke anger and blaming when ingroup members are faced with negative outgroup behaviors. Considering that anger produced by the outgroup motivates group members to take action against the outgroup (Gordijn, Wigboldus, & Yzerbyt, 2001), it is reasonable to assume that such anger will inhibit the willingness to forgive the outgroup. Therefore, we expect a negative correlation between anger and forgiveness for the respective victimized and perpetrator groups.

In the case of reparation, a different pattern is predicted for each group. Because reparation is perceived in the Chilean context as benefiting the victimized group, intergroup anger is expected to correlate positively with reparation in the left-wing group because the ingroup is the likely recipient of reparation. In comparison, intergroup anger is expected to correlate negatively with reparation in the right-wing group because the outgroup is the likely recipient of reparation.

Intergroup Guilt and Shame

Guilt and shame are negative, self-directed emotions that are associated with a number of positive reactions, including reparation for harm produced by one's misdeeds. Although most research on guilt and shame has focused on interpersonal contexts (see Tangney & Dearing, 2002), the study of these two emotions has been extended to the intergroup domain. Doosje et al. (1998) were among the first to study collective guilt from a social identity perspective (Tajfel & Turner, 1986). Based on the idea that social categorizations lead people to internalize the attributes associated with their category, they assumed that people would vicariously experience a sense of shared guilt about the negative actions of other ingroup members. In line with their predictions, several studies have shown that feelings of collective guilt prompt intergroup reparation in different contexts (Brown et al., 2008; Doosje et al., 1998; Iyer, Leach, & Crosby, 2003; Iyer, Schmader, & Lickel, 2007).

Lickel, Schmader, and Barquissau (2004) proposed and subsequently supported (Lickel, Schmader, Curtis, Scarnier, & Ames, 2005) a model that distinguishes collective guilt from collective shame on the basis of the appraisal group members make regarding the negative action of their ingroup. They proposed that when group members interpret negative actions as under their control, collective guilt is more likely to be experienced. But if negative actions are seen as stemming from some "essential" characteristics of the ingroup, the group image is threatened, and collective shame is more likely. Collective guilt and shame are expected to motivate different reactions to negative ingroup actions, with guilt promoting reparation for the wrong-doing and shame leading people to distance themselves from the misdeed (Brown et al., 2008).

The direction of findings in this recent but small literature provides some basis to hypothesize a stronger correlation with positive outgroup outcomes, such as forgiveness and reparation, for intergroup guilt than for intergroup shame. In our case, considering the different role of the groups in the conflict and that reparation would be perceived as benefiting mostly the left-wing group, we expect that intergroup guilt (and to a lesser extent intergroup shame) will be positively correlated with reparation and forgiveness for the right-wing group. For the left wing, however, this positive correlation is expected only for forgiveness. Since reparation focuses on the ingroup in this case, intergroup guilt or shame is not expected to be correlated with the willingness to make reparations for the ingroup.

Intergroup Empathy

In both the interpersonal and intergroup literatures, empathy (perspective taking and/or empathic emotions) has a consistent and positive association with a number of positive intergroup outcomes (Dovidio et al., 2004; Finlay & Stephan, 2000). People with an empathic orientation are able to better understand the perspective of another group, which translates into more positive attitudes toward them. More specific to our own model, some previous research has demonstrated a positive link between empathy and forgiveness in the intergroup context (Čehajić, Brown, & Castano, 2008; Noor, Brown, & Prentice, 2008). Therefore, we predict that empathy will generally be positively associated with forgiveness. Following previous reasoning about the role of groups in conflict and the focus of reparation, intergroup empathy is expected to have a positive correlation with reparation only for the right-wing group. In the case of the left-wing group, no correlation is expected between empathy and willingness to make reparations.

Intergroup Trust

Prolonged and violent conflicts usually undermine intergroup trust. According to Nadler and Liviatan (2004), generalized distrust is a common emotional consequence of protracted violent conflicts, representing a major obstacle to reconciliation. Distrust usually consists of negative expectations about the outgroup's intentions for the ingroup (Mitchell, 2000). Trust has been also been conceptualized as an intergroup emotion (Brewer & Alexander, 2002) that facilitates cooperation among groups. The creation of trust among groups motivates a number of positive outcomes. Although the study of trust in real intergroup conflict settings is very recent, the studies are consistent in showing its positive role in promoting positive outgroup attitudes (Čehajić et al., 2008; Noor, Brown, & Prentice, 2008; Tam et al., 2009). On the basis of the above evidence, we predict that trust and support for reparation should have the same asymmetric pattern of correlations mentioned previously: a positive correlation in the case of the perpetrator group and no correlation in the case of the victim group.

TESTING THE FRAMEWORK

Starting with our framework, we used structural equation modeling to test whether intergroup emotions mediate the relationship between group identity and intergroup forgiveness and reparation (González, Manzi, & Noor, 2010). This model shows the importance of considering identity and emotions when predicting forgiveness and reparation in situations of intergroup conflict (Manzi & González, 2007; Noor, Brown, Lewis, et al., 2008; Noor, Brown, & Prentice, 2008). Before testing the meditational role of intergroup emotions, we first tested the direct links between the two levels of identity and the outcomes of forgiveness and reparation. As expected, ingroup identity significantly predicted both outcomes. It correlated negatively with forgiveness and showed the anticipated asymmetry regarding reparation: The ingroup identity–reparation path was positive for the left-wing and negative for the right-wing groups. Common identity, on the other hand, was associated only with forgiveness in both groups.

We then tested the mediation model. Considering the asymmetric role of groups in the conflict, we used a multigroup model to test whether the paths within the model were similar for the left- and right-wing groups. We confirmed that group status (perpetrator vs. victim) moderated the pattern of relationships in the model. This means that the model predicted forgiveness and reparation differently, depending on the group status. Therefore, we present the results for the mediation model separately for each group.

In the right-wing group, the data fit the model well (normed fit index [NFI] = .98; comparative fit index [CFI] = .99; root-mean-square error of association [RMSEA] = .046). The hypothesized model explained significantly more variance in reparation than forgiveness. As shown in panel (a) of Figure 11.2, for the right-wing group, ingroup identity and common identity were related to each other. However, only ingroup identity was related, in the expected direction, with all emotions but guilt. At the same time, four of the five emotions (with the exception of anger), were significantly related to support for reparation, whereas only empathy was significantly connected with forgiveness. As predicted, the observed interrelationships between predictors, mediators, and outcomes were more often observed in the identity-emotions-reparation pathway than in the identity–emotions–forgiveness pathway.

In the left-wing group, the data also fit the model well (NFI = .99; CFI = 1.00; RMSEA = .00) and explained a significant proportion of the variance in forgiveness and reparation. In this case, the model explained a higher proportion of variance in forgiveness than in reparation. However, as shown in panel (b) of Figure 11.2, the fitted model looks very different for the left-wing group from that for the right-wing case. In the left-wing group, ingroup and common identities were not related to each other, but both levels of identity were significantly correlated with all emotions (with the exception of the ingroup

Right-Wing Model

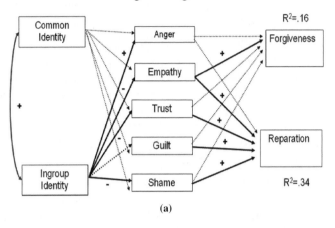

Left-Wing Model

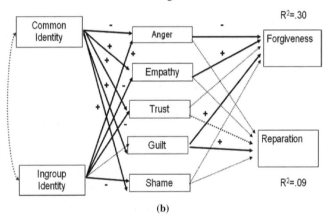

Figure 11.2. Identity predicting forgiveness and reparation: the mediating role of intergroup emotions.

identity–guilt link). The model also showed a very different pattern regarding the emotions–outcomes links. As expected, for the left-wing group, most of the significant paths involved the emotion-forgiveness side, indicating that anger, empathy, and guilt were related to forgiveness. In the case of reparation, we expected only anger to be significant, but we found that guilt was the only emotion with a significant and positive link. This unexpected correlation suggests that feelings of guilt in the left-wing group could have motivated them to include right-wing people among the victims. This explanation is consistent with the fact that intergroup guilt was the only emotion that mediated the relationship between common identity and reparation in this group.

The observed patterns of results were generally consistent with the expected asymmetry derived from the role that both groups played in the conflict. If we assume that people who identify with the groups involved in the conflict are aware of this asymmetry, then different aspects of the reconciliation process will be more psychologically relevant for each group. For the right-wing group, which is aware of its association with the perpetrator side and the harm caused to the victims, the main concern is about reparation. For the left-wing group, the victim side, the main dilemma concerns the possibility of forgiving the other group. What these findings suggest is that the very same intergroup emotions can work in different directions depending on who is experiencing them: the perpetrator group or the victimized group. The reported pattern of results supported the important differential role that identity and emotions play when dealing with forgiveness and reparation after a traumatic conflict.

An additional interesting and unexpected finding was the absence of a relationship between the common identity and intergroup emotions in the right-wing group. Contrary to the CIIM (Gaertner & Dovidio, 2000); endorsing an inclusive category did not predict forgiveness and reparation, mediated by intergroup emotions. However, as we mentioned earlier, common identity had a direct positive link with forgiveness in both groups. We can rule out the possibility that the lack of expected associations between common identity and intergroup emotions was due to disidentification with this category. Indeed, compared to left-wingers, right-wing participants exhibited a higher identification with Chile (the common identity). One way of explaining these results is that the right-wingers have not sufficiently differentiated the content of the common ingroup identity from the content of their ingroup identity. This is plausible both politically and empirically. Politically, the military coup and subsequent actions were always defended by the military regime as extreme actions undertaken to protect the country from an external threat (i.e., communism). All patriotic symbols were "claimed" by the military regime in an attempt to associate it with national interest and identity. As a consequence, a positive link was created between identifying with the right wing and identifying with the country. Empirically, we found support for this line of reasoning in the simple correlations between identification with the political ingroup and the common ingroup (being Chilean). There was a positive correlation in the right-wing group and a nonsignificant, nearly zero, correlation in the left-wing group.

CONCLUSION

This chapter has provided a theoretical framework and empirical evidence for understanding the role of emotions in two of the most prominent outcomes of any reconciliation process: willingness to forgive a perpetrator group and to make reparations to the victim group. On the basis of the data obtained from young Chileans who identified with one of the two groups involved in the conflict (left- and right-wing groups), the results reveal the important role that intergroup emotions play in mediating the identity–forgiveness and identity–reparation links. In addition, the evidence also supports the central idea of considering social identities when understanding these processes—particularly the role those groups played in the conflict. The results presented in this chapter provide support for the mediational role of intergroup emotions, which in turn is moderated by the groups' roles in the conflict (Shnabel & Nadler, 2008; Shnabel et al., 2009).

The evidence indicates that social identities are very relevant to an understanding of the Chilean conflict, even 2 decades after the end of the Pinochet regime. New generations who identify with the groups associated with past conflict keep approaching the other side from an intergroup perspective. Either directly or indirectly—that is, mediated through emotions—ingroup identities undermine positive intergroup attitudes (i.e., the willingness to forgive and offer reparation to the other group) and emotions (e.g., empathy and trust). Ingroup identity also stimulates negative emotions (e.g., anger). The evidence reviewed in this chapter also offers support for the positive role of a common national identity in bringing about positive intergroup emotions and attitudes. Common identity directly favored forgiveness, but not reparation, in both groups, and also had an indirect effect on forgiveness in the case of the victimized group. Altogether, our results indicate that social identity and intergroup emotion act together in complex forms when predicting positive outgroup attitudes, depending on the role of groups in the conflict.

Another relevant result concerns the role of intergroup emotions. Different patterns of mediation emerged for the two groups, confirming the relevance of emotions in understanding positive intergroup attitudes. Although all of the emotions showed significant relationships with at least one of the two identities and one of the outcome variables, empathy was the most consistent mediator. It mediated the relationship with forgiveness in both groups and the relationship with reparation in the perpetrator group. An unexpected result is that intergroup guilt was not a consistent mediator across the two groups. However, it was directly associated with reparation in both groups and with forgiveness in the victim group, and the association validates the general idea that collective guilt motivates people toward positive intergroup outcomes (Brown et al., 2008; Lickel et al., 2005; Wohl & Branscombe, 2005).

Future intervention programs might benefit from our general framework. Both forgiveness and reparation are important aspects of reconciliation and might be differentially predicted from social identities and intergroup emotions. For example, among perpetrators, attempts to focus on the promotion of common identities, the stimulation of awareness of the ingroup's past misdeeds and the encouragement of empathy with victims could increase the willingness to forgive and repair. Thus, understanding and accepting that the conflict involved two or more sides—that it caused negative and sometime severe consequences for all of them, alongside negative emotions—would provide the starting point of reconciliation. Indeed, we can assume that severe intergroup political conflicts often produce a strong tendency to associate negative emotions to intergroup situations, even many years after the conflict has stopped. These negative emotions are difficult to deal with and require systematic efforts to regulate or change them.

The evidence presented in this chapter suggests that the reconciliation process might benefit significantly if interventions in postconflict contexts are focused on intergroup empathy. For instance, we suggest that when societies decide to openly recognize past conflict or promote awareness in new generations (through memorials, history textbooks, and other cultural symbols), special care should be taken to include recognition of the suffering experienced by all parties involved in the conflict, even when the conflict has been clearly asymmetric. By doing so, people will be more willing to accept and understand the perspective of the outgroup, a precondition for forgiveness, and ultimately for the reconciliation process. Thus, taking the perspective of the outgroup—a central aspect of empathy—will virtuously promote both positive emotions and attitudes toward them. In addition, as the contact literature has confirmed (Čehajić et al., 2008; see also Swart et al., this volume), fostering positive intergroup contact between ingroup and outgroup members promotes empathetic feelings, which in turn are associated with positive emotions and attitudes toward the outgroup as a whole. Thus, empathy also mediates the contact–attitude link.

In terms of policy implications, we think that any intervention aimed at fostering positive intergroup relations in a postconflict society might benefit if common and ingroup identities, as well as emotions associated with the past conflict, are considered as proposed in the framework. Finally, it is important to acknowledge that the efforts toward actively preparing postconflict societies to move from destructive intergroup relations toward more constructive ones are complex and highly sensitive. In this chapter, we have aimed to make a contribution toward disentangling and understanding some of the important factors and their interrelationships underlying such efforts.

REFERENCES

Allport, G. W. (1954). *The nature of prejudice*. Reading, MA: Addison-Wesley.

Ashmore, R., Jussim, L., & Wilder, D. (2001). *Social identity, intergroup conflict, and conflict reduction*. New York, NY: Oxford University Press.

Barkan, E. (2000). *The guilt of nations*. London, England: Johns Hopkins University Press.

Bar-Tal, D. (2000). From intractable conflict through conflict resolution to reconciliation: A psychological analysis. *Political Psychology, 21*, 351–365. doi:10.1111/0162-895X.00192

Brewer, M. B. (1999). The psychology of prejudice. *Journal of Social Issues, 55*, 429–444. doi:10.1111/0022-4537.00126

Brewer, M., & Alexander, M. G. (2002). Intergroup emotions and images. In D. M. Mackie & E. R. Smith (Eds.), *From prejudice to intergroup emotions: Differentiated reactions to social groups* (pp. 209–226). New York, NY: Psychology Press.

Brown, R. (1995). *Prejudice: Its social psychology*. Oxford, England: Blackwell.

Brown, R., González, R., Zagefka, H., Manzi, J., & Cehajic, S. (2008). Nuestra culpa: Collective guilt as a predictor of reparation for historical wrongdoing. *Journal of Personality and Social Psychology, 94*, 75–90. doi:10.1037/0022-3514.94.1.75

Čehajić, S., Brown, R., & Castano, E. (2008). Forgive and forget? Antecedents and consequences of intergroup forgiveness in Bosnia and Herzegovina. *Political Psychology, 29*, 351–367. doi:10.1111/j.1467-9221.2008.00634.x

Doosje, B., Branscombe, N. R., Spears, R., & Manstead, S. R. (1998). Guilty by association: When one's group has a negative history. *Journal of Personality and Social Psychology, 75*, 872–886. doi:10.1037/0022-3514.75.4.872

Dovidio, J. F., ten Verget, M., Stewart, T. L., Gaertner, S. L., Johson, J. D., Esses, V. M., . . . Pearson, A. R. (2004). Perspective and prejudice: Antecedents and mediating mechanism. *Personality and Social Psychology Bulletin, 30*, 1537–1549. doi:10.1177/0146167204271177

Enright, R. D., & Zell, R. L. (1989). Problems we encounter when we forgive one another. *Journal of Psychology and Christianity, 8*, 52–60.

Exline, J. J., Worthington, E. L., Hill, P., & McCullough, M. E. (2003). Forgiveness and justice: A research agenda for social and personality psychology. *Personality and Social Psychology Review, 7*, 337–348. doi:10.1207/S15327957PSPR0704_06

Finlay, K. A., & Stephan, W. G. (2000). Improving intergroup relations: The effects of empathy on racial attitudes. *Journal of Applied Social Psychology, 30*, 1720–1737. doi:10.1111/j.1559-1816.2000.tb02464.x

Gaertner, S., & Dovidio, J. F. (2000). *Reducing intergroup bias: The common ingroup identity model*. Philadelphia, PA: Psychology Press.

González, R., & Brown, R. J. (2003). Generalization of positive attitude as a function of subgroup and superordinate group identifications in intergroup contact. *European Journal of Social Psychology, 33*, 195–214. doi:10.1002/ejsp.140

González, R., & Brown, R. J. (2006). Dual identities in intergroup contact: Group status and size moderate the generalization of positive attitude change. *Journal of Experimental Social Psychology, 42*, 753–767. doi:10.1016/j.jesp.2005.11.008

González, R., Manzi, J., & Noor, M. (2010). *Social identity and intergroup emotions: Testing a mediational model to predict intergroup forgiveness and reparation in Chile*. Manuscript in preparation.

González, R., Manzi, J., Saiz, J., Brewer, M., de Tezanos-Pinto, P., Torres, D., . . . Aldunate, N. (2008). Inter-party attitudes in Chile: Coalitions as superordinate social identities. *Political Psychology, 29*, 93–118.

Gordijn, E., Wigboldus, D., & Yzerbyt, V. (2001). Emotional consequences of categorizing victims of negative outgroup behavior as ingroup or ingroup. *Group Processes & Intergroup Relations, 4*, 317–326. doi:10.1177/1368430201004004002

Hewstone, M., Cairns, E., Voci, A., McLernon, F., Niens, U., & Noor, M. (2004). Intergroup forgiveness and guilt in Northern Ireland: Social psychological dimensions of "The Troubles." In N. R. Branscombe & B. Doosje (Eds.), *Collective guilt: International perspectives* (pp. 193–215). Cambridge, England: Cambridge University Press.

Hewstone, M., Rubin, M., & Willis, H. (2002). Intergroup bias. *Annual Review of Psychology, 53*, 575–604. doi:10.1146/annurev.psych.53.100901.135109

Iyer, A., Leach, C. W., & Crosby, F. (2003). White guilt and racial compensation: The benefits and limits of self-focus. *Personality and Social Psychology Bulletin, 29*, 117–129. doi:10.1177/0146167202238377

Iyer, A., Schmader, T., & Lickel, B. (2007). Why individuals protest the perceived transgressions of their country: The role of anger, shame and guilt. *Personality and Social Psychology Bulletin, 33*, 572–587. doi:10.1177/0146167206297402

Lickel, B., Schmader, T., & Barquissau, M. (2004). The evocation of moral emotions in intergroup contexts: The distinction between collective guilt and collective shame. In N. Branscombe & B. Doosje (Eds.), *Collective guilt: International perspectives* (pp. 35–55). Cambridge, England: Cambridge University Press.

Lickel, B., Schmader, T., Curtis, M., Scarnier, M., & Ames, D. R. (2005). Vicarious shame and guilt. *Group Processes & Intergroup Relations, 8*, 145–157. doi:10.1177/1368430205051064

Lira, E. (2009). Legado de las violaciones de derechos humanos: Políticas de verdad, justicia, reparación y memoria en Chile, 1990–2007 [The legacy of human rights violations: Chilean politics of truth, justice, reparation, and memory, 1990–2007]. In C. Arnson, A. Armony, C. Smulovitz, G. Chillier, E. Peruzzotti, & G. Cohen (Eds.), *La nueva izquierda en América Latina: Derechos humanos, participación política y sociedad civil* (pp. 20–45). Washington, DC: Woodrow Wilson International Center for Scholars.

Mackie, D. M., & Smith, E. R. (2002). *From prejudice to inter-group emotions: Differentiated reactions to social groups*. New York, NY: Psychology Press.

Manzi, J., & González, R. (2007). Forgiveness and reparation in Chile: The role of cognitive and emotional intergroup antecedents. *Peace and Conflict, 13*, 71–91.

Marques, J. M., Abrams, D., & Serodio, R. (2001). Being better by being right: Subjective group dynamics and derogation of ingroup deviants when generic norms are undermined. *Journal of Personality and Social Psychology, 81,* 436–447. doi:10.1037/0022-3514.81.3.436

McAuley, J., McGlynn, C., & Tonge, J. (2008). Conflict resolution in asymmetric and symmetric situations: Northern Ireland as a case study. *Dynamics of Asymmetric Conflict, 1,* 88–102. doi:10.1080/17467580802284712

Mitchell, C. (2000). *Gestures of conciliation factors contributing to successful olive branches.* London, England: Macmillan Press.

Nadler, A. (2002). Post resolution processes: An instrumental and socio-emotional routes to reconciliation. In G. Salomon & B. Nevo (Eds.), *Peace education worldwide: The concept, underlying principles, and research* (pp. 127–143). Mahwah, NJ: Erlbaum.

Nadler, A., & Liviatan, I. (2004). Intergroup reconciliation processes in Israel: Theoretical analysis and empirical findings. In N. R. Branscombe & B. Doosje (Eds.), *Collective guilt: International perspectives* (pp. 216–235). Cambridge, England: Cambridge University Press.

Nadler, A., & Saguy, T. (2003). Reconciliation between nations: Overcoming emotional deterrents to ending conflicts between groups. In H. Langholtz & C. E. Stout (Eds.), *The psychology of diplomacy* (pp. 29–46). New York, NY: Praeger.

Noor, M., Brown, R., Lewis, C., González, R., & Manzi, J. (2008). On positive psychological outcomes: What helps groups with a history of conflict to forgive and reconcile with each other? *Personality and Social Psychology Bulletin, 34,* 819–832. doi:10.1177/0146167208315555

Noor, M., Brown, R., & Prentice, G. (2008). Precursors and mediators of intergroup reconciliation in Northern Ireland: A new model. *British Journal of Social Psychology, 47,* 481–495. doi:10.1348/014466607X238751

Roccas, S., Klar, Y., & Liviatan, I. (2004). Exonerating cognitions, group identification, and personal values as predictors of collective guilt among Jewish-Israelis. In N. Branscombe & B. Doosje (Eds.), *Collective guilt: International perspectives* (pp. 130–147). Cambridge, England: Cambridge University Press.

Shnabel, N., & Nadler, A. (2008). A needs-based model of reconciliation: Satisfying the differential emotional needs of victim and perpetrator as a key to promoting reconciliation. *Journal of Personality and Social Psychology, 94,* 116–132. doi:10.1037/0022-3514.94.1.116

Shnabel, N., Nadler, A., Ullrich, J., Dovidio, J. F., & Carmi, D. (2009). Promoting reconciliation through the satisfaction of the emotional needs of victimized and perpetrating group members: The needs-based model of reconciliation. *Personality and Social Psychology Bulletin, 35,* 1021–1030. doi:10.1177/0146167209336610

Staub, E. (2000). Genocide and mass killing: Origins, prevention a, healing and reconciliation. *Political Psychology, 21,* 367–382. doi:10.1111/0162-895X.00193

Stephan, W. G., & Stephan, C. W. (2000). An integrated threat theory of prejudice. In S. Oskamp (Ed.), *Reducing prejudice and discrimination* (pp. 23–45). Hillsdale, NJ: Erlbaum.

Tajfel, H., & Turner, J. C. (1986). The social identity theory of intergroup behavior. In S. Worchel & W. G. Austin (Eds.), *Psychology of intergroup relations* (pp. 7–24). Chicago, IL: Nelson Hall.

Tam, T., Hewstone, M., Kenworthy, J., & Cairns, E. (2009). Intergroup trust in Northern Ireland. *Personality and Social Psychology Bulletin, 35*, 45–59. doi:10.1177/0146167208325004

Tangney, J. P., & Dearing, R. L. (2002). *Shame and guilt.* New York, NY: Guilford Press.

Wohl, M. J., & Branscombe, N. R. (2005). Forgiveness and collective guilt: Assignment to historical perpetrator groups depends on level of social category inclusiveness. *Journal of Personality and Social Psychology, 88*, 288–303. doi:10.1037/0022-3514.88.2.288

CONCLUSION: POSITIVE THOUGHTS ABOUT POSITIVE APPROACHES TO INTERGROUP RELATIONS

SAMUEL L. GAERTNER AND JOHN F. DOVIDIO

Collectively, the preceding chapters persuasively argue that knowledge about improving intergroup attitudes and relationships can benefit from reframing the primary research question. These chapters explore the utility of shifting the focus of research from examining negative outgroup attitudes, and especially how to reduce them, to understanding the development and promotion of positive outgroup attitudes. The shift in paradigm advocated in the current volume offers new insights theoretically, as well as practically, for contributing to harmonious and respectful cross-group relationships. We agree that much can be gained by focusing on positive attitudes and the factors that encourage interest in other groups. In this concluding chapter, we consider the promise of this perspective.

Prejudice has traditionally been considered to be an unfavorable attitude toward another group, involving negative beliefs, feelings, and behavior. For example, Allport (1954) defined prejudice as "an antipathy based on faulty and inflexible generalization" (p. 9). Perhaps as a consequence of this classic perspective, the prejudice of Whites toward Blacks has typically been measured

Preparation of this chapter was facilitated by National Science Foundation Grant 0613218 to Samuel L. Gaertner and John F. Dovidio.

241

using attitude scales reflecting Whites' degree of endorsement of statements about negative attributes of Blacks, negative feelings toward the group, and support for policies that restrict opportunities for Blacks (Brigham, 1993; Henry & Sears, 2002; McConahay, 1986). The attention directed by the present volume to positive intergroup attitudes, not simply negative forms, constitutes a major paradigm shift in this area.

Promoting positive orientations toward members of other groups offers a particularly valuable perspective for approaching intergroup relations for several fundamental reasons. First, although outgroup enmity represents the traditional emphasis for understanding intergroup relations, Brewer (1999) observed that differential "love" for ingroup members over outgroup members has critical implications for trust, greed, and altruism that determine both intragroup and intergroup relations. Second, expressions of intergroup bias are frequently driven by more positive qualities associated with one's own group than in terms of more negative characteristics of another group (Mummendey, Otten, Berger, & Kessler, 2000). Thus, interventions directed at positive attitudes have the potential for a greater impact on intergroup relations. Third, because discrimination violates egalitarian norms, people are often guarded about directly mistreating others based on group membership, but they more freely offer special benefits and advantages to members of their own group (Gaertner et al., 1997). Laws protect people from many forms of discrimination against them, but they rarely prohibit others from behaving especially positively toward their ingroup members.

Besides the shift in emphasis from negative to positive attitudes, the redirection of orientation from a prevention focus, involving an inhibition of negative behavior, to a promotion focus, emphasizing the value of positive action, can have a fundamental motivational impact. As Higgins's (1999) work reveals, a prevention focus involves sensitivity to negative outcomes, arouses negative emotions such as guilt and anxiety, and produces an avoidance motivation. Cognitively, attempts to suppress negative thoughts in intergroup interaction can result in a "rebound effect" in which negative associations become even more accessible—and potentially more influential—than normal (Macrae, Bodenhausen, Milne, & Jetten, 1994). Behaviorally, these concerns can lead to avoidance of intergroup contact and greater self-concern than interest in the outgroup person (Vorauer, 2006). By contrast, a promotion focus directs attention to potential positive outcomes and benefits, generates an approach orientation, and produces greater concern for others. Moreover, when people adopt a promotion focus, progress toward achieving their goals elicits positive emotions that are self-reinforcing and strengthen their positive motivation.

Each of the chapters in this volume addresses this core issue in a different way. In this chapter, we reflect on the novel ideas of these chapters, note some common themes that link them to each other as well as more broadly to other works (including our own), and explore how the new insights contained in this volume may guide future research. Our goal is not to summarize each but to highlight particularly distinctive insights that relate to and illuminate the importance of promoting positive intergroup attitudes and motivations.

REFLECTIONS ON THE PRECEDING CHAPTERS

In this section, we suggest one way that the different contributions of the chapters can be conceptually organized, which is presented schematically in Figure 1. Collectively, the chapters examine how different individual-level and social factors, historical as well as contemporaneous, shape expectations, needs, and goals that are activated as people prepare for intergroup interaction. A critical aspect of the interaction involves how members of different groups come to perceive their relations cognitively and the degree to which they develop emotional connections with each other. These expanded connections then contribute to multiple facets of positive intergroup attitudes.

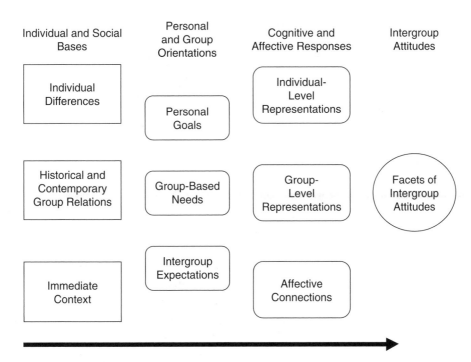

Figure 1. Processes contributing to intergroup attitudes.

Bases of Prejudice and Nonprejudice

For the most part, social psychologists have addressed the problem of prejudice by asking what causes people to be prejudiced. Much of the previous research in social psychology on intergroup relations has been concerned with historical and contemporary factors that arouse competitive relations between groups over material resources (i.e., realistic group conflict; Sherif & Sherif, 1969), ideology (symbolic conflict), and relative group position (Tajfel & Turner, 1979). Individual differences in orientations to power (Adorno, Frenkel-Brunswik, Levinson, & Sanford, 1950) and zero-sum relations (Sidanius & Pratto, 1999) have been studied as important contributors to intergroup bias and conflict. It seems reasonable to assume that if we understand the processes underlying why people *are* prejudiced, we could reframe this body of knowledge to answer the provocative question Livingston addresses in this volume: "(Why) are some people not prejudiced?" Specifically, Livingston asks, "What is unique about these individuals?" Livingston finds that nonprejudiced people are less apt to form negative associations and more likely to develop positive associations to neutral stimuli on paired-associate learning tasks than other people.

Whereas traditional research on prejudice in social psychology has focused on individual differences that are associated with especially negative orientations toward other groups, Livingston draws attention to individual differences that distinguish people as well, but in terms of an unusual, non-prejudiced intergroup orientation. Psychologists have debated the "normality" of prejudice (Fox, 1992), but Livingston also raises complex questions about the normality of not being prejudiced. In addition, this work suggests the value of looking more deeply into fundamental dimensions of personality, such as the Big Five dimension of Agreeableness (see Graziano, Bruce, Sheese, & Tobin, 2007) and its relationship to especially low levels of intergroup bias.

Personal and Group Orientations

The prospect of intergroup interaction is fraught with anxiety. This anxiety is rooted, in part, by the potential threats associated with outgroups (Riek, Mania, & Gaertner, 2006) and negative expectations of outgroup members. In some cases, when social norms emphasize egalitarian treatment of members of other groups, anxiety originates from self-image maintenance concerns. The chapters by Mallett, Wagner, and Harrison; by Migacheva, Tropp, and Crocker; and by Butz and Plant in this volume all detail how negative expectations about others and oneself, as well as needs and goals (see Figure 1, column 2), contribute to a person's motivation to avoid cross-group interactions.

Just as important, however, each chapter also reveals how the motivation to avoid intergroup interaction can be overcome and ultimately how people can become motivated to approach outgroup members.

Mallett et al. (this volume) describes an intervention that induces participants to expect a more pleasant intergroup interaction (Mallett & Wilson, 2010). In this intervention, White college students watch a video of cross-group interaction in which a Black student and a White student become friends, despite initially having negative expectations about forming a friendship. Participants are then asked to connect the story to their own experiences in which an interaction went better than expected. Mallett and colleagues report that this intervention subsequently facilitated White participants' positive interaction with Black students, and it also increased the number of cross-race friendships participants formed over the next week. Apparently, this intervention is successful because it leads people to be more relaxed and have more cognitive resources to devote to making their laboratory interaction go smoothly, which in turn increased positive expectations and motivation regarding cross-race friendships. Thus, as Higgins (1999) proposed, whereas a prevention focus elicits negative affect and avoidance, with a promotion focus people experience positive emotion that reinforces their approach motivation. Although much of the contemporary research on intergroup relations emphasizes the fragility of intergroup relations and how they can spiral negatively (Dovidio, Gaertner, Kawakami, & Hodson, 2002), Mallett et al. show that when expectations are reoriented from negative to positive, people may show successive increases in their motivations to engage members of other groups.

Butz and Plant's chapter reveals that concerns over potentially negative outcomes can have a particularly detrimental impact on intergroup interaction. One type of negative expectation involves perceptions of one's own behavior. People who have concerns about their ability to behave in a nonprejudiced manner in interracial interactions experience stress and anxiety, which motivates avoidance of these interactions. Indeed, experimentally providing negative efficacy feedback (vs. positive or no feedback) about White participants' ability to respond in a nonprejudiced manner during a forthcoming interaction with a Black participant heightened their desire to avoid the interaction. This negative efficacy feedback not only influenced participants' interracial anxiety during the interaction and their desire to avoid future interracial interaction, it also affected the Black partner's perceptions of the participant's anxiety. Another type of negative expectation, one focused on the partner, is also detrimental to constructive intergroup interaction. Participants who learn that a Black interaction partner is likely to reject them show negative approach responses, such as anger and hostility.

Nevertheless, increasing internal motivation to respond without prejudice seems to have a palliative effect in these contexts. Blascovich and Mendes (2000) demonstrated that people who perceive that their personal resources for responding to a stressful situation exceed the demands of the situation regarded these situations as a challenge to be overcome rather than as a threat. Plant and Devine (1998) proposed that people high on internal motivation to respond without prejudice would have greater confidence (i.e., greater feelings of self-efficacy) in regulating behaviors reflective of prejudice during interracial interactions. Consistent with this hypothesis, people high on internal motivation to respond without prejudice experienced lower levels of anxiety and behaved more positively in the cross-race interactions relative to those people who were externally motivated to respond without prejudice.

The chapters by Mallett et al. and by Butz and Plant focus on people's personal (i.e., self-oriented) needs during intergroup interactions. Whereas Mallett et al. consider expectations about how pleasant people will find the interaction, Butz and Plant discuss the importance of perceived self-efficacy to respond without prejudice during these interactions. By contrast, Migacheva, Tropp, and Crocker consider the possibility that people may have other-oriented, as well as self-oriented, motivations in cross-group interactions. Egosystem motivations involve self-image management and the achievement of personal goals, whereas ecosystem motivations involve a focus on the other person's needs and concerns. Migacheva et al. propose that changing a person's primary motivational perspective from a self-oriented goal (e.g., the desire to appear and behave as one who is nonprejudiced) to a goal that also includes concerns for others (e.g., to understand or learn about others) has dramatic positive effects on intergroup relations. Thus, Migacheva et al.'s position goes beyond the perspectives described by Mallett et al. and by Butz and Plant by advocating both the benefits of reducing self-concerns in interracial interactions and of increasing concerns for others with whom they are interacting.

Cognitive and Affective Responses

Once motivational concerns about entering intergroup interactions have been mitigated or supplemented by other-oriented motivations, there is a greater opportunity for cross-group interactions to produce cross-group friendships. Cross-group friendships are an important way in which prejudice can be reduced (Pettigrew, 1997). Nevertheless, there is a concern that close interpersonal relationships may decrease the salience of group identities and thus disable a critical link necessary for the generalization of positive attitudes from these personal relationships to the groups as a whole (Brown and Hewstone, 2005). Even in close friendships, though (or with common identity, considered by González, Manzi, and Noor in this volume), it is unlikely that group memberships will be entirely ignored; they may be deemphasized but not entirely eliminated, and thus generalization will still occur (Miller, 2002). At one level, having friends from another group can create more positive expectations of intergroup interactions (Figure 1, column 2); at another level, it can substantially alter the way intergroup relations are cognitively represented (Figure 1, column 3).

Davies, Wright, and Aron review a secondary benefit of cross-group friendship, an extended contact effect. The extended contact effect represents the finding that knowledge of an ingroup and an outgroup members' friendship can increase favorable outgroup attitudes among ingroup members who are aware of their relationship. While this connection provides the potential for more positive outgroup attitudes, generalization is more likely to occur when the member of the other group involved in the relationship is perceived as a typical outgroup member. Thus, cross-group friendships can have cascading effects.

Creating stronger connections to particular outgroup members through the development of cross-group friendships (see Swart et al., this volume) or common identity (see González et al., this volume) that generalize to the group as a whole also facilitates positive *intergroup* responses, such as greater willingness to forgive immediate or historical transgressions by the outgroup. Swart et al. show that positive interpersonal contact contributes to the development of cross-group friendships, which predicts a greater willingness to forgive the outgroup in Northern Ireland (see also Noor, Brown, & Prentice, 2008). González, Manzi, and Noor find that, in Chile, a stronger national identity (as opposed to a left-leaning or right-leaning subgroup identity) fosters forgiveness by reducing anger and increasing feelings of trust, empathy, collective guilt, and shame. In a different intergroup context, Wohl and Branscombe (2005) observed that increasing the salience of Jewish students' "human identity," in contrast to their "Jewish identity," increased their perceptions of similarity between Jews and Germans, as well as their willingness to forgive Germans for the Holocaust and their interest in associating with contemporary German students.

The processes by which cross-group friendship, either directly for the friends or indirectly through the extended contact effect, promotes more positive intergroup attitudes are not fully understood. While close cross-group friendship can elicit goals relating to learning about and caring for the other (ecosystem motivations), the process by which these friendships relate to generalization is believed to be more self-centered. According to self-expansion theory (see Page-Gould & Mendoza-Denton, this volume), inclusion of one's own cross-group friend as part of the self or knowledge of an ingroup friend's cross-group friendship connects the self to the outgroup as a whole (see Figure 1, column 3). That is, these interpersonal (friendship) or intergroup (recategorization with a common identity) *unit formations* bring outgroup members closer to the self (see Brewer, 1979; and Gaertner, Mann, Murrell, & Dovidio, 1989), perhaps integrating them into the self concept (see Davies et al., this volume), thereby activating motivations involving concerns for the other. When the other becomes part of the self, it is more likely that communal, compassionate motivations and goals will be activated (see Migacheva et al., this volume). Also, these interpersonal and intergroup unit formations are likely capable of reducing the anxiety and concerns about entering cross-group interactions discussed by Mallett et al. and by Butz and Plant. Thus, contact with outgroup members leading to friendships or perceptions of common ingroup identity may have additional positive effects on intergroup behavior.

Stronger other-oriented motivations, which may be stimulated by cross-group friendship or an inclusive common identity, can, in turn, increase sensitivity to the needs of outgroup members and elicit greater interest in satisfying the distinct needs of victim and perpetrator groups, as specified in Nadler and Shnabel's contribution to this volume. Thus, these interpersonal or intergroup unit formations may increase the likelihood that members of victim groups would offer forgiveness and moral acceptance to members of the perpetrator group, whereas perpetrators would be more likely to empower victims. As detailed by Nadler and Shnabel's needs-based model, this mutual exchange promotes intergroup reconciliation. Purdie-Vaughns and Walton further discuss how different prevailing intergroup perspectives—specifically colorblindness and multiculturalism—relate to the psychological needs and goals of members of minority groups. Purdie-Vaughns and Walton challenge the view that multiculturalism is necessarily beneficial for minority-group members and emphasize that people from different social groups can experience the same social context in different ways, contingent on how they perceive their identity is valued. Minority group members' perceptions of "identity safety," in which their group identity is not only recognized (as Nadler & Shnabel, this volume, propose for victims) but is also respected by majority group members in a given context, is critical to minorities' well-being and promoting positive intergroup attitudes.

Facets of Intergroup Attitudes

Because of the traditional emphasis on negativity in prejudice, conventional scales of prejudice conceptualize the relevant continuum to run from high levels of antipathy to feelings approaching an absence of negativity, or neutrality (i.e., from high to low prejudice). If nonprejudiced people are predisposed to develop strong associations between neutral stimuli and positive affect, as Livingston (this volume) finds, outgroup attitudes might extend beyond just attitudinal neutrality and indeed be very positive (Figure 1, column 4). Pittinsky, Rosenthal, and Montoya's Allophilia Scale (this volume) recognizes the potential existence of positive feelings toward outgroup members, thus complementing in an innovative way the conventional emphasis on the negativity of intergroup attitudes. The Allophilia Scale provides a valuable taxonomy of the specific facets of outgroup attitudes to capture a variety of positive beliefs and feelings. These facets or factors (i.e., affection, comfort, kinship, enthusiasm, and engagement) can singly or together predict a range of intergroup behaviors. These facets of positive attitudes are better predictors of positive behaviors, such as allocations to charity, than are negative attitudes, whereas negative attitudes are better predictors of negative behaviors toward outgroups, such as limiting antidiscrimination policies.

The taxonomy of positive attitudes offered by Pittinsky and colleagues in the Allophilia Scale can permit more detailed understanding of some of the issues discussed in the other chapters, particularly concerning ways of promoting positive intergroup attitudes. For example, future research might productively explore how direct and extended contact, cross-group friendships, and revised intergroup goals affect specific facets of allophilia. By including allophilia items as well as items geared to measure more negative outgroup sentiments, we could determine, for example, whether cross-group friendships increase positive outgroup attitudes or decrease negative outgroup attitudes, or both, and more specifically, which facets of positive and negative attitudes are changed uniquely by this strategy. Understanding both the antecedents and consequences of different facets of allophilia can theoretically elucidate the various ways that different interventions can promote positive intergroup attitudes and ultimately behavior, and, practically, help tailor interventions to address those processes most central for ameliorating a particular intergroup problem.

The insights contained in the chapters in this volume can help reorient the field to consider the relatively neglected aspect of intergroup relations, the potential of positive intergroup attitudes. As we depicted in Figure 1, the preceding chapters suggest a series of processes that may operate sequentially to shape intergroup relations. The current volume thus offers novel perspectives on the conceptual processes in intergroup relations. In the next section, we illustrate the applicability of many of these points by considering how they shed new light on our own work.

APPLYING NEW PERSPECTIVES

Our earlier work on aversive racism challenged the assumption that Whites who appear nonprejudiced on self-report instruments and who may truly believe that they possess egalitarian principles are nonracist. Specifically, our research on aversive racism (see Dovidio & Gaertner, 2004; Gaertner & Dovidio, 1986; see also Kovel, 1970) revealed that many of these presumably nonprejudiced Whites have not entirely escaped cultural and cognitive forces that promote racial bias despite their genuinely egalitarian value system. Rather, those who appear nonracist on these measures do discriminate in subtle, rationalizable ways that insulate them from awareness of their own racial biases (see Crosby, Bromley, & Saxe, 1980; Devine, 1989). To maintain and reaffirm this nonprejudiced image, in interracial contexts aversive racists are motivated to avoid acting inappropriately (e.g., thinking of stereotypes, feeling racial hubris, or discriminating behaviorally).

On the basis of this presumed motivation to avoid acting inappropriately in interracial contexts, we predicted when aversive racists would and would not be likely to discriminate. Namely, we hypothesized that they would tend not to discriminate in situations containing strong, clear social norms that explicitly define behavior that is inappropriate. Racial discrimination would be more likely in the absence of these normative guideposts. Furthermore, discrimination becomes more likely when nonracial factors permit rationalizing a negative response on the basis of factors other than race.

Mallett et al.; Butz and Plant; and Migacheva, Tropp, and Crocker all emphasize the different ways that self-focus and self-image concerns can adversely affect intergroup interaction, undermining the goal of aversive racists to appear nonprejudiced and to have, at least superficially, positive and smooth interracial interactions. Negative expectations of one's ability to appear nonprejudiced and concerns about how one will be viewed by partners of a different race can cause aversive racists to "choke" (see Vorauer, 2006) and can interfere with their ability to convey their egalitarian values and intentions effectively in interracial interactions. Thus, whereas our work focused on the intentions of aversive racists, these chapters in the present volume highlight the importance of examining the unintended consequences of the concerns of aversive racists about appearing nonprejudiced on intergroup dynamics.

The chapters in the current volume also offer an alternative perspective on the nature and dynamics of aversive racism more generally. Our traditional assumption has been that the subtle bias manifested by aversive racists primarily reflects their unconscious anti-Black (or anti-outgroup) attitudes. However, as the present volume suggests, modern forms of bias, such as aversive racism, may characterize a significant component of pro-White (i.e., pro-ingroup) attitudes that do not seem racist to aversive racists. Indeed, we began to suspect that at least some aversive racists did not have more negative attitudes toward Blacks than toward fellow Whites, but rather they had more positive attitudes toward Whites than toward Blacks (Gaertner et al., 1997). Thus, Blacks and other minorities were regarded as "strangers" for whom aversive racists had no sense of emotional attachment, affection, and kinship—

elements that facilitate the delivery of prosocial, positive behaviors, as Pittinsky et al. reveal in their chapter.

In one study (Gaertner & Dovidio, 1977), for example, we conceptually replicated the famous Darley and Latané (1968) "diffusion of responsibility" study, but we also varied the race of the victim (as Black or White). In their classic study, Darley and Latané discovered that when a person is alone at the time of an emergency, all of the responsibility for helping is focused on this one bystander; the appropriate behavior—to help—is clearly defined. However, as the number of additional bystanders increases, the responsibility for helping becomes diffused, or shared, among the various bystanders. In the multiple-bystander condition, the forces propelling intervention on any one bystander become weaker.

In our study, the presence of other bystanders provides White participants a non-race-related justification allowing them to rationalize a failure to intervene. When the victim of the emergency is Black, the presence of other bystanders, not bigoted intent, could be used to justify a decision not to help. Thus, there should be hardly any awareness that the victim's race influenced the participants' behavior. When the participant is the only bystander, however, the situation is quite different. In view of the clarity of the emergency, failure of the single bystander to help a Black victim could very easily be self-attributed to bigoted intent, an outcome that would be very costly to aversive racists whose motivation, we proposed, involves *avoiding inappropriate behavior in interracial situations*. Therefore, we expected that the forces propelling action on behalf of a Black victim would be especially strong and effective when the White bystander was alone.

The results were supportive of these predictions. Whites believing themselves to be the only bystander helped Black victims somewhat more than White victims (94% vs. 81%). White bystanders who believed that two other White bystanders could also intervene, however, helped White victims more frequently than they helped Black victims (75% vs. 38%). But does this reflect participants' anti-Black sentiment, as we initially believed? The tendency to diffuse responsibility more readily for Black victims than for White victims could perhaps more likely inform us of participants' relatively positive attitudes toward fellow Whites and does not necessarily suggest that our bystanders were anti-Black.

When pressure to take action is weak (e.g., other bystanders are present) or when the situation inhibits action (e.g., emergency technicians ask people to stand back), a person's failure to help would not be particularly revealing of his or her negative feelings toward the victim. However, taking action under these circumstances, particularly when it is nonnormative, would be very informative about a person's positive attitude toward the victim. Thus, greater positivity for ingroup members, rather than greater negativity for racial outgroup members, may have played a role in this experiment. Only when the situation strongly encourages intervention (e.g., when a person is the only bystander or a person calls directly for assistance) would inaction be potentially revealing of a person's negative outgroup attitudes.

Nevertheless, it is important to emphasize that bias rooted in positive feelings for one group over another group can be as pernicious as discrimination based on antioutgroup orientations (Murrell, Dietz-Uhler, Dovidio, Gaertner, & Drout, 1994). Thus, the development of allophilia toward the outgroup may represent an additional strategy for reducing intergroup bias. In addition, the Allophilia Scale may differentiate nonprejudiced Whites from aversive racists. Both groups score low on self-report prejudice measures, but nonprejudiced Whites would likely be much higher on allophilia than aversive racists, who are mainly concerned with appearing nonprejudiced. Although there may be social norms discouraging antioutgroup prejudice, it is not socially required to have strong feelings of affection and enthusiasm for members of a particular group. Therefore, in our opinion, the study of allophilia is a theoretically and methodologically important development in the field of intergroup relations.

Understanding the role of positive attitudes in intergroup bias can also critically inform strategies to reduce tension and conflict between groups. Mallett et al. and Butz and Plant directly indicate the value of creating more positive expectations of intergroup contact. Other chapters, including those by Davies et al. and by Page-Gould and Mendoza-Denton, implicate the role of intergroup friendships in creating more positive expectations and interpersonal connections.

However, the chapter by González, Manzi, and Noor relates most directly to our approach. The common ingroup identity model (Gaertner & Dovidio, 2000, 2009) was developed primarily to address the issue of how to change the racial attitudes of aversive racists, who already understand that racism is wrong but who believe that they are not racially biased. The model, which was derived from the social categorization approach to intergroup behavior (Brown & Turner, 1979; Tajfel & Turner, 1979), asserts that intergroup bias and conflict can be reduced by factors that transform members' cognitive representation of the memberships from two groups to one group. This change in members' perceptions of group boundaries thus enables some of the cognitive and motivational processes that may contribute initially to intergroup bias (i.e., ingroup favoritism) to be redirected toward establishing more harmonious intergroup relations.

Theoretically, the process by which a more inclusive superordinate identity can reduce bias rests on two related conclusions of Brewer's (1979) analysis, as well as on the basic premises of social identity theory (Tajfel & Turner, 1979) and self-categorization theory (Turner, 1985). First, intergroup bias frequently takes the form of ingroup enhancement rather than outgroup devaluation. Second, group formation brings ingroup members closer to the self. Thus, factors that induce a more inclusive, common ingroup representation are able to extend processes that produce positive feelings toward ingroup members to former outgroup members. We have consistently found among children, high school and college students, participants in corporate mergers, and members of blended families that a common ingroup identity reduces intergroup bias by increasing positive attitudes toward former outgroup members while having limited effects on attitudes toward former ingroup members (Gaertner & Dovidio, 2000, 2009).

Because a common ingroup identity focuses on redirecting the forces of ingroup favoritism, it can potentially change the motivational orientation of aversive racists from self-oriented (self-image) goals, such as to avoid wrong-doing, to an orientation concerned with goals involving *doing what is right for group members*, including former outgroup members. Migacheva et al. highlight the importance of changing intergroup goals in this way. In one of our studies (Dovidio, Gaertner, & Kawakami, 1998; Gaertner & Dovidio, 2000), we examined the issue of how motivations to appear nonprejudiced can result in an increased accessibility of the negative thoughts that people are trying to suppress—a "rebound effect" (Macrae et al., 1994). White participants who were about to interact with a White or a Black confederate were (a) asked to try to avoid wrongdoing, (b) instructed to try to behave correctly toward the other person, (c) informed that they were part of the same team with their partner and competing against a team at a rival institution, or (d) given no instructions. The dependent measure of interest was the relative accessibility of negative thoughts, as assessed by responses on a Stroop color-naming task. We hypothesized that because the primary motivation of aversive racists in interracial interaction is to avoid wrongdoing and thus to suppress negative thoughts and feelings, participants explicitly instructed to avoid wrongdoing and those given no instructions would show relatively strong accessibility of negative thoughts after interacting with a Black confederate. In contrast, we expected participants instructed to behave correctly and those in the "same team" condition (who were hypothesized to adopt a positive orientation on their own) would escape such a rebound effect.

The results revealed that when the confederate was White, the experimental conditions did not affect the accessibility of negative thoughts. When the confederate was Black, however, the increased accessibility of negative relative to positive characteristics (from a pretest to the posttest) in the "avoid wrongdoing" and "no instructions" conditions was significantly greater than in the "do right" and "same team" conditions. The latter two conditions showed an increase in the accessibility of positive relative to negative thoughts. The pattern of these findings suggests that the development of a common ingroup identity can alter motivation in interracial situations from one involving concerns about a nonprejudiced self-presentation to one that is more appetitive and prosocial in terms of concerns for the other (see also Migacheva et al., this volume). Creation of the positive outgroup attitudes and associated perceptions and motivations can further create a foundation of forgiveness for past injury and trust in future interaction across group lines (see Swart et al., this volume). Forgiveness and trust are critical for establishing stable, and perhaps positively reinforcing, intergroup relations.

Future research might consider exploring the different effects of interpersonal (friendship) and group-based (common identity) unit formations in promoting positive intergroup outcomes. For example, one of the fascinating findings reported by González, Manzi, and Noor (this volume) is that common national identity, while effective for the left-wing victim group, did not lead to forgiveness among members of the right-wing perpetrator group. They propose that this difference occurs because the right-wing identity is synonymous with the national identity. Thus, future research could examine the possibility that, in such instances of subgroup and superordinate group identity overlap, cross-group friendships relative to common identity may be more effective in eliciting guilt, shame, and trust—which in turn promote forgiveness and reconciliation among perpetrator groups.

From a practical standpoint, although intergroup friendships can be encouraged in the laboratory with friendship-building exercises (Aron, Melinat, Aron, Vallone, & Bator, 1997), a vexing problem is how to facilitate the occurrence of mutually self-revealing interactions during intergroup contact in more natural settings. Our research suggests that creating a common ingroup identity increases self-disclosure and prosocial behavior across group lines (Dovidio et al., 1997). In addition, an elementary school antibias educational program that emphasized increasing the inclusiveness of children's circles of caring and sharing, using principles compatible with developing a common ingroup identity, increased the willingness of children to choose a child who was of a race and gender different from their own to be their most preferred playmate (Houlette et al., 2004). Thus, conditions of contact that can induce perceptions of a common ingroup membership, such as those identified by contact theory (Allport, 1954; see Gaertner & Dovidio, 2000), can initiate more self-revealing interactions, which facilitate the development of cross-group friendships (West, Pearson, Dovidio, Shelton, & Trail, 2009). Thus, these interpersonal and intergroup unit formations discussed by Davies et al. and by González et al. activate related but potentially different pathways to more positive intergroup attitudes.

Finally, while Pittinsky et al. (this volume) propose that allophilia develops when separate group identities are salient, we suggest that a dual identity, in which both original subgroup identities and a common ingroup identity are salient simultaneously, may be especially conducive to developing allophilia. When a dual identity is achieved in a way that recognizes subgroup identities as complementary elements contributing positively to superordinate group functioning, members of the different groups do not experience threat to their subgroup identities; they feel that their distinctiveness is valued along with their commonality (Dovidio, Gaertner, & Validzic, 1998). In the terms of Purdie-Vaughns and Walton (this volume), an identity-safe environment is established. Moreover, recognition of the uniqueness of other subgroups within a common identity facilitates recognition of their different needs, including those associated with past conflict between the groups (see Nadler & Shnabel, this volume), and motivates efforts to satisfy those needs for the common good.

CONCLUSION

Traditionally, research on intergroup relations and prejudice has emphasized the role of antipathy between groups and how to eliminate it. However, as we learned from our work on aversive racism, successfully avoiding acting inappropriately is insufficient for developing stable and productive intergroup relationships. The present volume highlights the benefits of adopting a focus that basically begins when negative feelings, beliefs, and behavioral orientations toward outgroup members are no longer prevalent; it asks, "How can we promote positive outgroup attitudes, as well as forgiveness and reconciliation between groups?"

This perspective, as demonstrated by the preceding chapters, creates new theoretical and practical opportunities and challenges for social scientists and policymakers. Theoretically, the chapters in this volume establish the importance of understanding and promoting positive intergroup attitudes, and they identify a range of causes and consequences of these attitudes. Collectively, they suggest promising new directions for future research, such as the value of understanding developmental influences and the importance of studying how intergroup friendships can form and be maintained over time. The present volume provides a solid conceptual foundation for stimulating new initiatives and insights for investigating positive approaches to intergroup relations.

In practical terms, this emphasis on positive approaches to studying intergroup relations complements recent developments at more micro- and macrolevels. At the individual level, "positive psychology" focuses on nurturing psychological well-being and health for achieving a more efficacious and rewarding life (Seligman, Steen, Park, & Peterson, 2005). At the level of international relations, work on conflict and conflict resolution amply demonstrates that the absence of conflict is fundamentally different from true reconciliation and peaceful coexistence (Kelman, 2008). Similarly, the chapters in the present volume reveal that a focus on eliminating negative responses—whether motivated by individual effort, social norms, or formal policy—does not necessarily result in more harmonious intergroup relations. In the context of relations between different groups within the same society, the central topic in the current volume, intergroup tension may simply be replaced by avoidance and group segregation. Thus, the theme of this volume—promoting positive approaches to intergroup relations—represents a distinctly promising initiative that can help transform theoretical perspectives in this area and guide the development of new interventions to create truly respectful, stable, and productive relations between groups in increasingly multicultural societies.

REFERENCES

Adorno, T. W., Frenkel-Brunswik, E., Levinson, D. J., & Sanford, R. N. (1950). *The authoritarian personality*. New York, NY: Harper.

Allport, G. W. (1954). *The nature of prejudice*. Cambridge, MA: Addison-Wesley.

Aron, A., Melinat, E., Aron, E. N., Vallone, R., & Bator, R. (1997). The experimental generation of interpersonal closeness: A procedure and some preliminary findings. *Personality and Social Psychology Bulletin, 23*, 363–377. doi:10.1177/0146167297234003

Blascovich, J., & Mendes, W. B. (2000). Challenge and threat appraisals: The role of affective cues. In J. P. Forgas (Ed.), *Feeling and thinking: The role of affect in social cognition* (pp. 59–82). New York, NY: Cambridge University Press.

Brewer, M. B. (1979). Ingroup bias in the minimal intergroup situation: A cognitive-motivational analysis. *Psychological Bulletin, 86*, 307–324. doi:10.1037/0033-2909.86.2.307

Brewer, M. B. (1999). The psychology of prejudice: Ingroup love or outgroup hate? *Journal of Social Issues, 55*, 429–444. doi:10.1111/0022-4537.00126

Brigham, J. C. (1993). College students' racial attitudes. *Journal of Applied Social Psychology, 23*, 1933–1967. doi:10.1111/j.1559-1816.1993.tb01074.x

Brown, R., & Hewstone, M. (2005). An integrative theory of intergroup contact. In M. P. Zanna (Ed.), *Advances in experimental social psychology* (Vol. 37, pp. 255–343). San Diego, CA: Academic Press.

Brown, R. J., & Turner, J. C. (1979). The criss-cross categorization effect in intergroup discrimination. *British Journal of Social and Clinical Psychology, 18*, 371–383.

Crosby, F., Bromley, S., & Saxe, L. (1980). Recent unobtrusive studies of Black and White discrimination and prejudice: A literature review. *Psychological Bulletin, 87*, 546–563. doi:10.1037/0033-2909.87.3.546

Darley, J. M., & Latané, B. (1968). Bystander intervention in emergencies: Diffusion of responsibility. *Journal of Personality and Social Psychology, 8*, 37–383. doi:10.1037/h0025589

Devine, P. G. (1989). Stereotypes and prejudice: Their automatic and controlled components. *Journal of Personality and Social Psychology, 56*, 5–18. doi:10.1037/0022-3514.56.1.5

Dovidio, J. F., & Gaertner, S. L. (2004). Aversive racism. In M. P. Zanna (Ed.), *Advances in experimental social psychology* (Vol. 36, pp. 1–51). San Diego, CA: Academic Press.

Dovidio, J. F., Gaertner, S. L., & Kawakami, K. (1998, October). *Multiple attitudes and contemporary racial bias*. Paper presented at the annual meeting of the Society for Experimental Social Psychology, Lexington, KY.

Dovidio, J. F., Gaertner, S. L., Kawakami, K., & Hodson, G. (2002). Why can't we just get along? Interpersonal biases and interracial distrust. *Cultural Diversity & Ethnic Minority Psychology, 8*, 88–102. doi:10.1037/1099-9809.8.2.88

Dovidio, J. F., Gaertner, S. L., & Validzic, A. (1998). Intergroup bias: Status, differentiation, and a common ingroup identity. *Journal of Personality and Social Psychology, 75*, 109–120. doi:10.1037/0022-3514.75.1.109

Dovidio, J. F., Gaertner, S. L., Validzic, A., Matoka, A., Johnson, B., & Frazier, S. (1997). Extending the benefits of recategorization: Evaluations, self-disclosure, and helping. *Journal of Experimental Social Psychology, 33*, 401–420. doi:10.1006/jesp.1997.1327

Fox, R. (1992). Prejudice and the unfinished mind: A new look at an old failing. *Psychological Inquiry, 3*, 137–152. doi:10.1207/s15327965pli0302_12

Gaertner, S. L., & Dovidio, J. F. (1977). The subtlety of White racism, arousal, and helping behavior. *Journal of Personality and Social Psychology, 35*, 691–707. doi:10.1037/0022-3514.35.10.691

Gaertner, S. L., & Dovidio, J. F. (1986). The aversive form of racism. In J. F. Dovidio & S. L. Gaertner (Eds.), *Prejudice, discrimination, and racism* (pp. 61–89). Orlando, FL: Academic Press.

Gaertner, S. L., & Dovidio, J. F. (2000). *Reducing intergroup bias: The common ingroup identity model*. Philadelphia, PA: Psychology Press.

Gaertner, S. L., & Dovidio, J. F. (2009). A common ingroup identity: A categorization-based approach for reducing intergroup bias. In T. Nelson (Ed.), *Handbook of prejudice* (pp. 489–505). Philadelphia, PA: Taylor & Francis.

Gaertner, S. L., Dovidio, J. F., Banker, B. S., Rust, M. C., Nier, J. A., & Ward, C. M. (1997). Does pro-Whiteness necessarily mean anti-Blackness? In M. Fine, L. Powell, L. Weis, & M. Wong (Eds.), *Off white* (pp. 167–178). New York, NY: Routledge.

Gaertner, S. L., Mann, J. A., Murrell, A. J., & Dovidio, J. F. (1989). Reduction of intergroup bias: The benefits of recategorization. *Journal of Personality and Social Psychology, 57*, 239–249. doi:10.1037/0022-3514.57.2.239

Graziano, W. G., Bruce, J., Sheese, B. E., & Tobin, R. M. (2007). Attraction, personality, and prejudice: Liking none of the people most of the time. *Journal of Personality and Social Psychology, 93,* 565–582. doi:10.1037/0022-3514.93.4.565

Henry, P. J., & Sears, D. O. (2002). The Symbolic Racism 2000 Scale. *Political Psychology, 23,* 253–283. doi:10.1111/0162-895X.00281

Higgins, E. T. (1999). Promotion and prevention as motivational duality: Implications for evaluative processes. In S. Chaiken & Y. Trope (Eds.), *Dual-process theories in social psychology* (pp. 503–525). New York, NY: Guilford Press.

Houlette, M., Gaertner, S. L., Johnson, K. M., Banker, B. S., Riek, B. M., & Dovidio, J. F. (2004). Developing a more inclusive social identity: An elementary school intervention. *Journal of Social Issues, 60,* 35–55. doi:10.1111/j.0022-4537.2004.00098.x

Kelman, H. C. (2008). Reconciliation from a social-psychological perspective. In A. Nadler, T. Malloy, & J. D. Fisher (Eds.), *Social psychology of intergroup reconciliation* (pp. 15–33). New York, NY: Oxford University Press. doi:10.1093/acprof:oso/9780195300314.003.0002

Kovel, J. (1970). *White racism: A psychohistory.* New York, NY: Pantheon.

Macrae, C. N., Bodenhausen, G. V., Milne, A. B., & Jetten, J. (1994). Out of mind but back in sight: Stereotypes on the rebound. *Journal of Personality and Social Psychology, 67,* 808–817. doi:10.1037/0022-3514.67.5.808

Mallett, R. K., & Wilson, T. D. (2010). Increasing positive intergroup contact. *Journal of Experimental Social Psychology, 46,* 382–387. doi:10.1016/j.jesp.2009.11.006

McConahay, J. B. (1986). Modern racism, ambivalence, and the modern racism scale. In J. F. Dovidio & S. L. Gaertner (Eds.), *Prejudice, discrimination, and racism* (pp. 91–125). Orlando, FL: Academic Press.

Miller, N. (2002). Personalization and the promise of contact theory. *Journal of Social Issues, 58,* 387–410. doi:10.1111/1540-4560.00267

Mummendey, A., Otten, S., Berger, U., & Kessler, T. (2000). Positive–negative asymmetry in racial discrimination: Valence of evaluation and salience of categorization. *Personality and Social Psychology Bulletin, 26,* 1258–1270. doi:10.1177/0146167200262007

Murrell, A. J., Dietz-Uhler, B. L., Dovidio, J. F., Gaertner, S. L., & Drout, C. E. (1994). Aversive racism and resistance to affirmative action: Perceptions of justice are not necessarily color blind. *Basic and Applied Social Psychology, 15*(1), 71–86. doi:10.1207/s15324834basp1501&2_4

Noor, M., Brown, R., & Prentice, G. (2008). Prospects for intergroup reconciliation: Social psychological predictors of intergroup forgiveness and reparation in Northern Ireland and Chile. In A. Nadler, T. Malloy, & J. D. Fisher (Eds.), *Social psychology of intergroup reconciliation* (pp. 97–115). New York, NY: Oxford University Press. doi:10.1093/acprof:oso/9780195300314.003.0006

Pettigrew, T. F. (1997). Generalized intergroup contact effects on prejudice. *Personality and Social Psychology Bulletin, 23,* 173–185. doi:10.1177/0146167297232006

Plant, E. A., & Devine, P. G. (1998). Internal and external motivation to respond without prejudice. *Journal of Personality and Social Psychology, 75,* 811–832. doi:10.1037/0022-3514.75.3.811

Riek, B. M., Mania, E. W., & Gaertner, S. L. (2006). Intergroup threat and outgroup attitudes: A meta-analytic review. *Personality and Social Psychology Review, 10,* 336–353. doi:10.1207/s15327957pspr1004_4

Seligman, M. E. P., Steen, T. A., Park, N., & Peterson, C. (2005). Positive psychology progress: Empirical validation of interventions. *American Psychologist, 60,* 410–421. doi:10.1037/0003-066X.60.5.410

Sherif, M., & Sherif, C. W. (1969). *Social psychology.* New York, NY: Harper & Row.

Sidanius, J., & Pratto, F. (1999). *Social dominance: An intergroup theory of social hierarchy and oppression.* New York, NY: Cambridge University Press.

Tajfel, H., & Turner, J. C. (1979). An integrative theory of intergroup conflict. In W. G. Austin & S. Worchel (Eds.), *The social psychology of intergroup relations* (pp. 33–48). Monterey, CA: Brooks/Cole.

Turner, J. C. (1985). Social categorization and the self-concept: A social cognitive theory of group behavior. In E. J. Lawler (Ed.), *Advances in group processes* (Vol. 2, pp. 77–122). Greenwich, CT: JAI Press.

Vorauer, J. D. (2006). An information search model of evaluative concerns in intergroup interaction. *Psychological Review, 113,* 862–886. doi:10.1037/0033-295X.113.4.862

West, T. V., Pearson, A. R., Dovidio, J. F., Shelton, J. N., & Trail, T. (2009). Superordinate identity and intergroup roommate friendship development. *Journal of Experimental Social Psychology, 45,* 1266–1272. doi:10.1016/j.jesp.2009.08.002

Wohl, M. J. A., & Branscombe, N. R. (2005). Forgiveness and collective guilt assignment to historical perpetrator groups depend on level of social category inclusiveness. *Journal of Personality and Social Psychology, 88,* 288–303. doi:10.1037/0022-3514.88.2.288

INDEX

Accentuation, 23
Acceptance
    and allophilia, 41, 42
    enhancement of, 7, 8
    need for, 210
    of perpetrators, in moral community,
        226
    and social orientation, 212
    third party as source of, 213
Advantaged groups, 210–213
Affect generalization, 125
Affective component (tripartite model
        of attitudes), 44, 45
Affective conditioning, 28–33
Affective empathy, 184–185, 188
Affective orientation
    disadvantages of, 33
    and nonprejudice, 28–30
    origins and malleability of, 31–33
Affective processes, 119
Affective responses, 246–248
African Americans
    achievement of identity safety by,
        170–171
    complimentary stereotypes of, 44
    effects of multiculturalism on, 160,
        163–169
    and intergroup forecasting error, 66
    learning goals, 103, 104n1
    measures of attitudes toward, 43n1,
        45, 46, 51, 55, 241–242
    measures of prejudice toward, 29–30,
        49, 52
    and motivation in intergroup contact,
        89–90
    reporting of racism by, 70
    responses to cross-race interaction
        partners, 85–86
    and sense of belonging, 172
    in university settings, 151, 152
Agency, 210
Aggression, 190, 202, 204, 223
Allophilia
    and decategorization, 49, 51
    defined, 42
    for reducing prejudice, 252

self-disclosure for inducing, 186
    and tripartite model of attitudes, 48
    and violence, 202
Allophilia Scale, 44–56
    development of, 44–48
    differentiation of nonprejudiced
        Whites and aversive
        racists, 252
    factor structure, 44–48
    purpose of, 249
    relationship to other measures,
        48–51
    subscales, 45, 46, 48, 52–54
Allport, Gordon, 5, 21, 120, 183, 241
Anabolic balance, 146, 147
Anger
    and affective orientation, 33
    detection of, 31
    and forgiveness, 190, 225
    intergroup, 228–229
Anti-Black effect, 24–25
Anti-Semitism, 204
Anxiety, intergroup. See Intergroup
        anxiety
Apology–forgiveness cycle, 208
    and forgiveness, 208
    public, 203
Approach-related responses (intergroup
        contact), 43, 84–87
Arab Israeli citizens, 51
Asian Americans, 30, 103
    attitudes toward, 123–124
Assimilation, 22
Attitudes
    and classical conditioning, 29
    and cross-group friendships, 119,
        122–123, 140–142
    negative. See Negative attitudes
    positive. See Positive attitudes
    tripartite model of, 44, 48
Austen, Jane. See Pride and Prejudice
        (Jane Austen)
Aversive racism, 24–25, 139–140,
        249–250
Avoidance, of intergroup contact, 43,
        82–85, 87, 145

Balkan Wars, 202
Barriers
    and identity safety, 160, 161
    to intergroup contact, 65, 133–134
    to reconciliation, 204
Behavior
    and attitudes, 43, 44
    and bias, 68
    monitoring of, 106
    motivation vs., 109
    negative attitudes as predictor of, 249
    nonverbal, 102
    toward outgroup members, changes
        in, 183
Behavioral component (tripartite model
    of attitudes), 44, 45
Belonging, sense of, 171–173
Benevolent sexism, 44–45, 212
Bias(es)
    and behavior, 68
    expressions of, 242
    ingroup, 191–192
    intergroup/discriminatory.
        See Prejudice
    and motivation, 6–7
    negativity, 32
    racial, 21–22
    and recategorization, 227
    selection, 184
Black Americans. See African Americans
Black South Africans, 184, 191
Blame, 86, 228
Bogardus, Emory, 5, 6
Brown v. Board of Education, 81, 150
Buddhist meditation, 32–33

Calculus-based trust, 192, 193
Categorization, 65, 127, 229. See also
    Decategorization; Recategorization
Catholics, 23, 148, 149, 191, 193
Chile, 221–226, 231–233
CIIM (common ingroup identity
    model), 227, 233
Civil Rights, 168
Cognitive component (tripartite model
    of attitudes), 44
Cognitive depletion, 109
Cognitive empathy, 126
Cognitive responses, 246–248
Cold War, 205

Colorblindness. See also Nonprejudice
    Color-Blind Racism Scale, 49
    and diversity without oppression, 167
    and group identities, 170
    preference for multiculturalism
        over, 163
    self-presentation styles in workplace,
        168–169
    strategic, 28
Color-Blind Racism Scale, 49
Colored South Africans, 184, 193
Common identity, 231, 233, 254
Common ingroup identity model
    (CIIM), 227, 233
Compassionate goals, 101–102, 107–109
Compensation, 70
Conditioning, 28–33
Conflict, 23, 201–203, 221, 244. See also
    Postconflict societies
Conflict resolution, 201, 203, 204, 228
Conflict settlement, 201
Conservatism, political, 31. See also
    Right-wing bloc (Chile)
Constructivism, 149
Context, 69–70
Cook, S. W., 55
Cooperation, 120, 206, 230
Corporate settings, 161, 168–171
Cortisol, 141, 146
Cross-group friendship, 4, 119–134,
    139–154
    accessibility of, 144–147
    and aversive racism, 139–140
    benefits of, 142–145, 147–150,
        246–247
    desire for, 130–132
    early studies on, 120
    effects of, 120–127, 140–142
    empathy in, 188, 189, 191
    and extended contact, 127–130
    indirect, 148–149, 153
    institutional effects of, 150–152
    and intergroup attitudes/experiences,
        140–142
    and policy changes, 194
    and positive intergroup relations,
        182–185
    and romantic/family relationships,
        132–133
    and same-group friendship, 152–153

self-disclosure in, 185–187
and self-expansion, 121–125,
130–132
in South Africa, 184–185, 193
trust in, 193
Cross-group interactions. *See* Intergroup
contact
Cross-race interactions. *See* Intergroup
contact
Cultural groups, 160–161

Decategorization, 48, 49, 51
Dehydroepiandrosterone-sulphate
(DHEA-S), 146
Demographics, 70
Destruction, 202
DHEA-S (dehydroepiandrosterone-
sulphate), 146
Differentiation, 226
Direct violence, 202–203, 205,
207–211, 213
Disadvantaged groups, 210, 212
Discomfort, 100
Discrimination, 211, 212, 242
Discriminatory bias. *See* Prejudice
Distinctiveness, 22
Distrust, 192, 230
Diversity
increase in, 83
and multiculturalism, 160, 161, 165
without oppression, 167

Ecosystem orientation (motivation),
99–101, 108–110
Education, 161. *See also* Schools
Efficacy, 83, 84, 87, 89, 106
Egalitarian self-image, 25
Egalitarian values, 68–69
and discrimination, 242
and intergroup anxiety, 139, 244
and multiculturalism, 168
Egosystem orientation (motivation),
99–101, 108, 109
Emotions. *See also* Socioemotional
reconciliation
and forgiveness, 223, 225
intergroup, 125, 228–230
negative, 242
and reparation, 223–225
Empathic response, 187–189

Empathy, 187–189
affective, 184–185, 188
cognitive, 126
and compassion, 110
in cross-group friendships, 126
disadvantaged groups' desire for, 212
and forgiveness, 225
intergroup, 230, 235
and self-disclosure, 186, 187
and universal orientation, 27
Empathy–altruism debate, 108
Empowerment, 162, 208, 210, 212, 213
Engagement, 51
Enmity, outgroup, 242
Environment, identity-safe, 162
Equality, 168–169
Equity, 223
Essentialism, 149
European Americans. *See* White
Americans
Evolutionary perspective, 22
Executive function, 91–92
Expectancies, 81–95
and anger, 228
and approach-related responses,
84–87
and avoidance-related responses,
83–84
and intergroup forecasting error, 68
negative response, 85–88, 90, 91, 93
Expectations
and avoidance of intergroup
interactions, 145
improving, 71–73
and metastereotypes, 66
negative, 82
of negative emotions, 69
Explicit prejudice, 25–26, 29, 30
Extended contact, 127–130
Extended contact effect, 148, 183

Facial expressions, 67
Fair treatment, 169
Family cross-group relationships, 132–133
Fast-friends procedure, 123–124, 126
Favoritism, 128, 140
Forgiveness, 189–191
achieving, 195
apology–forgiveness cycle, 208
and empathy, 230

Forgiveness, *continued*
    and identity safety, 162
    positive effects of, 181–182
    and reconciliation, 223–225
    for violence, 190, 202
French people, 51
"Friend of a friend" effect, 128
Friendship
    cross-group. *See* Cross-group
        friendship
    same-group, 152–153
Functional separability, 42

Gay men, 171
Gay relationships, 129
Gender equality, 159, 171
Genetic basis, of race, 149–150
German–Jewish relations, 208–209
Goals (intergroup relations), 99–111
    compassionate, 101–102, 107–109
    directions for future research, 110
    and ecosystem/egosystem
        orientations, 99–101, 108
    evidence of positive effects of,
        104–106
    integrative model of, 106–109
    learning, 102–104, 107–109
    performance, 102–104, 107–109
    and reconciliation, 205
    and self-image, 101–102, 107–109
Graduated and reciprocated initiatives
    in tension reduction (GRIT), 205
GRIT (graduated and reciprocated initia-
    tives in tension reduction), 205
Group identity
    and Allophilia Scale, 48
    of Chilean groups, 224–227
    and colorblindness, 170
    and reconciliation, 204, 207–213
    subordinate, 165
    superordinate, 22, 225–227
Group membership, 147
Group orientations, 244–246
Guilt, 204, 214, 223, 229–230

Healing, 201, 203
Heterosexuals, 129
Hewstone, M., 125, 126, 187, 188, 193
Hierarchies, social, 23
Holocaust, 208

Hormonal responses
    to novel intergroup interaction, 146
    to stress, 141
Hostility, 82–83
Humanitarianism, 27
Human rights violations, 222
Humiliation, 202

IAT (Implicit Association Test), 25, 142
Identification, ingroup, 191
Identification-based trust, 192, 193
Identity(-ies)
    common, 231, 233, 254
    group. *See* Group identity
    ideological, 222
    ingroup, 225–227, 231
    multiple, 165–167
    national, 254
    political, 222
    social, 224, 225, 228. *See also* Social
        identity theory
Identity contingencies, 160, 162, 170, 171
Identity safety
    defined, 160
    and multiculturalism, 160–163,
        169–173
Identity threat, 204, 207
Ideological identities, 222
Ideologies, diversity, 165
Immigrants, 188
Implicit Association Test (IAT), 25, 142
Implicit prejudice, 25–26, 29, 35, 141
Inclusion
    enhancement of, 7, 8
    of other in the self (IOS), 119,
        121–125, 143
    of outgroup in the self (IOGS),
        121–125
    of perpetrators, in moral community,
        226
Indirect contact. *See* Extended contact
Indirect contact effect. *See* Extended
    contact effect
Indirect cross-group friendship,
    148–149, 153
Inequality, 31, 167–168, 173, 212
Infrahumanization, 191
Ingroup bias, 191–192
Ingroup favoritism, 128, 140
Ingroup identification, 191, 193

Ingroup identity, 225–227, 231
Ingroup members
    distinction between outgroup and, 22
    empathy of, 189–190
    friendship with outgroup members.
        See Cross-group friendship
    ingroup identification of, 191
    self-disclosure to, 186
Ingroup norms, 183
Inhibitory ability, 30, 31
Instrumental reconciliation, 204–207,
    225
Integration, 148
Integrative model of goals, 106–109
Intergroup anger, 228–229
Intergroup anxiety
    as barrier to positive attitudes,
        133–134
    and cross-group friendship, 139–142,
        145, 184–185
    as factor in future intergroup contact,
        71
    and indirect friendship, 148
    and motivation, 89, 109
    negative expectancies as predictor
        of, 82–84
    nonverbal behaviors with, 102
    and outgroup trust, 193
    role of empathy in reducing, 126
    and self-image, 244
Intergroup bias. *See* Prejudice
Intergroup conflict, 221
Intergroup contact. *See also* Cross-group
        friendship; Intergroup interactions
    approach-related responses to, 84–87
    avoidance-related responses to,
        82–85, 87
    benefits of, 81
    desire for, 140
    with immigrants in Italy, 188
    in Northern Ireland, 191
    overcoming negative expectancies
        of, 87–93
    role of intergroup forecasting error
        in, 65, 70, 71, 73, 74
    social benefits of, 81
    in South Africa, 184, 191
    trust in, 192–193, 205
Intergroup contact hypothesis, 120, 205
Intergroup contact theory, 5

Intergroup emotions, 125, 228–229
Intergroup empathy, 230, 235
Intergroup forecasting error, 63–75
    and improving expectations, 71–73
    and interaction partner, 65–67
    reasons for, 64
    and the self, 67–68
    and situation, 69–71
Intergroup friendship. *See* Cross-group
    friendship
Intergroup guilt/shame, 229–230
Intergroup interactions, 82–87. *See also*
        Intergroup contact
Intergroup reconciliation.
        See Reconciliation
Intergroup relations
    contemporary approaches to, 6–7
    and cross-group friendship, 182–185.
        See also Cross-group friendship
    early approaches to studying, 5–6
    emerging approaches to, 7–8
    goals in. *See* Goals [intergroup
        relations]
    and prejudice, 4, 5
    reconciliation for, 204
Intergroup trust, 205–207, 230. *See also*
    Trust
Intergroup violence. *See* Violence
Interpersonal relationships, 185–187
Interracial interactions. *See* Intergroup
    contact
Intersectional invisibility, 165–167
Ireland, Northern. *See* Northern Ireland
"Is Multiculturalism Bad for Women?"
    (Susan Okin), 159
Israeli citizens, 51, 205, 208, 209
Israeli–Palestinian relations, 205–206

Jewish–Arab relations, 208–209
Jewish–German relations, 208–209
Jewish Israeli citizens, 51
Justice, 214

Kelman, H. C., 204
King, Martin Luther, Jr., 3, 12, 150, 153
King, Rodney, 3

LaPiere, R. T., 6
Latino Americans (Latinos)
    attitudes toward, 123–124

Latino Americans (Latinos) *continued*
    learning goals, 103
    measures of positive attitudes
        toward, 46n2, 51
    measures of prejudice toward, 29–30
    in university settings, 151
Laws, antidiscrimination, 242
Learning, 183
Learning goals, 102–104, 107–109
Lee, Harper, 173
Left-wing bloc (Chile), 222, 229–232
Legitimization, 212
Legitimizing myths, 23
Lesbian women, 171
Los Angeles riots (1992), 3
Loving-kindness meditation, 32–33

Media, 149–150
Meditation, 32–33
Memory, 144, 190
Metastereotypes, 66
Metta (loving-kindness meditation),
    32–33
Middle East
    conflict in, 202
    relations between Jewish and Arab
        Israelis, 51
Minimal groups, 22
Modern prejudice, 24–26
Modern Racism Scale, 49
Motivation
    and biases, 6–7
    as factor in intergroup interaction,
        88–93
    and goal orientations, 102, 108, 109
    and negative expectations, 82
    in self-expansion model, 121
    and sense of belonging, 172
Motivational systems, 99–101, 108–110
Multiculturalism, 159–174
    defined, 28, 159
    effects of, on African Americans,
        160, 163–169
    and identity safety, 160–163,
        169–173
    limitations of, 164–169
Multiple identities, 165–167
Multiracial people, 51
Mutual trust, 185, 192
Myths, legitimizing, 23

National identity, 254
National Intelligence Directorate
    (Chile), 222
The Nature of Prejudice (Gordon Allport),
    5, 21
Needs-based model, 163, 207–214
Negative attitudes, 41–44
    and affective learning style, 29
    and Allophilia Scale, 48
    bias in psychology toward study of,
        41–42
    changes in, 43
    as predictor of behaviors, 249
Negative peacemaking, 211
Negative response expectancies, 85–88,
    90, 91, 93
Negativity bias, 32
Nonprejudice, 26–31, 34
    and affective orientation, 28–30
    and Allophilia Scale, 48, 252
    basis of, 244
    factors predicting, 30–31
    plausibility of, 21
    and universal orientation, 27–28
Nonverbal behaviors, 102
Norms, 127–128, 183
Northern Ireland, 148, 149, 182, 188,
    190, 191, 193

Obama, Barack, 169
The Office (TV series), 164
Old-Fashioned Racism Scale, 49
Olson, M. A., 35
Optimal distinctiveness theory, 22
Optimism, 68
Outgroup empathy. *See* Empathy
Outgroup enmity, 242
Outgroup members
    changes in behavior toward, 183
    distinction between ingroup and, 22
    empathy toward, 189–190
    friendship with ingroup members.
        See Cross-group friendship
    identity of, 225–227
    and multiculturalism, 164–165
    self-disclosure with, 186
Outgroups
    attitudes toward, 43
    learning about, 183
Outgroup trust. *See* Trust

Palestinian–Israeli relations, 205–206
Palestinians, 205
Peace-building efforts, 205
Peacemaking, 211
Performance goals, 102–104, 107–109
Perpetrators
    distinction between victims and,
        213–215. *See also* Victim–
        perpetrator dyad
    and forgiveness, 190
    in post-conflict Chile, 223–231, 233
    and reconciliation, 207–210
Personality, tolerant, 27
Personal orientations, 244–246
Perspective-taking, 27, 110, 188, 191
Police–community relations, 124
Policies
    for fostering positive intergroup
        relations, 194
    and identity safety, 162
Political conservatism, 31
Political identities, 222, 225
Positive affect, 126, 148
Positive affective orientation, 33
Positive attitudes, 41–45, 51–53. *See
        also* Allophilia
    and decategorization, 48
    and empathy, 230
    facets of, 243, 248–249
    processes contributing to, 243
    shift in emphasis toward, 242
    through extended contact, 183
Positive peacemaking, 211
Postconflict reconciliation.
        See Reconciliation
Postconflict societies, 181
    Chile, 221–226, 231–233
    Guatemala, 203
    Northern Ireland, 148, 149, 182,
        188, 190, 191, 193
    South Africa, 182, 184–185, 190,
        191, 193, 203
Power, 167, 207, 208, 210, 222, 244
Prejudice. *See also* Nonprejudice
    avoiding expressions of, 106
    basis of, 244
    contemporary approaches to, 6–7
    defined, 241
    emerging approaches to, 7–8
    explicit, 25–26, 29, 30

genesis and consequences of, 4
    implicit, 25–26, 29, 35, 141
    and intergroup anxiety, 139
    measures of, 49, 51
    modern, 24–26
    origins of, 22–26
    in postconflict societies, 181
    prevalence of, 21
    prioritizing study of, 221
    regulation of, 92, 93
    responding to interactions without,
        88–89
Prejudice reduction, 31–33
Pride and Prejudice (Jane Austen), 63,
        66, 67, 71, 73
Privilege, 210, 211
Pro-Black attitudes, 43n1
Promotion focus, 242. *See also* Positive
        attitudes
Protestants, 23, 148, 149, 191, 193
Prototypes, 165–166, 173
Psychology, social. *See* Social psychology

Race, 149–150
Race-sensitive topics, 104
Racial bias, 21–22
Racism
    aversive, 24–25, 139–140, 249–250
    combating, 168
    measures of, 49, 51
    and multiculturalism, 167
    reporting of, by African Americans,
        70
    and sexism, 34
    subtle, 24
    symbolic, 24
    ways of reducing, 202
Realistic group conflict, 23
Recategorization, 48, 49, 227
Reciprocal self-disclosure, 185–187
Reconciliation, 203–213
    aspects of, 223–224
    instrumental, 204–207, 225
    needs-based model of, 163, 207–213
    socioemotional, 203–205, 207–214
    and violence, 203
Regret, 203–204
Regulation, of prejudice, 92, 93. *See also*
        Self-regulation
Rejection, fear of, 99, 106

Reparation, 222–224, 227, 230
Respect, 41, 42, 210
Responsibility, admissions of, 214, 215
Revenge, 190
Reward, 32
Right-wing bloc (Chile), 222, 231–233
Robbers Cave study (Sherif), 5, 23
Roles, social, 214–215
Romantic cross-group relationships, 132
Rwandan genocide, 202

SAFCON. *See* Susceptibility to affective conditioning
Same-group friendship, 152–153
Schools, 103, 150–152, 161, 171. *See also* Education
Segregation, 81
Selection bias, 184
Self, the
    in ecosystem orientation, 100
    focusing beyond, 106, 108–109
    and group identity, 226
    and intergroup forecasting error, 67–68
    other in, 119, 121–125, 143
    outgroup in, 121–125
    self-affirmation as tool for transcending, 110
Self-affirmation, 110
Self-categorization, 127
Self-determination theory, 91
Self-disclosure
    in interpersonal relationships, 185–187
    as mediating process, 126
    trust inherent in, 193
Self-efficacy, 121
Self-expansion, 121–125, 130–132, 142–143, 191
Self-expansion model, 121
Self-image
    egalitarian, 25
    and goals, 101–102, 107–109
    intergroup interactions as threat to, 100
    monitoring of, 106
Self–other overlap, 143, 186, 189, 191. *See also* Inclusion of other in the self (IOS)

Self-regulation, 24, 109
Sexism
    benevolent, 44–45, 212
    and optimism, 68
    and racism, 34
    ways of reducing, 202
    women's reporting of, 70
Shame, 229–230
Sherif, Muzafer, 5
Situation (intergroup forecasting error), 69–71
Social change, 212
Social–cognitive research, 145
Social dominance theory, 23
Social exchange, 208
Social hierarchies, 23
Social identity, 224, 225, 228
Social identity theory
    and extended contact, 127
    and group identity, 226
    and identity threat, 210
    and tendency to join social groups, 22
Social power, 208
Social psychology
    and measuring positive attitudes, 44
    prioritizing study of prejudice and conflict, 221, 244
    reconciliation in, 203
Social rejection, 150–152
Social roles, 214–215
Socioemotional reconciliation, 203–205, 207–214
South Africa, 182, 184–185, 190, 191, 193, 203
South Asians, 187
Soviet Union, 205
Stereotypes
    and empathy, 126
    and intergroup forecasting error, 64, 65, 68
    meta-, 66
    and positive attitudes, 44
    reliance on, 189
Stereotyping, 23, 164–165. *See also* Subtyping
Strategic colorblindness, 28
Stress responses, 141, 152
Stroop task, 30
Structural inequality, 167–168

Structural violence, 202–203, 207, 209–214
Subordinate group identity, 165
Subtle racism, 24
Subtyping, 133–134, 164–165
Superordinate identity, 22, 225–227
Susceptibility to affective conditioning (SAFCON), 29, 31, 32
Symbolic racism, 24
Sympathy, 43n1. *See also* Empathy

Tatum, Beverly, 4
Third party, as source of empowerment, 213
Threat
    to agency and power, 209–210
    and attention to negativity, 32
    identifying setting cues that trigger, 170–171
    identity, 204, 207
    as response to situation, 88
    sensitivity to possible, 100
To Kill a Mockingbird (Harper Lee), 173
Tolerance, 41, 42
Tolerant personality, 27
Tripartite model of attitudes, 44, 48
Trust, 189, 191–194
    achieving, 195
    and identity safety, 162
    intergroup, 205–207, 230
    as mediator between intergroup interactions, 205
    positive effects of, 181–182
    and reconciliation, 213
    and self-disclosure, 185, 187
Truth and Reconciliation Commission (Chile), 222
Truth commissions, 203

Underrepresentation, 171–172
Unit formations, 248
Universal orientation, 27–28, 48
Universal Orientation Scale, 27, 49
Universities, 150–152

Valence congruence, 43, 44
Victimization, 33, 190

Victim–perpetrator dyad, 209, 213–214
Victims
    distinction between perpetrators and, 214
    and forgiveness, 190
    in post-conflict Chile, 222–233
    predicting reparation to, 227
    and reconciliation, 203, 204, 207–210
Violence
    Balkan Wars, 202
    in Chile, 222
    direct, 202–203, 205, 207–211, 213
    forgiveness for, 190, 202
    and indirect friendship, 148
    in the Middle East, 202
    prevalence of, 3
    Rwanda, 202
    structural, 202–203, 207, 209–214
Vulnerability, 33

White Americans
    attitudes toward African Americans, 55, 241–242
    learning goals, 104
    measures of prejudice toward African Americans, 29–30
    motivation of, in intergroup interaction, 89–90
    negative expectancies about interracial interactions, 82
    responses to cross-race interaction partners, 85–86
    and sense of belonging, 172
    in university settings, 151, 152
    views on multiculturalism, 163
White Britons, 187, 193
White prejudice, 24–25
White South Africans, 184–185, 193
Why Are All the Black Kids Sitting Together in the Cafeteria? (Beverley Tatum), 4
Withdrawal responses, 43
Working memory, 144
Workplace settings, 168–169

ABOUT THE EDITORS

Linda R. Tropp, PhD, is an associate professor of psychology and director of the Psychology of Peace and Violence Program at the University of Massachusetts Amherst. Her research concerns how members of different groups approach and experience contact with one another, and how group differences in status affect cross-group relations. She received the Allport Intergroup Relations Prize from the Society for the Psychological Study of Social Issues, the Erikson Early Career Award for distinguished research contributions from the International Society of Political Psychology, and the McKeachie Early Career Teaching Award from the Society for the Teaching of Psychology. Dr. Tropp is a fellow of the American Psychological Association, the Society of Experimental Social Psychology, and the Society for the Psychological Study of Social Issues. She has been a visiting scholar at the University of California, Berkeley; the Kurt Lewin Institute; the Marburg Center for Conflict Studies; and the International Graduate College on Conflict and Cooperation, where she taught seminars and workshops on prejudice reduction and intervention. She has collaborated with organizations in the United States to present social science evidence in Supreme Court cases on racial desegregation, worked on state initiatives designed to improve interracial relations in schools, and partnered with varied nongovernmental organizations to evaluate applied programs designed to reduce racial and ethnic conflict. She was coeditor of *Improving Intergroup Relations* (2008) and a 2006 special issue of the *Journal of Social Issues* on integrating intergroup research and practice.

Robyn K. Mallett, PhD, is an assistant professor of psychology at Loyola University Chicago. She completed her bachelor's degree at the University of Alaska Anchorage; her PhD in social psychology at the Pennsylvania State University, State College; and a postdoctoral fellowship at the University of Virginia, Charlottesville. Her research investigates pathways to positive intergroup relations by examining the cognitive, emotional, and behavioral components of intergroup contact—specifically, how the accuracy of intergroup expectations can be improved to increase the likelihood of positive future contact, how targets of discrimination can proactively protect themselves from the negative consequences of discrimination, and how emotions motivate majority group members to act on behalf of minority group members. Dr. Mallett's investigation of the intergroup forecasting error was funded by a grant from the Russell Sage Foundation.